THE MODERNISTS

Harry T. Moore (1908–1981)

THE MODERNISTS

Studies in a Literary Phenomenon

Essays in Honor of Harry T. Moore

Edited by Lawrence B. Gamache *and* Ian S. MacNiven

RUTHERFORD • MADISON • TEANECK
FAIRLEIGH DICKINSON UNIVERSITY PRESS
LONDON AND TORONTO: ASSOCIATED UNIVERSITY PRESSES

Associated University Presses
440 Forsgate Drive
Cranbury, NJ 08512

Associated University Presses
25 Sicilian Avenue
London WC1A 2QH, England

Associated University Presses
2133 Royal Windsor Drive
Unit 1
Mississauga, Ontario
Canada L5J 1K5

The paper used in this publication meets the
requirements of the American National Standard for
Permanence of Paper for Printed Library Materials Z39.48-1984.

Library of Congress Cataloging-in-Publication Data

The Modernists.

Bibliography: p.
Includes index.
1. English literature—20th century—History and
criticism. 2. Modernism (Literature) 3. American
literature—20th century—History and criticism.
4. Moore, Harry Thornton. I. Moore, Harry Thornton.
II. Gamache, Lawrence B. III. MacNiven, Ian S.
PR478.M6M64 1987   820'.9'1   85-45768
ISBN 0-8386-3257-2 (alk. paper)

Printed in the United States of America

Contents

Preface

This volume of essays, it should be made clear at the outset, does not attempt to explain modernism as a literary phenomenon or to propose a list of authors representative of the modernist period; such an attempt, even if done in a series of volumes, would be subject to inevitable arguments over definitions and selections. This collection, beyond its purpose to honor Harry T. Moore, attempts to contribute to a growing inquiry into the distinctive qualities of the literatures of Europe and the Americas of the late nineteenth and twentieth centuries—qualities that mark the works of that period as different from what preceded and what followed. Without denying the radical differences among the literatures and the individual works that constitute them, it is possible to distinguish in them what is reflective of the momentum of their time from the expression of human sensibilities derived from earlier and later cultural influences.

The editors have made their selections with the intent not only to range more widely in the kinds of studies than is usual in such collections, but also to maintain a focus to ensure coherence, a focus suggested by the scholarly career of Harry T. Moore. The essays reflect his concerns and the scope of his involvement in the study of the literature of the twentieth century and thereby reflect the scope and complex character of that literature. Moore is best known for his major contribution to the development of Lawrence studies, but his involvement was with far more than one author, one genre, one nation or one culture; he was able to generate scholarly investigations of many facets of modern literature and to stimulate a multitude of approaches by a multitude of scholars—those beginning their careers as well as seasoned veterans—through his work as teacher, editor, and sponsor of scholarly publications. This volume reflects something of the variety of Harry T. Moore's interests as teacher and as scholar. If our selection seems skewed because of the attention paid to D. H. Lawrence, the reason should be apparent: a volume dedicated to Moore and contributed to by many of his friends will inevitably give Lawrence a special place, particularly since his centenary year, 1985, has generated so much fresh interest in his work. In addition, however, it should be noted that we have used Lawrence as a point of focus for the range of studies of modernist phenomena included, as will become apparent in the rationale for the selection and arrangement of the essays.

From Paul Tillich's description of the twentieth-century mind as having "lost a meaningful world and a self which lives in meanings out of a spiritual center," some commonly ascribed notes of "modernism" can be inferred. The fragmentation of reality, of experience, and a concomitant compulsion for experimentation in many of the authors of this period has led to the attribution of a sense of desperation in the tone of their works; the joy and the beauty of this earth and of the universe have also been affirmed, however, often by those same authors we think of as most modernist, e.g., Joyce and Eliot. The editors hope to convey a balanced sense of the modern tradition through the essays included.

Although used with increasing frequency to refer to literary matters, the term *modernism* has been employed for almost a century to identify nonliterary as well as literary phenomena. Two of the earliest uses derive from widely differing origins both in place and in referent; one is Latin American and literary and the other is European and religious in context. Rubén Darío, the Nicaraguan poet, called his attempt to introduce European literary developments of the late nineteenth century into Latin American poetry *modernismo;* Pope Pius X, in 1907, condemned what he termed the "modernist heresy," which referred to a complex of ideas and attitudes questioning a number of traditional positions of the Roman Catholic Church. Despite the wide separation between these usages of modernism, certain common ground can be detected: both reveal a need to explore new ways of responding to an increasingly complex and difficult world, and an equally strong need to discover the grounds for maintaining contact with a cultural past. In a variety of ways the essays in this collection reflect both the differences in the application of the term *modernism,* deducible from a study of analyses of the period, and the bases of the common ground of meaning that can be equally inferred. Their selection and arrangement by the editors is intended to reflect the unity in diversity the term *modernism* itself suggests.

Following Suzanne Henig's memoir of Harry T. Moore, we begin with an essay by Carl Bode, a dedicated teacher-scholar not unlike Moore, who writes out of that background about the students he has met, each of whom has shared the experience of living in and coping with the modernist's world. The following four essays deal with larger views of the phenomena of modernism that can be revealed through the study of one or two writers: the first (Lawrence B. Gamache) tentatively defines what modernism is by examining the lives of nonliterary figures who very clearly represent a modernist response to the events—particularly religious and intellectual—of the last century and, at the same time, identifies one of the earliest uses of the term to gain wide currency; Paul Marcotte's essay discusses the "new critical" ideas of Cleanth Brooks and Robert Penn Warren through the successive editions of their highly influential textbook on the reading of poetry; Richard Lehan's essay, although it does treat Joyce at some length, considers the modernist novel in broader terms as well; James Flannery's essay discusses the growth of drama from modernism to postmodernism. The time span covered in these articles ranges across the late nineteenth and twentieth centuries; each one tends to focus on a slightly different era to give some sense of the breadth of the modernist period, taking up successively the novel, drama, and poetry of the modernist period from very particular points of view.

The next sequence of articles presents studies of major British-based writers of the early twentieth century: in addition to Lehan's work on Joyce, we include a Conrad study by Ted Boyle, a Forster study by Alan Warren Friedman, and five essays on Lawrence, representative of the range of approaches included in the collection: biographical (Keith Sagar), comparative (Armin Arnold), movement (Emile Delavenay), and two different critical approaches, the psychological and mythopoeic (James Cowan and Evelyn Hinz-John Teunissen). The next sequence crosses the ocean to include three major American writers: Eliot (E. L. Epstein), Faulkner (Walter Taylor), and Hemingway (Mark Spilka). We have included three articles on figures who come later in the century: Durrell (Ian MacNiven), Lessing (Paul Schlueter), and Vargas Llosa (Charles Rossman). In addition to extending the coverage in time, these writers expand the contexts of our coverage in place. The final article, Keith Cushman's discussion of Margaret Drabble and George Eliot, brings us full circle by relating a current writer to a major nineteenth-century author.

The final inclusion in this collection is an annotated bibliography of some fifty items, chosen rather idiosyncratically but necessarily so, given the multitude of possible worthy texts that could arguably be included, with the intention of offering some guidance to the study of a fascinating and complex subject. Space limitations required us to be more selective than we would rather have been. The editors believe that the bibliography forms a fitting conclusion to our effort to honor Harry T. Moore and to contribute to the study of the literature of our century.

We wish to thank the contributors for their generous cooperation in the preparation of the collection, and also Gerry Turcotte and Susan S. Mac-Niven for their diligent assistance in the editorial process. We also thank the D. H. Lawrence Society of North America for its support, through a special grant, of this publication. We would like to make a special dedication of this volume honoring her husband to Beatrice Moore, herself a distinguished editor.

Lawrence B. Gamache
Ian S. MacNiven

Acknowledgments

The authors and the publisher are grateful for permission to quote or reproduce material from the following sources:

Umberto Boccioni, *Development of a Bottle in Space*, 1912, a photograph of the sculpture, by permission of The Museum of Modern Art, New York.

Cleanth Brooks and Robert Penn Warren, *Understanding Poetry*, by permission of the authors.

Lawrence Durrell, correspondence, by authority of Curtis Brown Ltd. *Monsieur*, copyright 1974 by Lawrence Durrell; *Livia*, copyright 1978 by Lawrence Durrell; *Constance*, copyright 1979, 1982 by Lawrence Durrell; *Sebastian*, copyright 1983 by Lawrence Durrell; *Quinx*, copyright 1985 by Lawrence Durrell; *Collected Poems 1931–1974*, copyright 1980 by Lawrence Durrell, by permission of Faber and Faber Ltd. and Viking Penguin, Inc.

T. S. Eliot: *Collected Poems 1909–1962* by T. S. Eliot, copyright 1936 by Faber and Faber Ltd. and Harcourt Brace Jovanovich, Inc.; copyright © 1963, 1964 by T. S. Eliot. Reprinted by permission of the publishers. "Little Gidding" in *Four Quartets*, copyright 1943 by T. S. Eliot; renewed 1971 by Esme Valerie Eliot. Reprinted by permission of Faber and Faber Ltd. and Harcourt Brace Jovanovich, Inc.

Ernest Hemingway, correspondence and manuscripts, and Grace Hall Hemingway, correspondence, by permission of Mary Welsh Hemingway. Madelaine Hemingway Miller, correspondence, by permission of the author.

D. H. Lawrence, granted to this edition by Laurence Pollinger Ltd. on behalf of the Estate of Mrs. Frieda Lawrence Ravagli, specifically for the following works: *Phoenix*, copyright 1936 by Frieda Lawrence, renewed 1964 by the Estate of Mrs. Frieda Lawrence Ravagli; *Phoenix II*, copyright 1959, 1963, 1968 by the Estate of Frieda Lawrence Ravagli. *The Rainbow*, copyright 1915 by David Herbert Lawrence and 1943 by Frieda Lawrence, by permission of Laurence Pollinger Ltd. and Viking Penguin, Inc. All rights reserved.

Harry T. Moore: The Last Tycoon of Scholarship

A Memoir

SUZANNE HENIG

(This memoir was written in 1981 for a *Festschrift* in honor of Harry T. Moore's retirement from academic life. I had every expectation he would read it. It was recently revised with a Postscript as a memorial instead. Harry, unhappily, never was to read the first part which follows.)

Little did I know when I first met Harry T. Moore in 1971 at the annual meeting of the Modern Language Association of America in Chicago that we would grow to be the closest of friends, for his name had been an awesome legend to me for many years. As an undergraduate, I had learned literary scholarship and criticism from his books and later, as a professor, I had used in my classes the many volumes to issue from his pen. As a poet, I valued his criticism of my work before I published. He was a true Renaissance scholar, as much at home with British as with Russian and other literatures. His erudite mind has traversed the vast panorama of world literature, and he was also a gifted fiction writer.

Harry had met John Lehmann the previous year at Taos, New Mexico, at a D. H. Lawrence conference. He had made an abiding impression on the brilliant Britisher who had been Leonard and Virginia Woolf's partner in the Hogarth Press as well as an important poet in his own right. When John was my guest in late 1971 as he began a year in California as Distinguished Visiting Professor at my university, San Diego State, we founded the *Virginia Woolf Quarterly* together; he suggested I meet Harry and obtain his cooperation and advice in running our magazine. So it was with a request that I shyly approached the formidable Harry in the halls of the Palmer House, the convention headquarters.

"Sure," he responded without hesitation, "let's meet and talk it over. And, of course, feel free to use my name in any capacity that will help you." We met later that day for a drink and Harry agreed to serve on our editorial board; he was the first of what was to become a distinguished list of interna-

tional writers, scholars, and artists. His name, I later discovered, turned out
to be an "open sesame" to our initial funding. The real significance to our
meeting was to be evident, however, in the years to come: Harry was to be
among the inner circle of the dearest and truest friends I have ever had.

We began a long-distance correspondence and I gradually learned about
his "wonderful wife Beatrice" and their nine cats. Here we were on common
ground: I had five cats (and two collies who thought they were really cats).
We compared detailed notes on their respective personalities, feeding and
sleeping habits: all slept in his bed, while only three slept in mine. He was
more popular than I.

Usually we would meet at each annual Modern Language Association
Convention in New York, Chicago, Denver, or San Francisco, with common
friends, for dinner or drinks, whichever our busy schedules would permit.
We caught up with each other's lives and kept in touch the rest of the year,
Harry by long and fascinating letters that I have kept and treasure and I, a
poor correspondent, by telephone. Our really close friendship, however,
began in 1974.

I was chairing the Fiftieth Anniversary Conrad Commemorative Meeting.
Jacob Bronowski, author of *Ascent of Man,* was to deliver the opening
address and Harry was to be the keynote speaker. Delegates were coming
from Poland, Russia, Africa, England, France, and South America, as well as
from all over the United States. We were scheduled to do a CBS television
program as well as a Radio Free Europe and a Voice of America broadcast on
Conrad. The conference itself was being held on the campus of the University of California, La Jolla, not my own university, and so I was especially
anxious that everything should go exceptionally well.

Harry arrived early and stayed at my home, along with the late Dr. Vera F.
Beck of Harvard and Hofstra universities and an eastern European professor
with his wife. Then disaster struck, the first of many problems: "Bruno"
Bronowski died suddenly in New York of a heart attack three days before our
conference. In a panic, I asked Dr. Jonas Salk, a scientist without any Conrad
connection, to substitute, and he kindly agreed. I was certainly presuming on
our friendship, but as an added bonus he suggested that he give the delegates
a personal tour of Salk Institute. As a result, for the moment the conference
went smoothly, but at the old homestead more disasters were to strike.

Our eastern European guests did not wish to see Salk Institute, just as they
did not wish to leave my pool except for the hour the professor was scheduled to read his paper. Cultural shock was probably the root cause, but in the
five days they stayed with us, they broke our sliding glass doors to the patio
by walking, Superman style, through them (they were unhurt); they turned
our bathroom into a swimming pool each morning by letting the tub overflow;
they broke the flushing apparatus in the toilet; they ran up a $60 bill for a
phone call to Mexico City and an equal amount for another call to Washington to obtain permission from their embassy to speak about Conrad over
Voice of America.

Back at the campus, however, things were not tranquil either. Local anti-communist Polish groups (there are three in the San Diego area) began picketing the conference to protest the presence of the Iron Curtain delegates. As I would return each evening to find a new crisis at home, Harry would be the epitome of equanimity and would soothe my very frayed nerves.

At the convention he delivered a brilliant keynote speech, never using notes, stepped in without prior warning to discuss Conrad on the Voice of America when our eastern European guest demanded payment (which was not forthcoming) and, in general, was the most amiable, witty, and wonderful participant possible. Dr. Florence Talamantes and I, who were in charge of all arrangements, will always be grateful to him for his marvelous help during that trying week.

Evenings, Vera, Florence, her husband Eduardo, my elderly mother, and I would sit around the pool with our cocktails, Harry with his favorite Old Fashioneds, and he would enchant us with memories and anecdotes of Frieda Lawrence, Bunny Garnett, Harry Crosby, Middleton Murry et al.—figures legendary to us but whom Harry had known intimately. Someone asked, "Did Frieda ever make overtures to you, Harry?" "No, but I wish she had," he laughed.

The eastern Europeans were never in attendance during these fascinating evenings, but preferred to retire early after the rigors of wrecking some other area of my home or demolishing the leftovers in the refrigerator (while managing to break the refrigerator door). Harry told us again of his divine Beatrice, how they met, how she was an "Italian princess" (which she denies), how wonderful she was, and how much he adored her. He also told us of his early acting career and showed us photographs of himself on the stage. Harry was devastatingly handsome and, as he recited Shakespeare to us from memory for hours, it was easy to see how his early success as a tragedian might have led him in the tracks of Gielgud instead of Kittredge. It was strange how he maintained this dual side of himself that few people knew about: he had many important theatrical friendships with the famous actors and actresses and playwrights of our time, but he also seemed to know everyone in modern literature and just about every recognized or undiscovered writer of ability.

And when Harry would finally retire for the night, after a last few laps around the pool in moonlight, my four literary cats (one had died)—Sacheverell, Mrs. Dalloway, Lucrece, and Deirdre of the Sorrows—would desert my bedroom for his at the other end of the house. He always took precedence.

For years afterward, we kept in touch during various apogees and vicissitudes in both our lives. In 1977, on my way to Poland to chair a section of the International Association of University Professors at the University of Poznan, by way of England, I planned a surprise birthday party on 1 August for him in London, after his annual visit to his beloved Rome. Like most of my closest friends, he was a Leo. But Harry never arrived; instead his cable did, telling us he was ill. How he would have enjoyed seeing John Lehmann and Dame Rebecca West again, old friends who had been invited. And when I went through an unhappy love affair, it was to Harry that I wrote for advice and consolation.[1] Harry was then hard at work on two novels and I attended the birth of pages and chapters as midwife, anxiously reading Harry's many letters about their progress and then seeing the early drafts of chapters until they were safely berthed with a Houghton Mifflin contract. He was even going to permit me to publish a chapter or two in the *Virginia Woolf Quarterly*. How touched I was. Alas, he was to die leaving both novels unfinished.

In 1979 when the Modern Language Association met in San Francisco, Harry flew in and we had perhaps the best of our many reunions over the years. Would I, he asked, accompany him to Oakland on a tour of his boyhood haunts? I was so honored.

We drove out immediately after breakfast with another friend, Cheri Hoffman, and viewed his birthplace, the school he attended, the house where he later lived after his father's appointment as Ambassador to Iran, the Christian Science Church he worshiped in as a boy and left as an adult, and the creek where he had played. Some of the houses of his past remained; others had been razed and more modern personality-less ones had replaced them. Harry took pictures of everything and I took pictures of Harry. He was very quiet, introspective, not the usually loquacious friend I knew; but when he spoke, his parents, his friends, his boyhood activities came alive. A picture of a rural California burst forth and I could see Harry as a youngster climbing trees, fishing in the creek, and walking to the still-small grammar school. Harry told us about the last meeting with his father in Paris before his father's death, and how his grandparents had come west across the prairies in a Conestoga wagon to settle during the last century. I had a sudden feeling, almost a premonition, that he was making this pilgrimage to the places of his past for the last time, that he probably would not return to California; and I felt like his beloved Lawrence at the sight of the golden serpent, so blessed, so honored, to share that experience and his memories with this exceptional, sensitive, gifted literary man who had become a cherished friend, almost a family member, over the years.

In all the time I knew Harry, he had never said an unkind word about anyone. But to paraphrase Conrad, "Life seems but a series of betrayals," and many were the people, authors he first helped to publish and promote, who said and did unkind things behind his back. If he was aware of this, he never let on but continued to speak kindly of the offenders and help them whenever he could. This was typical of Harry.

We drove down the California coast after the convention and his reunion with old friends. On the way back, we had a memorable lobster dinner at Monterrey where we watched the seals and otters pirouette below us in the bay. Later that evening I dropped Harry off at the home of an old wartime buddy in Santa Barbara, a retired general with whom he had served in World War II. I was continually discovering things about Harry I had never known.

A week later I drove up to Malibu from San Diego where I then lived and picked him up at another friend's home, that of Carroll O'Connor (of Archie Bunker fame) and his lovely wife, Nancy. He had known them since his theatrical days. We drove back to San Diego, and my mother and I were delighted to have Harry entirely to ourselves at last, although only for two days. He saw some of his old California friends, Florence and Eduardo Talamantes; the last day we drove down to Rosarito, Mexico, for an exquisite dinner with another old friend, Carvel Collins, the Faulkner scholar. Later that evening we memorialized that day at the Coronado Hotel watching the sunset come in over the Pacific. Little did I know that within six months I would be moving to Mexico permanently and both our lives would take unexpected turns.

Harry was bubbling with news of the forthcoming film that was to be made from his D. H. Lawrence biography, *The Priest of Love*. It was called by the same name. My mother and I were as excited as he. The two days passed more quickly than the turning of a leaf, and it was soon time to take Harry back to Lindbergh International Airport for his departure flight home to Beatrice. As usual, we dared not offer Harry a hearty breakfast: he hated breakfasts passionately, a vestigial reminder of his unhappy childhood when his mother forced cereal and eggs on him before he trotted off to classes. We had a defiant Old Fashioned instead.

With my great remove to Mexico, the Sunday two-hour phone calls were no longer possible, for I had no telephone. But the magnificent and vivacious letters still arrived with the large, elliptical script, always ending with the familiar "love to your wonderful mother." And just this week, as I was searching for an ending that would not really be a termination to this memoir, the mails brought another epistle from Harry with news of Houston where I've never been ("unutterably dull; you'd hate it"), of the Lawrence film, then ready for release, and of his own movie debut in it.

So often *Festschriften* turn out to be very dry, tedious, tiresome, scholarly exercises in honor of a distinguished scholar whose career is at an end. But nothing will ever end for Harry or for those of us who know him: he is a tireless, indefatigable scholar who, naturally, is in the middle of another book, an eloquent and gifted creative writer, a marvelous belletrist, a brilliant orator, a man whose genius and charisma inculcate and inform everything he touches, an inspiration to those of us who can never really follow in his footsteps however much we emulate him. But more than any of these, Harry is a loyal, devoted, dear human being I shall always be deeply honored to cherish simply as my very own dear friend.

Rosarito Beach, Mexico
1981

POSTSCRIPT

Unhappily, this memoir which was written in honor of Harry's retirement from academic life must now serve as his memorial. In the spring of 1981, I called to congratulate Harry on the film that Christopher Miles, the British producer, had made. The week before, over the telephone, Harry had told me to watch for a cameo of himself as the man who collides with Pino Orioli on a street in Florence. This was to be in the style of Hitchcock, who always signs his pictures with a cameo in some unexpected crowd scene. Harry was a great admirer of Hitchcock. When I saw the film with Florence Talamantes, Ramón Sender, the late Spanish novelist, his wife (the Senders had known Lawrence personally), and my mother at the La Jolla Museum of Contemporary Art where all the seats had been sold out, we watched intently for Harry's cameo. Finally there he was—a tourist in a dark pin-striped suit bumping into Orioli—but only for two seconds (we counted).[2]

I excitedly dialed Illinois from Florence and Eduardo's apartment. Someone picked up on the second ring. It was Harry's voice.

"Harry, we loved the movie," I could honestly say. I was interrupted.

"This isn't Harry. This is his son. Harry died last week of a stroke. He had been in a coma for three days."

I couldn't continue the conversation.

Later that night I called back and told Harry's son how proud Harry had been of him and his completion of the Ph.D. in history. And I spoke to Beatrice, who had become an old friend by now, his beloved "Italian Princess." Nothing would ever be the same.

A literary era had passed. Harry left his great imprint on it, not as a creative artist, as he would have wished, but as a critic and scholar. And we who loved him, whom he pushed as poets and novelists, will forever miss the kind, unselfish literary and personal friend. He always unselfishly encouraged anyone with talent. Somewhere in the dim hereafter (God and an afterlife were the only topics we never discussed, for some strange reason), I would like to think of Harry in a pure white gown and halo, light enveloping him, meeting Lawrence and Frieda, Mansfield and Murry in a great celestial celebration.

San Diego
1984

NOTES

1. About a year before his death, Harry sent me a large packet of these personal letters, suggesting I destroy them. "I know you would never wish to see them published." How sensitive he was. I did as he suggested.

2. Editors' Note: A later shortened version of the *Priest of Love* film lacks Harry T. Moore's cameo appearance.

THE MODERNISTS

1

Literature at Work

CARL BODE

Every now and then my professional cheerfulness comes bang up against some heavy evidence that we're in trouble. I value stability, and institutions we can depend on. But nearly all the signs, exact and inexact—statistics, news reports, personal observations—show that some of our major institutions are eroding. The family, for one. Parental authority seems to me to crumble while I watch it. The broods of children without one strong parent, let alone two, are multiplying. Divorce rates boom. See the latest HHR figures.

The church, for another. In my Anglican parish the congregation shrinks, dignified but declining. The college students who used to crowd the pews, especially before examinations, have disappeared. Even the Rock of Rome is weathering. In my seminars nowadays I have Jesuits in bluejeans who concede, over coffee, that they're divided about such key issues as abortion and birth control. And the Catholic young, who used to go to mass even when lounging at Fort Lauderdale, now turn over and sleep an extra hour. The born-again young Protestants and the Charismatic Catholics provide the notable exception to all this, but they are a small if visible minority.

The schools, for still another, are in decline. We've laid an impossible burden on them. We blandly expect them to perform miracles on our children that we ourselves have never been able to perform at home. We grow huffy if the schools don't transform the dull into the brilliant, the untidy into the tidy, the nasty into the nice.

Finally, the older generation—if you'll accept that as an institution. Me certainly, you maybe. We've not only surrendered to the young, we've adopted some of their salient values along with some of their insignia. Take the case of hair. The cashier in my local bank has grown sideburns down to his jawline and his gray locks dangle over his collar. Or the case of sexual permissiveness. All too often we look with envy at situation ethics, particularly with its permit for sexual exploration.

Still, the consequence of all this is worse for the younger than the older generation, I believe. We have some standards still internalized deep within us. I don't think many of our students have. Yet I'm sure they feel the need for something. On my campus, where church is concerned—to pick one of our eroding institutions—my students turn to personalized movements that either promise them peace or sanction pleasure. They turn hopefully to Zen Buddhism, to Transcendental Meditation or its successors, to chemicals, to astrology—above all to astrology. Each has its drawbacks as well as its advantages.

Is there anything else that might meet the need these students feel? And some of the rest of us also? Well, I have a bizarre suggestion. It's that we try learning from literature.

I know it's a suggestion that comes on with a thud. Most students will merely raise a tired eyebrow. Most faculty members, especially members of the English department, will react as if they'd found a hair in their consommé. Over the years I've gotten to know a considerable number of my colleagues throughout the country who teach American literature. They'd rather be caught wearing white cotton socks than sharing with their students the so-called lessons of literature. I imagine that they'd equate learning from literature with memorizing the shorter lyrics of Longfellow: "Life is real! Life is earnest! And the grave is not the goal." Or memorizing the end of Bryant's "Thanatopsis," whose stately, old-fashioned lines I admit to liking.

And yet I think I have history on my side, from the time of the ancient Greeks down to the present. If we look at the great classical critics of literature, we find nearly all of them saying that literature instructs. They also say that literature entertains: that is, it instructs pleasurably, sugar-coating its lessons. Where they disagree with one another is about whether literature can give bad instructions. Most don't think so, or don't care, but a distinguished minority, captained by Plato, believe that literature not only can but will. The most famous place where Plato says so, you recall, is in the *Republic*. Speaking through Socrates he charges the poet, who is the essential author, with misrepresenting life. The poet tells us, and I'm quoting Socrates, that "wicked men are often happy, and the good miserable; and that injustice is profitable when undetected, but that justice is a man's own loss and another's gain." The more gifted the poet, the more persuasive his misrepresentations. Socrates concedes that Homer is the greatest of poets but he still must be expelled from the ideal state.

So what do we do with Homer? We perfume him with myrrh, we crown him with a wool hat, and we send him away to another city. The only poetry we can permit in our Republic must pass a board of censors. We find in the last part of the *Republic* that all they'll leave is poetry that either hymns the gods or lauds famous men.

However, most of our noted critics, through the centuries, have preferred to keep Homer. And they haven't itched to censor him either. I'd like to trace with you the way the critics in England and on the continent of Europe saw the purposes of literature. But I haven't the space, so I'd better jump a good many eras and one ocean and come down to twentieth-century America.

When our century opened, the idea that literature should teach had won such wide acceptance in the United States that it was collapsing of its own weight. The "Life is real, life is earnest" preachments were beginning to sound embarrassing. Consequently our critics in the first quarter of the century either ignored the issue or praised the realistic description of the life we knew. The new era was announced by Theodore Dreiser, whose fiction, in spite of its off-putting literalness, would have confirmed Plato's worst fears. If the novel *Sister Carrie* taught anything, it taught that a woman could sin and get away with it.

There was one firm, well-modulated voice raised in opposition, the voice of Irving Babbitt, professor of French at Harvard. He was deadly serious in asserting that literature taught. The problem as he saw it was that literature could all too easily teach bad things. Far more than most of his colleagues— comfortable, tweedy Unitarians—he believed both in the power of literature and the power of evil. In testimony to those two facts Babbitt's world had a villain, real if half-conscious, alarmingly potent even if fool as well as knave, a Swiss-born French writer who'd flourished a century and a half before Babbitt.

It was of course J.-J. Rousseau. To Babbitt, Rousseau combined the pernicious permissiveness, the selfish individualism, and the foolish belief in the goodness of human nature which conservatives of our 1960s thought they saw in that widely read and heeded author, Dr. Benjamin Spock. Babbitt was especially outraged at the effect, as he felt it, of Rousseau's doctrines upon Harvard College. It was Rousseau who'd done away with the required courses, substituting the elective system instead. Junk food for the mind! He'd attracted as his disciples, Babbitt writes bitterly in a 1908 book entitled *Literature and the American College*, "all those who, like him, trust to the goodness of 'nature,' and so tend to identify the ideal needs of the individual with his temperamental leaning; who exalt instinct and idiosyncrasy; who, in their endeavor to satisfy the variety of temperaments, would push the principle of election down to the nursery [ah Spock!], and devise, if possible, a separate system of education for every individual."

If Rousseau's disciples have their way on campus, "the A.B. degree will mean merely that a man has expended a certain number of units of intellectual energy on a list of elective studies that may range from boiler-making to Bulgarian." The only place at Harvard where strict discipline and common effort will survive is in intercollegiate athletics.

But Babbitt and his few followers made more ripples than waves. They hoped that the literature they taught in their lectures and advocated in their reviews would instill the qualities of rationality and self-restraint. Perhaps it could have but nobody gave it a chance.

The Roaring Twenties made Irving Babbitt almost a figure of fun, he seemed so fusty in his idea of putting literature to good use. But the Great Depression, which commenced in 1929, gave the usefulness of literature a sanction it hadn't enjoyed since Puritan days.

In literary studies the followers of Karl Marx had made, up to then, as small a dent as the followers of Irving Babbitt. The Depression gave them their gilded opportunity. Art for art's sake or art to teach self-restraint were scored as idle aberrations. Art should teach economics, particularly proletarian economics. A poem or a novel should advance the dictatorship of the proletariat. The new Marxist poets proved to be as full of lessons as Longfellow, though the lessons themselves would have made Longfellow wince.

The leftist poet Joseph Freeman published a typical group of four poems in the *Partisan Review* in 1934. Here's the final stanza of the final one:

> Beat, drums of the world!
> let the workers storm from the factories,
> the peasants from the farms;
> sweep the earth clean of this nightmare,
> build new cities, a new world,
> ringing with the clear voices of new men!

However, it was the novelists more than the poets whom the Marxist critics focused on. In 1933 the radical critic Granville Hicks provided us with one of the strictest statements of the Marxist position. In an essay called "The Crisis in American Criticism," published in the *New Masses,* he proclaimed that to be praiseworthy a novel had to meet three stiff requirements. First, it had to have what he termed "centrality of subject matter." By that he meant it had to deal with the class struggle. According to Marxist doctrine the class struggle was central to life and so "no novel that disregarded it could give an adequate portrayal of life." Second, the novel had to have "intensity," by which Hicks meant that the tone, in harmony with the plotting and characterization, had to be one of class-consciousness. Third, the author's point of view had to be that not only of the proletariat but of "the vanguard of the proletariat."

Proletarian novels poured from the pens of such authors as Myra Page, Arnold B. Armstrong, and Clara Weatherwax, and were appreciatively reviewed. Thereafter most of these books sank without a trace. A few survived, among them Jack Conroy's novel *The Disinherited.* He'd done a piece on the Depression in Toledo, Ohio, for of all things the *American Mercury.* H. L. Mencken, its editor, encouraged him to write his autobiography, which he later turned into the novel issued in 1933. *The Disinherited* showed enough life to reach a paperback edition, but it's hardly required reading today. Here's a brief passage (the author is speaking): "Autumn was sharpening the air and the . . . crowd had thinned out. The Market had just crashed to the cellar, leaving a sick and empty feeling in the stomachs of the cockroach capitalists, rolling in unaccustomed wealth and firm in the conviction that a perpetual saturnalia was written in America's destiny. Now they were scurrying to cover, perishing beneath the wreckage, or jumping from eighteenth story windows."

Throughout the 1930s the number of bad novels that passed the Marxist test was considerable; so was the number of good ones that failed it. But no critical system can be unproductive all the time. Applied to the novels of John Steinbeck, the Marxist critique worked handsomely. Take the powerful *In Dubious Battle* (1936), where a young communist named Jim Nolan joins a strike of California fruit pickers, rises to leadership in it, and at the end is murdered. Or *Of Mice and Men* (1937), equally tragic, a pastoral in reverse; it too conforms to Hicks's tenets. And *The Grapes of Wrath,* hailed as a proletarian masterpiece when it appeared in 1939. It has kept its high stature, I think, and we can still read it with appreciation.

World War II put an end to literature for use, and literature for use slept quietly through the Eisenhower years. In the 1960s it reawakened. Two massive issues charged the decade with dynamite: civil rights in the first half of the decade and Vietnam in the second half. Some of us remember the struggles in Mississippi, the demonstrations in Washington, the voice of Martin Luther King resounding along the Ellipse. The surge of psychic energy resulted in more nonfiction than fiction; with a few exceptions, such novels as appeared were not very good. The exceptions came, I think, from Black authors. The poetry that appeared, varying from good to dreadful, came from both Blacks and whites.

To take the poetry first, I hazard the suggestion that the poetry by whites was better to begin with but that the poetry by Blacks has shown more intensity and more staying power. Here for instance is a lyric by Don L. Lee, now known by his African name Haki Madhubuti, printed in 1969:

> I ain't seen no poems stop a .38,
> I ain't seen no stanzas break a honkie's head,
> I ain't seen no metaphors stop a tank,
> I ain't seen no words kill
> & if the pen was mightier than the sword
> Pushkin wouldn't be fertilizing russian soil,
> & until my similes can protect me from a night stick
> i guess i'll keep my razor
> & buy me some more bullets.

This Black poetry tended to be stark, simple in idea, and pyramidal in form. And it was imbued, I think, with a sense of history and a conviction that now, at last, history was on the side of Blacks. Even sensitive, inactive, academic Blacks. Here's the last third of Nikki Giovanni's "My Poem":

> if i never write
> another poem
> or short story

> if i flunk out
> of grad school
> if my car is reclaimed
> and my record player
> won't play
> and if i never see
> a peaceful day
> or do a meaningful
> black thing
> it won't stop
> the revolution
>
> the revolution
> is in the streets
> and if i stay on
> the 5th floor
> it will go on
> if i never do
> anything
> it will go on

Much Black poetry of the time was exemplified in Haki Madhubuti's tough-talking stanzas. But I can't leave this part of the discussion without quoting a couplet by that eminent Black poet and politician Julian Bond:

> Look at that gal shake that thing—
> We can't all be Martin Luther King.

Black fiction reached many more readers than Black poetry did. James Baldwin became the best Black novelist and—once he got past *Giovanni's Room*—his novels became, of all Black literature, the most effective politically. *Another Country,* which he published in 1962, ranked as a bestseller. Though it lacked the power of *Go Tell It on the Mountain,* it showed an awkward strength that impressed both the critics and the public. It portrays the love-hate relationship between Blacks and whites, between men and women, and between men and men. At the end of the novel the only promising relationship is homosexual.

Marching in step with the Black poets and novelists were the Black critics. About two allied points they were generally insistent: that Black literature is closer to Blacks than white literature to whites; and that Black literature has as its prime purpose the advancement of the Black race. Addison Gayle says flatly in the introduction to his 1971 anthology *The Black Aesthetic:* "The question for the Black critic today is not how beautiful is a melody, a play, a poem, or a novel, but how much more beautiful has the poem, melody, play, or novel made the life of a single Black?"

The protest about Vietnam that emerged in the mid-1960s and crescendoed in the late 1960s provided the second great resurgence of literature for use. It began with the poets, many poets in fact, led I think by Denise Levertov and Robert Bly. Nearly all of them were white. Vietnam developed into a white issue although many Black soldiers fought there. No Black poet came close to being as deeply involved as Levertov or Bly. To me Bly's strident voice epitomized the protest; the psychic energy of his anger gave us both good poetry and bad. But the bad was seldom consistently bad; even the ephemeral poems had passages that had some claim on preservation. In point, this passage from a lyric he called "Lies" and printed in the *Nation* in 1968:

> As soon as Rusk finishes his press conference,
>   Black wings carry off the words,
> bits of flesh still clinging to them; somewhere
> in Montana near Hemingway's grave,
> they are chewed by timid hyenas.

Or this image from his book *Light around the Body* (1967), which won a National Book Award:

> Underneath all the cement of the Pentagon
> There is a drop of Indian blood preserved in snow:
> Preserved from a trail of blood which once led away
> From the stockade, over the snow, the trail now lost.

In the literature of causes during the 1960s, our colleges and universities became widely involved. I suspect that the teachers, for the most part, became involved because their students were involved. Regardless, the causes affected even the teachers' professional organizations. The repercussions of the civil-rights struggle showed in more programs related to the struggle, in more prominence for Black professors. You could see white guilt at every convention. The repercussions of Vietnam were far more dramatic. Many a professional organization found its leadership under attack. There was a series of coups. A crucial one involved the Modern Language Association, to which most members of English departments belong. At its December 1968 convention in New York, I watched the attack erupt and indeed took a small part in it. Its aim was revolution; its watchword, as we remember, was "relevance."

During the next several years the revolutionaries won many a battle. They even elected a pair of presidents to the Modern Language Association. Their fiery speeches were often reported by a breathless *New York Times;* their printed polemics were respectfully reviewed, often in the *New York Review of Books.*

Professor Louis Kampf of MIT was the first of the two protest presidents of the MLA. He and a like-minded friend, Paul Lauter, edited a book published in 1972. They titled it *The Politics of Literature: Dissenting Essays on the Teaching of Literature,* and they composed a fifty-page preface that describes the rationale for relevance.

They start with the conviction, almost as gloomy as mine, "of the accelerating disintegration of American social and political institutions" and then announce that their main concern is "the specific social effects of literature." These have been ignored so far, to our culture's cost. Now through a helpful combination of action and thought, the social effects are not only being restudied but redirected. For ten years Paul Lauter has been thinking of writing an essay on Henry David Thoreau's effort "to awaken and change his readers." He hasn't put it on paper because he hasn't known enough about the dynamics of social change. But he's learning, fast.

For Lauter and Kampf the opposition to Vietnam is basically a weapon for social change. The call for relevance is really a call for revolution. It's time for all of us to play our part. As the editors see it, "Both self-interest and commitments to social justice lead, we would argue, toward altering our roles as students or critics of literature." We must offer courses such as "Revolutionary Literature" or "Imperialism." We must make contact with the proletariat. To teach "Wobbly songs or slave narratives or women's writings," we must—and I'm quoting again—"participate in the struggles of such people."

And they warn that we must recognize our limitations as critics. Women write best about women's literature. Blacks write best about Black literature. Moreover, whites need to take notice that Black writing is, as the Black critics claim, "much more fully integrated with the lives and struggles of Black people." So the scope of the typical professor of English is narrowed in one way but broadened in another. According to Kampf and Lauter we must hereafter be mindful of the workers, peasants, and soldiers; and we must mingle with them regularly to refresh our understanding of literature.

Sound familiar? Of course. It's Chairman Mao who's being drawn on. Properly too, for our campus socialism in the early 1970s was no longer the Russian Stalinism that dominated for decades but the Chinese variety of Chairman Mao.

Anyhow, Mao was their fountain. He was explicitness itself and had been for thirty years. My copy of his little red book is out of date because it contains the preface by Lin Piao. But the message is unaltered. "In the world today all culture, all literature and art belong to definite classes and are geared to definite political lines. There is in fact no such thing as art for art's sake, art that is detached from or independent of politics. Proletarian literature and art are part of the whole proletarian revolutionary cause."

Yet Mao's doctrines were corrupted by success, just as our academic revolutionaries have been corrupted. I remarked earlier that they'd won their battles. But I must now add that I think they lost the war. They succeeded, for instance, in opening up the MLA, in raising its awareness of Blacks, of women, of students. But when I sat in on one of the new delegate assemblies resulting from the revolution, I discovered that the rank and file of the membership had merely, and temporarily, changed masters.

And yet the revolution helped to confirm my view that literature should teach. Out of strong preference I turned: not forward to Chairman Mao but back to Henry David Thoreau and Ralph Waldo Emerson, writers I had read, enjoyed, and thought about for quite a while.

Early in the 1970s I devised a course which I hoped would do something with literature for use. I've given it periodically since then. I based it on the writings of Emerson and Thoreau but made the mode experimental. I diminished my own responsibility. Despite misgivings I turned over the conduct of the course to members of the class. I did what the class asked me to, whether it was to lecture or to discuss, to inform or to speculate. When the class didn't ask me to do anything I kept quiet. That put the responsibility on the shoulders of the class, and its members soon learned how heavy that burden could be. They'd been used to the teacher who either addressed them for fifty minutes or led a class discussion. Not here. As a rule a teacher is as terrified of dead air as a television talk-show host, but I managed to restrain myself. The typical result at the outset was awkwardness personified. For long minutes nobody said a word. However, as the semester went along, the class got used to the periods of silence. I'm sure some students used the time for thought; others wandered away into fantasy-land. On balance I believe the silences were for the good. They underlined the fact that the calculus in the course was Spartan: if the students didn't provide the psychic energy for their education in Emerson and Thoreau, nobody provided it.

What did they learn during the decade that they could use in their lives? I can give you some rough generalizations, with—I confess at once—few surprises among them.

From Thoreau and especially from his seminal essay "Civil Disobedience," they learned a theory of protest. They encountered the idea that if you're going to protest against something you believe to be wrong, you've got to be ready to pay a penalty. Your conscience must be your guide, but your working assumption must be that it's not infallible. After all, someone else's conscience may say that what you're protesting should be applauded. From *Walden* some of the students obviously learned that property is a trap and that to be without possessions can be a boon. Not that they all threw away their stereos or guitars or earth catalogues. However, they'd already experienced the genteel poverty of bluejeans. Some of them realized that they were part of that mass of people who "lead lives of quiet desperation." A few dropped out of school and went looking for Walden. Many of them, I think, learned something about nature.

In fact they still learn. Today the psychic energies behind rebellion have subsided; our campus demonstrations, with the arguable exception of apartheid, bring out only a handful of students and teachers. But the interest in nature has risen. More of my students backpack than ever before. This interest in nature, though, is a national trend, as is backpacking, and I mustn't claim too much for Thoreau. Anyway, plants abound in many of the dormitories, student apartments, and the occasional communes I visit. Even the campus bookstore now boasts a counter full of plants as well as a selection of paperbacks on gardening and plant care.

And Emerson? He's the American writer for the 1970s and early 1980s, just as Thoreau was for the 1960s and early 1970s. His essays appeal most to those students who are attracted to Zen, to oriental mysticism of several kinds, and to withdrawal into themselves. Some of my students say that marijuana finds sanction in Emerson, though I don't see it. It is to the contrary for the poet as Emerson defines him, even if not for the reader of the poetry.

One of Emerson's strongest appeals lies in his unwearying attempt to help the individual soul merge with the Over-Soul. Nearly as strong is his attempt to prompt us into self-reliance, to develop our individuality. He's suspicious of groups, societies, and even communes. He never joined that most notable commune, Brook Farm, and he didn't apologize for it.

Even more than Thoreau he's a teacher. Thoreau's *Walden* is a how-to-do-it book despite his denial. But Emerson labels one of his volumes, outright, *The Conduct of Life*. Naturally it's an Emersonian conduct of life. Its counsels are grand. The book is nothing like such bestsellers of yesterday as *Winning through Intimidation* or *The Joy of Sex*. It won't advise us on how to be aggressive or sexually effective.

How shall we live? Emerson puts the question promptly. His answer is that we should live by obeying "our own polarity." That means we must be both self-reliant and God-reliant. We must admit both free will and fate. This comes as no surprise—it's standard Emerson. Though we can't reform mankind, we can ennoble ourselves. Then if others will ennoble themselves, we can enjoy a utopia without slavery, without wickedness, and even without dissension.

Throughout his book Emerson speaks, often eloquently, at times beautifully, about the polarities he sees between self-reliance and God-reliance, between the working of free will and fate. But he never shows us how to reconcile the two and he never proposes that we choose only one. Here we meet the main characteristic of the literature of advice whenever it becomes truly literature. That characteristic is a large ambiguity. Only at the subliterary level, as a rule, do we find specific directions, concrete proposals—the kind of Monday-morning advice we incline to hope for. I don't deny that some books are both specific and grand, above all the Bible for our Western culture. A charming instance in our own literary history is Benjamin Franklin's *Autobiography,* with its well known "art of virtue." But these are exceptions: the literature of advice at Emerson's level is marked by its ambiguity.

That ambiguity naturally tempts us to pick and choose, not for inspiration but for confirmation. The poet-prophet tells us what we yearn to hear. But Emerson himself knows that and is resigned to it. He believes that our yearnings have been planted within us at birth. Calling his first chapter "Fate," he gives fate, including genetic fate, its due. And so he writes that "we doubt we can say anything out of our own experience whereby to help each other." His modesty, however, has its own appeal. It diminishes though it doesn't remove our dismay at his exquisite irresolution. What diminishes our dismay further is that he remains an optimist, in spite of the fact that the hard truths of daily life force themselves on him. "The first lesson of history," he says looking straight at us, "is the good of evil."

Clearly the experiment I've sponsored has its weaknesses as well as its strengths. But I come away from it continuing to believe that education— through literature, by literature, and sometimes around literature—is going on.

So I end where I began, by affirming that literature can and should teach; that when it tries flat-out it's apt to be poor literature but that when it's positive and profound—not simplistic—it may be embodied in a classic of our culture. But I also end by admitting again that literature probably can't help us on, say, a Monday morning. I remember what Plato says in the final book of his *Republic*. He has Socrates demand rhetorically of Homer, "Friend Homer, . . . tell us what state was ever better governed with your help?"

Reason and reality impel me to listen to Socrates. But emotion and, I trust, idealism draw me back to Emerson and above all to the prophetic Emerson. I don't believe I'm alone in this. Perhaps the touchstone for us is how we respond to the final paragraph of "Self-Reliance":

> So use all that is called Fortune. Most men gamble with her, and gain all, and lose all, as her wheel rolls. But do thou leave as unlawful these winnings, and deal with Cause and Effect, the chancellors of God. In the Will work and acquire, and thou hast chained the wheel of Chance, and shall sit hereafter out of fear from her rotations. A political victory, a rise of rents, the recovery of your sick or the return of your absent friend, or some other favorable event raises your spirits, and you think good days are preparing for you. Do not believe it. Nothing can bring you peace but yourself. Nothing can bring you peace but the triumph of principles.

2

Toward a Definition of "Modernism"

LAWRENCE B. GAMACHE

Because the ambition to define modernism completely would be almost Miltonic, I will begin this study with an explanation of its limitations. By considering the history of the words *modern* and *modernism* and by adumbrating the cultural context that defines their literary usage, I intend to suggest several essential constituents of both literary and nonliterary modernism and to provide several examples of modernists whose lives and works manifest those constituents.

My initial intent was to clarify the uses of *modernism* and *modernist* to describe some twentieth-century writers and their works. I considered referring to four major figures—Eliot, Yeats, Joyce, and Lawrence—to represent what I think are the constituents of a cultural phenomenon that reaches back at least several centuries in its genesis. This I found difficult: much clarification was needed before the examples could be discussed.

The word *modernism,* given its complex range of uses, has all the traps of others like it, for example, *romanticism;* it presents even greater difficulty just now because of the proximity in time of the phenomena it pretends to identify. My revised ambition has not been overreaching, I think, but it has, nevertheless, led to a very cumbersome project. Previous studies have dealt with rather limited literary and artistic applications of the word, and have discussed points of specific agreement and disagreement about the phenomena it usually refers to; but little has been done to relate nonliterary uses of the word, especially its earliest uses, to descriptions of the larger cultural context that frames recent literary history. A larger study might seem more appropriate than this attempt to outline a difficult subject, but in the context of the series of essays to which it will relate, what I have undertaken is apropos. The apparently disparate cultural phenomena referred to in a number of contexts by uses of *modern,* or many of the modifications of that word current in theological and religious, scientific and technical, linguistic, philosophical, and psychological study, in social, economic, and political practice as well as ideology, make an unequivocal usage impossible. Studies of the literature and art from origins other than Anglo-American, French, German, and Italian (most often treated as the mainstream sources of the "modernist tradition") and of its nonliterary uses can help to identify what is basic to the phenomena the word refers to. My final intent has been to clarify the literary meaning of this term by identifying its earliest usages, in particular the religious, the first context in which it gained currency, and to suggest parallels between appropriate literary and nonliterary figures who illustrate essential modernism.

It is the core of the meaning of modernism, then, for which I will suggest an explanation. I think there is a felt sense of crisis in human existence reflected in many late nineteenth- and twentieth-century cultural products to which the following constituents of modernism can be attributed: (1) a preoccupation with the present, usually urban and technical rather than rural and agricultural in its sense of place and time, is related to the loss of a meaningful context derived from the past, from its forms, styles, and traditions; (2) this sense of loss gives rise to a search for a new context—cosmopolitan, not provincial, in scope—and for new techniques to evolve an acceptable perception of reality, often, paradoxically, in the form of an attempt to rediscover roots in the depths of the past; (3) but this search tends to an increasingly relativistic, inward, often disillusioned vision and a compulsive need to develop techniques to embody it. As Monroe K. Spears suggests, however, the modernist may also react to modern cultural changes "as emancipation, a joyful release from the dead hand of convention, from stale pieties and restrictions."[1] The culmination for many modernists is the rejection of the present in favor of the values of the past (Eliot), a singular vision of the future (Lawrence), a substitute reality (Yeats), or the diminishing conviction that there is any stable external reality to which that inward search relates (Joyce). For a writer to be a modernist, each of these constituent elements should to a noticeable degree be not just arguable but evident preoccupations; someone may be modernistic in some ways without being a modernist, as is true of George Bernard Shaw, the early Yeats, Robert Frost (at least in much of his work), and the later Eliot.

My proposed description of modernism is really a fairly basic reduction to a common ground of what most commentaries on modernism state as defining constituents.[2] What has been most revealing during the study of this common ground is the extent to which it applies to the wide range of phenomena in our culture referred to above, that is, to our struggles as artists, scientists, philosophers, even technologists, to deal with that sense of crisis in our evolution that has increasingly pervaded human life through at least the last two centuries. Although a specifically modernist period, analogous to the romantic period of the late eighteenth and early nineteenth centuries, can be argued to have existed in the late nineteenth and early twentieth centuries, based on the prevalence to a significant extent of its defining characteristics in the rhetorical and poetical products of writers, be they artists, philosophers, or scientists, the word itself must be allowed to function descriptively, unfettered by temporal constraints, as are *romanticism* or *classicism*. Certain ancient authors, therefore, might be legitimately said to manifest modernist attitudes or responses, without the assertion being considered absurd.[3] For example, Euripides, for some critics, at times reflects very modernist reactions to certain human quandaries. In 1938, Robert L. Calhoun argued this point as he defined the meaning of *humanitarian modernism* in contrast to traditional Christian religious views. He applied his definition to several sociocultural contexts without limiting himself to a purely twentieth-century frame of reference. He said that "its key note is active, conscious preoccupation with the present" and that "the obstinate, urgent past embodied in living tradition is disparaged." Confidence in a "new critical insight," which may issue in "rationalism, in positivism, or in skepticism," he attributes to the modernists' cutting away of "spiritual bonds which else would hold present and future to the past."[4] While I would qualify Calhoun's sense of the modernists' perfectabilitarian optimism and decisiveness in divesting themselves of the past and a pride and confidence about themselves and their programs, his awareness that the phenomenon is not a "school of thought" and is a "particular recurrent mood of temper, which in essence is very old, which during the past two hundred years has become more widespread," are insights uncharacteristic of early considerations of the meaning of "modernism," especially in a religious context.[5]

It is very difficult to discuss any examples of modernism in isolation, and, for that reason, I will preface my examples of a prototypical form of modernism with a consideration of the word as such and with what I hope will be sufficient acknowledgment of the appropriate larger context necessary for a coherent discussion of representative patterns of moral, religious, and existential crises drawn by the examples I will cite. According to the *OED*, *modern* was first used in the sixth century A.D. by analogy with the modification of *hodie* to *hodiernus: modo* became *modernus,* meaning "just now." It would seem both by virtue of analogy and etymology that a preoccupation with "just now," rather than with the past or the future, is fundamental to what *modern* suggests, in particular when it is modifying statements of attitudes or states of mind, not simply designating what is coeval. In England, from the seventeenth to the nineteenth centuries, it usually referred to qualities of thought, style, or workmanship that were current rather than classical in sympathy or affinity, often with pejorative connotation.

This long history of usage is, in part, the source of some of the confusion in the use of *modernism* (that is, one that assumes apparently differing significations in differing contexts while, at the same time, retaining a core of meaning). When the suffixes *-ism* and *-ist* are added to *modern,* an irresistible and fascinating challenge to the ingenuity of lexicographers and semioticians develops. Defining it for use as a descriptive term in literary-cultural history is no less challenging. The addition of *-ism* and *-ist* to a word can make it refer to a set of tenets, an attitude or complex of attitudes held in common by a more or less identifiable group. Individuals, and the phenomena related to them for which the word is also used as a modifier, must in some significant measure adhere to those tenets or manifest those attitudes. The danger is to reduce complex human phenomena to the *-ism,* making it a vague tag, rather than to have it point at a perceivable propensity whose identification clarifies a complex idea; it can help us to be aware of an underlying coherence amid confusing diversity. Any definition of such a term that comes to grips with the fundamental problem—the relationship of the literary to the larger context of cultural influences that, in the final analysis, define it—will necessarily have to be relative: flexible, yet have the precision to suggest more than a meaningless set of ambiguities or, worse, a distorting category.

Some evidence of the scope of a study of Western intellectual traditions affected by modernism is provided by Richard Ellmann and Charles Feidelson in *The Modern Tradition,* a seminal anthology of source materials that goes as far back as the eighteenth-century roots of twentieth-century thought for evidence.[6] Their collection of bits and pieces suggests the range and richness of a modern tradition for which no single concept, no matter how complex its explanation, seems appropriate. Considering the multitude of *-isms* and *-ologies* they touch on (for example, in philosophy, Kantianism, Hegelianism, Marxism; in the arts, impressionism, surrealism; in psychology, Freudianism, Jungianism; in socioeconomic theory, socialism, liberalism), it might appear that this tradition is nothing more than an amorphous slagheap of ideologies that volcanizes out of the heat of human evolution. The tradition is, however, far more real and has, in its reality, touched individual lives far more powerfully than such a conception would allow for; such a conception admits no distinction between the living heat of the volcanic eruption and its residue.

The longstanding practice of identifying the time span from the early Renaissance to the present as "the modern period" (the source of much ambiguity in its current usages) to distinguish it from the medieval, was based on an awareness of a shifting focus of attention from a medieval God-centered to a man-centered vision of this world. In this context, the so-called modernist span, considered most broadly to begin in the last third of the nineteenth century, peaking between 1900 and 1930, and continuing to about World War II or shortly thereafter, is the period of the failure of Renaissance and post-Renaissance aspirations; but between the sixteenth and nineteenth centuries the center had shifted from man to nature—seen at first abstractly and analytically, then more imaginatively and emotionally by some and more empirically by others—in reaction to the incompleteness of the optimistic programs, for example, of the Baconians and Cartesians.

Valuable studies done earlier in the century by such scholars as Arthur O. Lovejoy, Erich Auerbach, Joseph Warren Beach, Basil Willey, Paul Oscar

Kristeller, and Meyer H. Abrams have helped to clarify this pattern: there has been a progression from the optimistic attempt to discover the real world, studied confidently as the proper object of philosophy and science and as the artist's guide, to man reduced to skepticism and to his own subjectivity. The individual, considered to be full of potential (as in the Renaissance), was gradually replaced by mass consciousness and individual subconsciousness or unconsciousness. Nature has changed from an object to know and control to a noumenal universe beyond our minds' direct grasp, and Nietzsche's "death of God" has been succeeded and completed by Michel Foucault's "death of man." The process of this succession constitutes the history of the modernist era.

The effects of these shifts on efforts to understand fundamental reality are primary indicants of the modernist temperament; by looking into the earliest attempts to embody these effects in the forms of our culture, especially in its religious forms, we can clarify them somewhat and apply them to literature by more precise use of analogy than is usual. The majority of studies of modernism thus far tend to isolate the object matter of the study—be it art, literature, philosophy, or religion—from the other areas of human activity that manifest the incursion of the modernist spirit, thereby rendering our perception of that phenomenon piecemeal and our understanding fragmentary. I have chosen to use the development of modernism in Roman Catholicism to exemplify what I think are its major constituents because religion touches most directly on those facets of human thought and feeling affected by modernism and because, historically, Roman Catholic intellectuals were the first to pursue consciously and deliberately the modernist enterprise as I am defining it.

Evidence of the spirit, the motivations, and the genesis of modernism can be studied in particular in the careers and thoughts of two exemplary figures from the history of the Roman Catholic modernist controversy, that is, in the personal and religious development of Alfred Loisy and George Tyrrell. Each of these men is considered the founder of Catholic modernism in his own country, France and England respectively; their lives suggest the terms of a crisis indicative of not only what religious modernism was at the turn of the century, but also of what it cost, and why it, too, is identified by those defining constituents mentioned above. These men were concerned with their own times, with the moral and intellectual issues they themselves felt and also saw others troubled by, both Catholic and not Catholic, in their own countries and beyond. They were aware of a loss of belief in the efficacy of religious traditions, in form and in content; they turned to new methods to discover new foundations for spirituality, but, in the case of Loisy in particular, became increasingly relativistic and disillusioned. Characteristic of the scholarly endeavors of each of these men was an awareness of the intellectual pursuits, in their own and in other fields, of colleagues in other countries. This cosmopolitanism was, in fact, the source of some of their difficulties with their more provincially-minded and ultramontane superiors. Each of these qualities contributed to Roman Catholic modernism and to the controversy surrounding it.

Pope Pius X, in his encyclical *Pascendi* (1907), identified a complex of attitudes and theories, especially certain avant-garde approaches to biblical study and to doctrine, as embodying the "modernist heresy." According to J. J. Heaney, a Catholic spokesman, "[*Pascendi*] condemned theories on dogma and Biblical criticism which had agnostic, immanentist-evolutionary and anti-intellectualist bases."[7] He also claims that "immanentism, neo-Hegelianism, and agnosticism were the terminal point rather than the *point de depart*" for some modernists only.[8] This judgment would apply to Loisy, but not to Tyrrell.

From such a point of view, *Pascendi* focused on the negative influence of current, often conflicting, varieties of epistemological phenomenalisms like those of Mill, Spencer, Pierce, and Comte; of philosophical idealisms like Bradley's, Hegel's, Bergson's or Croce's; of forms of scientific and historical determinism as preached by Thomas Henry Huxley or Hippolyte Taine; and of the religious historicism of such scholars of religion as Schleiermacher, Ritschl, von Harnack, and Renan. The views of these last supported, in varying measure, and paradoxically, scientific historicism in biblical and doctrinal studies—a relativistic development in matters of faith, and subjectivism, that is, feeling, as the basis for a commitment to religious belief in the absence of intellectual certitude. It is the force of intellectual currents such as these, in particular those that affected twentieth-century man's confidence in his knowledge of the world outside his mind, and, for that matter, the worlds of his mind as well, that have influenced modernists in literature from Joyce, the rational technician, to Lawrence, the intuitive man of feeling.

According to Leighton Parks, an early twentieth-century Protestant modernist, what was "somewhat contemptuously" condemned by Pius X was more than a series of explicit, highly formulated positions; it was, rather, a complex of "certain social, philosophical, and historical movements in the Roman Catholic Church"[9] that the Pope stigmatized as heretical. To Parks, modernism "is not a body of doctrine. It is a state of mind. It is an attempt to 'justify the ways of God to man,' that is, to man in the twentieth century."[10] To many, both inside and outside the Catholic Church, it was that "state of mind" the Pope condemned. The examples of Loisy and Tyrrell support Parks: they did not uphold the same theses; they were involved in different ways, as scholars and as idiosyncratic minds, with different areas. Yet they did share common attitudes, those I have cited above as specifically constituting the modernist spirit.

Alfred Loisy has often been called the father of Roman Catholic modernism. He was born in 1857 in Ambrières, Marne, and began studying for the priesthood at the age of seventeen. He was ordained five years later. He became a student and, later, Professor of Hebrew and Biblical Exegesis at the

Institut Catholique in Paris, between 1881 and 1893; he was dismissed in 1893
as a result of an article on the Bible and inspiration. He served as Chaplain to
the Dominican Sisters at Neuilly, Seine, from 1893 to 1899. In 1900 he was
Biblical Lecturer at the Ecole Pratique des Hautes Etudes in Paris but had to
retire in 1904 because of his controversy with Rome; a number of his books
were placed on the Index by Pius X in 1903. He was finally excommunicated
in 1908.

In 1909 he became Professor of the History of Religions at the Collège de
France. He abandoned Catholicism and eventually Christianity in any traditional sense, but continued to publish studies of the Bible and other religious
subjects until his death in 1940. His career spanned the modernist era, but his
earlier years are the most important.

In 1913, Loisy revealed his earlier torments while a student of theology:

> Just in the degree to which certain objects of faith had impressed me when
> employed as sources of religious emotion, to that same degree their Scho-
> lastic exposition in terms of naked intellect filled my mind with an ill-
> defined disquiet. Now that I was required to think all these things ra-
> tionally, and not merely to feel them, I was thrown into a state of prolonged
> disturbance. For my intelligence could find no satisfaction, and with my
> whole timid, immature consciousness I trembled before the query that
> oppressed, in spite of myself, every hour of the day: Is there any reality
> which corresponds to these doctrines?[11]

The conflict felt by Loisy as a sickly, delicate young seminarian might be
used, *mutatis mutandis,* to describe James Joyce during his adolescence.[12]

Loisy was but eleven years old when the doctrine of papal infallibility was
declared during Vatican Council I (1869–70); but the sources of tension
within and outside the Catholic Church that led to that declaration lie behind
Loisy's declared "four years of mental and moral torture,"[13] during which he
was introduced to the study of Roman Catholic theology. Joseph Ernest
Renan (1823–92), an agnostic and author of the highly controversial *Vie de
Jésus* (1863), had used textual-historical critical tools in treating the New
Testament story of Christ as a romance, reducing Christ to a purely human
historical figure; David Friedrich Strauss (1808–74), a German theologian,
had mythologized the Christ figure. These uses of "modern" textual-critical
approaches, compounding the effects of current archaeological discoveries in
the Middle East and the unsettling effects of popular Darwinianism, deeply
disturbed many of Loisy's contemporaries. It was as a response to such
influences that Rome declared infallibility and that Leo XIII published his
encyclical *Aeterni Patris* (1879) in support of neo-scholasticism for an ap-
proved method in philosophical and theological studies.

In his late adolescence, Loisy entered religious studies in a milieu of
heated controversy and a deeply-rooted historical division between "liberal"
and "fundamentalist" Catholicism. Those who stood on a middle ground or

who, like the Baron von Hügel and Giovanni Genocchi (both contributors to religious studies associated with Loisy during his controversy with Rome), attempted to mediate the "modernist" cause with traditionalists, were caught, often painfully, between two irreconcilable extremes. As Loisy developed in his studies of scripture, he became the spokesman of the "modernist" extreme. It was in his mid-twenties, after he took his degree in theology, that he embarked on his career as a modernist student of the Bible. By 1882, he expressed his awareness of the conflict that would eventually lead him to break with Roman Catholicism and, in the long run, with any traditional notion of Christianity:

> On the one hand [is] routine calling itself tradition; on the other, novelty calling itself truth. . . . These two attitudes are in conflict as to the Bible, and I wonder if anyone in the world is able to hold the scales even between faith and science.[14]

That same year, he became a student of Renan at the Collège de France.

By 1890, when he published his first piece of biblical scholarship, the way before him was becoming clearer and his direction was being set. In 1893 he lost his position at the Institut Catholique in Paris. In 1900 he criticized the notion of inspiration in Leo XIII's *Providentissimus Deus* (1893). Loisy's claim that theologians "are as able as others to write . . . free criticism, because in the field of biblical history, *as in every other subject* [emphasis added], faith directs scientific investigations" was, paradoxically, the source, according to Genocchi, of his pronouncements that contradicted traditional teaching. Genocchi warned Loisy against the inevitable conflict he would engender between biblical textual history and philosophical and theological analysis.[15] To Genocchi there was a fundamental difference between historical-critical and philosophical methods: they must not be confused or reduced the one to the other. Loisy began to treat purely philosophical and theological questions, "though protesting that he wished to write a purely historical work."[16] The philosophical and theological methods to which Genocchi referred were neo-scholastic, more specifically neo-Thomist. Genocchi was a declared devotee of Thomas Aquinas from his earliest years of study.[17] Loisy sought in these years to apply new, *nonscholastic* methods to biblical studies as an apologist; he in fact referred to his work concluded in 1899 as an "apologetic." The final section, according to Francesco Turvasi, served as the rough draft for chapters on the historical Jesus and on Christian dogma and worship in *L'Evangile et l'Eglise* and *Autour d'un petit livre* (1903), two works that seriously disturbed many of his confrères, and evidently caused a number of young clerics to question their religious convictions. This work was originally entitled *La crise de la foi dans le temps présent: essais d'histoire et de philosophie religieuses;* he clearly saw himself in the vanguard of a new approach to religious studies.

Loisy believed he was being maligned, not because of his audacity in implying radically different theological and philosophical (particularly implicitly epistemological) positions, but because of his accusers' ignorance of the true nature of the crisis and of the methods of modern study that might resolve that crisis. This seems, at least, to have been his sense of the conflict at the turn of the century. He was moving consistently toward an evolutionist view of church teaching, and an immanentist (anti-transcendent) view of God's relationship to the world and man, and toward a "Catholic" agnosticism in his view of the person of God and of Christ's divinity: he evidently wanted to remain *in* the Church while, at the same time, teaching views inconsistent with its traditions in theology. In 1913, he acknowledged the impossibility of maintaining these two positions.

Loisy's "ill-defined disquiet," his intense sense of a mission,[18] felt early in his intellectual development, to find new techniques for dealing with the issues of faith he recognized as increasingly troublesome for his contemporaries, and his desire to open his quest to the discovery of new, rational grounds for a new kind of religious faith offered by research outside the strict confines of traditional religious study, are the areas I think suggestive of analogies to be drawn to the urgency shared by literary and visual artists contemporary with him in their thematic preoccupations, and in their search for new techniques to embody those themes (whether products of thought or of feeling or, in Pound's words, of an "intellectual and emotional complex [experienced] in an instant of time."[19] Loisy's gradual movement away from the given heritage of his religious ancestry toward an agnostic, relativistic approach to biblical and doctrinal interpretations presages similar developments in other, equally sensitive products of late nineteenth- and early twentieth-century cultural evolution.

George Tyrrell and Alfred Loisy have often been linked in studies of Roman Catholic modernism as the leading lights of the movement, because both were excommunicated after *Pascendi* was promulgated and because both resisted the attempt to stop their endeavors to change basic conceptions of Catholic teaching; however, these two men could hardly have differed from each other more completely in their backgrounds and personalities. Loisy was born into a peasant farm family, very traditionally French Catholic, was destined very early in life for the priesthood, and was educated from his earliest years wholly in Church schools; Tyrrell was born in Dublin, in 1861, into a Protestant Irish family, made fatherless just before his birth, and was constantly moved about (eighteen times by the age of eighteen). He was exposed "to a variety of religious traditions, including Methodism, Calvinism, and Evangelicalism."[20] His older brother, a very important influence during his formative years, was an agnostic. Between the ages of ten and fourteen, George Tyrrell claimed he did not believe: "It was simply my first self-chosen attitude in regard to religion; I did not cease to be a believer, but, from a non-believer, I became an unbeliever at about the age of ten."[21] His family were believers, except for his brother Willie, but they were not aware of his attitudes. A childhood friend later wrote, "for Tyrrell, his change of religion was a necessary precondition to his gaining of his soul spiritually or intellectually."[22]

Tyrrell found his direction toward religious faith in his fourteenth year; he discovered Grangegorman, an Anglican High Church in Dublin. Of this experience, he said he "felt instinctively what I, long afterwards, understood clearly, namely: that the difference between an altar and a communion table was infinite."[23] Ellen Leonard describes Tyrrell's progress toward Catholicism by contrasting it with that of Newman, a figure of importance in Tyrrell's early modernist thought: "Whereas Newman began with a belief in God's presence in the voice of conscience, which led him ultimately to a belief in Catholicism, Tyrrell began with Catholicism, which led him to Christianity and then to Theism."[24] He became a Roman Catholic after having moved to London in 1879, and almost immediately he decided to become a Jesuit priest.

Tyrrell's "spiritual odyssey," according to Leonard, was the result of his "strong 'wish to believe' "; it was an urgent search for a conception of order that would provide meaning for people living in a modern, not medieval, world. He was guided by a "strong sense of mission, a conviction that his search was not for himself alone. . . . His concern was for others who were experiencing the same darkness through which he had come."[25] The introduction, during his seminary studies, to neo-scholastic methods had a long-lasting influence on him; he felt St. Thomas Aquinas gave him the intellectual instruments to pursue his quest:

> Whatever order or method there is in my thought . . . I owe . . . to St. Thomas. He first started me on the inevitable, impossible, and yet not all-fruitless quest of a complete and harmonious system of thought.[26]

It is ironic that his condemnation was, in part, for not acquiescing to the authority of neo-scholasticism in the teaching of Church doctrine.

Tyrrell's acceptance of the Jesuit discipline was based on a conviction "that the originality of Ignatius [founder of the Jesuits] lay in his willingness to adapt new means to meet the needs of his time."[27] It was to revive this Ignatian spirit, that is, to seek again the means, suitable to the realities of the turn-of-the-century, to speak to the people of a modern world, that he dedicated himself. He gradually came to believe that what he called Jesuitism had become "the maintainer of the *status quo,* rather than an innovative force within the Church."[28] He felt it contributed to an exaggerated sense of Church authority that stultified attempts to accommodate Church teachings to the research of modern science and scientific criticism. It became his hope to "historicize" St. Thomas, who "represents a far less developed theology than that of the later Schoolmen. . . . I would study Aquinas as I would study

Dante, in order that knowing the mind of another age we might know the mind of our own more intelligently."[29] Tyrrell here sounds much closer to a Gadamer than to any neo-scholastic of his own time. His attempts to use this critical approach to Thomas as a teacher of philosophy at Stonyhurst, between 1894 and 1895, led to his removal from teaching and to his early difficulties within the Society. At this point he began to search for alternative ways of understanding and interpreting Catholicism.[30] John Henry Newman seemed to offer such an alternative.

From Newman, Tyrrell adapted the conception of Christianity as developmental, that is, that the teachings of the Church in any age are the articulation of Christ's revelation for that age—that the Church itself evolved and is evolving continuously. He said that Newman recognized "the fluctuating character of science and religion" and that Newman wanted "to make the preambles of faith in some sort independent of, and indifferent to, those very fluctuations."[31] Tyrrell wanted to establish the critical bases of faith upon which subsequent studies, such as Loisy's adaptation of German criticism in his work on the Bible, could rest without need or fear of authoritative censure from Church officialdom. His was the position of mediator: "The Church may neither identify herself with 'progress' nor isolate herself from it. Her attitude must always be the difficult and uncomfortable one of partial disagreement and partial assent."[32]

At the close of the century, Tyrrell published an article on the dogma of Hell; in the course of his statement, rejecting the scholastic position, he remarked:

In a saner spiritual philosophy born of a revolt against materialism—the last and lowest form of rationalism [e.g., scholasticism]—a basis is found for a certain temperate agnosticism, which is one of the essential prerequisites of intelligent faith; . . . the essential incapacity of finite mind to seize the absolute and which governs and moves everything towards itself, the natural necessity of seeming contradictions and perplexities in our estimate of God's thoughts and ways are accepted as inevitable.[33]

This article led to the conflict with the authorities of his Society and of the Church in Rome that culminated eight years later (22 October 1907) in his excommunication, a little more than a month after *Pascendi* was promulgated.

Tyrrell's way of dealing with this conflict—without denying his basic acceptance of Catholicism, on the one hand, or of acquiescing to the pressures of authority, on the other—was to see himself as one who "will stand on the doorstep and knock and ring and make myself a nuisance in every possible way."[34] He had a sense of his own faith that echoes Newman's of *A Grammar of Assent* (1870), in rejecting "extravagant claims for what reason can prove about God. We have assents based . . . on the total response of the whole person to a concrete fact."[35] He also had to deal with uncertainty:

As to faith, it is my hope that there is a solution yet to be discovered; and that not very far hence. I think there are crises in human thought comparable to those in evolution when life, sense and reason first come on the scene; and that after such crises there are seasons of great confusion pending readjustment; . . . How far away even Newman seems to one now! How little he seems to have penetrated the darkness of our day![36]

His answer to the darkness, and his urgent reason for knocking at the door of the Church rather than retiring, is contained in his conception of the proper relationship between Catholicism and the modern world:

If a religion is to influence and leaven our civilization and culture it must be recognized as a part of it, as organically one with it; not as a foreign body thrust down from above, but as having grown up with it from the same root in the spirit of humanity.[37]

Death did not come to Tyrrell suddenly; he had expected to die even sooner than he did, but the spectre did not deter him from his convictions or his chosen course of action. Up to 1909, when the effects of Bright's disease and, undoubtedly, the strain of the conflict he was in took their toll, he continued to adhere, within himself, to his Catholicism, hoping that he might contribute to making it adapt more coherently to the ways of the modern world.

Earlier in the nineteenth century, Tennyson had expressed his fears of the image of nature being proffered by biological science (*In Memoriam*) and technology ("Locksley Hall Sixty Years After"), but he did not grasp the challenge to his most basic perception of reality that would evolve by the time of Tyrrell and Loisy. And Arnold's "darkling plain" in "Dover Beach" was perhaps his most extreme expression of human prospects after the withdrawal of the "Sea of Faith." On the whole, Victorians saw the direction of coeval developments in human knowledge positively or, at worst, fearfully; but the fearful did not realize the radical effect on their sense of the past and of the present about to invade their basically stable perceptions of the right order of things. The apparent darkness of modern human horizons became evident to religious searchers sooner than it did to most of their contemporaries, and their perception of that darkness—unlike, for example, a Hardy's—was framed by a modernist's sense of place and time and of the general human condition in a modernized world. The careers of both Tyrrell and Loisy echo the mind and world of a Stephen Dedalus or a Paul Morel far more than they do a Michael Henchard, or any of the Forsyths for that matter.

The patterns of the modern novel described by Frank Kermode in *The Sense of an Ending* or Alan Friedman in *The Turn of the Novel*, that is, their open-endedness and apocalyptic, urgent struggles for an intellectual and emotional vision to give a meaningful context of belief in which to act out human life, are more applicable to Loisy's and Tyrrell's biographies than they would be to their mentors' life stories, such as, for example, Renan's or

Newman's. The descriptions of literary modernism presented by such commentators as Spears, who acknowledges the importance of religious modernism in his *Dionysus and the City,* or Bradbury and McFarlane, who never allude to it in their collection of essays entitled *Modernism: 1890–1930,*[38] are clearly relevant to a study of religious modernism; and a knowledge of religious modernism does make clearer and more vividly real the intensity and nature of the human conflict the growth of modernism in our culture represents. I have attempted to sketch, briefly, the outlines of that conflict, in particular as it is represented by the lives of two of its most famous and most painfully intense figures.

In discussing the attempts of modern artists to produce their works, William Graham Cole offers the following description of modernists:

> Many modern artists have portrayed the predicament of twentieth-century man with jarring expressiveness. . . . In [all the arts], the creative mind has found the old forms hollow and mute. They no longer communicate; they have ceased to contain or convey. The search for new media, new symbols, new techniques is everywhere painfully apparent. . . . Those who peer at the present age, penetrate its mask and probe into . . . themselves no less than [into] the world outside . . . : for [modern artists] there was a chaotic breakdown of all traditional forms of communication. Impressionism, Expressionism, Fauvism, Cubism, Surealism [*sic*], Dadaism are all late nineteenth-century and twentieth-century efforts to understand and to express what is happening to modern man and his world, they are exercises in the attempt to bring order out of disorder, to manage the unmanageable, to express the ineffable.[39]

Cole's remarks can be used to comment almost as well on the motivations and actions of Loisy and Tyrrell. It is his reference to the "painfully apparent" search of the artists for the means to voice their sense of the breakdown of meaning that is particularly apt in describing the religious quest of the two priests. It is, perhaps, the sense that the pain is no longer so acutely apparent in many works of writers and artists of more recent years that suggests the passing of the dominance of modernism. It is as though we have gotten used to a sore and are no longer quite so sharply conscious of its continued presence.

NOTES

1. Monroe K. Spears, *Dionysus and the City* (New York: Oxford University Press, 1970), p. 7.

2. One study that does attempt to define *modernism* in its literary and, to some extent, artistic uses is Spears's *Dionysus and the City.* Frank Kermode has also discussed the phenomenon extensively; see in particular his *The Sense of an Ending: Studies in the Theory of Fiction* (London: Oxford University Press, 1967).

3. Spears points out the flexible use of *modern* in the past; for example, the "twelfth-century Schoolmen . . . were called *moderni.*"

4. Robert L. Calhoun, "The Dilemma of Humanitarian Modernism," in *The Christian Understanding of Man,* ed. T. E. Jessop et al. (Chicago: Willett, Clark, 1938), p. 45.

5. Ibid.

6. Richard Ellmann and Charles Feidelson, Jr., *The Modern Tradition: Backgrounds of Modern Literature* (New York: Oxford University Press, 1965).

7. J. J. Heaney, *The Modernist Crisis: von Hügel* (Washington: Corpus Books, 1968), p. 230.

8. Ibid. See also Heaney's "Modernism," *The New Catholic Encyclopedia* (Washington, D.C.: Catholic University of America, 1967).

9. Leighton Parks, *What Is Modernism?* (New York: Charles Scribner's Sons, 1924), p. 1.

10. Ibid., p. 5.

11. Alfred Loisy, *My Duel with the Vatican,* trans. Richard Wilson Boynton (Westport, Conn.: Greenwood Press, 1968), p. 71.

12. Loisy does, in fact, describe a religious retreat in 1873, during which a Father Stumpf's talks so "deeply stirred" him, by making him "feel the fragility of everything human" and by exalting "the virtue of sacrifice," that he felt he was called by God (*My Duel,* p. 56).

13. Loisy, p. 67.

14. Ibid., p. 90.

15. Francesco Turvasi, *A Condemnation of Alfred Loisy and the Historical Method* (Rome: Edizioni de Storia & Letteratura, 1979), p. 41.

16. Ibid.

17. Ibid., p. 2.

18. Loisy, p. 56.

19. Ezra Pound, "A Few Don'ts by an Imagiste" (1913), excerpted in Ellmann and Feidelson, *The Modern Tradition,* p. 147.

20. Ellen Leonard, C. S. J., *George Tyrrell and the Catholic Tradition* (London: Darton, Longman and Todd, 1982), p. 8.

21. George Tyrrell and M. D. Petre, *Autobiography and Life of George Tyrrell,* 2 vols. (London: Edward Arnold, 1912), 1:68.

22. Leonard, p. 9.

23. Tyrrell and Petre, 1:98.

24. Leonard, p. 9.

25. Ibid., p. 11.

26. Tyrrell and Petre, 1:248.

27. Leonard, p. 13.

28. Ibid.

29. Tyrrell and Petre, 2:45.

30. See Leonard, pp. 14–15.

31. Michele Ranchetti, *The Catholic Modernists: A Study of the Religious Reform Movement, 1864–1907,* trans. Isobel Quigley (London: Oxford University Press, 1969), p. 48.

32. Tyrrell and Petre, 2:102.

33. Ibid., 2:117.

34. Ibid., 2:409.

35. David Schultenover, S. J., *George Tyrrell: In Search of Catholicism* (Shepherdstown: The Patmo Press, 1981), p. 74.

36. Tyrrell and Petre, 2:144.

37. George Tyrrell, *Through Scylla and Charybdis: or the Old Theology and the New* (London: Longmans, 1907), p. 383.

38. Malcolm Bradbury and James McFarlane, eds., *Modernism: 1890–1930* (Harmondsworth, Middlesex: Penguin Books, 1976).

39. William Graham Cole, *The Restless Quest of Modern Man* (New York: Oxford University Press, 1966), pp. 9–10.

3

What the "Ontological Critic" in the Authors of *Understanding Poetry* Adds to the "New Criticism" of Brooks and Warren

PAUL J. MARCOTTE

I
"WANTED: AN ONTOLOGICAL CRITIC"

The "new criticism" of Brooks and Warren is old now. Perhaps it is defunct or perhaps it is only playing possum. This judgment is difficult to make.

Forty-three years ago John Crowe Ransom wrote a book, *The New Criticism,* in which he evaluated gently but, for the most part, adversely, the critical theory and practice of four men whose works were then current. His in-depth studies of I. A. Richards, William Empson, T. S. Eliot, and Yvor Winters persuaded him that it was "time to identify a powerful intellectual movement that deserves to be called a new criticism."[1] However, his studies of these critics and his familiarity with the work of other critics, Cleanth Brooks and Robert Penn Warren among them, also persuaded him that it was time for someone to demonstrate "that a work of art fulfils its purpose and achieves its value simply by *being.*"[2] Indeed, Ransom devoted the final chapter of his book—a chapter significantly entitled "Wanted: an Ontological Critic"—to a discussion of his and the world's failure "to find a new critic with an ontological account of poetry" (*New Criticism,* 281). Unfortunately, his plea for an "ontological critic" to come forth seems to have gone unheeded.

II
THE "NEW CRITICISM" OF BROOKS AND WARREN

Neither Cleanth Brooks nor Robert Penn Warren is an "ontological critic"; however, the poetics that may be inferred from various parts of the first (1938), second (1950), and fourth (1976) editions of *Understanding*

Poetry is certainly moving in that direction. Progress is sporadic and unequal: the third edition (1960), for example, reveals very little; the fourth edition, a great deal.

If Brooks and Warren are not "ontological critics," they are "new critics," who have received far less scholarly attention than they deserve. This is, of course, because their names have become synonymous with a textbook, and scholars tend to regard members of their fraternity who author textbooks—particularly textbooks that make a lot of money—as second-class. Perhaps it is time to remedy both the oversight and the prejudice.

Understanding Poetry begins with a proclamation: "This book has been conceived on the assumption that if poetry is worth teaching at all it is worth teaching as poetry." Although acknowledging their awareness that "The temptation to make a substitute for the poem as the object of study is usually overpowering," and although listing the "Paraphrase of logical and narrative content," the "Study of biographical and historical materials," and the "Inspirational and didactic interpretation," as three of the most common substitutes for the teaching of poetry as poetry, Brooks and Warren nevertheless concede that none of these activities, even when most enthusiastically performed, need necessarily become a substitute for the study of poetry as poetry. On the contrary, they point out that "When . . . an attempt is made to treat the poem as an object in itself, the result very often is . . . the vaguest sort of impressionistic comment, or . . . the study of certain technical aspects of the poem, metrics for instance" (iv).[3] From these more or less conflicting considerations, Brooks and Warren infer that:

> a satisfactory method of teaching poetry should embody the following principles. 1. Emphasis should be kept on the poem as a poem. 2. The treatment should be concrete and inductive. 3. A poem should always be treated as an organic system of relationships, and the poetic quality should never be understood as inhering in one or more factors, taken in isolation. (ix)

In the "Letter to the Teacher," the part of *Understanding Poetry* which precedes the Introduction in the first and second editions, Brooks and Warren reveal that they have made a very serious and fundamental assumption about the nature of poetry: "These *analyses* [the poems they go on to analyze in their book] are intended to be discussions of the poet's adaptation of his means to his ends: that is, discussions of the relations of the various aspects of a poem to each other and to the total communication intended" (ix). The words, "the total communication intended," make it absolutely clear that they believe that poetry is *a mode of communication* and that the poet, therefore, must know what he has to say before he says it. Although initially expressed *en passant*, this assumption concerning the primary function of poetry is one of the major premises—if not *the* major premise—that determines the limitations of the particular species of "new criticism" which is explicitly promulgated by Brooks and Warren.

The very organization of the first edition of *Understanding Poetry* underscores its authors' conviction that poetry is a mode of communication: its first, second, third, and seventh sections are described in a manner which clearly implies that poetry communicates something from one person to another; its fourth, fifth, and sixth respectively employ the following phrases: "as means of communication," "communicated to the reader," and a "device of communication" (x). Of course, the authors go on to emphasize that there is an "organic relationship existing among these factors [narrative and theme, for example] in poetic communication" (xi); they do not, however, sufficiently emphasize that the story which the narrative poet tells and the idea which the thematic poet explores are, in the final analysis, only accidentally different means of performing what is essentially the same function. Indeed, even when they do explicitly acknowledge that such things as the paraphrasable story which a narrative poet communicates to his readers is only a means to an end and not an end in itself, they apparently do not recognize the necessity of identifying the nature of the end for which the story was told. Such missed opportunities are not uncommon in their critical theory.

Another factor that characterizes their particular species of "new criticism" is the tentative and negative tone with which Brooks and Warren often express their critical views. Having little faith in the efficacy of definition as a pedagogical device, they consciously try to avoid its *explicit* use: they tell us, for example, that

> The *Introduction* [to *Understanding Poetry*] does not attempt to arrive at a "definition" of poetry or to explain, for instance, the workings of imagery or meter. It attempts, instead, to dispose of a few of the basic misconceptions with which the teacher is usually confronted in the classroom, and therefore to prepare the student to enter upon an unprejudiced study of the actual poems. (xii)

When we read passages like this one, it becomes increasingly difficult to credit their claim that they will not "delude themselves [or anyone else into believing] that they have here provided, or could elsewhere provide, solutions for any of the fundamental problems of poetic criticism" (xiv); on the contrary, we reluctantly suspect that Brooks and Warren may be more interested in catering to the exigencies of the marketplace than they are in promoting a critical approach that is inextricably bound up with an epistemology that is very unpopular. Unhappily, when they go on to defend their analyses of individual poems against the charges of dogmatism or error by declaring that "disagreement is to be encouraged rather than discouraged" (xiii), and when they qualify this seeming capitulation of principle by adding "insofar as pure impressionism can be eliminated from the debate," our suspicions are escalated.

The "Letter to the Teacher" is reprinted in the second edition of *Under-*

standing Poetry, and a disturbing "Postscript (1950)" is appended to it. The overall impression conveyed, when these essays are read one after the other, is that Brooks and Warren are attempting to persuade their readers that something which was true in 1938 is no longer true—or, at least, is no longer *as* true—in 1950. The problem arises as a result of a statement that the authors introduce as if it were merely a minor concession to teachers and students using *Understanding Poetry* who are interested in relating criticism to other literary studies: "In this revised edition, therefore, though we continue to insist upon the need for a sharp focus upon the poem itself, we have tried to relate criticism to other literary studies" (2d ed., xxi). This statement has been taken to imply that its authors regard the study of biographical or historical material, for example, as activities that are somehow extraneous to "the study of poetry as poetry." Of course, even if Brooks and Warren do not mean to imply such a thing, the statement seems to deprive the phrase "the study of poetry as poetry" of a meaning which "new critics" already understood to encompass as much of the study of biographical and historical material as the analysis of a particular piece of poetry requires. The most probable explanation is that Brooks and Warren are merely exhibiting the dichotomy which exists between their considerable skill as practical critics and their frequent lapses as speculative critics. This phenomenon, incidentally, is so commonly encountered in the writings of "new critics" that it must be regarded as one of the chief causes of what appears to be the decline and fall of a critical methodology that deserves a far better fate.

What actually happened was this. When Brooks and Warren were young men, "the ordinary college course in poetry made little or no attempt to teach poetry except by paraphrase, by the study of biographical and historical material, or by didactic interpretation" (2d ed., xxi). The influence of their work and the work of other "new critics" managed to convince a very large number of teachers and students of poetry that a poem is something more than, and different from, what its words say about any subject (its author, the world, morals, or anything else). As might have been expected, however, the successful communication of this truth about poetry was not enough. People continued to paraphrase Donne, read biographies of Byron, learn history from Shakespeare, and be edified by Milton—but it was not the same as it had been before. Something had been altered by the preaching and arm-twisting of "new critics" like Brooks and Warren. Readers of poetry who continued to do these things felt guilty, on the one hand, and cheated, on the other. They knew, but only because they had been told, that there is more to a poem than what the words say. The problem, succinctly stated, is that they did not know what this mysterious *more* was; consequently, teachers, students, and lovers of poetry began to experiment in weird ways with the act of reading a poem. Nothing helped: drink, drugs, lights, music, company. The search for a common understanding of the *more* was gradually abandoned, and readers of poetry began to relish each his own individual and often highly idiosyncratic experience with poetry. The progress, the very real progress, that the "new critics" had made against certain critical fallacies inherited by the twentieth century from the nineteenth was, for the most part, obliterated.

These things happened primarily because the "new critics" in general, and widely read critics like Brooks and Warren in particular, offered "explanations" of poetry that were philosophically thin. Although their theories sometimes contained flashes of great insight—none more often than Eliot's— and although their brilliant analyses of particular poems tended to conceal the deficiencies of their theories, sooner or later most of their opinions were found to be significantly inadequate and were consequently rejected.

Our experience with other parts of *Understanding Poetry* validates these judgments. After having read, in the "Letter to the Teacher," that "The *Introduction* does not attempt to arrive at a 'definition' of poetry," most perspicacious readers discover that this is precisely what it does attempt to do. Brooks and Warren state that "Poetry is a form of speech, or discourse, written or spoken"; that it is a communication, "the saying of something by one person to another person" (1); and that the "something" which is communicated is "feelings and attitudes" (2)—not "information for the sake of information" (1). Such statements as these certainly sound like an attempt to identify the *genus* and *specific difference* of poetry. Of course, Brooks and Warren do not stop with these few concise comments. Poetry and scientific statement, we are told, have two things in common, namely, both employ language in a very precise manner and both communicate something from one person to another; but—and this is what distinguishes poetry from scientific statement—poetry is concerned with the communication of feelings and attitudes, scientific statement with the communication of information for the sake of information. Brooks and Warren have, moreover, also made a distinction between poetry and scientific statement, on the one hand, and ordinary speech on the other. What distinguishes poetry and scientific statement from ordinary speech is the differing "specializations of language" employed by poets and scientific writers. Thus it is clear that, in the opinion of Brooks and Warren, the *specific difference* that distinguishes poetry from scientific statement is *what* is being communicated, but the specific difference between poetry and ordinary speech is *how* language is being organized to communicate feelings and attitudes. Whether they realize it or not, therefore, Brooks and Warren are now identifying the essence of poetry as the specific "specialization of language," which enables a poet to communicate feelings, attitudes, or interpretations—what they call the "stuff of poetry"—to at least one other person.

Thus far in the Introduction, Brooks and Warren are clear and coherent; however, at this point, they begin to say things or to say them in a way which either obfuscates the position they have just established or suggests that they are not entirely happy with it. When, for example, they inform us, in a section entitled "Poetry as a Specialization of Ordinary Speech," that "both the impulse of poetry—that is, the impulse to communicate feelings, attitudes and interpretations—and some of the methods of poetry—that is, comparisons, associations with words, etc.—appear in a great deal of our discourse that is not ordinarily considered as poetic at all" (8), they are telling us that "comparisons, associations with words," and who knows what else— the "etc." is particularly troublesome—are not always "methods of poetry." As a result, the term "specialization of language," which supposedly distinguishes poetry from ordinary speech, suddenly loses much of its meaning.

Furthermore, in the section "Confusion Between Scientific and Poetic Communication," Brooks and Warren point out that readers "will often accept as sober scientific doctrine what is essentially a poetic statement, or they will judge formal poetry as if it were aiming at scientific truth" (9). That readers of poetry commit such errors is certainly true; how the distinction between poetry and scientific statement promulgated by Brooks and Warren helps readers of poetry to avoid such errors, however, is difficult to see, since—and this is the crux of the matter—it is often difficult for a reader who encounters a work that communicates information to know whether that information is being communicated *for the sake of information* or *for some other reason*. Because they sense that this is so, Brooks and Warren, when they talk about "Message-hunting," conclude that "A Psalm of Life" and "Expostulation and Reply" are poems, not because they communicate feelings or attitudes or interpretations, but because of the "specialization of language" which they employ; unfortunately, however, this same "specialization of language," we have just been told, is made up of "methods of poetry" which "appear in a great deal of our discourse that is not ordinarily considered as poetic at all" (8). If, at this point, any confidence is still inspired by their distinction between poetry and scientific statement, it is seriously undermined when they fail to acknowledge explicitly, during their discussion of "Pure Realization," that the communication of emotion is at least as much the business of poetry as is the communication of feelings, attitudes, and interpretations; and, if, at this point, any significance still clings to their distinction between poetry and ordinary speech, it is surely further diminished when they fail to acknowledge explicitly, during their discussion of "Beautiful Statement of Some High Truth," that "rhythmical language, figures of speech, [and perhaps even] stories and dramatic situations, etc." (17), are elements of the "specialization of language" which is, in their view, the essence of poetry.

Undoubtedly the reason Brooks and Warren do not explicitly acknowledge either of these things is that they have seen the trouble such admissions (or claims) have brought upon other critics. The distinctions between poetry and scientific statement and between poetry and ordinary speech that they draw with care and precision at the beginning of their Introduction actually play a very minor role, or no role at all, in the species of critical performance they themselves ultimately advocate and actually perform. Instead of thinking of a poem as a form of speech that communicates a feeling or an attitude from one person to another by means of a "specialization of language" which makes use of meter, rhyme, figurative language, idea, etc., Brooks and Warren suddenly surprise us with the announcement that such difficulties as those which they had previously attributed to the confusion between scientific and poetic communication might be avoided if we think of a poem "*as a piece of writing which gives us a certain effect in which, we discover, the 'poetry' inheres.*" Even when Brooks and Warren go on to point out that what they are here advocating "is very different from considering a poem as a group of mechanically combined elements . . . which are put together to make a poem as bricks are put together to make a wall" and, therefore, that "the question . . . about any element in a poem is not whether it is in itself pleasing, or agreeable, or valuable, or 'poetical,' but whether it works with the other elements to create the effect intended by the poet" (18–19), we sense that they are moving in the right direction, but that their progress is more seriously hampered by their inability (or unwillingness) to think about poetry in the abstract than it is by any other single factor. Of course, we are troubled by the connotation of the phrase "the effect intended by the poet"— we suspect that they are advocating the commission of the "intentional fallacy"—and we are troubled by their attempt to persuade us that "The relationship among the elements in a poem is . . . not a mechanical relationship but one which is far more intimate and fundamental," on the basis of no better evidence than their analysis of an excerpt from Shakespeare:

> the piling up of the *s* sounds in the second, third, and fourth lines helps give an impression of desperate haste and breathless excitement. The lines give the impression of a conspiratorial whisper. The rhythm and sound effects of the passage, then, are poetic in the only sense which we have seen to be legitimate: they are poetic because of a relation to the total effect of the passage. (19)

What they have to say about the speaker of the poem and the ultimate value of poetry, in the two superficial sections that complete their Introduction, does little to enhance our confidence in them as speculative literary critics. While we applaud their recognition "that every poem implies a speaker of the poem . . . and that the poem represents the reaction of such a person to a situation, a scene, or an idea" (23), we deplore their failure to infer anything significant from these truths; and, although we are delighted to hear them say that the ultimate value of poetry "springs from a basic human impulse and fulfils a basic human interest" (25), we are disenchanted when they tell us that the basic human interest which poetry satisfies is the one which science ignores and that, in any case, the answer to the question of the ultimate value of poetry lies outside their present concern.

Brooks and Warren assign a tantalizingly seductive title to an essay that appears for the first time in the second edition of their book and is reprinted without essentially significant changes in its third and fourth editions. "How Poems Come About: Intention and Meaning" purports to investigate the origin of a poem by taking a close look at the *materials* of the poem and the *process* whereby the poem is made. Actually, it does neither of these things very efficaciously. On the one hand, it merely catalogues, once again, the *materials* of poetry; on the other, it endeavors to elucidate the creative process by fancifully analyzing manuscript evidence of the genesis of actual poems and by quoting and commenting upon what a selection of poets have had to say about their own creative experiences. The comparison that Brooks and Warren make between the composition of poetry and the discovery of a scientific principle, how little they have to say about the meaning of the word *intend* even after having singled it out for special attention, and how utterly and absolutely oblivious they appear to be of the role played by the *unconscious* in the making of *fine* artifacts are three eloquent examples of their lack of perspicacity as speculative literary critics. All in all, "How Poems Come About: Intention and Meaning" adds very little to what Brooks and Warren have already told us about their understanding of the creative activity: to them, it remains "an infinitely complicated process of establishing interrelations" (2d ed., 607).

In another essay which was printed for the first time in the second edition of *Understanding Poetry* (but which was not reprinted in subsequent editions), Brooks and Warren direct our attention to "The Poem Viewed in Wider Perspective." A discussion of eight of Wordsworth's poems affords them an opportunity to illustrate their opinion that "The work of a serious and able poet springs from certain basic ideas and attitudes that give it unity and continuity even in the midst of variety and change." Thus, it follows, in their view, that the study of one of a poet's poems "tends to throw light upon another" (2d ed., 632). A discussion of *The Waste Land,* in which Brooks and Warren elucidate a large number of the literary allusions employed by Eliot, affords them an opportunity to prove by actual demonstration that there is a difference between the elucidation and the poem. And a discussion of Marvell's "Horatian Ode" affords them an opportunity to examine the relationship which exists between the poem and the man who made it; indeed, we are told that "if we do succeed in mastering the poem, we shall have the poem; and we *may* have gained some insight into the attitude of Marvell the man. For the poem was fashioned by him" (2d ed., 671). Although Brooks and Warren take advantage of all these opportunities to say things about poetry which they believe to be true by reiterating their conviction that they infer little or nothing from their conclusions that "The poet himself is audience as well as speaker" (2d ed., 662) and that "the rôle of the unconscious in the process of composition" (2d ed., 680) is a problem. On the contrary, they end what they have to say about "The Poem Viewed in the Wider Perspective" by reaffirming their conviction that poetry "is an effect of the poem as a whole" (2d ed., 639). This performance evinces a lack of speculative aggressiveness that is perfectly consistent with what readers of the second edition had come to expect from Brooks and Warren.

The third edition, which was published ten years after the second, conveys the impression that the poetics of Brooks and Warren is about as complete and comprehensive as they are capable of making it; but the fourth edition, which was published in 1976, twenty-six years after the second, says things about poetry that persuade us that they have never stopped trying to understand poetry as poetry. The old familiar Introduction has been almost entirely rewritten—only a few of its most favored paragraphs survive. In its place, we are presented with an introductory essay entitled "Poetry as a Way of Saying," and the phrase "a way of saying" appropriately sums up both their progress and their lack of progress.

Here is what they have to say—expressed as often as possible in their own words. Since "Poetry is a kind of 'saying,'" students of poetry as poetry are interested in the "way of the saying" and the "nature of the said." Rhythm, rhyme, and figurative language are the most obvious characteristics of the "way of the saying." The "nature of the said," because it assumes so many different forms (narrative, dramatic, thematic, descriptive, etc.), is even more difficult to define. Nevertheless, Brooks and Warren insist that the "nature of the said" is as relevant to life as the "way of the saying" is natural. The antiquity, continuity, and ubiquity of poetry, in their view, argue that "it does spring from deep human impulses and does fulfill human needs" (4th ed., 1). Rhythm, for example, "is a principle of all life and all activity and is, of course, deeply involved in the experience of, and the expression of, emotion. . . . Rhyme, too, has a direct connection with our human constitution. It is related, as is rhythm, to the very origins of language" (4th ed., 2). And, there is a third impulse that is natural, "the 'natural' impulse to create forms" by means of rhythm and rhyme. Man is "a form-making animal. . . . Man creates forms in order to grasp the world." In creating these forms, man is often seen to employ words "in figurative, nonliteral ways" (4th ed., 3)—and this metaphorical use of language is regarded as "a natural—even essential— way of expression" (4th ed., 4). However, "metaphor [we are told] represents not only the 'way of saying' but also the 'said'" (4th ed., 5); in other words— and this is an extremely important breakthrough—in poetry, metaphors are not only a means to an end, they are an end in themselves. If, therefore, as Brooks and Warren assert, "the act of perception is, in a complex way, a creation of forms" (4th ed., 3), then it would seem that the creation of a poem *ipso facto* affords its creator and other people an opportunity to experience an entity that is necessarily new and necessarily unique.

At this point, a tremendously significant question naturally arises: What common denominator do these new and unique perceptions share? Brooks and Warren are not unmindful of the question, but, unhappily, in answering it, they fall back upon what they have had to say from the beginning about the

"stuff of poetry." The old distinctions between poetry and "scientific statement" and between poetry and "ordinary speech" are dredged up, but seem
somehow even less perspicacious in the present context than they did in the
original Introduction. They do, however, make an effort to provide us with an
apologia for the "stuff of poetry," a concept that now frankly includes
emotions as well as feelings, attitudes, and interpretations. Poetry, we are
assured,

> is a response to, and an evaluation of, our experience of the objective,
> bustling world and of our ideas about it. Poetry is concerned with the
> world as responded to sensorially, emotionally, and intellectually. But . . .
> this response always involves all three of these elements: a massive, total
> response—what we have called earlier *the multidimensional quality of
> experience.* (4th ed., 9)

"Only poetry—in the broadest sense of the word—can help us to answer
such questions [as 'What does it "feel like" . . . to be in love, to hate
somebody,' etc.[4]], and help us, thus, to an understanding of ourselves and of
our own values"; consequently, the "specialization of language" which is
associated with poetry may be viewed as "the most complicated language
that man has invented for talking not only to others but to himself." That the
poet talks to himself is an insightful conclusion; that he communicates with
himself (and others) by means of a process called *imaginative enactment,*
" 'living into' the world portrayed by a poem," is also insightful; however, the
insistence that poetry "is not cut off from life, but is basically concerned with
life—that is, with the lived fullness of the world" (4th ed., 9), casts some
doubt upon the value of these insights. As if conscious that, however "lived"
the experience which may have been involved and however "lived" the truth
which may have been inferred, no communicated feeling, attitude, interpretation, or emotion constitutes satisfactory justification for the study of poetry
as poetry, Brooks and Warren, once again, direct our attention away from the
"nature of the said" and back toward the "way of saying": "The poem, in its
vital unity, is a 'formed' thing, a thing existing in itself, and its vital unity, its
form, embodies—*is*—its meaning." And then they try to tie the two together:
"Yet paradoxically, by *the fact of its being 'formed' and having its special
identity, it somehow makes us more aware of life outside itself.* By its own
significance it awakens us to the significance of our own experience and of
the world" (4th ed., 11).

Toward the end of their introductory essay to the fourth edition, Brooks
and Warren raise two questions that they say have thus far been postponed.
Having assumed that poetry is a "saying," they question "Who does the
saying?" and "What provokes the saying?" Actually, both questions have
already been answered. The poet does the saying, and the saying is provoked
by his experience of the objective, bustling world. Obviously Brooks and

Warren are not satisfied with these answers; however, what they go on to say about the poem as "a response to a particular situation" (4th ed., 13) and about the identity of the "sayer" varying all the way from a totally unidentified speaker to a speaker whose identity clearly belongs to the poet, adds very little to what they had said previously and falls far short of the limits of their demonstrated progress and sophistication as speculative literary critics.

So do many of the comments that they make about the title of their book. Brooks and Warren are right to say: "When we do truly make contact with a poem, when we are deeply affected by it, the experience *seems* to come with total immediacy, with total naturalness, without effort. It comes with the ease of a revelation" (4th ed., 15). When, however, they talk about how the "readiness" to experience poetry is achieved, they are far less insightful. The experience of life that is the product of living and the experience of poetry that is the product of reading are not regarded as very important causes of this "readiness." We are informed that this "readiness" is obtained "By trying to understand the *nature* and *structure* of poetry." Coming from Brooks and Warren, this is a strange and surprising conclusion, for they know that "there is no point at which a reader can say, 'I am now ready to experience poetry'" (4th ed., 16). On the contrary, they know that the most a reader can ever say is, "I have experienced this or that poem, and since I have, I must have been ready to experience it." Considering how widely *Understanding Poetry* has been used, Brooks and Warren have undoubtedly put more people in a position to experience particular poems than have any of their colleagues. They have not done so, however, by explaining the *nature* and *structure* of poetry—they have done so by elucidating particular poems and by equipping their readers with the ability to elucidate others. Indeed, their practical criticism has value precisely because it enables people to experience poetry as poetry. The fact that their speculative criticism has been unable to teach these same people the meaning of the phrase "poetry as poetry" is neither ironical nor paradoxical; actually, it is simply a straightforward illustration of what happens when the tools of science are employed to solve the problems of philosophy.

III
FOUND: AN "ONTOLOGICAL CRITIC"

As we have seen, Brooks and Warren are not "ontological critics"; as a matter of fact, between the lines and even in the text of *Understanding Poetry,* we sometimes sense a determination that seems strangely familiar. Perhaps it is best described by T. S. Eliot, when he declares that "This essay ['Tradition and the Individual Talent'] proposes to halt at the frontier of metaphysics or mysticism, and confine itself to such practical conclusions as can be applied by the responsible person interested in poetry";[5] for, "The extreme of theorising about the nature of poetry, the essence of poetry if there is any, belongs to the study of aesthetics and is no concern of the poet or of a critic with my limited qualifications."[6] This determination not to meddle with metaphysical investigation is a characteristic generally displayed by "new critics"; the truth is that they, like most of their educated contemporaries, have been thoroughly intimidated by the method, achievement, and influence of science. As a result, they scrupulously attempt to avoid philosophical speculation; but, in spite of their best efforts, they sometimes wander across the line that separates the study of poetry in its proximate causes from the study of poetry in its ultimate causes, and, when they do, more often than not, it is the point of view of the "ontological critic" which they spontaneously manifest. Brooks and Warren exactly illustrate this phenomenon.

For example, when the philosopher in Brooks and Warren—and there is a philosopher in every man and woman—tells us that "The poet himself is audience as well as speaker" (2d ed., 662), that "there is the problem of the rôle of the unconscious in the process of composition" (2d ed., 680), that poetry "does spring from deep human impulses and does fulfill human needs" (4th ed., 1), that "the act of perception is, in a complex way, a creation of forms" (4th ed., 3), that "metaphor represents not only the 'way of saying' but also the 'said' " (4th ed., 5), and, finally, when the philosopher in Brooks and Warren tells us that "The poem, in its vital unity, is a 'formed' thing, a thing existing in itself, and its vital unity, its form, embodies—*is*—its meaning" (4th ed., 11), we realize that they have committed—unpremeditatedly, of course—what David Daiches called the "ontological fallacy."

John Crowe Ransom would have applauded these "trespasses" had he written *The New Criticism* in 1976. Actually, he would have done a great deal more: he would have elucidated the speculative insights of Brooks and Warren by comparing them with some of those that may be discovered in the writings of Eliot, Richards, Wimsatt, Beardsley, and a host of other "new critics." He would certainly have noted Eliot's assertion that the poet "does not know what he has to say until he has said it,"[7] that "the bad poet is usually unconscious where he ought to be conscious, and conscious where he ought to be unconscious" (*Selected Essays,* 21), and that there is such a thing as "the voice of the poet talking to himself—or to nobody" (*Three Voices,* 6), Richards's obviously ontological contention that "It is never what a poem *says* which matters, but what it *is*,"[8] and the attention that Wimsatt and Beardsley focus upon the autonomy of poems when they define the "intentional" and "affective" fallacies.[9] And finally, before concluding his study of Brooks and Warren (the "objective critics"), Ransom would have constructed, out of all these things and a great deal more, a model of the species of "new criticism" that the "ontological critic" in Brooks and Warren was struggling to portray.

IV
THE MODEL: A SIMULATION

All men have a natural impulse to create forms. As a form-making animal, man creates forms in order to grasp the world or his responses to the world. The forms that he creates are made of images or ideas or a combination of images and ideas.

The forms that a man creates in order to grasp the world are produced in him automatically as a natural effect of the interplay between the world and his sense and/or intellectual faculties.

A man may respond to the world either consciously or unconsciously. Conscious responses to the world (feelings, attitudes, interpretations, or emotions) are the result of a clash between a man's personality and the world; unconscious responses to the world (what Maritain calls "poetic intuitions"[10] and Eliot calls "*significant* emotion"[11]) are the result of a clash between a man's essential humanity and the world.

Conscious responses to the world, feelings, attitudes, interpretations, and emotions, are immediately known to the subject in whom they come to exist; consequently, no impulse to create a form through which they may be grasped is experienced. Unconscious responses to the world, "poetic intuitions," "*significant* emotions," are not immediately known or knowable; consequently, an impulse to create a form through which they may be consciously grasped is experienced.

The mere presence of what Eliot describes as a "bodiless childful of life in the gloom [that is, in the unconscious] / Crying with frog voice, 'what shall I be?' " (*Three Voices,* 28), causes images and ideas to come to consciousness and to coalesce in a manner that enables a man to grasp his unconscious responses to the world. In other words, the forms that a man creates in order to grasp his unconscious responses to the world are produced in him automatically as an artistic effect of the activity of his imagination working under the direction of his intellect.

The artistic form that is thus produced may be composed of images and ideas of entities which have a great deal, or little, or nothing to do with one another in the world. In the artifact, however, they may be related to one another in a manner that tells a story, or explores a theme, or describes an object, or expresses an attitude, or they may be yoked together in any one of an infinite variety of ways that defies classification. However these images and ideas come together, the (organic) whole that they form enables a man to know his unconscious responses to the world. Whatever else it may do is purely accidental.

Sometimes the images and ideas that become conscious do not spontaneously coalesce. Upon such occasions the successful production of an artistic form may depend upon the craftsmanship of the artist. If he works with words, for example, he may be able to verbalize the images and ideas, mechanically juxtapose them in different ways, and eventually discover a pattern that *is* the form through which he comes to grasp a particular unconscious response to reality. In such cases, the product of his art and craft is a poem, a form (a special arrangement of images and ideas) that expresses its maker's hitherto unconscious response to the world by means of a use of language which may involve rhythm and/or rhyme and/or verbal texture and/or the association of words.

V
POSTSCRIPT

It will be noted that this conception of poetry, a conception of poetry toward which the "ontological critic" in Brooks and Warren and in most other "new critics" was steadily moving, validates not only many of the unexplained "insights" which have been quoted, but, also the method of elucidating particular poems that Brooks and Warren have consistently championed. For, although a poet makes a poem in order to know his own unconscious responses to the world, once he has made it, other people—if they are prepared to learn how—are capable of coming to know responses to the world, which, although not their own, contain a bit of essential humanity that belongs to them as much as it belongs to the poet. In the final analysis, therefore, poetry is found to be a "way of saying" almost anything in which the "nature of the said" is of absolutely no necessary importance to the speaker or to any member of his audience except insofar as it serves as a form(ula) that "fulfills its purpose and achieves its value simply by *being*"— but, by *being* in a manner that is essentially different from the manner in which a well wrought urn[12] is said to exist.

NOTES

1. John Crowe Ransom, *The New Criticism* (Westport, Conn.: Greenwood Press, 1941), p. 111. Subsequent quotations are taken from this edition, hereafter cited in the text as *New Criticism*.

2. David Daiches, *Literary Essays* (Chicago: University of Chicago Press, 1967), p. 173. The irony is, of course, magnificent: John Crowe Ransom beating the bushes to find someone—indeed anyone—who is capable of and willing to commit what David Daiches calls the "ontological fallacy."

3. Cleanth Brooks and Robert Penn Warren, *Understanding Poetry,* 1st, 2d (complete), 3d, and 4th eds. (New York: Henry Holt, 1938, 1950, 1960, 1976). All page references—inserted parenthetically throughout this essay—are to the first edition unless a different edition is explicitly cited.

4. Since Brooks and Warren have already convinced us that "The justification of poetry as 'pure realization' . . . breaks down even in simple cases, for the pure realization of an experience is the experience at the moment it occurs" (15), we are uncomfortable and embarrassed when

they attempt to justify poetry by telling us that poetry can help us to know what it feels like to love or to hate. Are not love and hate—like grief—emotions?

5. T. S. Eliot, *Selected Essays* (London: Faber and Faber, 1932), pp. 21–22. Subsequent quotations are taken from this edition, hereafter cited in the text as *Selected Essays*.

6. T. S. Eliot, *The Use of Poetry and the Use of Criticism* (London: Faber and Faber, 1933), pp. 149–50.

7. T. S. Eliot, *The Three Voices of Poetry* (New York: Cambridge University Press, 1954), p. 29. Subsequent quotations are taken from this edition, hereafter cited in the text as *Three Voices*.

8. I. A. Richards, *Science and Poetry* (New York: W. W. Norton, 1926), pp. 33–34.

9. In the introduction to *The Verbal Icon* (Lexington: University of Kentucky Press, 1954), W. K. Wimsatt explains that he and his friend Monroe Beardsley wrote the essays in which they define these fallacies in order "to expose as fallacies two very prevalent approaches to the critical object, that by way of its origins in the mind of its maker [the 'intentional fallacy'] and that by way of its results in the mind of its audience [the 'affective fallacy']" (xi).

10. According to Jacques Maritain in *Creative Intuition in Art and Poetry* (New York: Pantheon Books, 1953), "poetic intuition" is "an obscure grasping of his own Self and of things in a knowledge through union or through connaturality which is born in the spiritual unconscious, and which fructifies only in the work" (115). Although Maritain may well have been the "ontological critic" Ransom was searching for, *Creative Intuition in Art and Poetry,* his great work on aesthetics and poetics, appears not to have been *seriously* consulted by any of the best known of the "new critics."

11. *Significant* emotion, as described by T. S. Eliot, is "emotion which has its life in the poem and not in the history of the poet" (*Selected Essays,* 22). Incidentally, when Eliot insists that *significant* emotion, the emotion of art, is "impersonal," he is underscoring what Maritain is saying about the non-idiosyncratic Self of the poet, which the poet grasps, however obscurely, in his works. Indeed, both Eliot and Maritain, each in his own way, are bearing witness to a truth that is self-evident: "essential humanity," whatever it may be, is an entity that is possessed by all men.

12. The "ontological propensities" of Brooks and Warren that have been identified in *Understanding Poetry* are, I think, neither significantly more nor significantly less evident in other parts of their critical writings.

4

Cities of the Living/Cities of the Dead: Joyce, Eliot, and the Origins of Myth in Modernism

RICHARD D. LEHAN

I

The earliest cities had their beginning about five thousand years ago in Mesopotamia in that region between the Euphrates and the Tigris rivers. The first of these cities was Ur, located about 140 miles southwest of Babylon in what is today southern Iraq. In the eighteenth century B.C., the biblical Abraham was supposed to have lived there. After Ur and Uruk, the power moved up the Euphrates to Babylon—a city of twenty-five hundred acres which, like Ur, was located on the Euphrates in a region five miles south of present-day Baghdad. Again like Ur, Babylon took its being from the river and, as Ur declined, prospered under the inspired leadership of Hammurabi before reaching its greatest heights under Nebuchadnezzar (605–562 B.C.), before falling to the Persian king Cyrus in 539 B.C. Alexander the Great captured the city in 331 and died there in 323 B.C.

In these cities where the river touched the land, the river brought life; life and death—and the mythologies connected with these processes—could not be separated from the flow of the river. Each city became connected with a god or goddess, and the ziggurat (storied temple) with its sanctuary at the top was both the physical and spiritual center of the community. Uruk, for example, was the center of Anu-worship, although Anu's power was diminished when he shared it with Ishtar, whose story is connected with the death of Tammuz and has obvious parallels to the vegetative gods, Osiris in Egypt and Adonis in Syria and later Greece. Ishtar descends to the underworld, passing through seven gates as she goes, giving up a garment at each, until she appears naked before the underworld queen. In the meantime, the world above was withering away and remained a wasteland until Ishtar was freed, at which time the land was restored.

The Gilgamesh legend is also connected with the history of Uruk;

Gilgamesh may even be a city king whose life deeds have been elevated beyond legend to myth. Gilgamesh's journey involves a series of adventures, first against the monster Enkidu, who later becomes his devoted friend, then against Ishtar, whom he refuses to marry. Ishtar demands his death from Anu, who sends a heavenly bull which Gilgamesh subdues, although this fight takes Enkidu's life when he insults Ishtar. Gilgamesh's journey ends with a flight to the underworld and an unsuccessful search for eternal life and later for eternal youth. Gilgamesh returns to Uruk, where he recognizes his human limits and the way the city helps serve these limits. A city like Uruk thus took its meaning from the land and from the processes of life and death that were inseparable from the land and the people who made up the city— processes that were in turn encoded in a series of legends and myths which established a connection between the natural and supernatural planes of existence. Moreover, all of these cities gave rise to a mythology involving a journey to an underworld, a realm of the dead, where contact is made that has a direct relevance to the health and well-being of the people in the city above.

II

As strange as it may seem, such myths had a deep effect on the modern imagination. We know the consent that Nietzsche gave to the Dionysus myth, which is inseparable from the myth of Osiris and Adonis, and which Nietzsche saw as the basis for tragedy. Nietzsche pitted Dionysus against Christ and called himself "the last Disciple and initiate of the God Dionysus." In 1876, Walter Pater published an essay, "A Study of Dionysus,"[1] which, like Nietzsche but seemingly independent of him, stressed the need for Dionysian subjectivity as a counter to Apollonian order and control; and such writings probably influenced Yeats, who was certainly sympathetic to a philosophy of impulse. But the most systematic and influential use of these ideas came from James George Frazer, whose *Golden Bough* (1890) summed up the existing work in anthropology and comparative religion, discussed the journey to the underworld and the connection between the living and the dead as mediated by the dying king, and specifically treated the Dionysus story in part 5 of volume 1 in what eventually became a thirteen-volume study. Frazer's study directly influenced Carl Jung and T. S. Eliot, and probably influenced James Joyce, who could find in Irish mythology a world of gods who had been driven underground.

This obsession with the land of the dead, interestingly enough, was linked with an equal fascination with the city as a subject for literature. In his essay on Dante, T. S. Eliot tells us that it was after he had read Baudelaire that he realized he could use the city as a subject for poetry, just as Dickens had used it as a subject for his novels. It is thus interesting that Eliot was reading

Dickens's *Our Mutual Friend,* a novel about the connection between the living and the dead in London, when he was working on *The Waste Land.*

But the novel that makes the most direct connection between the modern city and an underground is Victor Hugo's *Les Misérables* in which Jean Valjean descends into the underworld of Paris sewers, carries the wounded Marius like a cross under the streets of Paris, crosses a symbolic River Styx, and is let out of hell by a kind of gatekeeper, Thenardier, who literally opens a gate and lets Valjean and Marius ascend into the city, where the father is eventually reconciled with his children. Since the Christ story is so deeply imbedded in the Osiris/Adonis/Dionysus myth, Hugo could easily baptize and use it in a Christian context, even making explicit references to the parallels between his story and Dante's. But more important, Hugo tells us that the principals in his story must descend into hell before they can once again enter and be redeemed in the city. Something very close to what was happening in *Les Misérables* also happened in Joyce's *Ulysses.* I do not mean that the stories are similar; Joyce abandoned melodrama for a sense of the commonplace. But like Hugo, Joyce sent his principal characters through mythic and metaphorical forms of hell before there could be a kind of symbolic reconciliation between father and son in the city. The "Hades" chapter sets this theme, after which Bloom enters the center of the city—the newspaper office, Davy Byrne's, the library, the Ormond Hotel, the tavern, and later the beach and the hospital. After this sequence of city episodes is another hell scene, the "Circe" episode, a hell of the mind, which Ezra Pound called "a new Inferno in full sail," in which the subconscious mind vents in hallucinatory form a sense of guilt that seems inseparable from the previous urban experiences. After the "Circe" episode, we have another kind of gatekeeper scene, the "Eumaeus" chapter, after which Stephen and Bloom return to 7 Eccles Street for that fleeting moment of reconciliation between father and son, just as there is an equally fleeting moment of reconciliation between Cosette, Marius, and Jean Valjean at the end of *Les Misérables.* The romantic realism of Hugo anticipated the mythic method of Joyce, and the connection here is more a matter of affinity than of influence, although it is interesting to note that the greatest influence on Hugo was the popular writer Paul de Kock, whose novel Bloom buys in a river kiosk because Kock's novels of sentimental prurience amuse Molly.

III

In order to understand the affinity between the moderns and the ancients, we have to go back to the moment of transition from the feudal city to the modern commercial city. That moment took place at 2:00 A.M. on 2 September 1666, when a fire in Pudding Lane led to a five-day blaze that burned the London of Chaucer and Shakespeare to the ground. Christopher Wren completed a plan for a new London, literally as the old London was burning. In the new plan, Wren substituted the Royal Stock Exchange for Saint Paul's Cathedral as the center of London, the commercial function of the city taking precedence over the religious. Wren also proposed a series of boulevards radiating from this center, much as Haussmann would bring forth two hundred years later in Paris. Charles II liked Wren's plan, but the real estate costs of implementing it would have been too great. As a result, London was rebuilt more or less along the lines of the old city. But if the new London resembled the old physically, there was a quantum change in mind between the two cities. The new London was a commercial center for a new class of merchants who were displacing some of the old, landed aristocracy, as a novel like Richardson's *Clarissa* would show. This new class made money in such speculative adventures as the East India House, the Bank of England, the Royal Exchange, and in trade with the American colonies. The rise of the coffeehouses, which served as offices of business, implemented this function, as did the newpapers, which were the commercial voice for the new city. And the rise of the commercial city cannot be separated from the rise of the new science with its emphasis upon empiricism and rational thought. Men like Francis Bacon led the attack on the old mythical way of ordering reality. In *Wisdom of the Ancients,* he sees such speculation as a kind of witchcraft and magic, and his attack on the mythmaking process is answered by Henry Reynolds in *Mythomystes* (1630). The whole relationship between the living and the dead is reexamined in works like Thomas Browne's *Urn Burial.* The debate over living and dying challenged the mythic imagination.

Other kinds of change were also afoot. The new commerce was closely connected with new forms of technology, especially in the eighteenth and nineteenth centuries. Perhaps the most important was the invention of the steam engine (1769), which allowed the workplace to be freed from rural water power and the factory to move into the city, which, of course, moved the work force with it, creating the terrible wens that sprouted in London. As cities like London took on more power and influence, they became centers for a new kind of nationalism; and as the need for raw materials and markets became greater, they in turn became centers for a new kind of imperialism. The movement from a landed to an urban economy thus was inseparable from a movement toward the new science and empiricism, commercialism and technology, nationalism and imperialism. And what was happening in England after the Puritan Revolution would happen in France after the French Revolution and in America after the Civil War.

The most important literary consequence of these matters was the rise of the novel. One can chart the way the novel took the world of commerce as its new subject by following the changes in that genre from Greene and Nashe to Deloney and Dekker, a culmination of sorts being reached in Defoe. A novel like *Robinson Crusoe* recapitulates this whole historical process. Once Crusoe overcomes his fright of the wilderness, he empirically observes how it works and begins to control it. This control is implemented by primitive forms of technology such as tools and glass and pottery making. When the island becomes populated, he organizes it socially with a contract form of government. By the end of the novel, when he returns to the island from his trip to England, he makes claim to the land as his property and begins to parcel it off for sale. Thus in the course of the novel, Crusoe comes to control both the land and the people and to turn that control into wealth.

What we see in Crusoe is the conflict between the mythic and scientific imagination. While Crusoe eventually becomes deeply religious, he also becomes confident that he can control his environment and turn that control into money. The Dionysian wilderness gives way to Apollonian order; indeed, his commercial success seems to confirm rather than mediate his good standing with a divine being. This confidence in reason and material prosperity would become, in part, the basis for democratic individualism and for Enlightenment optimism, would lead to the triumph of the middle class, and would eventually generate a countermovement, known as modernism, that begins with a novel like Flaubert's *Bouvard and Pécuchet* in which Flaubert attacks the smug systems of the bourgeois, and is carried on by Joyce and Eliot, who saw that man's limits challenged this sense of control, this trust in the system of profit and loss.

A subgenre of the novel that looked suspiciously on the stratified city was the gothic. Walpole's *The Castle of Otranto* (1764), Radcliffe's *The Mysteries of Udolpho* (1794), and Godwin's *Caleb Williams* (1794), treat the passing of the estate and locate the origins of so much evil in the city. In these novels, the estate is often claimed by a rich city merchant, and the world of the old father has been disrupted by the ways of the new; a curse is often put on the land which disrupts the natural processes in a mysterious, sometimes supernatural way. The victim of this sequence of events is usually a young woman who has been used as a pawn to acquire claim to the estate or to perpetuate its growth. If she is saved, it is usually by the man of sentiment who embodies the lost values of the estate in contrast to the libertine who embodies the new secular values of the city. The man of sentiment—a kind of diminished Squire Allworthy or Mr. Knightley—tests his values against his feelings and, through the power of his good heart, is repelled by the libertine and comes to the heroine's rescue—as does Belford in *Clarissa* or Valancourt in *Udolpho*. In *The Castle of Otranto,* Theodore is the prefiguration of this character, and in *Caleb Williams,* the role is played by Caleb himself and Falkland. These novels are hence resolved by repudiating the man of the city, who is the source of evil, and by reestablishing the man of sentiment, who is often the last vestige from the world of the estate. The estate is not only locked in the process of death, but such death, ironically, seems to challenge the authority of the city itself. As Mikhail Bakhtin has demonstrated in his book on Rabelais, when a disintegrating process begins, it often takes on a life of its own.

The man who brought the gothic novel to the city was, of course, Charles Dickens. Like Defoe, Dickens in his early novels did not seriously indict the commercial-urban order. Dickens was obviously sympathetic to those who had moved into the upper levels of the new middle class, like Mr. Brownlow, although he is less kind to the custodians of this class—such as its money-counters like Ralph Nickleby, Quilp in *The Old Curiosity Shop,* John Chester in *Barnaby Rudge,* and Jonas Chuzzlewit, or its functionaries like Bumble in *Oliver Twist* and Pecksniff in *Martin Chuzzlewit.*

Dickens clearly saw the city as a middle ground between nature and civilization. Over and over, he describes the city extending to a kind of middle ground between the city and the estate. This realm is a strange, eerie, primitive world of marshes—a world of water and mud with often a house sinking into the mud, or a sluice gate, or a mill. Where water and land meet, where the country and the city intersect, or where the past and the present verge, we have narrative flash points in Dickens's fiction. This becomes a kind of modern hell that many of Dickens's central characters enter before they enter the city itself. Out of this world comes a primitive evil, slink various human outcasts who are almost mutant forms of humanity. In *Oliver Twist,* Bill Sikes emerges and goes to his death in such a region, as does Quilp in *The Old Curiosity Shop,* and Bradley Headstone in *Our Mutual Friend.* In *Great Expectations,* Orlick slithers from such a realm with a primitive evil clinging to him. Such a realm is always on the verge of reclaiming the city into which it is about to sink. The image—and it is an obsessive one with Dickens—seems to suggest the tenuousness of the city, held together by force of will, and held off from a reclaiming, primitive nature, out of which all life, including urban, first emerged.

Dickens's city, which houses the commercial system, strikes a delicate balance. It is held together by money, by counting houses, the work of which is brokered by crafty lawyers like Tulkinghorn and Jaggers, who control others through secret information, often documents locked in secret places, to which keys open drawers that hold keys to other locked drawers. Such a system is always threatening to subvert itself from within, to violate what Dickens called the sanctity of the heart, his sentimental belief in man's capacity to do good in the face of evil. Dickens's sentimental heroes and heroines labor mightily against those who give in to the system and violate their sense of humanity. Such characters run from the beginning to the end of his canon: Pickwick, Brownlow, the Cheeryble brothers, Joe Gargery, Esther Summerson, Sydney Carton, and Lizzie Hexam. They strive to overcome the chilling effect of those who give themselves to the commercial system, accept its logic unquestioningly, and define themselves by the role they play: Ralph Nickleby, Tulkinghorn, Jaggers, Scrooge, Dombey, Murdstone, Guppy, Snagsby, Chadband, Smallweed, Gradgrind, Josiah Bounderby, Merdle, and James Carker.

Dickens began to challenge the logic of the city that created such a divide between an ideal system and ideal human conduct. The system encouraged the head over the heart, as he showed in *Hard Times;* the emphasis was upon one's place in the system and its function; efficiency was to be encouraged at all costs except where, as in the functioning of chancery, waste and delay could be turned to a profit. Information was power in this world and could be used to preserve one's place, secure a new place, or enlist favors—so secrecy, cunning, selfishness, and wily behavior were at a premium and helped assure order and control.

While the system might encourage such behavior, the heart held it in scorn because it elevated the inhuman over the human, judged others only by how they fit into a bureaucratic hierarchy, allowed suffering to go unattended, and all that did not fit into the system to be dismissed as failure. Moreover, it encouraged human indifference on the grounds that compassion was unprofitable. Dickens let the counting house or the lawyer's office embody the system, and the close-knit family to embody the heart. A novel like *Great Expectations* puts the two in suspension when Pip leaves Joe Gargery and his family and enters the world of Jagger's London. And Jagger's clerk, Wemmick, becomes schizophrenic as he moves between the office (where his conduct is based on the value of portable property) and his home (where he gives generously to the aged one and to his intended). Dickens was perhaps the first great Western writer to see the contradictions built into the urban experience and the way it could lead to waste and death. He showed that the commercial process created its own sense of waste, that junk and junk shops were the end result of this process, as is the case with Krook's junk shop in *Bleak House* and Boffin's Bower in *Our Mutual Friend*. The wilderness of nature is more than tamed, Dionysus is stuffed in a place like Mr. Venus's taxidermy shop in *Our Mutual Friend*. As Dickens's city became more unfriendly, its fairy tale quality gives way to a sense of the hostile, which becomes the basis for urban gothic.

The Dickensian novel was only one of many that began to question how commercial values came into being. Even on the other side of Europe, in Russia, Gogol showed in *Dead Souls* how the commercial, bureaucratic system promoted schemes that exploited the system itself rather than encourage useful production of goods. H. G. Wells carried this idea even further in *Tono-Bungay,* where the patent medicine that makes Uncle Ponderevo wealthy is only slightly injurious to one's health; and where schemes, like the search for quap, illustrate the process of imperialism (the invasion of the wilderness, the killing of the natives, and the exploitation of natural resources). Wells also showed how inhibiting and self-destructive this process could become: the sense of exploitation turns to guilt even before the quap eats the wood and sinks the ship. Kipling's optimism had given way even before Conrad, Wells, and others showed how the demands of the extremities could eat away the heart of the imperial city, another example in modern literature of Dionysus subverting Apollo from within. What we end with in all of these novels is a sense of waste—the waste of natural resources, of human dignity, and of the urban system itself. In trying to bring control over nature, modern man exaggerated his powers and lost a sense of his own limitations. Is it any wonder that the moderns were ready to turn back to the mythic imagination and to cyclical history and allow a voice from the city of the dead to speak about folly in the city of the living—a voice that could speak with wisdom and authority because it had already experienced such folly at an earlier moment in history—as Eliot's Tiresias comes from the underworld to foretell it all from the center of modern London.

IV

In many ways, T. S. Eliot's world begins where Dickens's leaves off. For Eliot the secular city has cut man off from his spiritual roots, the profit and loss has emptied modern man of meaning, created the walking dead who are called to their commercial tasks in King William Street, the Wall Street of London, by the bells of Saint Mary Woolnoth. Naturalism as a literary moment had intruded between the novels of Dickens and the poetry of Eliot. As a literary movement, naturalism was the first attempt to chart the transition from a commercial to an industrial society, freeing as it did the peasants from the land and creating in the city a new class, the proletariat. Zola, moreover, believed the writer should approximate the method of the scientist in his laboratory, rely on observation rather than imagination, and document his novels from the historical record. His *Rougon-Macquart* novels illustrate this process: a twenty-volume study of two families, written between 1871 and 1893 but covering the period of the Second Empire, 1851–70, or as Zola put it in his introduction, "from the perfidy of the coup d'état to the treason of the Sedan." Zola offended Eliot's imagination with his belief that he could reduce literary truth to scientific observation, and Zola gave a kind of begrudging consent to the new commercialism with its power brokers (although, to be sure, Zola depicted this world as totally corrupt).

While Eliot and Pound would occasionally depict middle- and lower-class life, their version of modernism turned away from the commercial world by either moving toward aestheticism or toward an upper-class kind of experience that excluded the trials of the middle and lower classes. We can see the origins of this movement in Flaubert's *Bouvard and Pécuchet* which ridiculed the bourgeois mind, saw it as encyclopedic empiricism in pursuit of commercial ends; in *Sentimental Education* which parodied the subject of sentiment and the sentimental hero; and in *The Temptation of Saint Anthony,* the first purely aesthetic novel, and a novel that turns on sensibility and not sentiment, felt impressions for the generosity of feeling.

What Flaubert was doing on the Continent, Pater was encouraging in England, especially in the Preface of *The Renaissance* in which he says that the critic must seek after impressions, experiences that produce "pleasurable sensations." "What is important, then, is not that the critic should possess a correct abstract definition of beauty for the intellect, but a certain kind of temperament, the power of being deeply moved by the presence of beautiful objects."[2] Novels like Henry James's *The Princess Casamassima* turn on moments like this, especially when Hyacinth Robinson decides to abandon his commitment to the anarchists in St. Mark's Square in Venice when he is moved by the beauty of the moment and commits himself to what culture has built up rather than what the anarchists want to tear down. And Virginia Woolf's *Mrs. Dalloway* opens with a series of discrete and mechanical impressions from the street and closes in the salon with Mrs. Dalloway organizing such impressions into an aesthetic whole, a felt moment, which gives to her a presence. And the idea of a felt moment takes us to the early poetry of T. S. Eliot where the salon and felt impressions come together, separated from the crassness of commercial pursuit—that is, where downtown (where the money is made) is separated from uptown (where the money is spent), where the world of men is separated from the world of women who come and go talking of Michelangelo. And it is Stephen Dedalus who brings this aesthetic consciousness into the city's streets, as we are told in *A Portrait of the Artist as a Young Man:*

> His morning walk across the city had begun; and he foreknew that as he passed the sloblands of Fairview he would think of the cloistral silver-veined prose of Newman; that as he walked along the North Strand Road . . . he would recall the dark humour of Guido Cavalcanti and smile; that as he went by Baird's stone cutting works in Talbot Place the spirit of Ibsen would blow through him like a keen wind. . . .[3]

Moreover, Eliot and Joyce also learned that they would preempt the scientific dogmatism of naturalism by employing a mythic method—that is, by superimposing upon a naturalistic or realistic plane a mythic series of events. One can chart the movement from naturalism to modernism in Joyce and Eliot's predecessors—writers like George Moore, who moved from early naturalistic stories to the worship of Richard Wagner, whose interest in German myths influenced Nietzsche and created momentum for a mythic method; or a writer like Samuel Butler, who abandoned Darwinian thought for a Lamarckian theory of evolution because he believed it did away with naturalistic determinism and allowed a more complete human consciousness and sense of instinct. But the writer who had most to do with returning the modern consciousness back to a mythic past was James Joyce.

Joyce himself had moved through a form of naturalism, and a work like *Dubliners* is illustrative of his changing technique. While the opening story "The Sisters" and the closing story "The Dead" are very similar in subject matter (both dealing with the effect of the dead on the living), the two stories could not be more different in terms of technique. "The Sisters" is a slice-of-life story while "The Dead" involves a plane of symbolic action layered over realistic detail, taking place as it does on Twelfth Night or the Feast of the Epiphany, the commemoration of Christ's revealing his divinity to the Magi. Given Joyce's theory of the epiphany—by which he meant the sudden revelation of the essence or special meaning of a common object or experience—the details are important. Critics like Richard Ellmann and Jackson Cope maintain that Joyce at this time learned the symbolic method from Gabriel D'Annunzio, which would make the details of this story even more important. The main character, named Gabriel Conroy (suggesting the announcement of the king) learns that his wife had known the meaning of love and passion before she met him and that she is still bound to the memory of her dead lover. Gabriel learns the mythic truth that the dead have a power over the living and that for all his sense of superiority he is as much in their grasp as anyone. The power of the dead blankets the living like the falling snow, a theme that Joyce would depict even more graphically in the "Circe" episode in *Ulysses.*

Another influence on Joyce at this time was Giovanni Battista Vico (1668–1744), whose cyclical theory of history (that civilization passes through three stages—theocracy, aristocracy, and democracy—before giving way to anarchy) had influenced Michelet before Joyce. The connection between Joyce and Vico is usually reserved for *Finnegans Wake,* but Ellmann tells us that Joyce was reading Vico as early as 1913, and certainly Vico's beliefs are consistent with Joyce's superimposing the mythic world of Homeric heroes onto the commercial world of modern Dublin, allowing the historical contrast between the two to speak for itself. Joyce also uses this contrast for ironic and comic purposes as Leopold Bloom, the modern canvasser for ads, becomes the modern equivalent of the heroic Ulysses. But if the dimensions between modern and ancient man have changed, their common bond of humanity—the humanity that links the living and the dead—has not. In his conversation with Mr. Deasy in the "Nestor" chapter, Stephen tells us that God is a shout in the street, and then Joyce takes us forth into the streets to prove it. Whatever the historical cycle, the flow of life—that power to which Molly says Yes in the "Penelope" section—goes on. The present is thus connected to the past, the living to the dead, as the "Circe" chapter so vividly demonstrates when Bloom encounters the ghosts of both his dead father and son, and Stephen the ghost of his mother. The theme of the father and the son had been running throughout the novel and comes into focus in the "Scylla and Charybdis" chapter when Stephen connects Shakespeare with Hamlet's father, and Hamlet with Shakespeare's son Hamnet, and Anne Hathaway with Shakespeare's brothers with whom she is supposedly having an adulterous affair. The disrupted family thus runs throughout history, Stephen and Bloom embodying two modern versions of it. The whole weight of Joyce's novel is thus to bring Stephen and Bloom, a version of father and son, together for a brief moment, before the flow of life carries them apart again.

In *Time and Western Man,* Wyndham Lewis criticized Joyce for this obsession with time, especially for separating time from space—that is, from practical, scientific pursuits and connecting it so directly with the unknown. Joyce gets his revenge in *Finnegans Wake* when he portrays Lewis as Professor Jones who finds in the anthropology of Levy Bruhl support for his giving priority to space-oriented man with his sense of linear time. The exchange clearly suggests the opposition between mythic and scientific thinking, Joyce's unwillingness to set the commercial society on a higher plane than the primal society, and his belief that the day-world can never contain the night-world. It is probably no accident that the "Circe" episode in *Ulysses* comes so late in the evening, releasing from memory the ghosts of the dead, just as such release for Earwicker also comes at the end of a riotous evening; and it is surely no accident that Bloom is not only the embodiment of the commercial man but also the man of science—belied, of course, by the banality of his scientific information. It is probably also not accidental that at the end of the "Circe" episode two men appear to resolve the confusion: Corny Kelleher, the undertaker or the custodian of the dead, and the policeman or the custodian of authority. As Bloom is the urban remanent of Ulysses, so they are remanents of Dionysus and Apollo, which is why Joyce's world has so many of the qualities that Bakhtin predicates of Rabelais, especially the way it seems to partake of degenerate forms that in turn are infused with life.

Deep in Joyce's imagination, from the first stories of *Dubliners* to *Finnegans Wake,* was a tension between the living and the dead, between Earwicker's daytime respectability and nighttime shame, between his daytime rationality and his nighttime dream, between what could be contained by authority and system and what escaped. Joyce's role as exile-artist is not inseparable from this duality, so also his obsession with mythic giants who can be freed from the buried past by the liberating imagination. Such forms mock the trivial pursuits of commercial man with his rational, analytical mind and his belief in the linearity of progress.

The tension between myth and reality had long before Joyce been a part of modern consciousness. Henry Adams discussed the problem in terms of the Virgin and the Dynamo—one a centripetal, mythic power; the other a centrifugal, entropic force. In T. S. Eliot's *The Waste Land* that sense of entropy has laid the land waste and the burden is to find release by breaking the hold of the imperial, commercial culture and to release the powers of the old mythology. London is only one of many imperial cities—Jerusalem, Athens, Alexandria, and Vienna are named as predecessors in the poem—about to fall from imperial grandeur. As an imperial center, it is being weakened by the demands made at its extremities and by the recent war that was directly the result of imperial power. As a commercial-industrial center, London has caused its people to become mechanized extensions of the system, neurasthenic and debilitated. As the facsimile edition of the poem reveals, the obsession with profit and loss has sent a ship on a death mission to the Arctic and reduced the living to a kind of life in death. As in Joyce, the hope for salvation seems to depend upon a mythic journey—this time the journey of the Percival knight, who must cross the urban landscape to the land of the dead—that is, the Chapel Perilous. The Chapel Perilous—as Jessie Weston, Eliot's source, tells us—is a combination cemetery-chapel, ruled over by a satanic knight, called the Black Hand, who has slain the three thousand knights who have come to the Chapel in search of the Holy Grail. The Percival myth obviously connects *The Waste Land* story with the journey to Nemi in Frazer's *The Golden Bough* and with Wagner's use of the Percival legend—both sources for the mythic impulse in the modern imagination. Moreover, *The Waste Land* is only one of a number of literary texts that sets the city against the land of the dead; the recurrence of this theme can be found on a spectrum as wide as that which takes us from Balzac's *Père Goriot,* where Eugène de Rastignac commits himself to battle in the city from the grave of Goriot in Père Lachaise cemetery on the heights of Paris, to Dreiser's *Sister Carrie* and Fitzgerald's *The Great Gatsby* where the urban struggles of Hurstwood and Gatsby take them directly to the grave. The opposition between city and grave, two modes of being, has its counterpart in a novel like *The Sun Also Rises* in the contrast between Paris and the bullfight arena in Pamplona—that is, the contrast between the secular city and the mythic ritual of the arena; just as Faulkner allows the contrast between the holy and profaned sanctuary to carry this irony in *Sanctuary;* similar to the way that both Dashiell Hammett and Raymond Chandler in *The Dain Curse* and *Farewell, My Lovely* set their action against the world of the temple whose holy function has once again become fraudulent in an urban, commercial, decadent society, whose emptiness is revealed by the detective, the modern equivalent of the dead priest.

V

I should like to conclude this paper not with more examples of modern texts that contrast the city of the living and the city of the dead (Pound's *Cantos* would supply another happy hunting ground), but with an example from what we call for better or worse the post-modern. Many critics deny a difference between early and late modernism, but I think that there is one, and that the difference cannot be separated from our discussion of mythic and rational consciousness. Sometime after the Second World War a number of major writers set the workings of the city against a technological rather than a mythic frame of reference. Gaddis's *The Recognitions,* Pynchon's

Gravity's Rainbow, and most recently Don DeLillo's *White Noise* are texts that come immediately to mind. But for purposes of compressing my discussion, I should like to illustrate my point from Pynchon's *The Crying of Lot 49.*

Pynchon's main concern in this novel is with Henry Adams's sense of entropy—that is, with a technological society that seems to be exhausting its resources and potentiality. The man who has brought this world into being, Pierce Inverarity, is now dead and once again we have a message from the grave—in this case in the form of a will that must be executed by Oedipa Maas, whose very name suggests that the woman (a remanent form of the Virgin) must come to terms with the legacy of the father in the maze of the modern city (the equivalent of the Dynamo). What Pierce has left behind, Oedipa comes to believe, is the very embodiment of modern America itself—a vast interlocked network of corporations and technological resources. Oedipa comes to see that this network lives off natural and human resources, which it turns into waste. She comes to believe that a secret organization, the Trystero, which had its being (as Weber and Tawney might tell us) simultaneously with Puritanism, is organizing what the system discards, is bringing into being a kind of city of the dead within the city of the living, and threatens to take over from within a system that is exhausting itself. But as Werner Heisenberg might tell us, Oedipa, as long as she is a part of her own equation, can never be sure that her suspicions are true, can never escape what seems to be the firm grip of paranoia. Every clue seems to be simply another item of random meaning in a sequence that has no way of being arrested into truth. In the course of her travels through the city, she meets a young actor-director named Randy Driblette, who before he can confirm her suspicions dies a suicide. She is told this by Gengis Cohen who has gone to Randy's grave and come back with some dandelions out of which he has made dandelion wine. They drink the wine and hope somehow the spirit of Randy will touch them. When that fails, Oedipa makes a pilgrimage of her own to Randy's grave in the hope that she can somehow reach him through the soil. In *The Crying of Lot 49,* Pynchon shows the limitations of the Robinson Crusoe legacy which Pierce Inverarity embodies—the limitations of that blanched realm of the modern city whose complexities are as great as the maze of circuitry which makes up an intricate radio, another medium of communication that cannot go beyond its physical limits. And it is exactly with this sense of human limits that Pynchon ends his novel. Despite Pierce's belief that he could control his environment, his world is subject to the forces of mechanical, communication, and human entropy—that is, the forces of mechanical waste, silence, and death. In trying to go beyond man, Pierce Inverarity confirmed the limits of what it means to be human.

From Ur to Los Angeles, from Gilgamesh to Pynchon—we seemingly have come a long way; but perhaps we have not come as far as we think. There may seem to be little connection between primitive man who worshiped the moon and modern man who walked upon it. But like his literary predecessors, Pynchon seems to be telling us that much still depends upon a confused woman on a lonely grave in Southern California. And much also seems to depend on that jar of cloudy dandelion wine.

NOTES

    1. Walter Pater, "A Study of Dionysus: The Spiritual Form of Fire and Dew," *Greek Studies* (London and New York: Macmillan, 1895), pp. 9–52.
    2. Walter Pater, Preface to *The Renaissance* in *Criticism: The Major Texts,* ed. Walter Jackson Bate (New York: Harcourt, Brace, 1952), p. 509.
    3. James Joyce, *A Portrait of the Artist as a Young Man* (New York: Modern Library, 1944), p. 204.

5

In Search of a Poetic Drama for the Post-Modernist Age

JAMES FLANNERY

I

By the end of the nineteenth century poetic drama, once the dominant mode of all serious playwrighting, was synonymous with closet drama: a purely literary form with no relation to either the actual life or the stage of its time. Like poetry itself, poetic drama became a silent art—an art that existed on the printed page but not on the tongue.

Symptomatic of the decline of poetic drama is the fact that the very term "poetic" has been used so loosely in modern times that it has all but lost any stable meaning. As an illustration, many critics and theatre practitioners would agree with Francis Fergusson that the "poetry" in the dramas of Chekhov resides "in the rhythmic relationship of the 'scenes' established by the performers' make-believe and appealing to the histrionic sensibility of the audience." Thus instead of a poetry of words one seeks for an equivalent value in "the coherence of the concrete elements of the composition."[1]

This essentially dramaturgical and theatrical point of view is accepted even by perceptive literary critics like Denis Donoghue, who goes so far as to claim that verse, traditionally an essential component of poetic drama, is now "a purely technical" consideration. Ironically, in making this assertion, Donoghue takes issue with T. S. Eliot, the one modern "poetic" dramatist whose work he fully admires.[2]

Eliot himself argued that what primarily distinguished prose from poetic drama is "a kind of doubleness in the action, as if it took place on two planes at once." On one level poetic drama appeals to "the conscious planning mind," as does any effective piece of theatre. On a deeper level, however, poetic drama gradually discloses "a pattern behind the pattern into which the characters deliberately involve themselves, the kind of pattern which we perceive in our own lives only at rare moments of inattention and detachment, drowsing in sunlight." To Eliot, the key to this double pattern of action is the rhythmic iterative power of verse.[3]

As will be evident, I hold that a genuine poetic drama must be concerned with an imaginative deployment of the language of theatre—music, symbolic gesture, and visual imagery in the form of sets, costumes, lights, and stage properties that have a resonant life and function of their own. Eliot fell short as a dramatist precisely because he ignored the language of theatre as it might have served his vision. However, I also believe that we have too easily accepted the idea that verse and effective theatre are mutually exclusive. Having staged some sixteen of the poetic dramas of W. B. Yeats as well as a number of Greek dramas, I have experienced for myself the double pattern of action noted by Eliot as a component of authentic poetic drama. What is involved is a dialectical process that engages the conscious and unconscious mind. The greater the drama the greater the struggle between these two modes of consciousness, each activated to its fullest power. For this to occur the dramatist must be a master not only of the arts of the stage but of language. And language raised to the highest power of the conscious mind is poetry.

Not surprisingly, the decline of poetic drama to closet drama coincided with the development of naturalism as the most vital new force in theatre. As we know, naturalism was based upon an effort by dramatists to apply scientific principles and methods in their work. In its most extreme forms naturalism aimed at reproducing life upon the stage with strict objectivity. This led to an exclusion of the artist's personal vision or attitude toward life. Poetry, as the traditional means by which personal utterance is most powerfully expressed, was virtually banned by the naturalists as too obvious an organization of language.

Henrik Ibsen viewed himself as a poet and, with his intense moral zeal, an enemy of naturalism. It is arguable that his most effective play is the tragicomedy, *Peer Gynt,* written in verse early in his career in 1867. Yet Ibsen's reputation rests largely upon the realistic social dramas that he wrote between 1877 and 1886 in which he lacerated the prejudices, pretensions, and hypocrisies of bourgeois society. By the time he wrote these plays Ibsen had come to reject verse as "injurious to dramatic art." Ibsen went so far as to proclaim that it was "improbable that verse will be employed to any extent worth mentioning in the future."[4]

Ibsen's views have been reflected by dramatists, directors, and critics to the present day. The psychological realism, linear plot, and colloquial speech wrought to perfection by Ibsen have provided a model for modern dramatists as seductive as were the plays of Shakespeare to his would-be successors in the field of poetic drama.

Ironically, even though Ibsen's dramatic intention was satiric, by placing the middle-class drawing room and middle-class characters squarely in the center of his stage picture he, in effect, pandered to the taste of his audience, thereby confirming their blinkered idea that reality exists solely on an objective, materialistic plane. Thus imagination—the source and essence of what we truly mean by the term poetic—was all but driven from the stage. The sheer popularity of realism as a dramaturgical form and way of seeing the world has been the greatest single obstacle to the revival of poetic drama in our century.

Nowhere has the influence of realism been more pervasive than in the American theatre. This is reflected in the training methods of conservatories and drama departments, the repertoire of major professional theatres, the predilections of the critics, and the taste of mainstream audiences in the United States.

In recent years, however, there has been a reactionary movement against realism that, although still far from occupying a dominant position in American theatre, nonetheless promises some exciting developments as we move into the next-to-last decade of the twentieth century. My purpose in this paper is to trace the development of this experimental movement as it moves into a post-modernist phase[5] and, as I see it, may be preparing the way for a revival of poetic drama in the classical traditions of the past.

II

Some forty years ago the brilliant designer, Robert Edmund Jones, issued a plea for American theatre artists to turn away from the realistic forms that had dominated the stage since Ibsen. Jones argued that the American theatre had grown up on a "photographic basis," but that film had superseded this function: "nothing can be so photographic as a photograph, especially when that photograph can move and speak." The challenge of film could only be met if theatre rejected literalness and the illusion of reality. "What we are now interested in is not illusion but allusion, and allusion to the most magical beauty," said Jones. To illustrate the kind of theatre he had in mind Jones cited verse passages and scenes from the plays of Shakespeare, Yeats, and the Japanese Noh.[6]

Jones's ideas on the reform of the American theatre were echoed by the poet Archibald MacLeish. MacLeish attacked realism for its concentration on the surface actions of life and consequent superficiality. "Realistic theatre is never anything more than description, detailed, precise and painstaking, but description nonetheless. The underlying reality, which all but the most cynical of us must believe to exist, is nowhere divulged and nowhere made visible." MacLeish was careful, however, to reject the sentimental notion of dramatic poetry as merely a kind of decorated prose.

Poetry is not ornament, is not flowers, is not the pumping up of language with metaphors, is not a lovely embroidered cover drawn across a dirty fact, is not a charm to make the mind forget, is not a paint, an enamel, a veneer. Poetry is revelation. . . . Its essence is precision, but precision of the emotions, not the mind. Its quality is to illuminate from within, not to describe from without. Its language is not communication but experience.

Making an obvious reference to the turgid dramaturgy exhibited in the verse plays of Maxwell Anderson, MacLeish concluded his essay with an extraordinarily prophetic and challenging statement:

If ever a true poetic drama is written for the modern stage it will make palpable and real what has never been palpable in our time. That it may, in the process, destroy the modern stage is a possibility which those who talk so pleasantly of the theatre's need for poetry would do well to ponder.[7]

The revolutionary ideas voiced by Jones and MacLeish did not begin to come to fruition until the late 1960s when, inspired by the example of Jerzi Grotowski's Polish Laboratory Theatre and the Living Theatre under the direction of Julian Beck and Judith Malina, a number of experimental companies developed with the avowed purpose of breaking the stranglehold of realism on the American theatre. Given its subsequent history, it is ironic that the Living Theatre was originally noted for its commitment to poetic drama. Productions during the 1950s included works by Lorca, Eliot, Auden, Racine, and Yeats as well as American poets such as Gertrude Stein, John Ashbery, and William Carlos Williams. By the midsixties, however, the Becks scorned the playwright as an oppressive enemy of free creative expression. Echoing Antonin Artaud, the philosophical father figure of the new theatre movement, the Becks cried "Beware the rational" and "Excellent form is a lie,"[8] and turned their energies toward collective creations evolved through improvisation in which theatre, politics, and the communal lifestyles of the performers were viewed as synonymous. In 1968 the Living Theatre returned to the United States following a voluntary exile in Europe and confounded many of their previous admirers with a series of productions that preached nonviolence yet violently assaulted the intelligence, aesthetic sensibility, and, in some instances, physical well-being of their audiences.

Other ensemble groups followed the lead of the Living Theatre in stressing emotional authenticity rather than professional training and active rather than vicarious participation by the audience. But perhaps the outstanding characteristic of the ensemble companies was their aversion to written texts. Playwrights, if they were involved at all, were generally considered little more than voting members of the collective. Critic and director Richard Schechner went so far as to claim that the traditional function of the playwright as the prime mover in the theatre was finished.[9]

There was, of course, nothing really new in the efforts of the American avant-garde to redefine theatre so as to limit the creative function of the playwright. At the turn of the century Gordon Craig argued that the dominance of the playwright had prevented theatre from becoming a popular art because difficult psychological thoughts expressed in words were less appealing and fulfilling than evocative visual images. Even Shakespeare was dismissed by Craig as a "bore" when staged because the luxuriousness of his language tended to overwhelm the spectator with a plethora of competing sensory appeals.[10] What Craig advocated was a reform of the theatre that placed the master director at the top of the theatrical hierarchy. Craig also called for the development of actors who, in the tradition of the great classical theatres of the Orient, would be supremely trained in the physical techniques of their art. The formalist theories of Craig exerted a profound influence on some of the most innovative theatre practitioners of the twentieth century, including directors such as Jacques Copeau, Louis Jouvet, Charles Dullin, Michel Saint Denis, Jean-Louis Barrault, Yvesold Meyerhold, Max Reinhardt, Etienne Decroux, the father of modern mime, and Martha Graham. Today the work of Peter Brook exemplifies a continuance of the Craigean tradition in his search for a theatre of "the invisible made visible" based upon a language deeper than words—a language comprised of actions and of "words-as-part-of-movement, of word-as-lie, word-as-parody, of word-as-rubbish, of word-as-contradiction, of word-shock or word-cry."[11] Like Craig, Brook has focused much of his research on actors rather than writers. A "poetic" impulse is unquestionably at work, but the tools are primarily theatrical rather than verbal.

Another notable attack on the dominance of language in the theatre was launched by the surrealists. In the preface to his pictorially spectacular comedy, *The Wedding on the Eiffel Tower* (1922), Jean Cocteau drew a distinction between what he termed "poetry of the theatre" and the conventional literary idiom of "poetry in the theatre." According to Cocteau, the problem of poetry in the theatre is that, depending primarily on words for its effect, it lacks sufficient power to engage the spectator's full attention. Cocteau compared poetry in the theatre to "a delicate lace, impossible to see at any distance." Poetry of the theatre, on the other hand, has the much rougher texture of "a lace of rope." Reflecting the surrealists' gleeful repudiation of rationalism in favor of a total submission to the forces of the unconscious, Cocteau suggested that poetry of the theatre would involve words juxtaposed with extravagant aural and visual images so as to create the disorienting effect of "a drop of poetry seen under a microscope."[12]

The great triumph of surrealism was in the visual arts where the tradition of French classicism preserved a sense of formal composition and refinement within even the most avowedly irrational work. In contrast, the facile gimmickry of most surrealist theatre can accurately be described as a highbrow rationalization of lowbrow tastes. Nonetheless, the theatrical innovations of the surrealists created a major influence on the modern French drama from Anouilh and Giraudoux down to the dramatists of the Theatre of the Absurd. What the surrealists also demonstrated was that if poetic drama is to succeed on the modern stage it must be concerned not with words alone but with all the arts of the theatre. In comparison with Cocteau's poetry of the theatre, the attempts to revive poetic drama by such well-intentioned literary dramatists as Maxwell Anderson, Eliot, and Christopher Fry are, from a theatrical standpoint, dull and ineffective.

The American experimental theatre of the sixties and early seventies was, in many respects, a transference of surrealist ideas into an American context. Like the surrealists, the theatre companies and playwrights of the American avant-garde deliberately shattered most of the conventions on which modern drama has been based in order to create what one critic has described euphorically as "mind-blowing beyond-the-rational insight into the human soul."[13] The experimental movements succeeded in undermining realism as the dominant force in the American theatre. But, like the surrealists, the avant-garde created little work of lasting dramatic value, for what was ignored in the excitement of revolutionary change was a sufficient regard for the function of intellect or the craft of language.

Without question, the theatre of the twentieth century needed to rediscover the awareness of the fact that poetic language, if it is to be fully resonant, cannot exist in isolation from the nonverbal arts. The very word *poet* in classical times often involved the twofold character of poet and musician.[14] Poetry was thus originally intended to be sung or chanted, a tradition that Dylan Thomas, the Russian poet Yevgeny Yevtushenko, Allen Ginsberg, Robert Bly, and Lawrence Ferlinghetti have reinstituted with considerable success. This tradition was kept alive, though usually in debased form, in musical comedy, which has been no small part of that genre's popular appeal. We tend to forget that a large part of the popular appeal of the theatre of the ancient Greeks, the Orient, and Shakespeare was also due to a musical delivery of verse within a highly theatrical context.

Obviously the American theatre experimentalists of the sixties and early seventies were on the right track in striving to provide an exciting aural and visual context for language and in their efforts to give fuller expression to the connotative as well as denotative or literal meaning of words. Too often, however, their exploration of the gut impulses beneath language resulted in abstract sound and movement patterns that were of value in actor training and in the rehearsal process but failed to communicate anything of significance in performance. It is interesting to note that the most memorable productions of the ensemble companies—the Open Theatre's staging of Jean-Claude Von Itallie's *American Hurrah,* The Manhattan Project's adaptation of *Alice in Wonderland* under the direction of André Gregory, Lee Breuer's interpretation of a series of Beckett plays with Mabou Mines, Richard Schechner's production of Brecht's *Mother Courage,* and even the productions of Jerzi Grotowski—were all based on texts with a strong life of their own. Thus from their very inception these productions were provided with an intellectual coherence and form. With rare exceptions, such as the stunning

"Greek Trilogy" staged by Andrei Serban at the La Mama Experimental Theatre in 1974, most of the experimental work in the direction of poetic drama degenerated into a hybrid mixture of poor man's dance and poor man's music.

The unusual success of Serban's production was due chiefly to his extraordinary visual imagination as expressed in collaboration with the equally brilliant musical talents of Elizabeth Swados. One of the most electrifying moments I have ever experienced in the theatre occurred in Serban's staging of *Electra* when Aegisthus made his first appearance and moved down a flight of stairs with a live snake twined around his neck toward Electra, who herself carried a white dove on her shoulder. As the two actors approached one another across the vast space that served as a playing area their voices rose and fell in a barbaric, guttural chant sung in ancient Greek. The effect was utterly primal. As in opera, no verbal cognition was necessary and would, in fact, have impeded our response to the stark emotional power of the action.

The entire production unfolded in a similar manner as the plays were stripped to their bare essentials and staged as a series of Jungian archetypal images. The action was accompanied throughout by a score ranging from solo voice to polyphonic choral singing, from a complex of instruments including the gamelan and hand bells to percussive sounds on wood blocks. It was impossible to avoid being caught in the spell cast by the performance. But as I left the theatre I found myself only partially satisfied. What makes the original plays great drama as well as great theatre is their characters, their language (as understood in our own tongue) and their linkage of poetry with inner action. Serban's production moved me as I have rarely been moved in the theatre, but my response was almost entirely on an emotional, even unconscious, level. One half of poetic drama's double pattern of action was missing, and I felt cheated as a result.

III

The primary failing of the American experimental theatre during the sixties and early seventies was not merely the lack of technique, particularly in characterization and verbal expressiveness. Those were only the outward symptoms of a much deeper lack that, as with much avant-garde art of the twentieth century, was rooted in basically false assumptions about the nature of the human personality. Anton Ehrenzweig in his brilliant study of the psychology of creativity, *The Hidden Order of Art*, has argued that prior to this century art did not exhibit an open conflict between surface and depth sensibilities. Western art historically has depended on conventional "schemata" existing in an unbroken tradition over several centuries. According to Ehrenzweig, the "sanity" of this tradition resided in its openness to rational analysis which allowed for the continual possibility of modification or even radical change. Ironically, the persistent attacks of avant-garde artists on reason have prevented newer traditions from emerging and then being assimilated by both spectators and the artists themselves. Thus the recurrent upheavals in modern art have tended to destroy the children of the new movements almost as soon as they were born. Moreover, the assaults on reason have, from a psychological standpoint, been self-destructive, resulting in the development of fragmented and even schizoid artistic personalities. This is because the conscious mind, or ego, violently repels attacks on its dominant function within the psyche. Ehrenzweig believes that the themes of modern art mirror these schizoid tendencies in their obsession with death and destruction, their hatred of life and the human condition itself.[15]

With rousing manifestos modern art sought to sweep aside all preexisting art as no longer meaningful. This hubris now has worn thin. In recent years there has been a determined effort by a number of artists to define and articulate a new, still very unsure, traditionalism, a new reverence for older values that their predecessors thought had been destroyed forever. In the theatre this post-modernist aesthetic has led to a revival of interest in the classics as well as the emergence of several artists who combine the innovative boldness of the previous avant-garde with a renewed respect for formalist ideas and craftsmanship.

In the theatre, perhaps the most outstanding example of the post-modernist aesthetic is the movement known as the Theatre of Images.[16] With its emphasis on powerful visual and aural effects as distinct from language, imagist theatre would appear to be a revival of the anti-literary, anti-rational poetry of the theatre advanced by Cocteau and the surrealists. On closer examination, however, it becomes evident that the work of artists like Robert Wilson, Richard Foreman, Meredith Monk, and Lee Breuer embodies many of the basic premises, attitudes, and techniques of classical poetic drama.

One of the first things to note is that imagist theatre both demands and evokes an extremely high intellectual involvement from the spectator. This is in vivid contrast to the aggressively emotional, space-invading experimental theatre of the sixties. It also contrasts with the passive, total surrender to the stage illusion demanded by realistic theatre as symbolized by the darkened auditorium with its picture-frame proscenium arch. As in the poetic theatre of ancient Greece and the Orient, imagist theatre strives to engage the spectator's attention primarily through the presentation of a series of extraordinarily refined and evocative dramatic images. Always, however, an aesthetic distance is preserved so as to induce a state of contemplation rather than total empathy.

This distancing process is most evident in characterization. Instead of representing psychologically motivated characters with whom the audience is expected to identify, performers in the Theatre of Images either function recognizably as themselves or present highly stylized versions of characters in the form of animals with certain human qualities or through the medium of puppets. The effect of these presentational devices is to focus the audience's attention as much on the way in which a story is being told or a metaphysical situation being explored as on the story or situation in itself. Thus, by emphasizing form as distinct from content, theatre is brought closer to the pure condition of music, the visual arts, mime, and modern dance.

Many of the same devices as well as the underlying reasons for their use are found in the performance techniques of classical poetic drama. The purpose of masks in Greek and Oriental theatre was not only to heighten the theatrical effect but also to emphasize the archetypal qualities of the characters and the corresponding mythopoeic dimension of the themes being explored. [17] This idea was reinforced by having the same actor play several roles simply by changing masks. A similar effect was realized in the Greek, Oriental, and Elizabethan theatres by having female roles performed by male actors. While the Elizabethan theatre was more representational than Greek or Oriental theatre, recent scholarship indicates that Elizabethan actors employed many more formalized conventions in the way of movement, gesture, makeup, and speech than was previously realized. [18] The effect of these conventions was, as Gordon Craig noted, to create "a visible expression of the poetic spirit" or inner life of man. [19]

Another technique borrowed from classical poetic drama by the Theatre of Images is that of exploring the action from multiple perspectives. In Lee Breuer's *Red Horse Animation*, [20] for instance, the story of the life of a horse is told by a chorus. The actors in the chorus not only portray the horse both physically and vocally but, as in the Greek and Oriental theatre, express and comment on his inner reactions to experience. Over and above all of this, the chorus expresses Breuer's ideas, as the author, on the epistemological process of learning through a continual dialectic between the conscious and unconscious mind. In *A Prelude to a Death in Venice,* the central character is a puppet manipulated, in the tradition of Japanese Bunraku theatre, by an actor in full view of the audience. Both the actor and the puppet are, in turn, manipulated by the sound system, all of these "characters" again functioning explicitly as stand-ins for the author.

In the work of Richard Foreman, Robert Wilson, and Meredith Monk, we find a similar effort to present the action on several visual and aural planes at once. The very process of assimilating and then combining a variety of fragmented images into a syncretistic whole becomes, as in the act of reading poetry, an essential part of the aesthetic experience enjoyed by the audience. Psychologically, this process is equivalent to bringing the undifferentiated contents of the unconscious mind into conscious focus. Unlike conventional realistic drama, there is no condescension toward the audience. The tacit assumption is that people are capable of doing many things at once, capable of projecting a personal meaning onto the screen provided by the dramatic action—capable, in effect, of completing the performance in their own heads.

Richard Foreman describes his art as being specifically concerned with the problem and structure of consciousness. He views conventional realistic drama as "an unconscious means of reinforcing emotional orientation towards security goals." Such an art is not interesting to someone who wants to understand and see things as they actually are in momentary and unique instances.[21] The subject matter of Foreman's theatre pieces is the creative process, and members of his audience are compelled to dig deep within their psyches and experience that very process for themselves during the course of a performance.[22]

Robert Wilson's work also deliberately draws attention to the conscious and unconscious dialectic involved in responding to art of a highly poetic nature. In the tradition of Oriental theatre Wilson employs reiterative chants, hieratic movement patterns, and an intensive slowing down of the action in order to induce an almost trance-like state of mind in the spectator. Yet just as soon as that meditative state is evoked the mood is deliberately broken in order to shock the spectator into a renewed awareness of where he is and what he is actually experiencing. From time to time Wilson mimics the very tendency of spectators to drop out of his marathon spectacles. "I KNOW IT AIN'T CRAZY BUT I'M GOING TO THINK ABOUT IT AS SOON AS I GET OUT OF HERE," shouts a character in *A Letter from Queen Victoria*.[23] A simple statement like "I SAVE TIME" becomes increasingly ironic—hence intellectually provocative—as it is repeated throughout the piece. Occasionally, an explicit theme line ("YOU ARE ON YOUR OWN") emerges only to dissolve into an abstract tonal pattern made up of seemingly disconnected words and phrases. Wilson's plays are not only about but also are an experience of the human struggle in cosmic time and space. Gradually, they succeed in breaking down the mind's reliance on linear, causal progression in order to induce an almost Zen-like heightened consciousness of the nowness of being.

Myth, metaphor, and allegory are other traditional poetic devices employed by post-modernist artists to create theatre pieces intended to extend the boundaries of consciousness and thereby break down the barriers that divide people from one another. More often than not, the mythic element in the work of the Theatre of Images as well as dramatists like Sam Shepard and Michael McClure is based upon popular culture: legendary material derived from tales of the Wild West and Hollywood movies, including gangster films, horror films, science fiction, and romantic epics. Other sources include comic books, animated cartoons, the idiom of country and rock music, and television. One advantage of drawing upon the mythology of popular culture is that, as Robert Brustein observes, it provides immediate access to a storehouse of knowledge shared by audience and artist alike. This enables the dramatist to dispose of the illusionistic settings and extended expositional scenes of realistic dramaturgy in order to explore his subject with greater imaginative freedom.[24] Thus it is possible, as Robert Edmund Jones suggested, to create a theatre of allusion in which the action possesses the ambiguous resonance of poetic metaphor.

Dramatists from Greek and Roman times and the Renaissance down to Cocteau, Eliot, Anouilh, and Sartre have employed classical myths in order to create an ironic contrast with their own culture. Post-modernist artists have given this idea a new twist through the allegorical device of overlaying images borrowed from popular culture with mythic images derived from traditional high culture. What this represents, according to art critic Craig Owens, is a deliberate attempt to bridge the gap between the present and a past that might have otherwise remained foreclosed. Allegory as an attitude as well as technique thus exists as a positive response to the overwhelming estrangement from tradition felt by modern artists and society alike.[25]

In post-modernist theatre this has led to the development of dramaturgical structures based upon the accumulation of details, each of which resonates both vertically and horizontally. An equivalent effect is achieved in classical music through the use of polyphony. Instead of striving to carry the audience's attention continually forward as in the linear structure of conventional dramaturgy, allegorical structure arrests the narrative flow, thereby concentrating the attention on a moment-by-moment apprehension of the art work. Gradually, the audience perceives all of the details, whether verbal, visual, or musical, as existing both autonomously and in close interrelationship with one another. The ultimate effect is an almost mystical awareness of the correspondence of all the elements of the universe—animate and inanimate, past, present and future.

IV

Obviously, it is not my intention to claim that the mere utilization of poetic devices by the post-modernist artists we have been discussing automatically transforms their work into a contemporary equivalent of classical poetic drama. To argue along these lines would be as absurd as to claim, as some do, that Ibsen, Chekhov, Williams, and Pinter are poetic dramatists simply because they happen to employ symbols. The fact remains that the actions of the plays written by these dramatists are based largely upon literal correspondences with objective reality. In comparison with the plays of Aeschylus, Sophocles, Euripides, Aristophanes, or Shakespeare, the dramaturgical form of these modern realists represents a reduction of the imaginative and spiritual dimension of the theatrical experience.

Conversely, my feeling is that imagist theatre errs in all but eliminating discursive speech and in reducing the mimetic function of the actor. Essentially, this deprives theatre of a sense of verifiable lived experience that separates it from the other arts and provides it with its lifeblood. As a result, imagist theatre sometimes tends to be self-contained and overly abstract. It thus lacks the emotional engagement and passion of authentic poetic drama.

The point I am really trying to make is that despite the drawbacks I have mentioned, the ideas and techniques involved in imagist theatre and in post-modernist art generally represent an important preparatory stage in the revival of poetic drama. We cannot expect such an ideal form of theatre to be developed overnight. As Eliot explained concerning his own efforts in this direction, "the creation of any form cannot be the work of one man or of one generation of men working together, but has to evolve by the small contribution of a number of people in succession, each contributing a little; Shakespeare himself did not invent suddenly. . . ."[26] Perhaps I can best show how far we have advanced since Eliot made this statement almost fifty years ago by describing my experience in staging three poetic plays by W. B. Yeats in New York during the 1979–1980 season.

V

Of all the dramatists since Shakespeare none had a better understanding than Yeats of the full theatrical and literary possibilities of poetic drama. At the same time, Yeats's plays exhibit, both thematically and dramaturgically, many of the qualities of the post-modernist aesthetic. Yeats is thus a pivotal figure in the revival of poetic drama. In his art he looked both forward and backward toward the creation of an avant-garde rooted in classical traditions and values. The theatre envisaged by Yeats is, as he once described it, "a memory and a prophecy."[27]

The principal theme of Yeats's plays is the quest of the individual for what he termed Unity of Being, meaning the harmonious integration of all the component parts of the personality—mind, body, sensibility, and imagination. Jung's term for Unity of Being was individuation, and he held this to be the primary goal of life. The fundamental purpose of Yeats's theatre is, like that of the surrealists, to provoke in a blinding flash of irrational insight a recognition of the latent powers of the unconscious mind. Yet Yeats's art, like that of the post-modernists, always retains an aesthetic distance so that both conscious and unconscious modes of perception are exercised to their fullest powers.

Theatrically and dramaturgically, Yeats drew much of his inspiration from the ideas of Gordon Craig and the example of Japanese Noh. Yeats was one of the earliest champions of Craig, recognizing that poetry could not return to the stage until there was an entire reform of all the arts of the theatre. Yeats also recognized that the Japanese Noh provided a dramaturgical model that was peculiarly appropriate for his theatrical purpose. This is because of the combination in the Noh of many of the qualities that Yeats was striving to achieve in his poetry: austerity, compression, and refinement on the surface that yet embodies a suggestive inner life of spiritual intensity together with an almost barbaric wildness. Perhaps most important, Yeats came to understand that by employing the theatrical conventions of the Noh he could exercise an imaginative control over time and space and give expression to the objective and subjective life of his characters with the same flexibility that he was able to enjoy in writing poetry. In the Noh a character can move from Japan to China with a six-inch stylized movement; a simple gesture accompanied by a turn of the mask can bring a character from a state of serenity to a nightmarish world where he is tormented by the demons of the underworld. In the fourteenth-century Noh, Yeats discovered a form comparable to film in its imaginative freedom. Yet what excited him most was that it was through human rather than technological means that the Noh fully exercised its power.

The chief distinction between the theatre of Yeats and most experimental theatre of the twentieth century lies in Yeats's reliance upon the actor and the power of the spoken word. For Yeats, the actor was no mere craftsman, but, as in the theatre of the Orient, a living embodiment of humanity's greatness and grief. Such an actor requires enormous facility in the technical skills of characterization as well as masks, dance, mime, and vocal utterance, including a mastery of singing, choral speech, verse-speaking, and dialects. But all of these physical techniques are merely the outward manifestation of internal qualities that can be attained only through an extraordinary discipline of the mind and spirit like that of contemplative religious orders.

Yeats once defined a play as "merely a bunch of acting parts. There must always be something for the actor to do."[28] That "something" was fundamentally to provide a public testimony, a living embodiment of all that Yeats meant by Unity of Being. In this respect, Yeats's intention was virtually identical to that of Peter Brook and his concept of a "Holy Theatre."[29]

In addition to acting, all the other arts of the theatre were drawn upon by Yeats—music, lighting, and even stage properties with resonant metaphoric associations—to realize this dramatic intention. Yeats was a brilliant poet of the theatre in every sense of the term. But, for him, the highest art of the theatre was language, "the most personal of things."[30] However valid the other arts might be within their own right, within the theatre they were merely "the applied arts of literature."[31] In renewing the historic claim of language—by which he meant dramatic poetry—to a preeminent position in the theatrical hierarchy, what Yeats essentially did was reaffirm the power of the human intellect to grapple with and articulate a sense of its own consciousness. Yeats was a tragic dramatist; the Yeatsian hero suffers and is ultimately defeated in the pursuit of his personal destiny—a destiny that, as in classical poetic drama, pits him against the darker forces of his own nature and the universe. The ultimate triumph of Yeats's heroes lies in the inviolability of the soul's integrity and in the ability not only to experience deeply but also to express the meaning of that experience in eloquent language.

For almost fifty years Yeats's dramas have been viewed as unplayable, their mythic themes of no interest to a general audience. My experience in New York four seasons ago controverted these opinions. The company of young professional actors assembled at the Open Space with the help of producer Lynn Michaels were the products of the kind of intensive training now available in the best American drama schools. All of the performers were schooled in the techniques of the Stanislavsky system, which provided them with a control over their emotions as subtle and delicate as a pianist has over his fingering. Unlike conventional "Method" actors, however, these performers were also skilled in the physical and vocal techniques of classical acting. This provided them with a solid basis upon which, during the course of rehearsals, we were able to add the specialized techniques required by Yeats's plays. Over and above all of these qualities, however, what was most impressive about the members of the company was their total intellectual and spiritual commitment to the ideas embodied in the plays. That something of this feeling was transmitted to the audience is evidenced in a review of the production by Elinor Fuchs, herself one of the foremost theoreticians and critics of postmodernism in the theatre:

> At the center of [Flannery's] production was—in the Buddhist sense— nothing. Not the dancer, not the actor, but the space itself . . . Flannery seemed to understand the dancer in the theatre the way Mallarmé does, not as a person who dances, but as a metaphor, summing up the elemental aspects of phenomena.[32]

VI

Herbert Read once suggested that "The future may have in store for us a form of poetic drama that imitates not so much modes of action as states of sensibility."[33] Regardless of where they have arisen and varied as the forms in which they have found expression, the basic intention of the artists and theatrical movements that have been the focus of this paper has been to reenergize the spiritual life of modern man. Excess of zeal, a willful satisfaction with merely attacking the existing norms and, above all, a failure to keep in mind what Goethe called "the best part of man"[34] has, at times, made the pathway of experimental theatre throughout the twentieth century a difficult one to follow. But, as the old Chinese saying has it, only evil follows a straight line. In the tradition of Goethe, Blake, Emerson, and Yeats, those revolutionary artists who have seen most clearly recognize the norms must be shattered, not out of disparagement or resentment, but in order to create new forms that respond to the psychic hunger of the modern age.

Increasingly, theatre artists and audiences are coming to understand that realism is a dead end because it does no more than reflect the tawdry values of modern civilization. Similarly, didactic art can only diagnose our social ills without suggesting meaningful cures. What is required is an art that affirms both the potential and actual stature of men and embodies rather than preaches the standards of a better society.

It seems to me that the most significant aspect of the work of the Theatre of Images is that it reaffirms the ancient mystical idea that the true frontiers of man's development lie within the realm of the mind. By striving to awaken the imaginative capacities of their audiences, these artists celebrate what has always been the proper subject of art—a heightened awareness of the very process of existence predicated upon the belief that, in the words of Joseph Campbell, "the whole universe is a reflection magnified of our own most inward nature."[35] The vision evoked in the work of these artists is not an all-purpose panacea but rather a challenge to the ideal self latent in the personality of every man. In the highest tradition of the great drama of the past, it is a nourishment to the soul on its lonely, difficult journey toward individuation.

NOTES

1. Francis Fergusson, *The Idea of a Theater* (Garden City, N.Y.: Doubleday 1953), pp. 160, 178.
2. Denis Donoghue, *The Third Voice: Modern British and American Verse Drama* (Princeton: Princeton University Press, 1959), pp. 3, 141–45.
3. T. S. Eliot, "John Marston," *Elizabethan Essays* (London: Faber and Faber, 1934), pp. 189–90, 194.
4. Henrik Ibsen, *Letters and Speeches,* ed. Evert Sprinchorn (New York: Hill and Wang, 1964), p. 218.
5. As many difficulties arise in trying to identify a distinctive post-modernist art and aesthetics as in trying to find a satisfactory definition of the term *poetic*. Part of the problem is that we do not always agree on the conditions of modernism. Another reason is that postmodernism in the theatre is not necessarily the same as in art, film, architecture, dance or music. Nonetheless, there are enough commonalities so that at least some of the following characteristics (selected from Ihab Hassan, "The Question of Postmodernism," *Performing Arts Journal* 16 [Vol. 6, No. 1], p. 34) are generally agreed upon:

Modernism	*Postmodernism*
Purpose	Play
Design	Chance
Hierarchy	Anarchy
Mastery/Logos	Exhaustion/Silence
Art Object/Finished Work	Process/Performance/Happening
Distance	Participation
Presence	Absence
Centering	Dispersal
Selection	Combination
God the Father	The Holy Ghost
Phallic	Androgynous
Determinacy	Indeterminacy
Transcendence	Imminence

In theatre perhaps the most perceptive observations are those of critic and theorist Elinor Fuchs. In an essay entitled "The Death of Character" (*Theatre Communications* 5 [March 1983]: 1–6), Fuchs argues that as drama passed from the primacy of plot in Aristotelian terms to that of character in the Renaissance, we have now moved into a new phase in which the inner psyche and spiritual realms control the focus of dramatic action. Fuchs points to the work of Samuel Beckett as the clearest demarcation of this new sensibility. After Beckett, who seemed to obliterate the perception of objective reality, it was impossible to *re-present* that reality with any meaning. Instead contemporary experimental artists are turning to forms of theatre in which performances are about the act of performance itself. Fuchs goes on to claim that this overt concern with theatre's own artifacts and techniques reflects the inversion and breakdown of historical cultural values as well as the global collapse of traditional boundaries between cultures, sexes, genres, performance and text, sign and signified, etc. The most intriguing suggestion of Fuchs is that the holistic vision of postmodernism corresponds to the reality of the Buddha who taught there is no such thing as a continuous self and that human suffering arises from grasping for permanence. All human functions are therefore impersonal weavings in the universal flux.

6. Robert Edmund Jones, *The Dramatic Imagination* (New York: Theatre Arts Books, 1941), pp. 131–48.

7. Archibald MacLeish, *A Time to Speak: Selected Prose* (Boston: Houghton Mifflin, 1940), pp. 79, 81.

8. Julian Beck, "Meditations 35 and 7," *The Life of the Theatre: The Relation of the Artist to the Struggle of the People* (San Francisco: City Lights, 1972).

9. Schechner based this claim upon a completely meretricious division between what he termed "craftsmen of words" (playwrights) and "craftsmen of actions" (directors). In this approach directors were encouraged to confront texts with actions that arose from the associations of performers rather than from "the dictates of authors." In other words, directors and performers were free to develop with absolute freedom their own actions. "On Playwriting & Environmental Theatre," *Yale/Theatre* 4 (Winter 1973): 28–40.

10. Edward Gordon Craig, *On the Art of the Theatre* (London: William Heinemann, 1958), p. 284.

11. Peter Brook, *The Empty Space* (London: MacGibbon and Keel, 1968), p. 49.

12. Jean Cocteau, Preface to *The Wedding on the Eiffel Tower,* in *Modern French Drama,* ed. and trans. Michael Benedikt and George Wellworth (New York: E. P. Dutton, 1966), p. 97.

13. Edward Parone, ed., *Collision Course* (New York: Random House, 1968), p. v.

14. Aristotle, *The Poetics,* trans. S. H. Butcher (New York: Dover Publications, 1951), p. 140.

15. Anton Ehrenzweig, *The Hidden Order of Art: A Study in the Psychology of Artistic Imagination* (London: Paladin, 1970), pp. 79–92.

16. Bonnie Marranca, ed., *The Theatre of Images* (New York: Drama Book Specialists, 1977), pp. ix–xv.

17. See William Arrowsmith's introduction to his translation of Euripides' *Alcestis* (New York: Oxford University Press, 1974, pp. 4–10) for a description of how masks were employed in Greek drama to express what he terms a "modal" rather than individual form of psychology.

18. See Leonard Pronko's essay, "Kabuki and the Elizabethan Theatre" (*Total Theatre,* ed. E. T. Kirby [New York: E. P. Dutton, 1969], pp. 187–96) for a fascinating analysis of Elizabethan stage conventions in the light of our knowledge of Japanese theatre of the same period.

19. Edward Gordon Craig, *Designs for the Stage,* ed. Janet Leeper (London: Penguin Books, 1948), p. 46.

20. Marranca, *Theatre of Images,* p. 123.

21. Richard Foreman, "Ontological/Hysteric Theatre: Third Manifesto," *The Drama Review* 68 (December 1975): 71–81.

22. On 13 July 1983 I attended a production of Foreman's *Egyptology* at the Public Theater, New York. The production was an hour in length. There were no plot and no characters. Instead we were presented with an astonishing array of visual and aural images that stimulated a continual shift in orientation. The setting itself consisted of a collage of hundreds of objects from past and present times: Persian rugs, family heirlooms, a skeleton, a Victorian pump organ, a Mickey Mouse clock with its hands pointing to 12:05, a red neon Exit sign above two doors,

posters of American film stars juxtaposed to faded daguerreotypes of presidents. The performers were themselves treated as other objects within the setting, with roles continually dissolving before our eyes. There were two major figures. One was a male dressed in a collage costume consisting of a medical orderly's apron, workman's boots, spectacles, a Roman collar, and a skullcap that reminded one of Pope Pius XII. The other was an aviator who had crash-landed in the play's Egypt and at other times appeared in the guise of a nurse, wife, mother, child, and lover.

Periodically the action was broken with harsh lighting changes, including a strobe effect. Throughout the piece one heard a repetitive drone which periodically swelled into the yelping of a dog interspersed with the unctuous moan of a 1930s crooner and snatches of classical pieces that sounded like Wagner, Mahler, Stravinsky, and Orff. Gradually the images grew more and more violent until, at the climax, a woman was pushed into a sphinx-like tomb while two rats danced frenetically on top of it. Suddenly there was silence. The Exit doors opened and the audience drifted out, walking through the set, which now appeared like a ruined antique storehouse in the glaring work lights of the theatre.

Three lasting impressions remain with me. One is of a fiercely satiric vision that pulled the vestiges of Western civilization apart in order to dissect the remains with a cold dispassionate precision. The second is that *Egyptology*, in form and content, was a signpost marking the end of an era. The third impression is that of a sheer inventive splendor, an intelligence, elegance of form, and ego-transcending imagination that was more provocative, inspiring, and fulfilling than almost anything I have ever experienced in the theatre.

23. Marranca, pp. 50–108.

24. Robert Brustein, *Critical Moments: Reflection on Theatre and Society 1973–1979* (New York: Random House, 1980), pp. 103–4.

25. Craig Owens, "The Allegorical Impulse: Toward a Theory of Post Modernism," *October* 12 (Spring 1980): 67–86.

26. D. E. Jones, *The Plays of T. S. Eliot* (Toronto: University of Toronto Press, 1960), p. 212.

27. W. B. Yeats, *Explorations* (London: Macmillan, 1962), p. 255.

28. W. B. Yeats, *The Letters of W. B. Yeats,* ed. Allen Wade (London: Rupert Hart-Davis, 1954), p. 658.

29. Brook, *Empty Space,* pp. 42–64.

30. W. B. Yeats, *Essays and Introductions* (London: Macmillan, 1961), p. 268.

31. W. B. Yeats, *Autobiographies* (London: Macmillan, 1955), p. 194.

32. Elinor Fuchs, "Yeats Fever," *Soho Weekly News,* 19 March 1980, p. 15.

33. Sir Herbert Read, *The True Voice of Feeling* (London: Faber and Faber, 1953), p. 150.

34. Bernard Dukore, ed., *Dramatic Theory and Criticism* (New York: Holt, Rinehart and Winston, 1974), p. 481.

35. Joseph Campbell, *Myths to Live By* (New York: Viking, 1972), p. 257.

6

Marlow's Choice in "Heart of Darkness"

TED BOYLE

At the end of *Waiting for Godot* Vladimir says to Estragon, " 'Let's go' "; the stage directions indicate *"They do not move."* They continue to wait for some external force to tell them if and why and when they should move—Beckett's image of the timidity and self-destructive stasis embodied in the predicament of the modern—"one world dead, the other powerless to be born."

In *The Stranger* Camus gives us a similar instruction by negative example. Meursault has turned completely against life, feels nothing when his mother dies, has no love for his girlfriend Marie, and murders an Arab cold-bloodedly. Only when he is to be executed does Meursault express emotion:

> I laid my heart open to the benign indifference of the universe. To feel it so like myself, indeed, so brotherly, made me realize that I'd been happy, and that I was happy still. For all to be accomplished, for me to feel less lonely, all that remained to hope was that on the day of my execution there should be a huge crowd of spectators and that they should greet me with howls of execration.[1]

He chooses the certitude of death over the freedom of life.

Conrad also saw very clearly the darkness and absurdity of existence in a world in which the old gods had died. He was sorely tempted by nihilism as exemplified in "An Outpost of Progress," an earlier version of "Heart of Darkness," but in the later story he clearly demonstrates the resiliency of the human spirit. Marlow goes to sea—as does Ishmael in *Moby Dick*—with "drizzly November" in his soul. He has, after all, sinned in his male Victorian eyes: "Then—would you believe it?—I tried the women. I, Charlie Marlow, set the women to work—to get a job. Heavens!"[2] His employment is not as he expected. Once in the Congo, he sees only disorder quite in contrast to his Tennysonian ideas of "progress":

> I came upon a boiler wallowing in the grass, then found a path leading up the hill. It turned aside for the boulders, and also for an undersized railway-

truck lying there on its back with its wheels in the air. One was off. The thing looked as dead as the carcass of some animal. I came upon more pieces of decaying machinery, a stack of rusty rails. To the left a clump of trees made a shady spot, where dark things seemed to stir feebly. I blinked, the path was steep. A horn tooted to the right, and I saw the black people run. A heavy and dull detonation shook the ground, a puff of smoke came out of the cliff, and that was all. No change appeared on the face of the rock. (63–64)

But his work, his Victorian notion of work, saves him, at least temporarily, from the despair of modern artifice gone awry.

Marlow's work offers him a secure position from which he can continue his quest for the redeeming idea, the small grain of truth that he is sure exists even in the depths of the Congo. His work is not a retreat but an opening out.

At the Central Station Marlow sees the degeneration of men who have no object in life except the accumulation of wealth, but now that he has firmly anchored himself in his work, they do not cause him discomfort. He can observe that their lack of any unselfish objective, not the illogic of the universe, accounts for their inhumanity. The station's brick-maker symbolizes the plight of all the pilgrims. He is apparently not an altogether unpromising young man, but deprived of any possibility of fulfilling his job of making bricks, he turns into a spy for the station manager. Marlow describes him as a papier-mâché Mephistopheles and comments ironically on his moral weakness:

The business intrusted to this fellow was the making of bricks—so I had been informed; but there wasn't a fragment of a brick anywhere in the station, and he had been there more than a year—waiting. It seems he could not make bricks without something, I don't know what—straw maybe. Anyway, it could not be found there, and as it was not likely to be sent from Europe, it did not appear clear to me what he was waiting for. An act of special creation perhaps. (77)

The brick-maker needs straw, and Marlow needs rivets. He has sufficient plates to cover the holes in the side of the ancient steamer, but he has no rivets, and the station manager is not particularly disposed to get him any. Rivets become an obsession with Marlow. He dreams of the wealth of rivets at the first station:

You kicked a loose rivet at every second step in that station yard on the hillside. Rivets had rolled into the grove of death. You could fill your pockets with rivets for the trouble of stooping down—and there wasn't one rivet to be found where it was wanted. (83)

In his conversation with the brick-maker, who apparently has some influence with the station manager, Marlow demands rivets. When he and the boiler-maker with whom he has been working are confident that they shall, indeed, have some rivets, they dance a grotesque jig on the deck of the steamer. Rivets have clearly become to Marlow a symbol of civilization, the ideas of humanity and solidarity that enable man to constrain hostile nature: "What I wanted was a certain quantity of rivets—and rivets were what really Mr. Kurtz wanted, if he had only known it" (84). It is also significant that in order to obtain rivets for his ship, Marlow goes "near enough to a lie" (82). When the brick-maker overestimates the importance of Marlow's connections in Europe, Marlow does not correct him. The brick-maker apparently reports that this influential man wants rivets desperately, and the station manager has them sent. If the symbolic significance of the rivets is accepted, Marlow's first "lie," then, enables him to gain access to the strength which he must have to front the elemental evil which would turn him into a scheming animal. His second "lie" is of much the same nature.

Though never ignoring the ever-present danger that the jungle represents, Marlow slowly comes to see order where before he could see only chaos. There is a certain fitness in the boiler-maker's tying up his waist-length beard in a serviette to keep it clean as he crawls in the mud underneath the ship to repair her. He immerses himself in the destructive element, the river's primeval ooze, but by the force of his imagination he keeps a part of himself clean.

When Marlow gets the ship under way, he travels further yet into the heart of darkness. During this part of his voyage, the exercise of his craft becomes even more important to the maintenance of his spiritual sanity, for now he realizes that he possesses a heritage in common with the savages whom he sees on the river banks:

> It was unearthly, and the men were—No, they were not inhuman. Well, you know, that was the worst of it—this suspicion of their not being inhuman. It would come slowly to one. They howled and leaped and spun, and made horrid faces; but what thrilled you was just the thought of their humanity—like yours—the thought of your remote kinship with the wild and passionate uproar. Ugly. Yes, it was ugly enough; but if you were man enough you would admit to yourself that there was in you just the faintest trace of a response to the terrible frankness of that noise, a dim suspicion of there being a meaning in it which you—you so remote from the night of first ages—could comprehend. (96)

Yet, since he is protected from the primeval ugliness by the ritual of his work, he can begin to discern the truth for which he is searching:

> What was there after all? Joy, fear, sorrow, devotion, valour, rage—who can tell?—but truth—truth stripped of its cloak of time. . . . You wonder I didn't go ashore for a howl and a dance? Well, no—I didn't. Fine sentiments, you say? Fine sentiments, be hanged! I had no time. I had to mess about with white-lead and strips of woollen blanket helping to put bandages on those leaky steam-pipes—I tell you. I had to watch the steering, and circumvent those snags, and get the tin-pot along by hook or by crook.

There was a surface-truth enough in these things to save a wiser man. (96–97)

In his fireman and his cannibal crew, Marlow reads the story of mankind's faltering and painful journey out of the dark jungle. The fireman tends the boiler with assiduous care because he believes that if he lets the water fall below a certain mark on the gauge, the spirit inside the boiler will become angry and devour him. He does not understand his work, but he is useful to the ship, and the knowledge of the ship's operation which he possesses is "improving knowledge" (97).

It is an indication of how far Marlow has pierced into the heart of darkness that not being eaten by a fellow human being is to him a hopeful sign. It is also a tribute to Conrad's ability to present the primary, unadorned realities of existence that, in describing the cannibal's restraint, he gives an infinitely more meaningful perspective on the solidarity of mankind than can volumes of preaching about the brotherhood of man. The cannibals have no inherited experience to teach them a code of behavior. They do not understand the contract under which they are bound, and their pay—three pieces of brass wire a week—is useless to them. They are hungry, yet they perform their duties and apparently never think of dining on Marlow and the pilgrims. Marlow jokes that he, if he were a cannibal, would not eat the pilgrims either—they are unwholesome in any sense of the word—but he is mystified by the cannibals' restraint:

Restraint! What possible restraint? Was it superstition, disgust, patience, fear—or some kind of primitive honour? No fear can stand up to hunger, no patience can wear it out, disgust simply does not exist where hunger is; and as to superstition, beliefs, and what you may call principles, they are less than chaff in a breeze. (105)

Marlow sees that the nobility of the human spirit is in fact a greater mystery than the nameless brute thing waiting in the jungle:

But there was the fact facing me—the fact dazzling, to be seen, like the foam on the depths of the sea, like a ripple on an unfathomable enigma, a mystery greater—when I thought of it—than the curious, inexplicable note of desperate grief in this savage clamour that had swept by us on the river-bank, behind the blind whiteness of the fog. (105)

He is beginning to fit the facts of his experience into some meaningful pattern, and Conrad skillfully guides the reader along the path of Marlow's ever-more-hopeful quest.

One of the most effective symbols in this, the second section of "Heart of Darkness," is the tattered book, *An Inquiry into some Points of Seamanship.* Marlow, when he discovers this volume in the deserted hut of the Russian harlequin, can be said to be almost cheerful:

> Not a very enthralling book; but at the first glance you could see there a
> singleness of intention, an honest concern for the right way of going to
> work, which made these humble pages, thought out so many years ago,
> luminous with another than a professional light. The simple old sailor, with
> his talk of chains and purchases, made me forget the jungle and the
> pilgrims in a delicious sensation of having come upon something un-
> mistakably real. (99)

He has in his hands at last a tangible manifestation of the honor which he has
been able to salvage from the chaos of Africa.

Marlow's devotion to his work is a code that enables him to find value in
life. In fact, some twenty years before Hemingway began to write, Conrad
had conceived in the Marlow of "Heart of Darkness" the "code hero."
Cayetano, Robert Wilson, the "non-messy" people in *The Sun Also Rises,*
and old Santiago are direct descendants of Marlow.

Conrad blends the first and second parts of the story together by bringing
the work imagery to the fore precisely at the moment when Marlow seems to
have lost all faith in making his mind triumph over the futility that he
observes around him. The second section of the story flows perfectly into the
third section, in which the emphasis is on Marlow as mythic hero. At this
point in the narrative, Conrad shifts the imagery to a mythic referent. Marlow
is transformed from the captain of a river steamer into a hero who has as his
mission the simultaneous discovery of his own destiny and a beneficent
talisman that will work for the good of all mankind. Keeping his ship on
course is no longer his primary task. He is to wrestle with the soul of Kurtz
and effect a return from the nether world with no powers to invoke save his
own inborn courage. Though it is now certain that Marlow will not succumb
to the powers of darkness over a thing as small as two black hens, his return
from Kurtz's hellish world is by no means assured. Marlow has already heard
the report that Kurtz once traveled almost three hundred miles downriver
before deciding to go back, and the significance of Kurtz's return, though at
first understood by neither the reader nor Marlow, becomes increasingly
apparent as Marlow continues his voyage upriver. Kurtz, in fact, did not
change his mind, but was recalled by the dark powers whose intimate he had
become.

The mythic theme of Marlow's journey is ever present in "Heart of
Darkness," but in the first two sections it plays a subordinate role. In the first
section of the narrative he sees the two knitters of black wool as preter-
natural creatures guarding the portal of darkness, but there are not yet
sufficient symbolic referents to render these two women full significance as
mythic figures. When, in the second section of the story, Marlow speaks of
Kurtz as an "enchanted princess," the mythic framework has been more
firmly established, but is, nevertheless, subordinate to the symbolism of
work as a saving grace. In the third section, however, the symbolic elements
emphasized earlier are submerged in the myth of the hero's discovery of the

saving talisman in the nether world, and his carrying it back to the upper world.

As Marlow travels up the Congo on the last stage of his journey, the jungle steps "leisurely across the water to bar the way for our return" (95). He has learned to look on the jungle as on a treacherous human being and has mastered it, at least temporarily, by never turning his back on it. It is clear, however, that Marlow will need to discover a more powerful stabilizing force than the ritual of work to return from the depths to which he has descended. When he brings Kurtz on board, Marlow is "numbered with the dead" (147) by the greedily complacent pilgrims, and he accepts this "unforeseen partnership" which has been forced on him. He, too, feels that he is a lonely spirit wandering in the land of the dead, and knows that he must learn the secret of the heart of darkness before he can return.

The ingress into the heart of darkness has been slow, and Conrad does not jostle the deliberately unhastened sequence of action in this last stage of Marlow's journey. Before Marlow meets Kurtz, he meets the youthful Russian harlequin, one of the most enigmatic characters in "Heart of Darkness." At first Marlow almost laughs at the young adventurer: "His aspect reminded me of something funny I had seen somewhere" (122). Marlow finally decides that the strange fellow reminds him of a harlequin:

> His clothes had been made of some stuff that was brown all over, with bright patches, blue, red, and yellow—patches on the back, patches on elbows, on knees; coloured binding around his jacket, scarlet edging at the bottom of his trousers; and the sunshine made him look extremely gay and wonderfully neat withal, because you could see how beautifully all this patching had been done. (122)

But this harlequin is not funny, for he is completely under the mad influence of Kurtz. He has given Kurtz his small hoard of ivory and has nursed him through two illnesses. In return, Kurtz has lectured him on love, justice, honor, and courage and has threatened to kill him. Kurtz is destroyed by his own egoism; the Russian is nearly destroyed by a supreme lack of self-consciousness. Marlow says:

> If the absolutely pure, uncalculating, unpractical spirit of adventure had ever ruled a human being, it ruled this be-patched youth. I almost envied him the possession of this modest and clear flame. It seemed to have consumed all thought of self so completely, that even while he was talking to you, you forgot that it was he—the man before your eyes—who had gone through these things. I did not envy him his devotion to Kurtz, though. He had not meditated over it. It came to him, and he accepted it with a sort of eager fatalism. I must say that to me it appeared about the most dangerous thing in every way he had come upon so far. (126–127)

The crazy quilt pattern of the harlequin's clothing seems symbolic of his moral and intellectual being. He has had experiences in the jungle that should have exploded his juvenile notions, but, unlike Marlow, he has been unable to assimilate these experiences. His ideas are as colorful as his clothing, but, like his clothing, they are an absurd and ineffectual superficiality with which he hopes to disguise his nakedness.

As the receptacle of Kurtz's noble ideas, the harlequin symbolically illustrates their impractical sentimental bases, but he also functions as a sort of guide to aid Marlow in his heroic quest. It is the Russian who has left the strange message for Marlow: "Hurry up. Approach cautiously" (98). And it is the Russian who confirms Marlow's suspicions about Kurtz's devilish practices, advises him about the influences of the savage woman, and tells him of the dangers of approaching the "pitiful Jupiter."

The harlequin is, however, a desperately lonely human being, and Marlow, who has sympathized with the oppressed Negroes in the grove of death, the cannibal crew of his steamer, and his incompetent helmsman, likewise sympathizes with this addled young man. In fact, it seems Marlow wishes to bring the young Russian, as well as Kurtz, out of the Congo. Towson's *An Inquiry into some Points of Seamanship,* which has come to possess such symbolic importance to Marlow, is the young man's property, and Marlow restores it to him. Perhaps this book on navigation will help the Russian to find his way out of the heart of darkness. It is also significant that Marlow, who has stepped into Fresleven's shoes, and has thrown a new but bloodstained pair of his own overboard, gives the harlequin a pair of his old shoes. It is, of course, a mythic tradition that an article of clothing retains the spiritual and physical attributes of its original owner. Perhaps, then, when the young man steps into Marlow's shoes he will be able to negotiate the painful ascent to the world of light even as Marlow does. In any case, Marlow's restoring of the Russian's book and his gift of a pair of old shoes echo the magical and magnanimous deeds of the mythic hero.

The jungle is ever present, ever ready to spring on the unwary; but Marlow, by this time, regards it almost affectionately, as one would an old enemy. He is ready for a severer test. He is ready to meet Kurtz himself. Conrad, of course, has to handle this meeting with consummate artistry to keep it from turning into a horrible anticlimax, for though the narrative of Marlow's journey is nearly over, we have still not seen Kurtz. A lesser artist than Conrad would, no doubt, at this point include some detailed accounts of the "unspeakable rites" and cruel atrocities in which Kurtz has indulged. Conrad, however, delineates Kurtz's character with a few direct strokes. Kurtz comes out of the jungle borne on a litter like a king. He is long and lean, belying his name: "Kurtz—Kurtz—that means short in German, don't it? Well, the name was as true as everything else in his life—and death. He looked at least seven feet long" (134). How better to indicate a man is not what he is supposed to be and how better to indicate that his failure is not a result of his conscious will than to note that his name is not fitting. Kurtz has with him a small arsenal—"two shot-guns, a heavy rifle, and a light revolver-carbine" (134), absurd when the only enemy from whom he needs protection is himself.

Kurtz is, indeed, a "hollow man." When he carries him out of the forest, Marlow reports that "he was not much heavier than a child" (145). Kurtz is also hollow in that his "gorgeous eloquence" is wholly ethereal. Ill as he is when he is brought on board the steamer, he has not lost the ability to expound his noble ideas:

> Kurtz discoursed. A voice! a voice! It rang deep to the very last. It survived his strength to hide in the magnificent folds of eloquence the barren darkness of his heart. Oh, he struggled! he struggled! The wastes of his weary brain were haunted by shadowy images now—images of wealth and fame revolving obsequiously round his unextinguishable gift of noble and lofty expression. My Intended, my station, my career, my ideas—these were the subjects for the occasional utterances of elevated sentiments. (147)

But these words are meaningless. In fact, the only words that he utters to Marlow which possess truth enough to mitigate his emptiness are his last: "The horror! The horror!" (149).

Kurtz has allowed himself to be regarded as a God. "He had kicked himself loose of the earth" (144), reports Marlow. He has murdered and robbed; he has crawled through the grass like a snake in order to reach those who would worship him. His last words, however, at least partially expiate. They represent for both Marlow and Kurtz a "supreme moment of complete knowledge. . . . an affirmation, a moral victory paid for by innumerable defeats, by abominable terrors, by abominable satisfactions" (151). Marlow discovers that the human spirit is stronger than the powers of darkness, and this is the ultimate boon which he must carry to the upper world.

Joseph Campbell, in *The Hero with a Thousand Faces,* describes the problem of the returning hero:

> How teach again, however, what has been taught correctly and incorrectly learned a thousand thousand times, throughout the millenniums of mankind's prudent folly? That is the hero's ultimate difficult task. How render back into light-world language the speech-defying pronouncements of the dark? . . . The first problem of the returning hero is to accept as real, after an experience of the soul-satisfying vision of fulfillment, the passing joys and sorrows, banalities and noisy obscenities of life. Why re-enter such a world? Why attempt to make plausible, or even interesting, to men and women consumed with passion, the experience of transcendental bliss?[3]

Conrad's description of the psychological state of his returning hero, Marlow, closely parallels that of the traditional mythic hero which Campbell describes above:

I found myself back in the sepulchral city resenting the sight of people hurrying through the streets to filch a little money from each other, to devour their infamous cookery, to gulp their unwholesome beer, to dream their insignificant and silly dreams. They trespassed upon my thoughts. They were intruders whose knowledge of life was to me an irritating pretence, because I felt so sure they could not possibly know the things I knew. Their bearing, which was simply the bearing of commonplace individuals going about their business in the assurance of perfect safety, was offensive to me like the outrageous flauntings of folly in the face of a danger it is unable to comprehend. I had no particular desire to enlighten them, but I had some difficulty in restraining myself from laughing in their faces, so full of stupid importance. (152)

Marlow's experience with Kurtz is not accurately one of "transcendental bliss"; although he has learned about the darkness of the human heart, he has also learned about the resilience of the human spirit, and it is his duty, though he is at first reluctant to acknowledge it, to translate his vision of truth into a form that will "redound to the renewing of the community, the nation, the planet." He "lies" to Kurtz's Intended.

When Marlow recounts his experiences at the Central Station, he says:

You know I hate, detest, and can't bear a lie, not because I am straighter than the rest of us, but simply because it appalls me. There is a taint of death, a flavour of mortality in lies—which is exactly what I hate and detest in the world—what I want to forget. It makes me miserable and sick, like biting something rotten would do. (82)

If, however, the nature of the truth that Marlow has learned in Africa is carefully examined, and if Marlow is viewed as a sort of mythic hero who has returned from the nether world with a restorative boon, his words to Kurtz's Intended do not constitute a lie, in the normal sense of the word.

At the Central Station Marlow sees Kurtz's painting of "justice":

I noticed a small sketch in oils, on a panel, representing a woman, draped and blindfolded, carrying a lighted torch. The background was sombre—almost black. The movement of the woman was stately, and the effect of the torchlight on the face was sinister. (79)

When Marlow stands before the door of Kurtz's Intended, he remembers one of the dying man's remarks: "I want no more than justice." One cannot tell whether Marlow is cynical or pensive as he repeats: "He wanted no more than justice—no more than justice" (156), but after his interview with the Intended, it is obvious that Marlow, at the last, perceives that Kurtz, in fact all mankind, wants not justice, but love. Justice, especially Kurtz's stark, sentimental type of justice, as symbolized in his painting, has a sinister countenance; it is not only dark, but terribly destructive.

When Kurtz's Intended says: "Don't you understand I loved him—I loved him—I loved him" (161), she in truth has little conception of the love that transcends sexuality—the solidarity that gives meaning to the universe. However, Marlow instantaneously perceives, when he hears the Intended speak of her love, that only in affirming the deeper meaning of Kurtz's expiating words "the horror" can he soothe his own troubled imagination, keep back the dark wilderness, and make the human adventure meaningful: "Hadn't he said he wanted only justice? But I couldn't. I could not tell her. It would have been too dark—too dark altogether" (162). If Marlow tells the "truth," his Congo experiences and Kurtz's life will be completely without value.

As Kurtz's savage consort symbolizes the soul of the jungle, the Intended, with her "great and saving illusion" (159) shining in the darkness, symbolizes the soul of civilization. The soul of the latter is, of course, not without its darkness also. As Marlow sits in the drawing room waiting for the Intended, the imagery is dominantly dark, but there are significant patches of light and whiteness:

> The dusk was falling. I had to wait in a lofty drawing-room with three long windows from floor to ceiling that were like three luminous and bedraped columns. The bent gilt legs and backs of the furniture shone in indistinct curves. The tall marble fireplace had a cold and monumental whiteness. A grand piano stood massively in a corner; with dark gleams on the flat surfaces like a sombre and polished sarcophagus. (156)

When Marlow meets the Intended, he has a vision of her and Kurtz united in the same being, and when she says: "I have survived" (157), though "The horror" still echoes in Marlow's ears, he perceives that a part of Kurtz, the noblest part, the part he "Intended" has in fact survived the powers of darkness. It would be deceitful of Marlow to kill this surviving nobility.

"And this also has been one of the dark places of the earth" (48), says Marlow before he begins the narrative of his Congo voyage. London, the city to which Marlow refers, is, however, no longer as devoid of light as the African jungle, for it has had light brought back to it by men like Charlie Marlow. A long and unbroken line of heroic adventurers have gazed into the pit and perceived this light where there seemed to be none. The illumination these knights-errant have brought back with them is imperfect and fleeting—in fact may be enfolded in a lie: "Yes; but it is like a running blaze on a plain, like a flash of lightning in the clouds. We live in the flicker—may it last as long as the old earth keeps rolling!" (49).

So to the chaos of the modern world, which Marlow sees laid bare in the Congo, Conrad offers a powerful challenge—humanity, without the bindingly cruel structures of Victorianism, can survive, choosing crepuscular good over certain evil. "He moves."

NOTES

1. Albert Camus, *The Stranger,* trans. Stuart Gilbert (New York: Alfred A. Knopf, 1954), p. 154.

2. Joseph Conrad, *Complete Works,* 22 vols. (London: J. M. Dent, 1946), 16:53. Subsequent quotations are taken from this edition, hereafter cited in the text.

3. Joseph Campbell, *The Hero with a Thousand Faces* (New York: Meridian, 1956), p. 218.

7

Forster and Death

ALAN WARREN FRIEDMAN

Death destroys a man, but the idea of death saves him. . . .

—Howards End

Many of the novelists of E. M. Forster's generation—Ford, Woolf, Joyce, Lawrence—wrote their major novels out of the detritus of the Great War. Death and destruction—massive, indiscriminate, and inevitable—provided the implicit context for *The Good Soldier; Jacob's Room, Mrs. Dalloway,* and *To the Lighthouse; Ulysses; The Rainbow, Women in Love,* and *Lady Chatterley's Lover* as much as they did explicitly for Dos Passos's *Three Soldiers,* Cummings's *The Enormous Room,* Ford's *Parade's End,* Hemingway's *A Farewell to Arms.* As Forster writes of such books, "even when they are not directly about a war—like the works of Lytton Strachey or Joyce or Virginia Woolf—they still display unrest or disillusionment or anxiety, they are still the products of a civilization which feels itself insecure. . . . [Such prose] is the product of people who have war on their mind."[1] Like Pound and Eliot, all of these writers—Forster very much included—fought in their own ways for what Pound called "an old bitch gone in the teeth" and, as Eliot put it, shored what fragments they could against their ruins.

Forster was both younger and older than his contemporaries, for though he outlived all of them he had all but finished writing fiction before most of them began, and five of his six novels were written before the war. (The exception, *A Passage to India,* which was published in 1924, was itself begun before the war, in 1912.) Though Forster's novels are closer to social comedy than to elegy (Woolf's term for her own fiction), death casts as long a shadow in them as in those of any of these other writers. Forster, in fact, for all his vaunted humanism, sometimes seems almost cavalier in disposing of his characters, displaying a profligacy that annoyed several of his early reviewers, one going so far as to say that Forster "deals out death to any one of his characters on the slightest provocation. . . ."[2] In one of the first extended essays on Forster after the publication of *A Passage to India,* Edward Shanks put it even more strongly: "Sudden death is worse than a commonplace with Mr. Forster, it is a vicious habit. . . . His sudden deaths, sudden as they are, are announced with all possible calm."[3] There is truth in this remark, but it is not all of the truth—just as it would be perverse to accuse Forster of unqualified gallows humor at his characters' expense because of his occasional mordant puns: in *Howards End,* Margaret Schlegel's thoughts about eternity for herself and her husband conclude with, "Thus gravely meditating, she was summoned by him";[4] in *A Passage to India,* Aziz, discovering that he and Mrs. Moore are both widowed, reacts with, " 'Then we are in the same box,' he said cryptically."[5] Death both is and inspires action central to all of Forster's plots, but it is playful as well as serious, usually appropriate even if shocking, its role and impact often ambiguous or at times even positive. A chronological look at the novels should demonstrate how this concept evolves for Forster.

Charles Herriton's death, before the beginning of Forster's first novel, *Where Angels Fear to Tread* (1905), impels his widow, Lilia, on an Italian journey—seeking both adventure and escape from her dead husband's continuing domination in the form of his family's stultifying conventionality and manipulation, and finding both in a precipitous Italian marriage. Her own death, which occurs shortly thereafter in childbirth, is dismissively announced: "As for Lilia, some one said to her, 'It is a beautiful boy!' But she had died in giving birth to him"[6]—though it provokes the novel's subsequent events, climaxing in the Herriton family's abducting and then, while fleeing, accidentally killing the baby whose birth had caused her death.

The suddenness and seeming whimsicality of these deaths, as well as many of those in the novels that follow, have provoked much negative discussion and some defense of Forster's work. Among the more interesting comments are those, like Lionel Trilling's, linking Forster's unmotivated deaths with the "crass casualty" of Hardy,[7] a writer with whom Forster shares several crucial antipathies, most notably toward the industrial revolution and organized religion (as well as, ultimately, the writing of fiction). The destruction of the rural world and society creates a widespread disorientation and unsettlement; the loss of faith results in an analogous spiritual restlessness. Characters so affected lack assurance regarding their place in both this world and the next. Chance and coincidence come to displace certitude and causality. As Jacques Barzun writes, "we blame Hardy for failing to show adequate cause when the lack of adequate cause is what Hardy is trying to show."[8] The comment applies equally to Forster.

The death of Gerald in *The Longest Journey* (1907) occurs gratuitously and is announced even more brutally than those of Lilia and her baby: "Gerald died that afternoon. He was broken up in the football match."[9] (This is especially startling since, for Forster, football of course meant soccer, a

generally nonviolent sport whose greatest danger normally is exhaustion.)
Yet, as Trilling argues, a humanizing duality of vision complicates Forster's
treatment of the death and its aftermath.

> Forster can despise Gerald of *The Longest Journey* because Gerald is a
> prig and a bully, but he can invest Gerald's death with a kind of primitive
> dignity, telling us of the maid-servants who weep, "They had not liked
> Gerald, but he was a man, they were women, he had died." And after
> Gerald's death he can give Agnes Pembroke her moment of tragic nobility,
> only to pursue her implacably for her genteel brutality.[10]

Gerald's startling death, just before he is to marry Agnes, frees him from all
mortal failings—those of the past as well as the present and future—at least
for the hero-worshiping Rickie. He becomes mythologized—forever young
and fair, an embodiment of ideal passion against which Rickie measures
himself—and inevitably fails. Like the death of the spouse in *Where Angels
Fear to Tread,* that of the fiancé here also leads to an inappropriate marriage
and the deaths of both child and parent—for Rickie marries Agnes, a serious
mistake from which he eventually flees (after the birth and death of a son)
and, in the process, he dies almost immediately.

The pattern is different in *A Room with a View* (1908), but it was a very
near thing. That unusual occurrence in Forster, a happy marriage, results
from events—beginning with the physical contact between George and
Lucy—initiated by death: that of a stranger they happen to witness together
in Florence. Waking with the knowledge that she was embraced after having
fainted, Lucy "thought that she, as well as the dying man, had crossed some
spiritual boundary,"[11] though it takes most of the rest of the book for her to
realize that she cannot return; and George, when he finally declares his love
for her, expresses it this way: " 'I have cared for you since that man died' "
(195). That Lucy both ends her engagement to the pompous and silly Cecil
and then marries the totally appropriate George represents a clear victory for
passion over conventionality, freedom over bondage, Italy over England. But
as the manuscript called "The Lucy Novels" shows, it almost did not
happen; for in it George is killed by a tree falling where he would not have
been had Lucy not suddenly canceled their elopement. Oliver Stallybrass,
Forster's editor, says that "One can only speculate on the reasons that
caused Forster, in *A Room with a View,* to reprieve George as well as his
father; perhaps *The Longest Journey* had sated for the moment his vicarious
death-wish. That his clemency later troubled his artist's conscience is suggested in the Introduction to *A Room with a View.*"[12] But it may also be that
Forster's harsh reviewers had a lasting effect on him. He responded to
Bertrand Russell's praise of *The Longest Journey* with, "You are gentle, too,
to the corpses. They, and other things, displease me a good deal."[13] And in
1958, in *A View without a Room,* a brief "prophetic retrospect" on *A Room*

with a View, Forster not only expressed no regret over the book's published ending, he actually describes George and Lucy as having had fifty years of happy marriage—including three children, all of whom survive.[14]

Howards End combines the sudden deaths of *Where Angels Fear to Tread* and *The Longest Journey* with the happy ending of *A Room with a View.* Mrs. Wilcox, who in many ways anticipates Mrs. Moore in *A Passage to India* as well as Woolf's Mrs. Ramsay in *To the Lighthouse,* remains a powerful presence after her death. In all three of these novels, the narrators treat the deaths of these women brusquely, even crudely, yet the effect is to render their dying less definite rather than more. The lack of warning or preparation reverses the chronology of events, seems to deny them ordinary causality and climax, and focuses attention on survivors rather than the dead or dying: first the telegram, then the explanatory letter. In *Howards End* we are suddenly told, "The funeral was over" (87); only afterward do we learn—obliquely, through the reactions of the local poor, the gravediggers, and then the family—that it is Mrs. Wilcox who has died. "She had gone," the narrator says as if commenting on Forster's technique, "and as if to make her going the more bitter, had gone with a touch of mystery that was all unlike her. . . . Without fully explaining, she had died" (90).

In an interview Forster was once asked about "the significance of Mrs. Wilcox's influence on the other characters after her death"; he replied: "I was interested in the imaginative effect of someone alive, but in a different way from other characters—living in other lives."[15] For Mrs. Wilcox, who is referred to as "this shadowy woman" (85) while she is still alive and about whom it is said, "How easily she slipped out of life!" (93), death alters very little. Like Mrs. Moore in *A Passage to India,* she finds life's common distinctions generally meaningless: "Mrs. Wilcox's voice . . . suggested that pictures, concerts, and people are all of small and equal value" (70); and she remains hovering—"that unquiet yet kindly ghost" (243)—to help sort out the muddle left by her death: "Mrs. Wilcox strayed in and out, ever a welcome ghost; surveying the scene, thought Margaret, without one hint of bitterness" (166). Yet her dying wish—to leave Howards End to Margaret because of a felt spiritual affinity between them, their shared commitment to the book's epigraph, "Only connect . . ."—is denied by her husband and son, and must somehow be accommodated despite them; for in Forster when the living interfere with the dead, the dead return the compliment. The sorting-out process ultimately requires another death, that of Leonard Bast, as well as the birth of a son he has with Margaret's sister, Helen. Ruined by a combination of the Wilcoxes' smug indifference to those they view as inferior beings and the Schlegels' well-intentioned but ignorant manipulation, Leonard becomes obsessed by his own "sense of sinfulness" (318). Abandoning all hope of this world—"Death alone still charmed him, with her lap of poppies, on which all men shall sleep" (319)—he desperately seeks Margaret in order to confess (in the mistaken belief that he had seduced Helen). Forster's analogy aptly expresses Leonard's true purpose:

> He did not suppose that confession would bring him happiness. It was rather that he yearned to get clear of the tangle. So does the suicide yearn. The impulses are akin, and the crime of suicide lies rather in its disregard for the feelings of those whom we leave behind. (319)

Leonard's death—"He was terrified but happy" (324)—is consummatory and clarifying: it fulfills and ends his dual quest, and it allows for the novel's satisfying resolution.

Through her continuing loyalty to her dead friend and predecessor as the first Mrs. Wilcox, Margaret attains a kind of identity with her—so that there is an inevitability (despite Henry Wilcox's hollowness and Forster's wrenching of his plot) about Margaret's marrying her widower, living in her place and with her name, even to being taken for her (202). In fact, the moral chasm that separates Margaret from Henry may be measured by their contrasting attitudes toward his dead wife: he takes her into account no more now than he did while she lived (259); Margaret, though she wonders if "perhaps it is superstitious to speculate on the feelings of the dead" (258), always considers her predecessor and acts with her in mind. Toward the end she concludes to Helen (who had earlier said that she loves death because it validates life [238–39]) that " 'Except Mrs. Wilcox . . . no one understands our little movements. . . . I feel that you and I and Henry are only fragments of that woman's mind. She knows everything. She is everything' " (313). Thus Margaret, who speaks for Forster's moral viewpoint, in the end gains her bequest without trying for it, without even knowing about it: she learns the truth only on the book's last page, by which time the Wilcoxes' betrayal of both the living and the dead has enfeebled and broken them.

Margaret's insight and final happiness invert those of Lady Anne in Shakespeare's *Richard III,* for the latter arrives on stage cursing first Richard, who has murdered her husband, and then any woman unfortunate enough to become his wife—curses shortly fulfilled, after her own marriage to him, by her subsequent miserable life and death. Margaret, who always refers to Henry's first wife as Mrs. Wilcox, is herself blessed, *as* Mrs. Wilcox, for the vision of the world she offers and sustains. Thus, although the end of the novel is in some ways as negative as it is positive (Charles in prison for manslaughter in Leonard's death; Henry, with his debilitating hay fever, forced indoors, hiding from nature; London's "red rust" creeping closer on the horizon, melting down differences by which we live), it nonetheless provides a sense of resolution and continuity in Margaret's moral triumph, the birth of Helen and Leonard's son (the only baby born in a Forster novel who actually survives), the abundant hay crop—a sense that, at least this once, the living and the dead may be at one and at peace.

Maurice (written 1913–1914; published 1971) is the Forster novel that has least to say about death, the only one whose title is not a metaphorical statement about it (though *Where Angels Fear to Tread* was a publisher's title to replace the presumably uncommercial "Monteriano" that Forster had wanted). The novel's strengths and weaknesses result from the major impetus behind his creation: sexual and literary frustration. After what he called his "awakening" from Christianity at Cambridge, Forster's second great self-discovery, his homosexuality, remained more troubling than liberating. With *Maurice* (as well as the posthumous short story collection, *The Life to Come*), however, Forster turned from what he felt he must write about to what truly possessed him. In his 16 June 1911 diary entry he writes: "Weariness of the only subject that I both can and may treat—the love of men for women & vice versa."[16] *Maurice* was begun shortly thereafter, having come to him wholly outlined, and as a cure for his sterility. "It was the only occasion that he would write a novel in this manner, without lengthy planning and premeditation."[17] Although it could not be published "until my death or England's,"[18] *Maurice* was made deliberately anachronistic, very much set during the period of its composition and remaining there through numerous revisions over the next several decades. The novel defines this time on the eve of war as the last moment of "the greenwood."

Yet for all its denial of death, *Maurice* too demonstrates the power exercised by the dead hand of a parent: in this case, the pressures on Maurice to grow up "like his father." The implication is clear that Maurice's rejection of him and his way of life leads eventually to his "marriage" to Alec Scudder, a gamekeeper who, as David Lodge first noted, "performs much the same service for Maurice as Lawrence's Mellors for Connie Chatterley (though, as one might expect, Forster is far less explicit)."[19] That "service," of course, is escape from the sterility of the modern industrial wasteland through what they feel to be full and reciprocated sexuality.

Forster's narrator also turns against the parent, who had died, we are told, as he had lived: without passion or struggle.

> Mr. Hall senior had neither fought nor thought; there had never been any occasion; he had supported society and moved without a crisis from illicit to licit love. Now, looking across at his son, he is touched with envy, the only pain that survives in the world of shades. For he sees the flesh educating the spirit, as his has never been educated, and developing the sluggish heart and the slack mind against their will.[20]

Again, as with *A Room with a View,* Forster initially had doubts about the happy ending, and he defends it in similar terms: "The only permanence that is not a theory but a fact is death. And perhaps I surfeited myself with that in *The Longest Journey*. At all events the disinclination to kill increases."[21] Like Adela in *A Passage to India* (206), Maurice at his lowest ebb·contemplates suicide (an action that no one in Forster actually commits—death perhaps being so pervasive that it requires no assistance); but just as Mrs. Moore's death seems in some sense to release Adela, so a surrogate is also offered for Maurice: he "would have shot himself but for an unexpected event. This event was the illness and death of his grandfather, which induced a new state of mind" (136).

Death in *A Passage to India* is heralded by a telegram that both announces Mrs. Moore's death and deflects our attention from its actual occurrence. In fact, the telegram even comes to us secondhand: Fielding says of Ronny, Mrs. Moore's son: " 'Fate has treated him pretty roughly to-day. He has had a cable to the effect that his mother's dead, poor old soul' " (246). (Even Fielding's "poor old soul" fails to distinguish the dead from the living since it could refer either to Ronny or to Mrs. Moore.) Only subsequently are we told directly, "Dead she was" (256), and that she died and was buried at sea. The angled and retrospective representation of death is the norm rather than the exception in Forster; and its effect is to deny full validation to death so depicted, and thereby help to create a sense of the characters' continuing presence—even as their absence is intensely felt—during the remainder of their respective novels. Thus, the deaths of Mrs. Wilcox and Mrs. Moore, like that of Mrs. Ramsay, attain a kind of limbo status: having happened and yet not being wholly addressed or accommodated, they seem to belong as much to the future as to the past. Such characters, though themselves beyond mortality, remain in and of the world, part of the context in which crises in the lives of others occur. In the book's last section, in fact, Mrs. Moore seems to preside over both the Hindu ceremony in celebration of God's birth and the death of the local Rajah, as well as to effect various reconciliations among the novel's survivors.

For T. S. Eliot's Apeneck Sweeney in "Fragment of an Agon," life's cyclical pattern—its central moments—may be summarized as "Birth, and copulation, and death"; for Forster, it seems largely a repeated alternation of death and marriage, with very little copulation and even less birth. Mrs. Moore, twice a widow, comes to India ostensibly to assist in arranging the marriage of Ronny to Adela Quested. But while Adela, after her engagement, thinks that "marriage makes most things right enough" (98), Mrs. Moore "felt increasingly (vision or nightmare?) that, though people are important, the relations between them are not, and that in particular too much fuss has been made over marriage" (135). (Forster himself would surely have agreed.) Her first experience in India, the meeting with Dr. Aziz in the mosque, contains a warning about death; during the climax of her stay, the expedition to the Marabar Caves, she develops a sense of meaninglessness (everything reduced to " 'bou-oum,' or 'ou-boum,'—utterly dull. Hope, politeness, the blowing of a nose, the squeak of a boot, all produce 'boum' " [147]) that causes her to be "sunk in apathy and cynicism" (158), which last until her death: "the echo began in some indescribable way to undermine her hold on life. Coming at a moment when she chanced to be fatigued, it had managed to murmur, 'Pathos, piety, courage—they exist, but are identical, and so is filth. Everything exists, nothing has value' " (149). Such a state may properly be called despair, and emergence from it seems impossible this side the grave. Thus, the train returning from the caves is described as a hearse carrying corpses in place of its live passengers; and Mrs. Moore, who wishes to "retire . . . into a cave of my own" (200), attacks all human connection and distinction, marriage most specifically:

"Why has anything to be done, I cannot see. Why all this marriage, marriage? . . . The human race would have become a single person centuries ago if marriage was any use. And all this rubbish about love, love in a church, love in a cave, as if there is the least difference, and I held up from my business over such trifles!" (201–2)

Her business, which is death, is crucial to the book's reiterated attempt to decide whether India—and life—is a mystery or a muddle. Like Mrs. Ramsay, she helps to muddle things by sponsoring an inappropriate marriage; by withdrawing, she escapes what she cannot control or sort out: not only the marriage, but also Aziz's trial, which she considers the torturing of an innocent man (204–5). At first her absence only adds to the muddle—confusion erupts at the trial when both sides invoke her; Aziz and Fielding begin to be at cross-purposes when the former refuses to believe the latter telling Aziz that she is dead—so that "it struck him [Fielding] that people are not really dead until they are felt to be dead. As long as there is some misunderstanding about them, they possess a sort of immortality" (255). Thus, Aziz insists that he will consult Mrs. Moore on the question of his suing Adela for compensation (253), and in a sense he does: "Fielding was not ashamed to practise a little necromancy. Whenever the question of compensation came up, he introduced the dead woman's name" (261)—until "Aziz yielded suddenly" (261), as Mrs. Moore presumably would have wanted. As for marriage, Fielding tells Adela that it " 'is too absurd in any case. . . . I suspect that it mostly happens haphazard, though afterwards various noble reasons are invented. About marriage I am cynical' " (262). Yet the book ultimately maintains otherwise: for Mrs. Moore's departure both helps to prevent the inappropriate marriage of Ronny and Adela (Ronny thinks: "What does happen to one's mother when she dies? Presumably she goes to heaven, anyhow she clears out. . . . And Adela—she would have to depart too" [257–58]), and also allows for the appropriate one between Fielding and her daughter. In both cases, proper judgments and connections are finally made, and crucial relationships sorted out in a way that suggests mystery rather than muddle.

"Death closes all," says Tennyson's Ulysses, but mostly things happen quite otherwise in Forster. Not that his dead characters continue to live in any transcendent or supernatural way—though they are sometimes spoken of in such terms—but that their sudden departure, which is emphasized by its invariably being announced before the dying is depicted, creates a gap, a hiatus, in the fabric of the living. (Forster's only depiction of the dying process itself is that of Aunt Juley in *Howards End*—but then she does not die.) The vacuum thus created seems to suck others in to replace those lost or gone before (Rickie for Gerald in *Longest Journey,* then Stephen for Rickie; Margaret for Mrs. Wilcox in *Howards End*), or else the sudden absence promotes an equally traumatic reaction (unlikely marriages in *Longest Journey* and *A Room with a View,* baby snatching in *Where Angels Fear to Tread*). Worst of all, it perpetuates postures of bad faith. Mr. Wilcox betrays his wife's dying wish—he fails generally to consider her, live or dead—which does not ultimately thwart her, but it does break him. Hypocritically, Harriet, Lilia's sister-in-law in *Where Angels Fear to Tread,* after Lilia's death, "thought that they should [mourn]. She had been detestable to Lilia while she lived, but she always felt that the dead deserve attention and sympathy" (109). And in *A Passage to India* Ronny decides, after learning of his mother's death, "to persist in unkindness towards her" rather than repent his ill-treatment of her while she lived (257).

This pattern, which seems peculiarly harsh and nasty, may be summarized by Margaret Schlegel's thoughts concerning "the senselessness of Death. One death may explain itself, but it throws no light upon another: the groping inquiry must begin anew" (276). And yet the refrain of *Howards End*—and Forster's central theme—is that hope survives "even on this side of the grave" (103; also 104, 206, 330); certainly, the successful pattern of Margaret's own life argues as much. Though supposedly obsessive, capricious, and vicious about death, Forster fully rewards with such happiness as the world has to offer those of his characters who act in good faith toward the dead (as well as, of course, toward the living, the two being corollaries in Forster): George and Lucy are well married at the end of *A Room with a View* (and still happy fifty years later); Margaret and Helen and Helen's child actually come to possess Howards End, and a piece of the future; Maurice thinks of Alec's ship sailing off, while Alec remains behind with him, as "heroic, she was carrying away death" (238); Aziz's loyalty to his wife, dead in childbirth, as well as to Mrs. Moore is validated by his moral victory; while Fielding, who had been cynical about marriage but also loyal to Mrs. Moore, marries her beautiful daughter. Forster's distinctions concerning how death deals with his characters, and vice versa, are, in the last analysis, meaningful and important. His attitude, while clearly one of fascination with death, is very far from mere bloody-mindedness.

What are we to make, finally, of Forster's linkage of death and sex, thanatos and eros? One critic writes, "An examination of Forster's fiction limited to the attitude revealed towards personal relations discloses the disintegration of Forster's optimism and the development of a pessimism generated by frustration."[22] But the heterosexuality that Forster felt compelled to treat is most disastrously expressed—in the form of destructive marriages, a death in childbirth, the demise of two infants—in his first two novels. Instead of the deadly marriages that seemed imminent, successful ones occur in both *A Room with a View* and *A Passage to India*, while Margaret makes something positive of hers in *Howards End*; and in, or after, two of these novels children do get born who survive. Nonetheless, Forster's heterosexual relationships are generally a distraction and a deflection, a stratagem for representing interests of real moment: not Lilia and her baby in *Where Angels Fear to Tread* but the violent scene in which Gino (ravaged by his son's death) first nearly kills Philip and then ends up nursing him back to health; not the Rickie-Agnes relationship in *The Longest Journey* but Rickie's intense identification with two mythologized males: the dead Gerald for whom he marries Agnes and the living Stephen for whom, in a climactic action, he gives his life; not even the more or less successful marriages in *Howards End* and *A Passage to India* but the relationships between Margaret and Helen in the former and Fielding and Aziz in the latter. Only *A Room with a View* is written totally against the grain—and it was changed radically during revision. In general and usually without their knowing it, Forster's men strive to couple with images of themselves rather than with their opposites. But except in the posthumous *Maurice*, that consummation is unavailable to them, and so Forster has to dispose of them as best he can— while often simultaneously destroying the women who fail to fulfill them. In so doing, Forster laid himself open to a number of charges—brutality, pessimism, sexism—none of which, as I hope I have demonstrated above, is *entirely* true. Though far from Forster's best novel, *Maurice* may well have been his most important: certainly writing it was congenial and cathartic. Had it been published early on, he might then have had the impetus to continue writing fiction, and to treat subjects that mattered most, while reaching a larger and more discriminating audience than himself. And had he, subsequently, both heeded the critics (whom Forster always heard) and continued to publish fiction, he would necessarily have improved on *Maurice*. To reverse my epigraph from Forster, then, it was not his homosexuality but the idea of his homosexuality that, although it did not destroy the man, made the novelist less than he might have been.

NOTES

1. E. M. Forster, "English Prose between 1918 and 1939," in *Two Cheers for Democracy* (New York: Harcourt, Brace and World, 1951), p. 272.

2. Unsigned notice in *E. M. Forster: The Critical Heritage*, ed. Philip Gardner (London and Boston: Routledge and Kegan Paul, 1973), p. 83.

3. Edward Shanks, "E. M. Forster," in *Critical Heritage*, p. 309.

4. E. M. Forster, *Howards End* (New York: Vintage, 1921), p. 332. Hereafter cited parenthetically in the text.

5. E. M. Forster, *A Passage to India* (New York: Harcourt, Brace and World, 1952), p. 22. Hereafter cited parenthetically in the text.

6. E. M. Forster, *Where Angels Fear to Tread* (New York: Alfred A. Knopf, 1944), p. 105. Hereafter cited parenthetically in the text.

7. Lionel Trilling, *E. M. Forster* (New York: New Directions, 1964), p. 64.

8. Quoted in Trilling, *Forster*, p. 64.

9. E. M. Forster, *The Longest Journey* (New York: Vintage, 1962), p. 55. Hereafter cited parenthetically in the text.

10. Trilling, p. 17.

11. E. M. Forster, *A Room with a View* (New York: Vintage, n.d.), p. 50. Hereafter cited parenthetically in the text.

12. Oliver Stallybrass, ed., *The Lucy Novels: Early Sketches for "A Room with a View"* (London: Edward Arnold, 1977), p. 131.

13. Quoted in P. N. Furbank, *E. M. Forster: A Life*, 2 vols. (London: Secker and Warburg, 1977), 1:151.

14. E. M. Forster, *A View without a Room* (New York: Albondocani Press, 1973 [1958]).

15. Malcolm Cowley, ed. "E. M. Forster," in *Writers at Work: The "Paris Review" Interviews* (New York: Viking Press, 1967), p. 30.

16. Quoted in Furbank, *Forster*, 1:199.

17. Furbank, 1:257.

18. Ibid., p. 259. This is quoted as "until my death and England's" by Francis King, *E. M. Forster and His World* (London: Thames and Hudson, 1978), p. 57.

19. David Lodge, "Before the Deluge," in *Critical Heritage*, p. 474.

20. E. M. Forster, *Maurice* (New York and London: W. W. Norton, 1981), pp. 151–52. Hereafter cited parenthetically in the text.

21. E. M. Forster to Lowes Dickinson, 13 December 1914. Quoted by P. N. Furbank, introduction to the English edition of *Maurice* (Harmondsworth: Penguin Books, 1975), pp. 8–9.

22. Richard Martin, *The Love That Failed: Ideal and Reality in the Writings of E. M. Forster* (The Hague and Paris: Mouton, 1974), p. 41.

8

D. H. Lawrence:
The Man and the Artist

KEITH SAGAR

Prefatory Note: Of the many assessments of Lawrence published at the time of the fiftieth anniversary of his death in 1980, one of the best was by Philip Larkin. Larkin spoke on the assumption that "the age of proselytizing is over. We are all Lawrence converts nowadays." It was on that same assumption that, the previous year, I had given a talk called "Beyond D. H. Lawrence" to a gathering of the faithful in Carbondale, Illinois. I had felt that after twenty years of preaching and praising Lawrence, it would be a salutary exercise for me, and perhaps a useful shock to the complacency of the assembled Lawrenceans, to talk, for a change, about his deficiencies and limitations, especially for us fifty years on. I did not try to put myself in the position of his enemies and detractors; indeed, I assumed that he no longer had any, not in the academic world and the informed literate public at any rate. I felt that he no longer needed to be defended, that his status as the greatest English writer of the century was assured; but that we did him no real service by idolatry, by taking him to be all-in-all sufficient and all subsequent literature supererogatory. I felt that by recognizing his weaknesses we should be better able to appreciate his strengths. That talk was, I know, a disappointment to some of those who heard it, particularly to George Zytaruk and Harry T. Moore.

A year later I knew that they were right, and Larkin and I were wrong. "The spirit of homage and affection" in which Larkin responded to the "sane and healthy spirit" of Lawrence was conspicuously absent elsewhere in all the thousands of words published and broadcast about Lawrence in England in 1980. There was scarcely another voice speaking up boldly for him; rather voice after voice niggling, belittling, vilifying. Instead of proselytizing, Larkin asked for a "balanced assessment, a sorting out of the acceptable from the unacceptable." Unfortunately, in the present state of English literary criticism, this is a recipe for just the sterile waste of trees Larkin

114

himself obviously deplored. If criticism is to count for anything, the job of the critic is to proselytize for all he is worth on behalf of every great writer who ever lived, and there will never be a great writer who does not need to be fought for again and again, every generation, against those who, afraid to meet his challenge, deny his greatness. It was heartening to hear Henry Miller say, in an interview just before his death, that the business of the Lawrence critic is "to love him, absorb him, and make others love him."

Lawrence's enemies are still numerous, perhaps even still a majority in the literary establishment. They kept a low profile in the sixties and seventies. Perhaps the death of F. R. Leavis gave them the courage to come into the open again. The phenomenon forced me into some radical new thinking, not only about Lawrence, but also about the teaching of literature in our universities, the business of criticism, the nature of the creative imagination, and the purpose of literature. Some of my first thoughts went into the essay that follows, intended as a counterweight to "Beyond D. H. Lawrence." I hoped that Harry Moore would read it and approve. At least he heard a little of it in Santa Fe in 1980, the last time I saw him. But perhaps, as Lawrence said, "The dead don't die. They look on and help."

"Lawrence the Man"—the phrase carries the implication, "as opposed to Lawrence the Artist." Yet in fact no such distinction is possible. If T. S. Eliot is right in his claim that "the more perfect the artist, the more completely separate in him will be the man who suffers and the mind which creates,"[1] then Lawrence is a most imperfect artist, yet in good company, since, by the same criterion, Eliot judges *Hamlet* to be an artistic failure. Lawrence created directly out of his living, and his work draws its vitality directly from his engagement with life. All his works are attempts to tell the truth about life as he was currently experiencing it.

Lawrence met, and dismissed, the Eliotic position early, in the works of Flaubert and Thomas Mann. In his essay on Mann, his first piece of serious literary criticism, written in May 1913, he wrote:

He has never given himself to anything but his art. . . . But then there are other artists, the more human, like Shakespeare and Goethe, who must give themselves to life as well as to art. And if these were afraid, or despised life, then with their surplus they would ferment and become rotten. Which is what ails Thomas Mann. He is physically ailing, no doubt. But his complaint is deeper: it is of the soul.[2]

Lawrence, like Keats, saw life as a vale of soul-making, and literature as a record of and contribution to that process.

In 1915 Lawrence was saddened by reading the letters of Van Gogh. Van

Gogh, it seemed to Lawrence, had destroyed himself by failing to reconcile "the artistic life" with "real life." The best, Lawrence says, is to

> *be the artist creating a man in living fact* . . . —and where the art was the final expression of the created animal or man—not the be-all and being of the man—but the end, the climax. And some men would end in artistic utterance, and some men wouldn't. But each one would create the work of art, the living man, achieve that piece of supreme art, a man's life.[3]

In a life that is an achieved work of art one would expect to find unusual significance and coherence. Nothing will be accidental or trivial. Every place and person, every choice, act, experience, will be symbolic, drawing universal significance from the fact that he acts and chooses from a depth of his own humanity at which we can recognize him as our representative or prototype, going naked into the unknown as both hero and scapegoat (like Prometheus, to whom Lawrence frequently compares himself).

Lawrence's life story, told simply and dramatically, allowed to find its own shape and follow its own rhythms, will be found to have the form, impetus, resonance, centrality, and inevitability of a work of art. More than anything else, what gives Lawrence's life these qualities is that it takes one of the oldest and most potent of all mythic forms, that of the quest. The hero ventures out from the visionless world of common reality, fights his demons, suffers an ego-death, is reborn into a world cleansed and respiritualized, returns to make his health-bringing visions available to his fellow men. This is a metaphorical account of the life of any great artist: but it is a literal account of Lawrence's.

The quest began with Lawrence's early rejection of Puritanism, industrialism, and materialism. He diagnosed that these and many other characteristics of the modern world were symptoms of a disease he came to call "the mental and spiritual Consciousness"; and he knew that the only cure was imagination, which, like Blake, he defined as the only true vision. As early as February 1913 he wrote to Ernest Collings:

> One needs something to make one's mood deep and sincere. There are so many little frets that prevent our coming at the real naked essence of our vision. . . . I often think one ought to be able to pray, before one works— and then leave it to the Lord. Isn't it hard, hard work to come to real grips with one's imagination—throw everything overboard. I always feel as if I stood naked for the fire of Almighty God to go through me—and it's rather an awful feeling. One has to be so terribly religious, to be an artist. (*Letters* 1:519)

What does Lawrence mean by throwing everything overboard and standing naked before God? What must be jettisoned is everything that works against the deepest sincerity—against what Birkin calls "the old effort at serious living": everything egotistical, cowardly, frivolous, superficial, self-indulgent, secondhand, inauthentic. What must be got out from under is the suffocating pillow of convention, especially in England; conventional morality and conventional art are both manifestations of the same inauthentic social being that Lawrence was to castigate in his last substantial piece of literary criticism, his essay on Galsworthy in 1928:

> Satire exists for the very purpose of killing the social being, showing him what an inferior he is and, with all his parade of social honesty, how subtly and corruptly debased. Dishonest to life, dishonest to the living universe on which he is parasitic as a louse. By ridiculing the social being, the satirist helps the true individual, the real human being, to rise to his feet again and go on with the battle. For it is always a battle, and always will be. (*Phoenix*, 543)

And how are we to recognize "the true individual," "the real human being"?

> While a man remains a man, a true human individual, there is at the core of him a certain innocence or naïveté which defies all analysis, and which you cannot bargain with, you can only deal with it in good faith from your own corresponding innocence or naïveté. . . .
>
> It is the essential innocence and naïveté of the human being, the sense of being at one with the great universe-continuum of space-time-life, which is vivid in a great man, and a pure nuclear spark in every man who is still free. (*Phoenix*, 540–41)

Lawrence comes extraordinarily close here not only to the ideas, but even to the terminology of existentialism. The existentialist hero is also involved in a lifelong battle against the social beings who deny life in the name of conformity and fixed moral principles, and the battle to create an area of freedom within which individuals can recover their own naïveté (an openness to life, an innocence on the far side of experience) and out of that relate to others in good faith.

The England of Lawrence's time was riddled with bad faith—Church and State, politics, the arts, public and private morality: "The English seem as if they can't help themselves. A lily-livered lot: that's where all their purity lies. Alas, that they should be a nation of poltroons in the face of life! But that's what they are: bossed by the witless *canaille* and offsweepings of a dead 19th century."[4] Every great writer has the obligation, the price of his gift, to keep up the fight with all the weapons at his disposal. The artist must always be an outlaw and troublemaker. His job, in Fiedler's phrase, is "to give valuable offence." He says No! in thunder to the most cherished beliefs of his society. He mercilessly exposes its falsehoods, sophistries, hypocrisies, and complacencies—and that means most of what we live by. Hence the hatred he aroused and still arouses: in *No! In Thunder,* Fiedler says:

> When the writer says of precisely the cause that is dearest to him what is always and everywhere the truth about all causes—that it has been imper-

fectly conceived and inadequately represented, and that it is bound to be betrayed, consciously or unconsciously, by its leading spokesmen—we know that he is approaching an art of real seriousness if not of actual greatness. The thrill we all sense but hesitate to define for ourselves—the thrill of confronting a commitment to truth which transcends all partial allegiances—comes when Dante turns on Florence, Molière on the moderate man, de Sade on reason, Shaw on socialists, Tolstoy on the reformers, Joyce on Ireland, Faulkner on the South, Graham Greene on the Catholics, Pasternak on the Russians, and Abraham Cahan or Nathanael West on the Jews.[5]

Surely Lawrence on England should have been in that list. Lawrence did not hate England. He hated "their" England, what the liars had made of it and were making of it. If he had not loved England so much, he would not have cared so much. But a man cannot be free and a true individual simply by repudiating society and his fellow men and becoming a hermit in his cell or an artist in his ivory tower.

Lawrence believed that man is essentially a social animal, that the societal instinct is stronger than the sexual or even survival instincts. By this he meant that man has a biological drive to involve himself in some communal creative activity—exploring, pioneering, building, shoulder to shoulder with the best men of his generation:

> It is the desire of the human male to build a world. . . . It is the pure disinterested craving of the human male to make something wonderful, out of his own head and his own self, and his own soul's faith and delight, which starts everything going. . . . That is, the essentially religious or creative motive is the first motive for all human activity.[6]

But that describes a perfect world. In reality it is only the brave few who keep up the great adventure. And they must fight for survival against the majority who have sold out or chickened out of the struggle toward consciousness and creativity in favor of power or possessions or comfort, or who, inadvertently, through loss of vision, are living without faith or in bad faith. Art is a means of keeping the spark alive, keeping the ark afloat, even "throughout the howlingest deluge": "Once all men in the world lost their courage and their newness, the world would come to an end" (*Phoenix,* 734).

But the artist cannot perform his task of initiating "a new venture towards God" alone. Lawrence wrote to Bertrand Russell: "If I know that humanity is chained to a rock, I cannot set forth to find it new lands to enter upon. If I do pretend to set forth, I am a cheating, false merchant, seeking *my own* ends. And I am ashamed to be that. I will not" (*Letters* 2:284). For the Christian idea of salvation Lawrence substitutes fulfillment. Fulfillment involves wholeness, and wholeness involves relationships, connections, interdependencies. Therefore the hermit life is not available to him, nor the ivory tower. He will withdraw from the world occasionally, but only temporarily, *pour mieux sauter,* to refresh himself at the source prior to a further effort in the world of men.

The great need, even more urgent now than in Lawrence's day, is to get the human race back into a viable vitalizing contact with the sources of life in the depths of the human psyche and in the nonhuman world. Evil, Lawrence's version of the Fall, is the denial of this larger, essentially religious life, and the attempt, almost completely successful now, to replace it with a sealed-off, airless, energyless, sterile world of the exclusively human—rational, secular, and mechanical. We have corrupted our own powers, spawned reptiles of the mind, and now spew out poison over the whole earth.

The artist is a healer, but what is the healer to do when confronted with a body wholly diseased: "Everything lies in *being,* although the whole world is one colossal madness, falsity, a stupendous assertion of not-being" (*Letters* 2:593). The artist becomes destroyer. The old, false world must be destroyed before a new world can come into existence: "The old world never tumbles down except a young world shoves it over, heedlessly" (*Letters* 2:575). But the young world cannot come into being without root-room or in poisoned earth. So the priority has to be to clear the ground, to raze the temples of arrogance, greed, and hypocrisy, to fight their guardians tooth and nail: "One must be an outlaw these days, not a teacher or preacher. One must retire out of the herd and then fire bombs into it" (*Letters* 2:546).

Frieda called Lawrence "the only revolutionary worthy of the name." But every great artist, as truth-teller (and art-speech, in Lawrence's words, is only the truth about the real world), is a revolutionary of a radical and total kind, committed to destroying not just institutions and governments and economic systems, but the falsity of our very thinking and feeling. The bombs are not just polemics and satires ("only satire is decent now") and tendentious books like *Lady Chatterley's Lover.* Every true word, every creative thought, every energizing image is a bomb fired into a false world.

Even within a living and respected tradition, even within a community of equally brave and dedicated souls, it is a daunting task, perhaps even a doomed one now, to take on the world in this way. But to be condemned to function in isolation and exile, with no sustaining comradeship and help, a voice in the wilderness, at best misunderstood, at worst hounded, is to put one's very sanity at risk. The prototypes here are Blake and Nietzsche. It is the central paradox of the role of the artist in the modern world. As with Cassandra, the god-given gift of prophesy carries with it the curse of never being heeded. In the very act of standing up for sanity and fullness of life, the artist is driven by rejection, by the gap between the urgency of his message and the general deafness to it, to wild extremes, eccentricities, cruelties.

Three things saved Lawrence's sanity during the worst times. He had Frieda to expend his rages against. He had nature to hold on to as a source of unfailing sanity: "It isn't my disordered imagination. There is a wagtail sitting on the gatepost. I see how sweet and swift heaven is. But hell is slow and creeping and viscous and insect-teeming: as is this Europe now—this England" (*Letters* 2:331). And he never lost his faith that the world in which the war was taking place was not as real as the world of his own imagination: "I know it is true, the book [*Women in Love*]. And it is another world, in which I can live apart from this foul world which I will not accept or acknowledge or even enter" (*Letters* 2:659).

For an artist to rest in resignation before "the facts" is escapism, since what is usually taken to constitute "reality" is merely the product of a local and temporal tendency to believe to be real whatever you believe that other people believe to be real:

> Realism is just one of the arbitrary views man takes of man. It sees us all as little ant-like creatures toiling against the odds of circumstance, and doomed to misery. It is a kind of aeroplane view. It became the popular outlook, and so today we actually are, millions of us, little ant-like creatures toiling against the odds of circumstance, and doomed to misery; until we take a different view of ourselves. For man always becomes what he passionately thinks he is; since he is capable of becoming almost anything.[7]

*   *   *

Lawrence recognized his isolation as "meaningless," and committed himself to a vision of the good life that would be communal, and the effort to set up an actual community, Rananim, to embody it. His efforts were all fiascos, partly because there was nothing more than an assumption of goodwill (which tended to mean willingness to be acolytes) in the members, and their dedication to a simple-minded utopian and pre-lapsarian dream: "The only way is the way of my far-off wilderness place which shall become a school and a monastery and an Eden and a Hesperides—a seed of a new heaven and a new earth" (*Letters* 3:71–72).

In spite of the fiascos, Lawrence clung to his dream, and embarked on his pilgrimage in 1919 partly in the hope of finding, somewhere on earth, a living people who would prove the dream to be a possibility. He thought he had found, and to a degree did find, what he sought in the New Mexico Indians. There was a community held together by a common deeply religious consciousness. And for Lawrence it was the only true religion—a religion not of theology or morality, but simply of contact with everything else that lives:

> For the whole life-effort of man was to get his life into direct contact with the elemental life of the cosmos, mountain-life, cloud-life, thunder-life, air-life, earth-life, sun-life. To come into immediate *felt* contact, and so derive energy, power, and a dark sort of joy. This effort into sheer naked contact, *without an intermediary or mediator,* is the root meaning of religion, and at the sacred races the runners hurled themselves in a terrible cumulative effort, through the air, to come at last into naked contact with the very life of the air, which is the life of the clouds, and so of the rain. (*Phoenix*, 146–47)

Yet even here, where Lawrence goes as far as he was able to go in entering the spirit of the Indian dances, there are still hints, in the "terrible" effort and "dark" joy, of a final step Lawrence was never able or willing to take into identification with them; there is still a residue of the categorical statement he had made in "Indians and Entertainment":

The Indian way of consciousness is different from and fatal to our way of consciousness. Our way of consciousness is different from and fatal to the Indian. The two ways, the two streams are never to be united. They are not even to be reconciled. There is no bridge, no canal of connection.[8]

Though he tried to do so, especially in *The Plumed Serpent,* Lawrence never quite overcame his initial spontaneous distaste for certain overtones in the Indian dances: ". . . the diabolical, pre-human, pine-tree fun of cutting dusky throats and letting the blood spurt out unconfined. . . . Just the antithesis of what I understand by jolliness: ridicule. Comic sort of bullying. No jolly, free laughter" (*Phoenix,* 95–96). Lawrence was too honest a writer not to put the same reservations into the mind of Kate in *The Plumed Serpent.* She detects behind everything a certain malevolence, "something dark, heavy and reptilian in their silence and their softness": "They did not belong to the realm of that which comes forth." Kate feels that she belongs, as they do not, to "the upper world of daylight and fresh air."[9]

It was a relief to Lawrence to get back to Europe, to the Mediterranean, in November 1925. He found there at once "a deep insouciance, which really is the clue to faith." Looking back at America in 1929 he wrote: "The spirit and the will survived: but something in the soul perished: the softness, the floweriness, the natural tenderness. How could it survive the sheer brutality of the fight with that American wilderness, which is so big, vast, and obdurate!" (*Phoenix,* 267).

In contrast, when Lawrence first entered the Etruscan necropolis at Cerveteri, he experienced at once the feeling that it was good for his soul to be there. In tombs, of all places, he met "a living, fresh, jolly people"; in those dark underground chambers he found daylight and fresh air: "You cannot think of art, but only of life itself, as if this were the very life of the Etruscans, dancing in their coloured wraps with massive yet exuberant naked limbs, ruddy from the air and the sea-light, dancing and fluting along through the little olive trees, out in the fresh day" (*Mornings,* 136).

The American Indians had not quite embodied Lawrence's dream. His attempt to adapt their religion and culture to the needs of a modern state with white leaders in *The Plumed Serpent* had led him into horrors. The Indian way, he had reluctantly decided, was right for them, but wrong, or not available, for him. He abandoned the leadership principle. He abandoned, it seems, Rananim. Yet he continued to travel, and traveling itself implied a residual hope. In November 1926 he wrote: "We do not travel in order to go from one hotel to another, and see a few side-shows. We travel, perhaps, with a secret and absurd hope of setting foot on the Hesperides, of running our boat up a little creek and landing in the Garden of Eden" (*Phoenix*, 343). In the Etruscan tombs Lawrence felt he had come face to face with unfallen man.

His long pilgrimage brought him at last to these tombs, and in them he found the vivid human life he had been seeking, a life of perfect awareness and relatedness, without the crippling dualism of mind versus body, human versus nonhuman, physical versus metaphysical, life versus death.

Aldous Huxley was one of Lawrence's most sympathetic critics, but in his review of *Etruscan Places* he completely misunderstood what the Etruscans meant to Lawrence:

> For the sake of the double flute and all that it stands for, he [Lawrence] was prepared to sacrifice most of the activities upon which, for the last two thousand years or thereabouts, humanity, at any rate in the West, has set the highest value. The philosophy and the practice of non-acceptance have made it possible for man to become, in some respects, more than human. But in the process he has had to sacrifice much of his former happiness; and while he has become spiritually and intellectually more, emotionally and physically he has, too often, degenerated and become less than human.[10]

This would be an accurate enough account of Lawrence's position in, say, 1913. But it is a parody of his position in 1927. The crude choice between the spiritual and intellectual on the one side and the emotional and physical on the other is no longer to be found in Lawrence's writings at this date. Nor is he searching for happiness—that is a desirable but not inevitable by-product of what he is seeking, which is wholeness. He wishes to reinstate the body and its emotions not because he values it more highly than the life of the spirit and of consciousness, but because he now knows that to pursue the life of the spirit or of the mind in opposition to the life of the body and to Nature, is to alienate, stultify, or pervert the spirit and to turn the mind into a sterile mechanism or juggling act. It is because they had a rich physical life that the Etruscans were able to have a rich spiritual life, or vice versa, since to distinguish between them at all is part of the Socratic sickness.

Lawrence's effort, in these last years, is to respiritualize the world. The Etruscans confirmed for him what he had always known, that it is futile hubristic perversity to seek the life of the spirit apart from the given world; for God is in everything that lives and nowhere else.

The grail Lawrence sought and found in his quest was wholeness. Wholeness means atonement. And atonement means imaginative vision. Only literature speaks the whole truth, because only literature speaks from the whole man. The imagination is simply a charge that links up again and makes operative those senses and powers of perception which our rationalistic culture has allowed to atrophy. "The mind is non-religious," Lawrence said.

The imagination is necessarily religious. Any genuine act of attention ("a man in his wholeness wholly attending"[11]) yields a revelation:

> All it depends on is the amount of *true,* sincere, religious concentration you can bring to bear on your object. An act of pure attention, if you are capable of it, will bring its own answer. And you choose that object to concentrate upon which will best focus your consciousness. Every real discovery made, every serious and significant decision ever reached, was reached and made by divination. The soul stirs, and makes an act of pure attention, and that is a discovery. (*Mornings,* 153)

This, for Lawrence, is the only valid way of thinking. He brought himself to a pitch of internal discipline that enabled him to channel life through his pen almost whenever he put it to paper. His genius is just as likely to manifest itself in a letter, or a little newspaper article, as in a poem or major novel.

Starting from the narrow world we all inhabit, with its hubristic human perspectives and habitual complacencies, the imagination reaches inward toward the roots of our being in the psyche and outward toward the powers of the nonhuman world. Its goal is atonement, the healing of the split between the mind and the rest of our faculties which has brought us to our present chronic, perhaps terminal, condition. The analytical reason, operating in a void, is absurd. It has no validating or vitalizing contact with either inner or outer realities. If thought were a matter of mind only, man would be a windowless monad, an ego-bound obscenity:

> . . . thought is an adventure, and not a practice. In order to think, man must risk himself. He must risk himself doubly. First, he must go forth and meet life in the body. Then he must face the result in his mind.
>
> . . . .
> Today men don't risk their blood and bone. They go forth panoplied in their own idea of themselves. Whatever they do, they perform it all in the full armour of their own idea of themselves. Their unknown bodily self is never for one moment unsheathed. All the time, the only protagonist is the known ego, the self-conscious ego. And the dark self in the mysterious labyrinth of the body is cased in a tight armour of cowardly repression. . . .
> And inside the armour he goes quite deranged. (*Phoenix II,* 616, 620–21)

All the great writers are visionaries and see this. They are not just busy-bodies and do-gooders. They see that this almost universal madness makes real living impossible for anyone, that it is responsible for most of the crime, war, and suffering in the world, and that it degrades the world with blasphemous living.

What is normally thought of as thinking, all those methods of "thinking" that have been developed and systematized over the centuries in Western civilization under the name of philosophy or science or mathematics, and whose methods and assumptions have been built into the very structure of our language, have been techniques for separating things from each other and then the parts of things from each other, atomizing, analyzing, vivisecting, labeling, and compartmentalizing. We have completely lost the capacity for thinking in a way that puts things together again, perceives relationships and patterns and wholes. We no longer have the language for it, except those few who have the language of the imagination, poetry, at their disposal.

And this is why poetry, imaginative speech, is so unremittingly metaphorical. The metaphor is the linguistic equivalent of touch. It is the link, the bridge, the meeting, the marriage, the atonement, bit by bit reconstructing the world as a unity, blissfully skipping over the supposed chasms of dualism. When God needed a token of his atonement with man after the flood, he made a metaphor, a rainbow, a visible sign of the harmony behind all apparent dualities.

Lawrence's use of sex, for example, is metaphorical or symbolic. He always insisted that *Lady Chatterley's Lover* was a phallic not a sexual novel. A phallus is a penis seen in its impersonal and symbolic aspect. For Lawrence it symbolized that life in us which even now resists or ignores the conscious mind, taking its orders from elsewhere: "It is far deeper than sex. It is the self which darkly inhabits our blood and bone, and for which the ithyphallus is but a symbol" (*Phoenix II*, 619). The phallus is also a bridge between the self and the other, an explorer into the darkness of the unknown, a way for the soul to escape from the ego without death.

If the language of the imagination makes connections, reveals patterns and interdependencies, strives to see wholes, the language of current criticism breaks down, divides into categories and sub-categories that can be neatly labeled and then dealt with by formulae. A writer sacrifices his ease, his freedom, perhaps even his life, in order to make his testimony, for the race, for the truth. A critic then takes up this work written in blood and plays the game with it of deciding whether it should be labeled modernist, anti-modernist or post-modernist.

> Man is always, all the time and for ever, on the brink of the unknown. The minute you realize this, you prick your ears in alarm. And the minute any man steps alone, with his whole naked self, emotional and mental, into the everlasting hinterland of consciousness, you hate him and you wonder over him. Why can't he stay cosily playing word-games around the camp fire? (*Phoenix*, 323)

Most academics are hostile to great literature; it bursts their carefully constructed pigeon-holes. It challenges their cherished habits, and makes greater demands upon them than they are willing to meet. If it is old and established, it becomes a "classic," which means that it need not be responded to at all, just taught and examined. If it is new, it is mocked, belittled, or ignored. They prefer the familiar and predictable. The great new work is always offensive, both morally and formally; but mediocrity doesn't rock the boat. Hence the approval of the critical establishment is the kiss of death.

Thus the more effectively art is doing its job, the more hostility it will arouse in the defenders of the status quo, the Establishment, the social beings, the ideologists, the *lâches,* and the *salauds*—that is, in the great majority which is always wrong. It is a measure of the extent to which Lawrence is still alive as man and artist that he can still offend and sting the defenders of civilized, liberal, and academic values, of reason and tolerance and impartiality and objectivity. They are against Lawrence not just as a quirky individual with obsessions and blind spots, but against him as archetypal artist and truth-teller. The fight for Lawrence is the fight for art, for the life of the imagination, which is our only hope of redemption.

NOTES

1. T. S. Eliot, "Tradition and the Individual Talent," in *Selected Essays* (London: Faber and Faber, 1951), p. 18.

2. D. H. Lawrence, *Phoenix: The Posthumous Papers of D. H. Lawrence,* ed. Edward D. McDonald (London: William Heinemann, 1936), p. 309. Hereafter cited in the text as *Phoenix.*

3. D. H. Lawrence, *The Letters of D. H. Lawrence,* 3 vols., in progress, ed. James T. Boulton et al. (Cambridge: Cambridge University Press, 1979, 1981, 1984), 2: 299. Subsequent references to this edition of the correspondence will be cited parenthetically in the text as *Letters.*

4. D. H. Lawrence, *The Collected Letters of D. H. Lawrence,* ed. Harry T. Moore (London: William Heinemann, 1962), p. 1180. Hereafter cited in the text as *CLM.*

5. Leslie Fiedler, *No! In Thunder* (London: Eyre and Spottiswoode, 1963), p. 7.

6. D. H. Lawrence, *Fantasia of the Unconscious and Psychoanalysis and the Unconscious* (Harmondsworth: Penguin Books, 1971), p. 18.

7. D. H. Lawrence, *Phoenix II: Uncollected, Unpublished and Other Prose Works by D. H. Lawrence,* ed. Warren Roberts and Harry T. Moore (London: William Heinemann, 1968), p. 281. Hereafter cited in the text as *Phoenix II.*

8. D. H. Lawrence, *Mornings in Mexico and Etruscan Places* (Harmondsworth: Penguin Books, 1960), p. 55. Hereafter cited in the text as *Mornings.*

9. D. H. Lawrence, *The Plumed Serpent* (Harmondsworth: Penguin Books, 1983), pp. 117, 144.

10. Aldous Huxley, "Lawrence in Etruria," *Spectator* (4 November 1932), p. 629. Reprinted in *D. H. Lawrence: A Critical Anthology,* ed. H. Coombes (London: Penguin Books, 1973), p. 273.

11. D. H. Lawrence, "Thought," in *The Complete Poems of D. H. Lawrence,* ed. Vivian de Sola Pinto and F. Warren Roberts (New York: Viking, 1971), p. 673.

9

D. H. Lawrence and Max Mohr

ARMIN ARNOLD

I

On 4 August 1927 Lawrence left Florence for Villach in Austria. Having spent most of August there, he moved on to Salzburg on 29 August and arrived at his sister-in-law's cottage in Irschenhausen (in the Isar valley near Munich) two days later. He stayed at the "Villa Jaffe" until 4 October, when he left for Baden-Baden to pay a two-week visit to his mother-in-law. On 20 October he was back in Florence.

During Lawrence's stay in Irschenhausen, Franz Schoenberner, who at the time was editor of the weekly *Jugend,* came to visit him two or three times. He knew Else Jaffe, Lawrence's sister-in-law, as a translator from English into German; it was she who had informed him about Lawrence's stay in Irschenhausen. When Schoenberner noticed signs of Lawrence's poor health, he asked Hans Carossa, a physician and well-known German poet and novelist, to have a look at him. On 27 or 28 September Lawrence underwent a medical examination.

One or two days later, Max Mohr, another German author with a degree in medicine, came to see Lawrence in Irschenhausen. Lawrence first mentions Mohr in letters to Schoenberner and Else written on 24 or 25 September. He tells Else: "I heard from England that a man who writes plays and thinks I am the greatest living novelist (quote) and who lives in Tegernsee, may come and see me: Max Mohr: do you know anything about him? I don't."[1] To Schoenberner he writes: "Do you know anything of Max Mohr, the dramatist? I hear he might possibly come and see me" (*CLM,* 1003). Who in England could have been in contact with Lawrence and Mohr at the same time? It was not Martin Secker, because Lawrence told him on 30 September 1927: "A dramatist Max Mohr came to see me, queer chap, writes queer plays, nearly good."[2] Neither was it Rolf Gardiner (see letter to Gardiner of 3 February 1928[3]), although Gardiner had been familiar with Mohr's name as early as 1922. Gardiner met Mohr later at the Châlet Beau Site in Les

126

Diablerets on 12 February 1928 and remembers him as a "youngish, stout man with a boyish face and glasses. . . . I had been to the première of his play *Improvisationen im Juni* at the Munich Residenztheater six years before."[4]

It is possible that Mohr had heard about the performance of Lawrence's play *David* in May 1927 and had obtained a copy of the play. Mohr had been a prisoner of war in England, knew English quite well, and might have tried to obtain permission to translate the play into German. If so, he was out of luck since Frieda Lawrence had already done the job.

When Mohr visited Lawrence in Irschenhausen, he presented him with two of his own plays: *Improvisationen im Juni* (1922) and *Platingruben in Tulpin* (1926). Lawrence wrote to Else in early October 1927: "Max Mohr came in a car from Tegernsee, where he has a pleasant house—with wife and child—a man thirty-six years old or so. . . . We have his plays, we send them to you" (*CLM,* 1005–6). On 10 October 1927 Lawrence wrote to Mohr from Baden-Baden: "I have already read your Tulpin play. It has a queer flavour of its own, you should not abuse it. But you are bad at heroes. Your Columbus always seems to be weeping into a wet pocket-handkerchief. Your villainous Christys are much more alive and frisky." Lawrence had let his mother-in-law read the play, and he reported her as remarking: "Aber das ist kein Kunstwerk! Und die Sprache, die sie sprechen! Aber nein, der Mohr, das ist kein gebildeter Mann!" [But this is no work of art! And the language they speak! No, no, this guy Mohr is not a gentleman!] He then quoted some other comments by the Baronin and went on: "But whatever your plays are, you have a queer power of putting one right into the scene, whether one wants to go or not. I am reading your *Improvisationen im Juni* now" (*CLM,* 1010).

In return for the two plays, Lawrence gave Mohr a copy of his and Frieda's German translation of *David*. Mohr felt that the play needed some cutting and the translation could be improved; nevertheless, he tried to get some German producers interested in *David*. On 31 October 1927 Lawrence wrote to Mohr:

> It's awfully nice of you to take so much thought and trouble for *David*. But don't you bother too much about it, you'll hate it and us in the end. I know the translation is very unsatisfactory: my sort of German, which, like your English, must go into a class by itself. And of course the whole play is too literary, too many words. The actual technique of the stage is foreign to me. But perhaps they—and you—could cut it into shape. I shall be very much surprised if they *do* play it in Berlin. The public only wants foolish realism: Hamlet in a smoking jacket. (*CLM,* 1016)

On 23 December 1927 Lawrence advised Mohr to abandon his attempts at having *David* performed in Berlin:

> Don't bother about *David*. Only my wife is sad. But I knew too well that you would never get past the commercial *Wurm* with it. I know, alas, even better than you do, the limits of possibility in the commercial-artistic

world. And the limits get narrower and narrower. Soon we shall either have
to start arse-licking or be squeezed out. But *courage mon ami! Le diable
vit encore!* We are still alive and kicking.[5]

It seems that Mohr was also taking a hand in placing *Aaron's Rod* with a
German publisher, since Lawrence wrote in the same letter: "If the sale of
Aaron's Rod comes off, well and good: but M. 10,000 they will *never* pay.
Aspettiamo! Let us wait and see!" (*THM*, 27). Up to 1928, Anton Kippenberg's Insel-Verlag had published all German translations of Lawrence with
the exception of *The Boy in the Bush*. Mohr felt that Kippenberg was paying
too little and suggested to Samuel Fischer that he (Fischer Verlag, Berlin)
become Lawrence's German publisher. Fischer and Curtis Brown (Lawrence's agent) did some bargaining, but in the end Lawrence remained with
Insel-Verlag. Neither *David* nor *Aaron's Rod* was published in German.

II

Mohr met Lawrence again a few months later. Mohr arrived in Les Di-
ablerets on 12 February and saw Lawrence daily but stayed less than a week.
After his return to Germany, Mohr sent Lawrence the manuscript of his novel
"Venus in den Pisces" (to be published as *Venus in den Fischen,* 1928).
Lawrence acknowledged receipt of the novel on 29 February 1928: "Today
Venus in the Pisces has come, so I shall read it—and many thanks—and I
shall tell you what I think" (*THM*, 29). It took Lawrence three weeks to read
the book. On 22 March he wrote to Mohr:

> No, I didn't really like *Venus in the Pisces:* it is too modern for me: you
> know I am a bit *"altmodisch"* really. And it is true, you have written drama
> so much, you are more concerned with the mechanism of events and
> situations, than with essential human character. That is where I think the
> novel differs fundamentally from drama. The novel is concerned with
> human beings, and the drama is concerned with events. A drama is *what
> happens,* and a novel is *what is.* And you don't care very much what *is.* You
> are not *really* interested in people: you don't care what they are, inside
> themselves. You only care for their "figure," in the American and in the
> Italian sense—of what they're worth and what they look like. So you write
> novels as if your characters were puppets: much more than when you write
> plays. But perhaps the public will like it: I am no judge. (*THM*, 30)

While in Les Diablerets, Lawrence corrected proofs of *The Woman Who
Rode Away*. On 12 May 1928, he sent Martin Secker a list of eight persons to
whom complimentary copies of the book should be sent; Mohr was one of
the eight.

Lawrence had not a very high opinion of Mohr's work, but he was fascinated by the man himself. While Mohr told Lawrence that all men must have
roots, he seems to have considered his farm-like home, "Wolfsgrube" in

Rottach-am-Tegernsee, only as a sort of starting point for his frequent perambulations. Lawrence once compared Mohr to "a bewildered seal rolling around" (Huxley, 832). Repeatedly, Lawrence mentions Mohr's playing the accordion, and he liked Mrs. Käthe Mohr's drawings.

Mohr was anything but a cheerful fellow. In a letter to Else, Lawrence characterizes Mohr as follows: "He wants to be a child of nature but we were disappointed in the nature. But he is good and interesting, but a last man who has arrived at the last end of the road, who can no longer go ahead in the wilderness nor take a step into the unknown. So he is very unhappy" (*CLM*, 1006). On 19 December 1928 Lawrence wrote to his mother-in-law: "Der Mohr schrieb etwas traurig von seinem [*sic*] Wolfsgrube—sagt er muss immer mit seinen Verlegern kämpfen, und hat wenig Geld" [Mohr wrote a rather sad letter from his Wolfsgrube home—he says he has to fight with his publishers all the time, and he has little money].[6] On 10 October 1929 Lawrence wrote to Else that Mohr is "always very nice and willing to do everything he can to help. But also his voice says the same thing over and over again: *Alles ist nichts!* Why must everybody say it?—when it is only *they* who are nothing, and perhaps not even they" (*CLM*, 1206).

In Les Diablerets, Max Mohr had invited Lawrence to visit him in Rottach. On 29 February 1928 Lawrence concluded his letter to Mohr with the hope of meeting him in "Wolfsgrube" the following summer (*THM*, 29). But Lawrence spent July and August in Gsteig (Switzerland), then went for a two-week visit to his mother-in-law in Baden-Baden. From there he traveled to the south of France and spent the winter in Bandol. He did not meet Mohr between February 1928 and August 1929, but the two men exchanged at least forty letters. On 22 March 1928 Lawrence sent Mohr some subscription forms for *Lady Chatterley's Lover*. Mohr tried to get several publishers interested in a German translation, including Daniel Brody's Rhein-Verlag (Zurich and Munich)—the publisher of Georg Goyert's German translation of Joyce's *Ulysses* (1927)—and H. R. Sauerländer (Aarau, Switzerland). Evidently, Mohr wanted to translate the book himself. Lawrence offered *Lady Chatterley* to Anton Kippenberg and told him that Frieda was "preparing a translation with the help of a friend, a German author, under my supervision" (*THM*, 33). Lawrence wrote to Mohr:

> Thank you very much for saying you will translate the book. I believe you could do it, and keep the tenderness and the freshness. But the dialect! And I am sure they will hate the *class* inference and the *industrial* analysis. They are more bourgeois than a bidet.
> The best will be if you will translate a chapter, and then send your translation to us, and we will go over it and say what we think. In that way chapter by chapter we could get the thing ship-shape.
> And of course you would have to have a proper share of the money: it will be a lot of work to you. But that we can arrange later. (*THM*, 33)

On 17 January 1929 Lawrence told Mohr that Kippenberg was "afraid of prosecution by law" (*THM*, 34) and that another publisher must be found.

But Mohr was not successful, and Lawrence consoled him on 25 May 1929:
"As for *Lady C.,* I'm sorry you have such endless bothers, you must be bored
stiff with the affair. Rheinverlag or Sauerverlag [H. R. Sauerländer], damn all
their eyes!" (*THM,* 35).

In May 1929 Mohr told Lawrence that he was writing a sort of
"Zauberphantasie." This might refer to Mohr's novel *Die Freundschaft von
Ladiz* which was published in 1931—with a dedication to Lawrence. As I
shall point out later, the novel contains fictitious portraits of Mohr and
Lawrence. Lawrence answered Mohr's letter on 25 May 1929. The beginning
of his letter, as it appears in *Collected Letters,* reads as follows:

> I was glad to get your letter and to know you were all right. I'm sorry about
> your troubles with the damned publishers. It's a pity they don't every single
> one go bankrupt, and stay there for evermore. But I am wondering what
> sort of weird fantasy your book is. When we get to a settled place, do send
> me the typescript that I can read it. And anyhow you have made money
> with medicine and comedies, and the roof is safe over your head. (*CLM,*
> 1156)

Harry T. Moore took this text from the first English publication of Lawrence's letters to Mohr in *T'ien Hsia Monthly.* The text of the same letter in
the first German publication of these letters is quite different.

When Aldous Huxley had asked for permission to publish Lawrence's
letters to Mohr, the latter had refused, "weil ihm der Tod von Lawrence noch
zu nahe schien" [because Lawrence's death seemed to him all too recent].[7]
But after the Huxley edition of Lawrence's *Letters* had appeared in 1932,
Mohr gave fourteen of the thirty-three letters Lawrence had written to him to
the editor of *Die Neue Rundschau.* They were published, in Mohr's German
translation, in the issue of April 1933, preceded by a short version of Aldous
Huxley's introduction to the *Letters,* translated into German by Kurt Fiedler.
The German version of the beginning of Lawrence's letter to Mohr of 25 May
1929 reads as follows:

> Ich habe mich sehr über Ihren Brief gefreut, und dass es Ihnen gut geht.
> Ich möchte gern wissen, was für eine Art Zauberphantasie Ihr Buch
> enthält. Wenn wir einen festen Wohnort haben, müssen Sie mir das Man-
> uskript schicken, damit ich es lesen kann. Und auf jeden Fall haben Sie mit
> Lustspielen Geld verdient, Sie haben ein sicheres Dach über dem Kopf:
> Gottseidank! *Ist man arm, isst man Judendreck; ist man reich, lässt man
> Juden weg.*

> [I have been very glad about your letter—and to hear that you are well. I
> would really like to know what sort of magic fairytale your book contains.
> As soon as we have settled down somewhere you must send me the
> manuscript so I can read it. And in any case you have made money with
> comedies, you have a solid roof over your head—thank God! *If one is poor,
> one has to eat the dirt of Jews; if one is rich, one can do without the Jews.*]

The second and the third sentence of the English version are missing in the German translation; much of the translation is quite inexact; the rhyming proverb at the end is missing from the English text.

Mohr is not a Jewish name, but Mohr's mother or grandmother might have been Jewish. Lawrence did not consider Mohr to be a Jew; surely, he would have mentioned the fact in one of the letters in which he refers to Mohr, and Lawrence would not have used the tactless rhyme in a letter to Mohr. In his *Geschichte der deutschen Literatur,* Adolf Bartels carefully distinguishes between Jewish and non-Jewish authors; he does not call Mohr a Jew.[8] In *The Intelligent Heart* (Penguin Books, 1960), Harry T. Moore states that "Mohr, though not a Jew, left Nazi Germany to begin a new career in Shanghai, only to die there a few years later of one of the diseases he was helping to combat."[9] Moore had taken this information from Erika and Klaus Mann's book *Escape to Life*.[10] The information was incorrect, since Moore changed his text in *The Priest of Love:* "Mohr, who was Jewish, left Nazi Germany to begin a new career in Shanghai, only to die there a few years later of a heart attack."[11] According to Elisabeth Castonier there is no doubt that Mohr was Jewish.[12] She had been working for the Georg Müller Verlag and had accepted *Improvisationen im Juni* for publication.

III

In June 1928 Lawrence wrote to Mohr that he might come to Rottach on the way from Florence to Baden-Baden; he would travel by train via Verona and Innsbruck to Munich. Later he would go on to Baden-Baden and visit his mother-in-law. But by the middle of July, Lawrence had changed his plans no fewer than three times. In the end, he went to Baden-Baden first to celebrate the Baronin's seventy-seventh birthday (19 July). In the meantime, *Lady Chatterley* had been refused by Rowohlt Verlag as well, and Mohr had given up the idea of translating the novel. He needed money and could not risk translating a book that seemed to have no chance of finding a publisher. Lawrence was quite upset, since he was afraid that a pirated German edition might appear. Finally, E. P. Tal in Vienna published an unexpurgated edition of *Lady Chatterley* for subscribers only in 1930, an expurgated edition in 1933. The translator was Herbert E. Herlitschka.

On 24 July 1929 Lawrence asked Mohr from Baden-Baden whether he was still welcome in Rottach. The answer must have been positive, since Lawrence wrote on 22 August that he would come to Munich on 25 August and arrive in Rottach the day after.

There are conflicting reports about the Kaffee Angermaier where the Lawrences took rooms. According to Else, Lawrence "was lying in a bare room in the mean village inn." She severely reprimands Mohr for having enticed Lawrence, "already then a very sick man, to stay with him in a shady valley by Tegernsee" (Nehls, 426). Lawrence, on the other hand, called the Kaffee "rather a lovely place—and very peaceful, a little inn smelling terrifically of cows—but we eat out of doors under the trees, and live in a little house to ourselves" (Huxley, 821). According to most of his letters from Rottach, Lawrence seems to have enjoyed the inn and the surroundings (*CLM,* 1188, 1191, 1194), but toward the end of his stay, he began hating the mountains (*CLM,* 1193, 1198).

Frieda had suffered for months from a dislocated bone in her foot; Lawrence had paid considerable bills for specialists in London and Baden-Baden—but there had been no improvement. Now a simple farmer and bone-setter shoved the bone back into its socket—a matter of less than a minute. Lawrence hoped that a similar miracle might happen in the case of his own health, and he agreed to try out a special dietary cure recommended by some doctors brought in from Munich by Mohr. It turned out that Lawrence was already too weak to absorb the prescribed quantities of arsenic and phosphorous; he abandoned the poison part of the cure, but went on with a diet of porridge, raw fruit, and carrots.

The poisons and the climate had done more harm than good to Lawrence;[13] he felt he would be better off in the south of France. Mohr felt responsible for Lawrence's deteriorating health and accompanied Lawrence and Frieda all the way. Most biographies of Lawrence indicate that Lawrence and Frieda traveled to Bandol by themselves, and that Mohr arrived later and stayed as a visitor. However, it is quite clear from Frieda's account in *Nur der Wind . . .* that Mohr accompanied the two on their slow trip.[14]

While the Lawrences first lived at the Hôtel Beau Rivage and then moved into a little house, the Villa Beau Soleil, Mohr was staying at Les Goëlands. He gave Frieda advice as to Lawrence's diet. When he felt he could no longer be of any use, he left Bandol (on 21 October), promising to be back in January and bring his wife Käthe and his daughter Eva along. On the day of Mohr's departure, Lawrence wrote a letter to Mrs. Mohr—an apology for having kept Mohr away from her for such a long period of time. He emphasizes the fact that he is very ill and in bed and cannot even accompany Mohr to Toulon, but that Frieda and Achsah Brewster are taking him there in a taxi. Lawrence hopes to see her, Max, and little Eva in Bandol in January 1930. He finally invited Käthe to inform him, "wenn etwas schweres kommt, wo ich helfen kann" [if there should be a serious difficulty in which I can help] (*THM,* 173).

A few weeks after Mohr's departure, Lawrence received several books in the mail—one a scholarly work on the Etruscans. Mohr also sent Lawrence a review of the German translation of *Fantasia of the Unconscious* (*Spiel des Unbewussten* [Munich: Dornverlag G. Ullmann, 1929]). In December 1929, Mohr told Lawrence that he would visit him in February. On 30 January 1930 Lawrence seems to discourage such a visit: Frieda's daughter Barbara is in Bandol, and Lawrence expects both his sisters. But from the sanatorium Ad

Astra in Vence, Lawrence sent a card ([18] February 1930) asking Mohr: "Perhaps you would like to come here, later?" (*THM*, 179).

Mohr did not see Lawrence again. When he heard that Lawrence had died, he wrote a commemorative essay that appeared in the *Vossische Zeitung* (Berlin, 21 March 1930).

IV

Die Freundschaft von Ladiz was published in 1931.[15] Rolf Gardiner read and enjoyed the novel "in which the hero is modelled on D. H. L." (Nehls, 183). The only scholar who mentions Mohr's book with regard to Lawrence is Robert Lucas; in his biography of Frieda, Lucas says that the hero of Mohr's novel is D. H. Lawrence.[16] But Mohr's "Zauberphantasie" has, as the title implies, two heroes; these are Dr. Xaver Ragaz (Dr. Max Mohr) and Philipp Glenn (Lawrence). Dr. Ragaz is, like Mohr, a man of many talents: he is an excellent mountain climber, a well-known Alpine guide who publishes successful books about his adventures in the Karwendel mountains. He holds a Ph.D. in geology and geography and lives in a farmhouse ("Wolfsgrube") in Ladiz (Rottach) with his small family. He is quite a philosopher, healthy, unconventional, and always on the move; Xaver's wife rarely knows where her husband is. Sometimes he disappears for days at a time—living on a lonely alp or climbing mountains. He would like to have more money, and in the end he accepts a position at the University of Munich that will permit him to continue living among his beloved mountains. Ragaz is forty-two years old, the son of a Bavarian Alpine guide. Before he had married and moved to Ladiz eight years before, he had taken part in geological expeditions to Labrador and China.

Not far from Xaver's farmhouse stands a sort of rural castle belonging to Mr. Fergus, a capitalist from Hamburg. At the moment, a number of guests are living in the house, among them Philipp Glenn, thirty-seven years old, a painter, a genius. Glenn is not married and does not suffer from tuberculosis; nevertheless, who would not recognize Lawrence from the following description:

> Philipp Glenn, wie er am Rand der alten Grube sass, kaum mittelgross, hager und zäh, den Katzenjammer über die Weibernacht in den Fuchsaugen, und die blaue Jacke war viel zu weit geschnitten für die schmale Brust, dadurch hing sie in besonders elegantem Wurf um die Schultern, der kurz geschnittene kastanienbraune Bart lag wie ein Helmriemen um das Kinn: das war ein Kavallerist, verspätet oder verfrüht. Er war abgesessen, und der Gaul war ihm davongelaufen. Wer weiss wohin, vielleicht den Göttern nach, auf einen anderen Planeten. (Mohr, 25)

> [Philipp Glenn, as he sat on the brink of the old pit, not quite of medium height, haggard, tough, the hangover from the night with the women still in

his eyes—the eyes of a fox; his blue jacket was much too wide in view of his narrow chest, but it left the impression of an especially elegant style as it hung from his shoulders; the short beard, chestnut brown, surrounded the chin like the strap of a helmet: this was a cavalryman—either a premature or a belated one. He had alighted, and the horse had run away from him; who knows where it had gone—maybe after the Gods or to another planet.]

Mohr's novel is largely ironical. Glenn does sleep with women from time to time, but he is not satisfied with the attitudes of women toward men and of men toward other men. The problems and conflicts resemble the ones discussed in *Women in Love*. Glenn is an obstinate person; if he is confronted by stupidity, he flies into a rage. He speaks in a falsetto, he reminds one of a fox, and he has a shambling sort of walk. He feels that the emancipation of women is at the root of many of today's evils:

Die Frauen wollen, dass der Mann vor ihnen her marschiert, wenn sie auch millionenmal das Gegenteil behaupten und Millionen Bücher über die Gleichberechtigung der beiden Partner schreiben. Die Frauen hassen die Männer, welche nicht vor ihnen her, sondern neben ihnen her oder hinter ihnen her marschieren. Ganz fürchterlich hassen sie solche Männer, bewusst oder unbewusst, mit einem mörderischen Hass. Das ist der grosse Hass, den man in allen Ehen sehen kann, wenn man näher hinschaut. (Mohr, 73)

[Women want men to march in front of them, although they assert the opposite millions of times and write millions of books about the equality of rights of both partners. Women hate men who do not march in front of them, but on their side or behind. They hate such men quite dreadfully, consciously or unconsciously, with a murderous hate. This is the great hatred which one may observe in all marriages if one looks at them closely enough.]

There is talk about the Apocalypse, Noah's Ark ("Wolfsgrube"), and the new, nonsentimental kind of love between men and men, men and women. Glenn and Ragaz agree that the modern world is sick, and that Germany is even sicker than the rest of the world. They are of the opinion that, as in ancient Mexico, there must be a region which should belong to men exclusively, a place where men can meet among themselves, a sphere to which women should not have (and should not wish to have) access. Such a "link" between men is missing today (Mohr entitles the second part of the novel "Das Missing-Link").

The contents of the novel are, indeed, quite weird. When Ragaz and Glenn meet in Ladiz for the first time, they quarrel; there is even a fistfight between them. Glenn travels to the south of France where he meets Fanny Purgasser, and the two plan to marry. Fanny resembles Frieda in many ways; she is down-to-earth, not sentimental, and she often laughs heartily. Fundamentally, her ideas are the same as Philipp Glenn's. Philipp and Fanny decide to leave the south of France and spend two weeks skiing in Ladiz. Fanny dies in an avalanche. At this point, Ragaz begins to take care of Glenn, who is by no means greatly upset by the death of Fanny. With Fanny out of the way and Xaver's wife safely in the background, the two men begin to develop an ideal, nonsentimental friendship. For weeks, they live on a lonely alp; when two pretty female tourists appear, the two men keep them overnight and make love to them. No woman can resist these new paragons of masculinity. In the end, Ragaz and Glenn undertake an extremely dangerous climb through the "Nordwand" of the Karwendel. The function of their rope is real and symbolic at the same time: it unites both men, and their very lives depend on the rope between them. It turns out that their new kind of male friendship withstands all trials; they arrive safely at the top.

The novel, at best amusing and, in the third part, thrilling, is no great work of art. The language is careless, the plotting pedestrian, and the descriptions superficial; the dialogues, on the other hand, are witty and entertaining. Still, if it were not for the fact that it contains fictional portraits of Lawrence and Mohr, the novel might well be forgotten.

When Lawrence read Aldous Huxley's novel *Point Counter Point* (1928) in which he and Frieda appear as Mark and Mary Rampion, he wrote to Martin Secker: "Did you read Aldous' *Counter-Point?* My word, the modern melodrama—East Lynne up to date! I thought the Rampions an unreal and wordy couple, but I suppose he meant well" (Secker, 112). To Huxley himself he wrote in a rage: "your Rampion is the most boring character in the book—a gas-bag. Your attempt at intellectual sympathy!—It's all rather disgusting, and I feel like a badger that has its hole on Wimbledon Common and trying not to be caught" (Huxley, 758). One wonders what Lawrence would have said if he had been able to read *Die Freundschaft von Ladiz!*

V

Not much is known about Mohr's later years. Literary histories and *Who's Who*s have ignored Mohr's name. We know from Peter de Mendelssohn that Mohr changed his publisher in 1933; he left Ullstein and joined the Fischer Verlag. Mendelssohn politely calls Mohr an "ausgezeichneter Romancier" [excellent novelist].[17] Fischer published *Die Neue Rundschau,* which brought out the selection of Lawrence's letters to Mohr in April 1933.

In 1934, Mohr decided to emigrate. In a letter to Thomas Mann he explained why he felt he had to leave. Mann answered on 5 November 1934.[18] In a note to this letter, Erika Mann says: "*Improvisationen im Juni* gehörte zu den meistgespielten Dramen seiner Art. Der Expressionismus, der den Autor bestimmte, ist hier mit viel liebenswerter Romantik durchsetzt" [*Improvisationen im Juni* was one of the most frequently performed plays of its kind. Expressionism, which formed the author, is here interspersed with much charming romanticism].[19] It seems that Mohr left Germany in December 1934. When he arrived in Shanghai in early 1935, he had ten dollars in his pocket, "my instruments, my medical training, a few photos of the family I had left behind in Germany, the letters of D. H. Lawrence, and a glorious feeling that I had finished with Germany."[20] Mohr died in Shanghai in 1944 at the age of fifty-three.

APPENDIX: A LIST OF LAWRENCE'S LETTERS TO MAX MOHR

Abbreviations

THM "The Unpublished Letters of D. H. Lawrence to Max Mohr." *T'ien Hsia Monthly.* Vol. 1, nos. 1 and 2 (August and September 1935): 21–36, 166–79.

NR "Briefe an Max Mohr." *Die Neue Rundschau* (vol. 44 of *Die freie Bühne*). Vol. 1 (April 1933): 527–40.

CLM *The Collected Letters of D. H. Lawrence.* Edited by Harry T. Moore. London: Heinemann, 1962.

Date of letter	Published on page(s) in		
	THM	*NR*	*CLM*
1927			
1 10 Oct.	22–24	528–29	1010–11
2 31 Oct.	24–25		1015–16
3 22 Nov.	25–26		
4 17 Dec.	26–27		
5 23 Dec.	27–28	529–30	
1928			
6 3 Feb.	28		
7 29 Feb.	29	530–31	
8 22 March	30–31	531–32	1047–48
9 7 June	31–32		
10 9 Dec.	32–33		
11 31 Dec.	33		
1929			
12 17 Jan.	34		
13 5 April	34–35		
14 18 May	35		
15 25 May	35–36	532-33	1156–57
16 8 June	166		
17 12 June	166		
18 ? June	166–67		
19 26 June	167		
20 2 July	167–68		
21 10 July	168	533	
22 [14] July	168		

Date of letter	Published on page(s) in		
	THM	*NR*	*CLM*
23 [17] July	169		
24 24 July	169–70	533–34	
25 6 Aug.	170–71		
26 [17] Aug.	171–72	534–35	
27 22 Aug.	172		
28 21 Oct.	172–73	535–36	
29 14 Nov.	174–75	536–37	1213–14
30 20 Nov.	175–76	537–38	1215–16
31 19 Dec.	177–78	538–39	
1930			
32 30 Jan.	178–79	540	
33 [18] Feb.	179	540	

Comments:

a) Letters 6, 16, 19, 23, 24, 25, 26 and 27 are written entirely in German.
b) Letter 1 in *NR* is erroneously dated 10 Dec. (instead of 10 Oct.).
c) Letter 28 is addressed to Mrs. Käthe Mohr.
d) Letters 29 and 31 are addressed to Max and Käthe Mohr.
e) The text of the six letters in *CLM* does not differ from the text of the same letters in *THM*.
f) The text of most letters in *NR* is inexact and incomplete.
g) The text of the letters in *THM* seems to have been cut in a few places; letter 21, for instance, has more text in *NR* than in *THM*.

NOTES

1. D. H. Lawrence, *The Collected Letters of D. H. Lawrence,* ed. Harry T. Moore (London: William Heinemann, 1962), pp. 1003–4. Hereafter cited in the text as *CLM.*
2. D. H. Lawrence, *Letters from D. H. Lawrence to Martin Secker 1911–1930* (privately published, 1970), p. 95. Hereafter cited in the text as Secker.
3. D. H. Lawrence, *The Letters of D. H. Lawrence,* ed. Aldous Huxley (London: William Heinemann, 1932), p. 702. Hereafter cited in the text as Huxley.
4. Edward Nehls, *D. H. Lawrence: A Composite Biography,* 3 vols. (Madison: University of Wisconsin Press, 1959), 3 (1925–30):183. Hereafter cited in the text as Nehls.
5. D. H. Lawrence, "The Unpublished Letters of D. H. Lawrence to Max Mohr," *T'ien Hsia Monthly,* no. 1 (August 1935), 27. The letters appeared in *THM,* nos. 1 and 2 (August and September 1935), 21–36 and 166–79. Hereafter cited in the text as *THM.*
6. Frieda Lawrence, *Nur der Wind . . .* (Berlin: Rabenpresse, 1936), p. 326.
7. D. H. Lawrence, "Briefe an Max Mohr," in *Die Neue Rundschau,* vol. 44 of *Die freie Bühne,* 1 (April 1933): 527–40.
8. Adolf Bartels, *Geschichte der deutschen Literatur,* 3 vols. (Leipzig: H. Haessel, 1928), 3:967.
9. Harry T. Moore, *The Intelligent Heart* (Harmondsworth: Penguin Books, 1960), p. 453.
10. Erika Mann and Klaus Mann, *Escape to Life* (Boston: Houghton Mifflin, 1939).
11. Harry T. Moore, *The Priest of Love: A Life of D. H. Lawrence* (Harmondsworth: Penguin Books, 1976), p. 546.
12. Elisabeth Castonier, *Stürmisch bis heiter. Memoiren einer Aussenseiterin* (Munich: Nymphenburger, 1964), pp. 137–38.
13. In his book *D. H. Lawrence* (London: Barker, 1957) Anthony West says: "a Bavarian dietetic quack got hold of him and bore him off to a pseudo-sanatorium where they dosed him with a course of drugs" (71). The fact is that the doctors visited Lawrence in Rottach and prescribed a diet including arsenic and phosphorous. Lawrence went to no sanatorium, and left out the poisons from his diet when he felt that they made him weaker. But Lawrence continued with this sort of diet in Bandol. See Frieda Lawrence, *The Memoirs and Correspondence,* ed. E. W. Tedlock (London: William Heinemann, 1971), pp. 239–40.
14. While Keith Sagar states the facts correctly in *D. H. Lawrence: A Calendar of His Works* (Manchester: Manchester University Press, 1979), Harry T. Moore has them wrong in *The Intelligent Heart* and *The Priest of Love.* Taking their cue from Moore, Emily Hahn (*Lorenzo* [Philadelphia and New York: Lippincott, 1975]) and others seem to go on perpetuating the mistake.
15. Max Mohr, *Die Freundschaft von Ladiz. Roman aus den Bergen* (Munich: Georg Müller Verlag, 1931). The novel was reprinted in 1933 for the Deutsche Buch-Gemeinschaft, Berlin. This version represents a "neue vom Verfasser durchgesehene Ausgabe." Quotations in the text are taken from this revised edition hereafter cited as Mohr. The dedication reads as follows:

Für David Herbert Lawrence
geb. 11. 9. 1885, Eastwood
gest. 2. 3. 1930, Vence.

16. Robert Lucas, *Frieda von Richthofen* (Munich: Kindler, 1972), p. 290.
17. Peter de Mendelssohn, *S. Fischer und sein Verlag* (Frankfurt am Main: Fischer, 1970), p. 283.
18. Thomas Mann, *Briefe I: 1889–1933,* ed. Erika Mann (Frankfurt am Main: Fischer Taschenbuch Verlag, 1979), p. 379.
19. Erika Mann, "Editor's Note," In *Briefe I,* p. 528.
20. Erika Mann and Klaus Mann, quoted in Nehls, p. 726.

10

Lawrence and the Futurists

EMILE DELAVENAY

In *The Intelligent Heart*, Harry T. Moore briefly refers to Lawrence's expressed interest in the Italian futurists, pointing out that his letter to A. W. McLeod of 2 June 1914 shows "how thoroughly he had looked into" them. And yet the stress has been laid so far on the divergences that Lawrence himself outlines. Now that the early works of Marinetti's group are more readily accessible, a closer study of the points of convergence becomes possible. The present attempt to do so is undertaken mainly in the hope that it may suggest further and deeper research. Explicit references to the futurists in two letters are the emerged tip of the iceberg, and I hope to show that Lawrence's writings offer evidence of interest from the autumn of 1913 to at least 1917.

BASIC DATA

Letters of 2 and 5 June 1914[1] give definite clues to Lawrence's reading and attest to his eagerness.

> I got a book of their poetry—a very fat book too—and a book of pictures—and I read Marinetti's and Paolo Buzzi's manifestations [*sic*] and essays and Sofficci's essays on cubism and futurism. It interests me very much. (279)

> I want to write an essay about Futurism, when I have the inspiration and wit thereunto. (281)

> Please keep this letter, because I want to write on futurism and it will help me. (283)

He was then working on *The Wedding Ring*: "I think the book is a bit futuristic, quite unconsciously so," he wrote to Garnett. Marinetti helped him to "see something of what [he was] after" (*CLM*, 281). These letters admit convergence of views and artistic aims, while also stressing divergence. While the projected essay was never written, parts of it run in filigree through "Study of Thomas Hardy," the next critical work undertaken after his return to England, showing that a continuing debate was running on in his mind about futurist views.

Two of the publications he read in 1914 are identified by Keith Aldritt.[2] The "very fat book" is *I Poeti Futuristi*,[3] published in Milan in 1913, indeed a fat volume of 428 pages. It contains:

a) An Introduction, "Giovanni Italiani" [Young Italians] (*IPF*, 7–12), in which is found the sentence quoted by Lawrence, in simplified form, as "Italy is like a great dreadnought surrounded by her torpedo boats" (*CLM*, 280).

b) Marinetti's "Technical Manifesto of Futurist Literature" (*IPF*, 12–23), dated Milan, 11 May 1912. Lawrence's letter to Garnett quotes from this.

c) "Rispósta alle Obiezióni" [Reply to the Objections] (*IPF*, 23–42), also found in other publications as "Supplement to the Technical Manifesto of Futurist Literature."

d) Paolo Buzzi's essay "Il Verso Libero" [Free Verse] (*IPF*, 43–48), dated Milan, 1908, originally published as part of Marinetti's inquiry on free verse in his review *Poesia*. This is the essay to which Lawrence refers.

Ardengo Sofficci's booklet, *Cubismo e Futurismo* (78 pp.), consists of a collection of short essays and was first published in Florence in 1914. Perhaps the fact that Lawrence obtained a copy so soon testifies to his keenness.

The peculiar use of the plural "manifestations" in his letter to McLeod suggests that he had read other futurist manifestos, such as Marinetti's original "Manifesto of Futurist Literature," first published in French in *Figaro* on 20 February 1909, and later in Italian. He could have read it in the "book of pictures," which I have identified as *Pittura, Scultura Futuriste, Dinamismo Plastico*.[4]

In "Study of Thomas Hardy" Lawrence discusses Umberto Boccioni's sculpture *Sviluppo di una bottiglia nello spazio*, which he translates as "Development of a Bottle *through* Space," slightly misconstruing the sculptor's intention. This plaster cast was originally shown at the Galerie La Boëtie in June-July 1913; Boccioni wrote an introduction for the Catalogue. While it is unlikely that Lawrence ever saw the actual sculpture, now at the São Paulo Museum, he probably saw its photograph and read the Introduction in the "book of pictures," another fat book containing reproductions of ten other sculptures by Boccioni, and of ten paintings by him and five other futurists, including Sofficci.

This book, *Pittura, Scultura, Futuriste, Dinamismo Plastico*, was published in Milan in March 1914. In addition to photographs of good quality on bond paper, it contains Boccioni's long paper "Dinamismo Plastico" (over three hundred pages), his Introduction to the Catalogue, and lists of all the

Umberto Boccioni, *Development of a Bottle in Space*, 1912. Silvered bronze (cast 1931),

manifestos and futurist works of art exhibited and sold; and it reproduces Marinetti's original manifesto of 1909 under the title "Fondazióne e Manifesto del Futurismo."

GENERAL JUDGMENTS ON THE FUTURISTS

Lawrence's letter to McLeod alludes to the contents and spirit of that 1909 Manifesto and its introductory piece, "Fondazióne e Manifesto del Futurismo":

> They want to deny every scrap of tradition and experience, which is silly. They are very young, college-student and medical-student at his most blatant. But I like them. Only I don't believe in them. I agree with them about the weary sickness of pedantry and tradition and inertness, but I don't agree with them as to the cure and the escape. (*CLM,* 280)

"Fondazióne e Manifesto del Futurismo" does read like a students' prank. It stresses the youthfulness of the group: "The oldest among us are thirty; we therefore have at least ten years to accomplish our task."[5] The allusion to "medical-student" may refer to their enthusiasm for Dr. Alexis Carrel, the precursor in human grafts, and to Marinetti's exaltation of "the creation of mechanical man with replaceable parts."[6]

Their program for the extirpation of the past, excessive though it may have seemed to Lawrence, is not without resemblance to some of his reactions against his recent experience. Section 10 of the 1909 Manifesto reads: "We want to demolish museums, libraries, to combat moralism, feminism, opportunist and utilitarian cowardice." The second chapter of the so-called "Study of Thomas Hardy" denounces feminism and utilitarian cowardice:

> It is so sad that the earnest people of today serve at the old, second-rate altar of self-preservation. The woman-suffragists . . . even they are content to fight the old battles on the old ground, to fight an old system of self-preservation to obtain a more advanced system of preservation.[7]

People seeking utilitarian self-preservation are "cabbages" rotting at the heart in "a winter of cowardice" (*Phoenix,* 405, 408). Rather than attacking "moralism," Lawrence attacks the laws: "Let there be a parliament of men and women for the careful and gradual unmaking of laws." His general attack on suffragists and parliament is not unlike Marinetti's piece "Le Mépris de la femme"[8] [Contempt for Woman], which circulated in various forms and languages before 1914. Some of its passages should be compared with Birkin's thoughts on love and woman, conceived if not written during those months of 1914.

Just after he wrote the "Hardy," Lawrence was rewriting *The Rainbow,* describing Ursula's bitter disappointment with her suddenly meaningless university studies. Was he thinking, at Greatham where he was finishing his novel, of Marinetti's phrases, read in the spring?

We want to liberate Italy from its gangrene of professors, archeologists, cicerones and antiquarians.

To admire an old painting is to pour out our sensibility into a funeral urn instead of thrusting it forward in violent jets of creation and action. Do you want us to spoil the best of our strength in useless admiration of the past, which fatally leads to your being exhausted, diminished, downtrodden?

Indeed daily attendance at museums, libraries and academies (those cemeteries of wasted efforts, those calvaries of crucified dreams, those registers of broken impulses! . . .), is to artists what the prolonged tutelage of parents is to intelligent young men inebriated with their own talent and their willful ambition. (MF, 178–79)[9]

Ursula resents her parents' prolonged tutelage as she tries to launch out into "the man's world"; and before her, Will Brangwen's admiration for old paintings had "spoiled the best of [his] strength in useless admiration of the past." While Ursula's awakening to the emptiness of her college studies needs no prompting from the futurists, her thoughts run on lines parallel to Marinetti's:

The professors were not priests initiated into the deep mysteries of life and knowledge. After all, they were only middle-men handling wares they had become so accustomed to that they were oblivious of them. . . . The life went out of her studies, why, she did not know. But the whole thing seemed sham, spurious; spurious Gothic arches, spurious peace, spurious Latinity, spurious dignity of France, spurious naïveté of Chaucer. It was a second-hand dealer's shop, and one bought an equipment for an examination.[10]

Birkin's and Ursula's struggle toward "some condition of blessedness" will be Lawrence's illustration of his own idea of the "cure and escape" away from the love of machinery, of vibrating airplanes and speeding motor cars. The futurists wished to "sing the man who holds the steering wheel, whose ideal stem crosses the Earth launched itself on the circuit of its orbit." Ursula is looking for the Sons of God. She finds Birkin, who in the chapter "Excurse" sits next to her steering his car "like an Egyptian Pharaoh," combining the Egyptian "deepest physical mind" with "a sort of second consciousness" and "a free intelligence to direct his own ends" as he drives to his chosen destination.[11] This sole concession made by Birkin to machinery is neither a compromise with Marinetti, nor completely alien to the Italian's interest in parapsychology; in *Women in Love* it is to be read as a sign of the integration of the machine into a culture as the servant of man, not his master.

Lawrence sees the futurists as

ultra-ultra intellectual, going beyond Maeterlinck and the Symbolistes, who are intellectual. . . . It's the most self-conscious, intentional, pseudo-scientific stuff on the face of the earth. . . . Italy has got to go through the most mechanical and dead stage of all—everything is appraised according to its mechanic value—everything is subject to the laws of physics. (*CLM,* 280)

This last sentence, expressing an idea later developed in *Twilight in Italy,* aptly sums up a recurrent theme of futurist propaganda, anxious to see Italy catch up with the industrial civilization of more advanced European countries.

On the destructive element Lawrence has no reservations: "This is the revolt against beastly sentiment and slavish adherence to tradition and the dead mind. For that I love it" (*CLM,* 280). He is more specific in his agreement on certain positive values in the letter to Garnett. To McLeod, who to some extent represents Lawrence's own recent past, he states his sympathy with the attempt to apply "to emotions . . . the purging of the old forms and sentimentalities. I like it for its saying—enough of this sickly cant, let us be honest and stick by what is in us" (*CLM,* 279). To Garnett, he outlines in justification of *The Wedding Ring* his own "different attitude to [his] characters."

AN INTUITIVE *PHYSICOLOGY* OF MATTER

"I don't think the psychology [of the new novel] is wrong: it is only that I have a different attitude to my characters, and that necessitates a different attitude in you, which you are not prepared to give" (*CLM,* 281). He finds partial convergence with Marinetti, who wanted to "destroy all psychology" (MT, 187) and had written in the *Daily Mail* (21 November 1913): "this foul thing and foul word, psychology." Lawrence quotes paragraph 11 of the Technical Manifesto of 1912: "But when I read Marinetti—'the profound intuitions added one to the other, word by word, according to their illogical conception, will give us the general lines of an intuitive physiology of matter'—I see something of what I am after" (*CLM,* 281).

Marinetti's word, it should be recorded once and for all, *was not "physiology,"* for which Italian has a word, *fisiologia,* and French also, *physiologie.* The 1912 Italian text and its original French version, both published from Marinetti's personal address in Milan, use *"fisicologia"* and *"physicologie,"* excluding all suggestion of a mistake. Marinetti was French-speaking and wrote in French before he did so in Italian. He coined the words deliberately. Lawrence probably did not realize that *"fisicologia"* was not current Italian. Recent editors of Marinetti's works, rejecting the neologism, now print *"psicologia,"* making total nonsense of the passage and leading certain critics in turn to "correct" Lawrence's translation and print "psychology" instead of his "physiology."

What Marinetti had in mind is perhaps not abundantly clear; Lawrence finds "his Italian . . . obfuscated." But the general sense is perceptible and close enough to what he himself was after. This long section of the Technical Manifesto proposes to "replace the psychology of man, from now on exhausted, by the **lyrical obsession of matter.**" Marinetti wishes to give expression to "movements of matter outside the laws of intelligence, and therefore of more significant essence." Hence his recourse to "intuition." Literature should, he thinks, take into account, for instance, elements so far neglected by it, such as "noise (the manifestation of the dynamism of things);[12] weight (the faculty of flight) and odor (faculty of dispersion). For instance, endeavor to render the environment of smells perceived by a dog. Listen to motors and reproduce their discourse" (MT, 187).

An attentive reading of various scenes in *The Rainbow* could not fail to discover passages inspired, within reasonable limits, by similar preoccupations, motors excepted. But Lawrence, ready as he was to assimilate some of the Italians' techniques, and as dissatisfied as they were with traditional psychology and conventional aesthetics, was, at least in this letter, more concerned with justifying, against Garnett's criticism, his own treatment of human character: "Somehow—that which is physic—non-human, in humanity, is more interesting to me than the old-fashioned human element—which causes one to conceive a character in a certain moral scheme and make him consistent. The certain moral scheme is what I object to" (*CLM, 281*).

Here again he follows Marinetti some of the way, gathering from him strength in his opposition to what he wants to do away with; but his emphasis is more on the "moral scheme," and the Italian's on the shift from traditional psychology (he fights D'Annunzio's type of literature) to a new, scientific approach to objects and their dynamics. Marinetti wanted to "combat moralism." Since writing the foreword to *Sons and Lovers,* Lawrence had adopted an antinomianist attitude neither very different from nor incompatible with Marinetti's Nietzschean preaching of "the love of danger, the practice of energy and temerity" (MF, para. 1), which was later to lead the Italian to active support of fascism. But he is fascinated by machinery, by the materials of which it is made; while the Englishman, at heart a novelist–poet of the individual and the fugitive, tries to apply futuristic techniques to the portraying of characters, remaining essentially interested in people even if he depicts "inhuman" or "non-human" aspects of their behavior, and insists on the accurate, detailed description of their features and gestures, as in the scenes between Tom Brangwen and Lydia Lensky at the beginning of *The Rainbow.* Striving to show in them the secret "physic" workings of their innermost being, he does not declare war on psychology, but seeks expression for a new psychology:

When Marinetti writes: "It is the solidity of a blade of steel that is interesting by itself, that is, the incomprehending and inhuman alliance of its molecules in resistance to, say, a bullet.[13] The heat of a piece of wood or iron is in fact more passionate, for us, than the laughter[14] of a woman"— then I know what he means.

He does, in spite of his minor mistranslations. He goes on, forging his own doctrine on the way:

He is stupid, as an artist, for contrasting the heat of the iron and the laugh of the woman. Because what is interesting in the laugh of the woman is the same as the binding of the molecules of steel or their action in heat; it is the inhuman will, call it physiology, or, like Marinetti, physiology of matter, that fascinates me. I don't so much care about what the woman *feels*—in the ordinary usage of the word. That presumes an *ego* to feel with. I only care about what the woman *is*—what she IS—inhumanly, physiologically, materially—according to the use of the word: but for me, what she *is* as a phenomenon (or as representing some greater, inhuman will), instead of what she feels according to the human conception. That is where the futurists are stupid. Instead of looking for the new human phenomenon, they will only look for the phenomena of the science of physics to be found in human beings. They are crassly stupid. (*CLM*, 281–82)

To this, one might object that they were not interested in the phenomena of physics to be found in humans, but anxious to describe matter and objects with a minimum of interference from human emotions. Lawrence's overriding preoccupation with people and their conscious or unconscious psychology clouds his perception of their aim, with which he is not in sympathy. And so he goes on to what has always been treated as a significant personal discovery: his conception of a new "*ego* of the character." The starting point is also to be found in the 1912 Manifesto.

MARINETTI AND LAWRENCE'S *EGO* OF THE CHARACTER

The same paragraph 11 of the "Technical Manifesto" begins (and Lawrence does not quote this) with the prescription: "**Destroy the 'I' in literature, that is to say, all psychology.**" (**Distruggere nella letteratura l' "io".**) Lawrence will say the "ego"; the French text says *"le Je"* and *"le moi."* Marinetti has in mind both the "I" as subject for literature and as the "I" of the author, for instance in D'Annunzio. Immediately following this, Marinetti introduces the equivalent of what Lawrence will call the "certain moral scheme":

Man, completely spoiled by library and museum, *submitted to a frightful logic and wisdom*, is now of no interest whatsoever. Therefore abolish him in literature. Replace him at last by matter, the essence of which has to be reached by dint of intuition, a thing physicists and chemists can never do. (MT, 187; emphasis added)

Rather than "abolish man," Lawrence aims at studying and presenting him in a new light. But Marinetti's imagery drawn from the sciences of matter has made an impression: he goes on to develop his often–quoted theme of the allotropic states, of diamond and carbon,[15] and his simile of the Chladny figures:

You mustn't look in my novel for the old stable *ego*—of the character. There is another *ego,* according to whose action the individual is unrecognizable, and passes through, as it were, allotropic states which it needs a deeper sense than any we've been used to exercise, to discover are states of the same radically unchanged element. (*CLM,* 282)

More interested, it would seem at this stage, in the new Freudian psychology of unconscious states than in the somewhat utopian idea of developing an "intuitive physiology of matter," he begins to work out his own artistic problems, following a train of thought started by the Manifesto. Convergence with the futurists in wanting to make a clean sweep of the past does not mean that he adopts their aims and rather wild literary ambitions. Lawrence is not prepared to follow Marinetti in his typically Italian obsession with matter, machinery, and industry: his attitudes are post-industrial, whereas the futurists are anxious to enter the industrial age, to wipe out what they resent as three centuries of artistic stagnation in their own country. Futurist writing on the plastic arts throws light on Marinetti's recommendation to poets to "hate intelligence" and to awaken in themselves "divine intuition," on his rejection of psychology, his call for intuition centered, not on the animal kingdom, but on "the mechanical kingdom" and leading to "knowledge of and friendship with matter." Boccioni wants to do away with what he calls "il sublime tradizionale dei soggetti," the traditional sublime of subjects, to "destroy the whole literary and traditional nobility of marble and bronze" as well as "the systematic nude," the traditional notion of statue or monument. He sees more truth in the intersection of the surfaces of a book with the angles of a table, or the straight lines of a matchstick, than "in all the twining muscles, all the bosoms and all the buttocks of heroes and venuses which inspire the modern idiocy of sculpture."[16] Similarly, Marinetti declares war on syntax and the "Latin period," on all forms of the grand style, asserting that there is no hierarchy of images, "noble or coarse, elegant or low, eccentric or natural"; "Let us courageously create the 'ugly' in literature and kill in all places the solemn. . . . We must daily spit on the *Altar of Art*" (MT, 186; his emphasis). "Words in freedom" will be to prose what free verse is to poetry.

As "obfuscated" (to use Lawrence's word) as much of this may seem, there is a link between this general demolition campaign against "the old forms and sentimentalities," and his endeavor to portray human character in an English context in a novel manner. Of course there is a difference of temperaments. He emphasizes the "moral scheme," in typically English and post-Victorian reaction, where Marinetti and his artist friends rebel rather against Latin, i.e., Italian and French, formalism, academic style in art and letters, and a worn-out type of discourse. But what encouragement, nonetheless, to Lawrence to find his own path!

For the futurists, matter, "ugly" if necessary—that is to say not conforming to academic notions of beauty—must come before tradition and classical psychology. Lawrence's very metaphor of diamond and carbon, one noble, the other common, his use of the figures made by a bow on a tray of sand, suggest that what distinguishes his new psychology from the old is its *materialism.* The words he uses to define his portrayal of a woman are "inhumanly, physiologically, materially."

Like the Italians, he rejects *hierarchy:* Marinetti does in style, syntax, images, subjects; Boccioni, in materials for sculpture, in subjects. Unlike Garnett, Lawrence refuses to recognize any hierarchy of psychological states, some perceived as "noble" because admitted into consciousness or integrated into the "certain moral scheme." His objection, made in the letter to McLeod, to the futurists "[sticking] by those things that have been thought horrid, and by those alone," is not fundamental. The divergences are elsewhere.

Marinetti, the Italian with a French education, reacts more strongly against aesthetic and stylistic formalism; the Anglo-Saxon, against a moral scheme that he now perceives as concealing, or failing to recognize, certain aspects of human nature. Steeped as he is in "the great tradition," how could he agree to "abolish man in literature"? He wants to extend the field of psychology, to show a character according to what he is rather than what he feels: that is, has been educated to feel in the moral scheme. We can take him at his word when he says that Marinetti shows him something of what he is after.

BOCCIONI'S DYNAMISM AND PLASTIC STATES OF MIND

Letters written several months before the first mention of the futurists reveal Lawrence's familiarity with their ideas. Baffled by drawings of Ernest Collings, he wrote to him on 22 March 1914:

Don't tell me it is merely beautiful form and space-filling: that means *tour de force.* The thing must be *the expression of some strong emotion or idea.* . . . You don't use the human figure to express any individual emotion—not dramatically. Don't say it is *just a decorative* use.[17]

According to Sofficci an artist wants, above all, to make whoever looks at his work "see, or better, *feel* . . . the emotional relations between . . . elements coordinated in an artistic composition, that is to say a plastic unity both vital and self-sufficient." His instinct "as painter *and not illustrator*" (emphasis added) dictates his projection of his inner vision, so that he will "render exactly perceptible, to whomever is capable of receiving it, *the sensation and the lyrical-pictorial emotion which objects have provoked* in his essence as painter."[18] Even if such ideas were fairly current, the coincidence is remarkable, and it is all the more so when in the same letter Lawrence probably echoes Marinetti:

> You want to use the human body to express—what?—something elementary in nature, *something non-organic, or of the realm of physics*—what? What property of the human soul do you want to express?—*the mechanicalness of thought, as one of the natural forces?* (Huxley, 185; emphasis added)

In his friend's drawings he finds "something that is like *the intellectual ego,* something *frozen like death* which survives life, and knows nothing of life or resurrection" (Huxley, 183; emphasis added). Marinetti not only wanted to "destroy the ego" but also to "hate intelligence, by waking up in you divine intuition," and "to free man from the idea of death, and therefore from death itself, that supreme definition of logical intelligence" (MT, 188). Again, is this mere coincidence?

In June when Lawrence says he "has been" interested in the futurists, not only the use of the past tense but also a comment on James Stephens in a letter of 2 December 1913 date his familiarity with their writings: "I think in Italy one is interested in different things from England—one can't stand so much woolliness, and fluffiness, as there is in Stephens" (*CLM,* 250).

Started in 1913, the debate with the Italians continues nearly to the end of his life: traces of it, as we shall see, can be detected in his comments on Cézanne, the acknowledged ancestor of futurist art according to Sofficci and Boccioni. A frontier of disagreement, drawn from the very first, should not obliterate some deep sympathies. It is delineated by Lawrence's growing preoccupation with the relations of the sexes. "The futurists," he wrote to McLeod, "will progress down the purely male or intellectual or scientific line" (*CLM,* 280–81). Did he have any reason, other than in his own incipient theorizing, to stress the "purely male"? Did he in particular know of what Giovanni Lista calls Marinetti's and his group's "latent sodomy" and his "maternal attitude towards" Boccioni,[19] a subject which, according to Lista, "remains to be studied"? Lawrence's first explicit reference to homosexuality is in a letter to Henry Savage of 2 December 1913, about the poet Richard Middleton, some of the terms of which are recalled by passages on Michelangelo in "Study of Thomas Hardy": "I should like to know why every man that approaches greatness tends to homosexuality, whether he admits it or not: so that he loves the *body* of a man better than the body of a woman—as I believe the Greeks did, sculptors and all, by far" (*CLM*, 251).

"But from a woman [a man] wants himself re-born, re-constructed": this letter contains the germ of the positive statement to McLeod, which follows his basic criticism of futurist art:

> They will even use their intuition for intellectual and scientific purpose. The one thing about their art is that it *isn't* art, but ultra scientific attempts to make diagrams of certain physic [*sic*] or mental states. . . .
>   I think the only re-sourcing of art, revivifying it, is to make it more the joint work of man and woman. (*CLM*, 280)

Substantial sections of "Study of Thomas Hardy," written in the autumn of 1914, expand this theme of male and female, including allusions to homosexuality in artists. It could in fact be argued that in that respect as well as in its discussions of Italian art, that long and complex work, if not the projected essay on the futurists, contains elements originally intended for it. In *Pittura, Scultura Futuriste, Dinamismo Plastico,* which has been identified as the "book of pictures" mentioned in June 1914, Lawrence had seen forty reproductions of paintings by six members of the group and eleven photographs of Boccioni's sculptures, the most striking and the most seminal of which was *Sviluppo di una bottiglia nello spazio, Natura morta,* to which Lawrence devotes a whole page, declaring himself fascinated and confused.

Point by point comparisons could be made between details of his general argument in sections VI to IX of his "Hardy," and Boccioni's ideas and actual phrases. I must here limit myself to showing the persistence in those sections of a debate begun in the spring of 1914. Like Boccioni, Lawrence takes a racial view of art. The Italian sees in a work of art a finality closely related to the historic moment of its creation, and to racial characteristics: "When we speak of Greek sculpture, of Italian painting or of Flemish painting, our mind immediately embraces homogeneous cycles, historical continuities *in the plastic expression of a race*" (DP, 56; emphasis added). Artistic tradition, according to him, is "the logical, fatal and continuous unfolding of a race's ideality," notwithstanding influences from fashions or foreign schools. Such racial conceptions were of course widely current, disseminated by Gobineau, and by Houston Chamberlain who, as H. G. Wells has pointed out, became by the end of 1914 "the material of countless articles and interminable discussions."[20]

Lawrence differs from Boccioni mainly in that he introduces a sexual element in the debate on art. He sees everywhere the action of the male and female principles. What he calls "the race conception of God" depends upon "whether in that race the male or the female element triumphs, becomes predominant" (*Phoenix*, 448). There is, according to him, a "will-to-motion" expressing, in a race, the assertion of the male or an aspiration toward it, and a "will-to-inertia" expressing the female principle or its attraction. "And

everything we see and know and are is the resultant of these two wills. . . .
The artistic effort is the portraying of a moment of union between the two
wills" (*Phoenix*, 447).

Allowing for basic differences, some of his reasonings sound strangely like
Boccioni's. Lawrence writes:

> The division into male and female is arbitrary, for the purpose of thought.
> The rapid motion of the rim of a wheel is the same as the perfect rest at the
> centre of the wheel. . . . Motion and rest are the same, when seen com-
> pletely. . . . Infinite motion and infinite rest are the same thing. . . . But
> this table on which I write, which I call at rest, I know is really in motion.
>   So there is no such thing as rest. There is only infinite motion. But
> infinite motion must contain every degree of rest. So that motion and rest
> are the same thing. Rest is the lowest speed of motion which I recognize
> under normal conditions. (*Phoenix*, 448)

And Boccioni:

> Absolute motion is a dynamic law axed in the object. The plastic con-
> struction of the object considers . . . the motion which is in the object,
> whether immobile or in motion. I make this distinction between immobility
> and motion for convenience of exposition, but in reality there is no such
> thing as immobility; motion alone exists, immobility being mere ap-
> pearance or relativity. . . . Relative motion is a dynamic law axed on the
> motion of the object. It is accidental in that it concerns, rather, mobile
> objects or their relation to immobile objects. In reality however nothing is
> immobile according to our modern intuition of life. (DP, 69–71)

Boccioni was the first to apply the word "abstract" to the plastic arts. In
fact he sees the history of art in the light of four great "abstractions," a word
that Lawrence also uses frequently in his art criticism: "Greek plastic abstraction" makes the outer man the center of the universe; with "Christian
plastic abstraction" art passes from depicting the outer to the inner man, the
climax being the Gothics and Michelangelo. "Naturalist plastic abstraction,"
from Rembrandt to the fauves and cubists, exteriorizes the inner man.
Finally, "Futurist plastic abstraction," coming after the impressionists, will
culminate in "dynamism" and "states of mind."

With differences caused by the injection of the "male and female" theme
as determinant of the conception of God in each race, there are parallels
between this scheme and Lawrence's outline of great periods of art, from
"the movement into the conscious possession of a body," through "the
cathedrals" to the Renaissance, Corregio who leads "to the whole movement
of modern art" (*Phoenix*, 456) and Raphael "the end of the Renaissance in
Italy; almost . . . the real end of Italy" (*Phoenix*, 458): "Raphael the evil-
doer," says Boccioni (DP, 125); then on to the landscape painters, Corot,
Turner who achieves "pure light" and dissolves the body, as do the impres-

sionists in Boccioni's scheme: "Turner is a lie, and Raphael is a lie," says Lawrence, both being "abstraction from . . . truth."

Boccioni's aim is what he calls the "solidification of Impressionism." He reacts against the dissolution of painting into shapeless colors and wishes to "create form definitely linked to color" (DP, 50), without returning, like the cubists, to a solid, static construction of volumes. Cubism he sees as the denial of the conquests of impressionism, atmosphere, motion, lyricism. An object to be painted or sculpted is a "nucleus (centripetal construction)" from which there radiate forces that "define its environment (centrifugal construction) and determine its essential character" (DP, 52). He aims at creating, as an indivisible unit, an "object-environment . . . inner and outer seen in . . . compenetration." By this he means that an object and its surroundings are seen as one:

> Thus, where the impressionists see an object as a nucleus of *vibrations* appearing as color, for us, futurists, an object is also a nucleus of *directions* appearing as shape. In the characteristic potentiality of these *directions*, we find *the plastic state of mind*. (DP, 52)

This new conception of the motions of matter seen as "plastic equivalents of life *in itself*," permits, according to this theory, "a dynamic definition of an impression, that is, the intuition of life."

The layman may be confused by Boccioni's style, but his artistic intentions in the sculpture that Lawrence discusses are somewhat clarified by the above summary. The bottle, resting on a plate, is shown not as a complete, finished object, but as ascending spiral lines, massively outlined but open, as part and parcel of its "environment": it is both solid and dynamic, defined by lines of force that suggest motion.

Lawrence, it is clear from his comments, is familiar with Boccioni's language, "absolute" and "relative" motion, centripetal and centrifugal directions, "power-forms" (in French, *formes-force*) expressive of "the instant of plastic life" and "pure plastic rhythm" which is alone capable of "constructing the action of bodies." Boccioni opposes "sensation" or "appearance" to "construction" or "knowledge" of an object, knowledge meaning mass or centripetal direction, and appearance, the centrifugal direction.

Lawrence's criticism of the sculpture of the bottle follows a long discussion of Italian art culminating in Raphael's "geometric abstraction." Extensive quotation will, I am afraid, be necessary. In terms of the relations of the sexes, Raphael expresses the "conception of a long, clinched, timeless embrace . . . from which there is no escape," a conception that "has arrested the Italian race for three centuries." Lawrence writes:

> In marriage, in utter, interlocked marriage, man and woman cease to be two beings and become one, one and one only, not two in one as with us, but absolute One, a geometric absolute, timeless, the Absolute, the Di-

vine. . . . But the Italian is now beginning to withdraw from his clinched and timeless embrace, from his geometric abstraction, into the northern conception of himself and the woman as two separate identities, which meet, combine, but always must withdraw again.

So that the Futurist Boccioni now makes his sculpture, *Development of a Bottle through Space,* try to express the withdrawal, and at the same time he must adhere to the conception of this same interlocked state of marriage between centripetal and centrifugal forces, the geometric abstraction of the bottle. But he can neither do one thing nor the other. He wants to restate the real abstraction. He must insist on the male spirit of motion outwards, because, during three static centuries, there has necessarily come to pass a preponderance of the female in the race, so that the Italian is rather more female than male, now, as is the whole Latin race rather voluptuous than passionate, too much aware of their utter lockedness male with female, and too hopeless, as males, to act, to be passionate. (*Phoenix,* 463–64)

So Lawrence shows his familiarity with Boccioni's terminology, and, to some extent, with his artistic aims, while Lawrence's preoccupation with a sexual explanation of racial psychology partly blinds him to the exact artistic and intellectual pursuits of the futurist writer. There is a duality in his argument. He follows his own line of approach, based on his idea of the expression in art and religion of the male and female principles, and at the same time he is responding to Boccioni's aesthetic theory:

So that when I look at Boccioni's sculpture, and see him trying to *state the timeless abstract being* of a bottle, the *pure geometric abstraction* of the bottle, I am fascinated. But then, when I see him driven by his desire for the male complement into portraying motion, simple motion, trying to give expression to the bottle in terms of mechanics, I am confused. It is for science to explain the bottle in terms of forces and motion. (*Phoenix,* 464; emphasis added)

And yet he is aware of the theory of "plastic states of mind":

Geometry, pure mathematics, is very near to art, and the vivid attempt to render the bottle as a pure geometric abstraction might give rise to a work of art, because of the resistance of the medium, the stone. But a representation in stone of the *lines of force* which *create that state of rest called a bottle,* that is a model in mechanics.

And the two representations require *two different states of mind* in the appreciator, so that the result is almost nothingness, mere confusion. And *the portraying of a state of mind* is impossible. There can only be made scientific diagrams of states of mind. (*Phoenix,* 464; emphasis added)

While he is a little unfair to a work of art he had not seen except in a photograph, and not a very good photo at that, his judgment on futurist art is not without merit: it was, according to Herbert Read, "fundamentally a symbolic art, an attempt to illustrate conceptual notions in plastic form."[21]

But he must continue to assimilate the Italian's "scientific attitude" with "the departure of the male from the female . . . the act of withdrawal" (*Phoenix*, 464), thus confusing what is a valid appreciation of the sculpture.

The futurists meant to take painting and sculpture "beyond cubism," the title of one of Sofficci's essays. Section VII of Boccioni's "Dinamismo Plastico" is headed, "What separates us from Cubism." In brief, he objects to it, and in particular to Picasso, because of their decomposing the object and enumerating its various aspects, thus "arresting the life of the object." "They extract dead elements from which it will never be possible *to compose something alive*" (DP, 53). Picasso "kills emotion," his pictures are without lyricism: "We disagree with Picasso when he wants to destroy painting. . . . he is greatly mistaken when he does not see that *the search for abstract elements* does not lead to an *abstract construction*" (DP, 55; first emphasis added).

On 27 January 1915 Lawrence writes to Ottoline Morrell, apropos of his visit to Duncan Grant's studio:

> One cannot *build a complete abstraction,* or absolute, *out of a number of small abstractions,* or absolutes. Therefore one cannot make a picture out of geometric figures. One can only build a great abstraction out of concrete units. Painting is *not* architecture. It is puerile to try to achieve architecture—third dimension—on a flat surface, by means of "lines of force"! The architecture comes in painting only with the suggestion of some whole, some conception which conveys in its own manner the whole universe. (*CLM*, 308; first and second emphases added)

He has worked out his own position, accepting the futurists' criticism of the abstract and analytical aspect of cubism, but rejecting Boccioni's plea, to which we shall revert, that painting and sculpture must be architectural.

In his 1929 "Introduction to these paintings," Lawrence wrote penetratingly about Cézanne; he had no words hard enough for his imitators, "tricksters," "all the Matisses and Vlamincks, of his following" (*Phoenix*, 570). Cézanne had been claimed by Sofficci and Boccioni as a precursor. The latter goes so far as to claim for his genius Italian racial origins (DP, 59). An important phase in his evolution, shortly before his death in 1916, was his "return to Cézanne," whose name is the most frequent in "Dinamismo Plastico," even if he is called "more dangerous than Phidias" (DP, 97).

Boccioni also objects to the disciples and imitators, in their pursuit of form and immobility, that lead to cubism. Further comparison between his views and those of Lawrence in his 1929 Introduction might be worthwhile, even if more recent discussions of art may have inspired Lawrence. He says, for instance, that with Cézanne "landscape 'crystallized,' to use one of the favourite terms of the critics, and it has gone on crystallizing into cubes, cones, pyramids, and so forth ever since" (*Phoenix*, 565). Boccioni's aim was "the solidification of Impressionism," meaning very nearly the same. And

Lawrence's argument in the Introduction follows in various respects his analyses on art in his "Hardy." Is it too much to suggest that the debate with the futurists was still active in his mind in 1929?

THE SYNTHESIS: LOERKE AND MODERN ART

In his effort to renew sculpture and abolish the old type of "subjects," Boccioni stresses its necessary relationship to architecture:

> The pursuit of form over so-called *"truth"* has estranged sculpture (like painting) from its origin and therefore from the goal towards which it is moving today: architecture. *Architecture is for sculpture what composition is to painting.* And the want of architecture is one of the negative characteristics of impressionist sculpture.[22]

True enough, he does not so much see sculpture as a decorative contribution to architecture, but is more concerned with the architectonics of the sculpture itself. But, seen in conjunction with Marinetti's list of subjects fit for modern art, the above passage may have contributed to a highly significant scene in *Women in Love*. Marinetti wants to

> sing the great crowds agitated by labor, by pleasure or revolt; the multicolored and polyphonic currents of revolutions in modern capitals; the nocturnal vibration of arsenals and work sites under their fierce electronic moons; the voracious stations swallowing smoking serpents; the factories hanging from the clouds by the strings of their smoke. (MF, 178)

Boccioni, almost tracing a program for Gudrun's excursions in the main street of Beldover in the chapter "Coal-dust" and outlining Loerke's idea of art, expatiates on

> the need to become brutal, rapid, precise; the need to Americanize ourselves, by entering the frenzied turmoil of modernism, through its crowds, motorcars, telegraphs, its bare popular quarters, its noises, stridency, violence, cruelty, cynicism, its ruthless will to succeed; in other words, the exaltation of all barbarian and anti-artistic aspects of our time. (DP, 87–88)

In *Women in Love*, Loerke, a character admirably compounded of diverse elements, some of which date back to Lawrence's life in Italy, expresses views largely contained in the above quotations and other futurist statements:

> Sculpture and architecture must go together. The day for irrelevant statues, as for wall pictures, is over. As a matter of fact sculpture is always part of an architectural conception. And since churches are all museum stuff, since industry is our business, now, let us make our places of industry our art—our factory-area our Parthenon, *ecco!* (*Women*, 447)

The fact that his last word is Italian may be an admission of the source of his ideas. The frieze that he describes, a granite sculpture on a great factory in Cologne, is "a representation of a fair, with peasants and artisans in an orgy of enjoyment, drunk and absurd in their modern dress, whirling ridiculously in roundabouts, gaping at shows . . . a frenzy of chaotic motion" (*Women*, 446–47). And what follows is almost a parody of Marinetti, always more extreme than Boccioni: "Art should *interpret* industry, as art once interpreted religion," says Loerke. His man at the fair "is fulfilling the counterpart of labour—the machine works him, instead of him the machine. He enjoys the mechanical motion, his whole body. . . . It is nothing but this, serving a machine or enjoying the motion of a machine—motion, that is all." These sinister views are in effect a brilliant if caricatural synthesis of some of Lawrence's impressions of the futurists, gathered in the spring of 1914, and matured during the final period of gestation of *Women in Love*.

BUZZI AND LAWRENCE ON FREE VERSE

Writing to Edward Marsh on 19 November 1913, Lawrence vigorously asserts his views on scansion and poetic rhythm. He reads his poetry, he says,

> more by length than by stress—as a matter of *movements in space* than footsteps hitting the earth. . . . I think more of a bird with broad wings flying and *lapsing* through the air, than anything, when I think of metre. . . . It all depends on the *pause*—the natural pause, the natural *lingering* of the voice according to the feeling—it is the hidden *emotional* pattern that makes poetry, not the obvious form. . . . It is *the lapse* of the feeling, something *as indefinite as expression in the voice carrying emotion.* It doesn't depend on the ear, particularly, but on the sensitive soul. And *the ear gets a habit, and becomes master, when the ebbing and lifting emotion should be master,* and the ear *the transmitter.* . . . "It satisfies my ear," you say. Well, I don't write for your ear. This is the constant war, I reckon, between new expression and the *habituated, mechanical transmitters and receivers* of the human constitution. (*CLM*, 242–44; emphasis added, except for *pause, lingering,* and *emotional*)

The futurists, as we have seen, emphasized "movement in space," dynamism, the expression of the living instant. Lawrence's metaphor, "mechanical transmitters and receivers," even calls to mind the "Technical Manifesto of Futurist Literature": "We shall invent together what I call **wireless imagination**" (*"senza fili"* in Marinetti's bold type): "We shall attain one day an art even more essential, when we dare suppress all first terms of our analogies and offer only the uninterrupted sequence of second terms. For this, we shall have *to renounce being understood.* It is not necessary to be understood." By doing away with the dead form of syntax, "a sort of interpreter and monotonous cicerone . . . literature may enter the universe directly and become one with it" (MT, 188).

Lawrence is not ready to renounce understanding, but he has acquired enough temerity to tell his patron Marsh, "I don't write for your ear." His idea of the pulse of poetry, movements in space, flying and lapsing through the air, is remarkably close to Buzzi's definition of poetic rhythm. According to the futurist poet, free verse can give poetry a chance "of being the true and unique expression of a poet's soul" (*IPF*, 43). A whole sentence, in conversation, may be governed by a general intonation (*accento*). Similarly in declamation, a given tone "governs a whole stanza and fixes for you the measure of the auditive values." The whole world over, all passions "produce almost the same effect of *acceleration or slowing down*." This *"accento"* or tone "is communicated to the words through the sentiment which moves the speaker or poet, regardless of *any tonic stress or fixed value* the actual words might in themselves command."

Commenting on the French poet Gustave Kahn's writings on free verse, Buzzi declares that this "impelling tone" is capable of liberating powerful energies, through a poem, provided it is "appropriate to the importance" and the *temporaneita* (fleetingness, "momentaneity") "of the sentiment evoked or sensation to be conveyed" (*IPF*, 44). Thus all poets can conceive their original stanzas and write in their own, personal and typical rhythm "instead, so to speak, of donning an already overworn uniform which reduces them in the best of cases to the status of pupils of some glorious predecessor."

Allowing for a chance meeting of great minds, Lawrence's and Buzzi's thinking runs on parallel lines. Like Buzzi, Lawrence minimizes tonic stress in favor of "the lapse of the feeling," "expression of the voice carrying emotion"; to the mechanical effect on the ear he prefers "the sensitive soul," "the ebbing and lifting of emotion": "I can't tell you what *pattern* I see in any poetry, save one complete thing. But surely you don't class poetry among *the decorative or conventional arts*" (*CLM*, 244; second emphasis added). These ideas and phrases are related to his remarks to Ernest Collings already quoted.

Buzzi pleads for a poetry liberated from the patterns set by the old masters:

> Today, there surges in Italy, virginal, a free poetry understood as it should be, that is to say the purest expression of ethic and aesthetic feeling, with all the native sincerities and all the liberties in structure and sound of which the nature of our evolved soul is capable under the eternal kiss of the sun. [Such poetry should] reveal all the psychic and musical mystery of life in its highest and at the same time deepest essence. [The poet is no inheritor, but is sure] to thrust himself upon the souls born for the sole joy of hearing the word, and to subjugate them with the simple charm and complex purity of the rhythm which governs his own inner universe. (*IPF*, 46)

Free verse lends itself to "the painting of landscape, the sculpture of the human form, the complex architecture of things and happenings." "Whoever has sung [in free verse] and reads his song over, finds himself in it continually new and is convinced that he has created *with the very eternal stuff of life*" (emphasis added).

When Lawrence wrote "Poetry of the Present"[23] in 1917, he may well have forgotten all about Buzzi's essay. Whitman, the common inspirer of Gustave Kahn and Buzzi, was foremost in his thoughts; yet he mentions that "much has been written about free verse." And his magnificent prose takes up the Lawrentian theme of *"temporaneita"*: "The seething poetry of the incarnate Now is supreme, beyond even the everlasting gems of the before and after. In its quivering *momentaneity* it surpasses the crystalline, pearl-hard jewels, the poems of the eternities" (*CP*, 183; emphasis added). For him free verse

is, or should be, direct utterance from the instant, whole man. It is the soul and the mind and body singing at once, nothing left out. . . . Free verse toes no melodic line, no matter what drill-sergeant. Whitman pruned away his clichés—perhaps his clichés of rhythm as well as of phrase. And this is about all we can do, deliberately, with free verse. We can get rid of the stereotyped movements and the old hackneyed associations of sound and sense. We can break down those artificial conduits and canals through which we do so love to force our utterance. We can break the stiff neck of habit. (*CP*, 184)

As for Buzzi, for him the nature of free verse is "instantaneous like plasm." Any "externally applied law" (rhyme or rhythm) "would be mere shackles and death" (*CP*, 185): according to Buzzi Italy had "always made its various metres so many various shackles of one same prison" (*IPF*, 45).

Both poets plead the same case: the essence of poetry is the expression of "the pure present," "the quick of all time is the instant. The quick of all the universe, of all creation, is the incarnate, carnal self" (*CP*, 185). Superficially different, Buzzi's preoccupations are essentially the same. His art of poetry is "eminently aristocratic and difficult." It is "the most severe assertion . . . of the noblest canons of synthesis and rule, both in its conception and in its form." It alone can "eliminate . . . the unworthy crowd of graphomaniac pygmies who attempt to infest and bewilder the way to the stars of Poetry" (*IPF*, 48). Lawrence condemns the common run of "free versifiers" who "do not know that free verse has its own nature, that is neither star nor pearl, but instantaneous like plasm" (*CP*, 185).

Had he read Buzzi before he wrote to Edward Marsh? I incline to think he had. Did he remember this essay on free verse when he wrote "Poetry of the Present"? Possibly. Nothing he wrote to Marsh in 1913, or in his "introduction for *Look, We Have Come Through!*, needed inspiration from another. Similarities may be the result of separate technical reflection, the expression of individual experience as writers. And yet when Lawrence wrote, in June

1914, "I think the book [*The Wedding Ring*] is a bit futuristic—quite unconsciously so" (*CLM*, 281), we may ask ourselves whether his futuristic approach was quite as unconscious as he said.

A FIELD FOR FURTHER RESEARCH

I have tried here, with the help of texts now more readily available, to
present prima-facie evidence of resemblances between Lawrence's writings
and some of the futurists'. Other fields could be explored. I have briefly
mentioned Lawrence's and Marinetti's views on women, love, and feminism.
To what extent are some of Birkin's ideas on love the expression of Marinetti's piece entitled "Contempt for Woman"? Even his stoning of the moon
may recall the theme of "Tuons le Clair de Lune." There is room for a close
and detailed study of the effects of futurist aesthetics and theory on Lawrence's treatment of scenes and objects. When in December 1913 he writes,
"I don't care much more about accumulating objects in the powerful light of
emotion, and making a scene of them. I have to write differently" (*CLM*,
263), or "I shan't write in the same manner as *Sons and Lovers* again, I
think—in that hard, violent style full of sensation and presentation" (*CLM*,
259), he had in all probability read Marinetti's recommendation to hear the
pulse and respiration of "objects at liberty," i.e., not bound to human
emotions, to "Beware of lending human feelings to matter" (MT, para. 11), or
again his statement that "man tends to soil, with his youthful joy or ageing
sorrow, matter which is neither young nor old."

To what extent was Marinetti's wish to do away with "human psychology"
in literature reflected in Lawrence's conscious change of style? A close study
of stylistic devices in those parts of *Women in Love* and *The Rainbow* that are
now known to have been written in 1914 might provide an answer. The "going
beyond Maeterlinck and the Symbolistes" (*CLM*, 280) which he detects in
the futurists, may well have contributed to the change in his own method of
presentation of scenes, after the dominant influence of the symbolists in *The
Trespasser* and *Sons and Lovers*.

Lawrence agreed, on the whole, with the destructive aims of the futurists,
and on the need for a new approach to literary subjects, even when he
disagreed on method. As for reconstruction, his own temperament led him to
a highly personal and, in the end, essentially English conception. Already
immersed through Frieda and her sister's circle in a European philosophical
and aesthetic atmosphere wholly different not only from his native Midlands
but also from the Edwardian London he had known, he was confronted in
Italy with a movement aiming at a complete break with the past three
centuries of art and literature. He was prompt to assimilate some of those
iconoclastic tendencies, while retaining a sense of measure and his native
Englishness. Characteristically, he used futurism as an anvil on which to

hammer into shape his own idiosyncratic idea of art. The areas where he stressed difference were those where he felt most attracted and fascinated.

I hope to have shown, in amplification of Harry T. Moore's calculated understatement quoted at the outset, the extent and depth of the fascination that the young Italians of 1909–14 exercised over Lawrence's active, agile mind, and the considerable importance of Marinetti and his group in the process of self-discovery of the greatest English writer of this century.

NOTES

1. *The Collected Letters of D. H. Lawrence,* ed. Harry T. Moore (London: William Heinemann, 1962), pp. 279–83. Hereafter cited in the text as *CLM.*

2. Keith Aldritt, *The Visual Imagination of D. H. Lawrence* (London: Edward Arnold, 1971).

3. *I Poeti Futuristi . . . con un proclamo di F. T. Marinetti e uno studio sul verso libero di Paolo Buzzi.* Edizione futuriste di *Poesia* (Milan: Corso Venezia, 1912). Hereafter cited in the text as *IPF.*

4. *Pittura, Scultura Futuriste, Dinamismo Plastico, con 51 Riproduzioni quadri sculture de Boccioni, Carro, Russolo, Balla, Severini, Sofficci.* Edizione futuriste di *Poesia* (Milan: Corso Venezia, 1914).

5. Filippo T. Marinetti, "Fondazióne e Manifesto del Futurismo," as quoted by Giovanni Lista, *Marinetti et le Futurisme: Etudes, documents, iconographie réunis et présentés par Giovanni Lista,* Cahiers des Avant-gardes (Lausanne: L'Age d'Homme, 1977), p. 179. Unless otherwise noted, all translations from French and Italian are mine. Hereafter cited in the text as MF.

6. Filippo T. Marinetti, "Manifesto tecnico della letteratura futurista" (1912), as quoted by Giovanni Lista, *Marinetti.* Collection "Poètes d'aujourd'hui" (Paris: Seghers, 1976), p. 188. Hereafter cited in the text as MT.

7. *Phoenix: The Posthumous Papers of D. H. Lawrence,* ed. Edward D. McDonald (London: William Heinemann, 1936), p. 404. Hereafter cited in the text as *Phoenix.*

8. Filippo T. Marinetti, "Le Mépris de la femme," in *Le Futurisme* (Paris: Sansot, 1911).

9. Originally published as "Manifeste du futurisme," *Le Figaro,* 20 February 1909.

10. D. H. Lawrence, *The Rainbow* (London: Martin Secker, 1930), p. 410. Hereafter cited in the text as *Rainbow.*

11. D. H. Lawrence, *Women in Love* (London: Martin Secker, 1930), p. 335. Hereafter cited in the text as *Women.*

12. "Noise" is not included in the text as printed in *I Poeti Futuristi* (1912) but is found in the French text, also 1912.

13. Marinetti says "incomprehensible" and "in resistance to a shell" (the allusion is to the steel plate of a warship).

14. Marinetti says "henceforth," not "in fact"; *appassionante,* i.e., "impassions us more," "more seductive for us"; and *sorriso,* "smile," not "laughter." Perhaps he is thinking of the *Mona Lisa?*

15. On the probable indebtedness of Lawrence to Weininger for the "diamond, carbon" metaphor, see my "D. H. Lawrence, Otto Weininger and Rather Raw Philosophy," in *D. H. Lawrence New Studies,* ed. Christopher Harwood (London: Macmillan, 1987).

16. Umberto Boccioni, "Manifesto Tecnico della Scultura Futurista" (1912) in Raffaele Carrieri, *Il Futurismo* (Milan: n.p., 1961), pp. 69–70.

17. *Letters of D. H. Lawrence,* ed. Aldous Huxley (London: William Heinemann, 1932), p. 183. Emphasis added, except the first. Hereafter cited in the text as Huxley.

18. Ardengo Sofficci, *Cubismo e Futurismo* (Firenze, 1914), reprinted in *Opere*, Vol. 1 (Firenze: Valechi, 1959), p. 657. Emphasis added.

19. Umberto Boccioni, "Dinamismo Plastico" (1914), in *Pittura, Scultura Futuriste, Dinamismo Plastico, con 51 Riproduzioni quadri sculture di Boccioni, Carro, Russolo, Balla, Severini, Sofficci*. Edizione futuriste di *Poesia* (Milan: Corso Venezia, 1914), pp. 13, 145. Hereafter cited in the text as DP.

20. H. G. Wells, *Mr. Britling Sees It Through* (London: Morley-Baker, 1969), p. 264.

21. Herbert Read, *A Concise History of Modern Painting* (London: Thames and Hudson, 1959), p. 112.

22. Raffaele Carrieri, Preface to the Catalogue of the "Exhibition of Futurist Sculpture in Paris" (1913), p. 73. Emphasis added except for *truth*.

23. *The Complete Poems of D. H. Lawrence*, ed. Vivian de Sola Pinto and F. Warren Roberts (New York: Viking, 1971), pp. 181–86. Hereafter cited in the text as *CP*.

11

Phobia and Psychological Development in D. H. Lawrence's "The Thorn in the Flesh"

JAMES C. COWAN

In D. H. Lawrence's story "The Thorn in the Flesh" (1914), Bachmann, a young German soldier, is unable, during an attack of anxiety, to write his weekly postcard to his mother. The soldier, who suffers from an almost incapacitating fear of heights, is confronted in a training exercise with the task of scaling a high rampart. Groping his way up the swaying ladder, he is so sick with fear that he cannot control his bladder. Feeling himself violated by his sergeant's enraged face, aggressive jaw, and shouted orders, Bachmann involuntarily strikes the non-commissioned officer, knocking him over the fortifications into the moat below. Running away from the barracks to his sweetheart, Emilie, who works as a maid-servant in the house of a baron, Bachmann plans, with the help of Emilie and her friend Ida Hesse, the governess, to desert and go to America. In Emilie's bedroom, the sweethearts make love, and Bachmann feels restored and resolves to accept his phobic affliction and live with it. Traced to the baron's house by the postcard to his mother, which Emilie has mailed for him, the soldier is taken into custody by the military search party. Although the baron tells Emilie that Bachmann is "done for now," the youth departs confident in the knowledge of what he has shared with the girl: "They knew each other. They were themselves."[1]

The romantic art of the story, the way Lawrence carefully develops his theme, opposing the mechanistic, uniformitarian values of the military with the organicist, instinctual values of individual differences and young love, is admirably contained in the symmetry of the story's structure. The story turns, however, on a single element of character, Bachmann's acrophobia, which I should like to consider in the light of a brief review of several conceptions of phobia, with particular emphasis on Sigmund Freud's psychoanalytic theory.

The first recorded case history of a phobic patient is attributed to Hippo-

crates, and John Locke is credited with making one of the earliest attempts
to deal with the phobic reaction systematically. According to Locke, " 'Antipathies' and fears . . . often arise from an association of ideas, and, if such
'antipathies' were acquired in childhood, their causes may later be forgotten."[2] This view anticipates the psychologically oriented theories of twentieth-century psychologists and psychoanalysts. In accord with Locke's
associationist theory, the behaviorist John B. Watson held that such fears
were acquired by conditioned response. Pierre Janet, who thought the fear
response a secondary effect rather than a cause, related the phobic reaction
to hysterical paralysis in that both function to prevent the individual from
doing something that he does not want to do anyway.[3]

It was Sigmund Freud, however, who originated the first truly dynamic
conception of phobia as a part of anxiety neurosis. In the first of his classic
papers on the subject, "Obsessions and Phobias: Their Psychical Mechanism
and Their Aetiology" (1895), he divides phobias

> into two groups according to the nature of the object feared: (1) common
> phobias, an exaggerated fear of things that everyone detests or fears to
> some extent: such as night, solitude, death, illnesses, dangers in general,
> snakes, etc.; (2) contingent phobias, the fear of special conditions that
> inspire no fear in the normal man; for example, agoraphobia and the other
> phobias of locomotion.[4]

At that time, Freud thought obsessions and phobias "entirely different" in
mechanism. Substitution was a predominant feature in obsessions, but what
the phobic individual actually fears, Freud thought, is neither the object of
his phobia in itself nor the incompatible ideas which the object represents but
simply the occurrence of an anxiety attack "under the special conditions in
which he believes he cannot escape it."[5]

By the time he wrote the second of his classic papers on phobia, "Analysis
of a Phobia in a Five-Year-Old Boy" (1909), Freud had revised his theory to
include substitution, the replacement of incompatible ideas with an object
that is feared because it represents those ideas. The patient, little Hans, is
afraid to go out because, as he tells his mother, *"I was afraid a horse would
bite me."*[6] The case history of the analysis, with the boy's father acting as
intermediary, is an engrossing story followed by Freud's critical analysis.
Piece by piece, the basic information is unfolded: one learns that little Hans
is afraid of big animals that have big "widdlers," that is, penises (33–34); that
he is afraid of white horses because he knows one that bites; that Hans's
mother had once threatened to "have his widdler cut off if he went on playing
with it" (35); that he is "most afraid of horses" with "something black on
their mouths" (49) like a dray horse's thick harness; that he is particularly
afraid that a dray horse may fall down and make *"a row with its feet"* (50) as
he had seen a horse drawing a furniture van do; that he fantasizes that his
little sister Hanna lived and traveled about before birth in a "stork-box" (76);

and that he associates the falling dray horse with Hanna's arrival and rivalry with him. Analysis reveals that both the biting horse and the falling horse represent Hans's father, whose white skin and mustache Hans associates with the white horse and the dray harness. As Freud analyzes it, "Behind . . . the fear of a horse biting him" was the "more deeply seated fear . . . of horses falling down," and both were "his father, who was going to punish him for the evil wishes he was nourishing against him" (126). Hans is "afraid of buses and luggage carts . . . when they're loaded up" (91), an image which analysis shows to be associated with his mother's pregnancy. Hence, the image of the falling dray horse is "over-determined," since it represents "not only his dying father but also his mother in childbirth" (128). His father correctly interprets his wish, despite his jealousy, for his mother to have another baby: "You'd like to be Daddy and married to Mummy; you'd like to be as big as me and have a moustache; and you'd like Mummy to have a baby" (92). Hans's phobia lasted for about five months. When he is at last able to go out for a walk with his father in the Stadtpark, he points out a bus with wary humor: "Look! A stork-box cart!" (97).

To return to "The Thorn in the Flesh" in this context, as the story opens, Bachmann sits trying to write his weekly postcard to his mother, but he breaks off at the line " 'We are just off to drill on the fortifications—.' " The very thought calls up his paralyzing fear of what is to come, and he sits "suspended, oblivious of everything, held in some definite suspense" that remains unbroken because what lies behind it remains repressed and therefore unverbalized: "Out of the knot of his consciousness no word would come" (22).

The relation of speech and silence to anxiety invites a comparison between the story situations in "The Thorn in the Flesh" and Herman Melville's *Billy Budd, Sailor,* though of course Lawrence was not influenced by that novella, since it was not published until 1924.[7] Melville's "Handsome Sailor" has "a lingering adolescent expression in the as yet smooth face all but feminine in purity of natural complexion but where, thanks to his seagoing, the lily was quite suppressed and the rose had some ado visibly to flush through the tan."[8] Similarly, Lawrence's young soldier is "almost girlish in his good looks and his grace. . . . There was also a trace of youthful swagger and daredevilry about his mouth and his limber body, but this was in suppression now" (22–23). Billy Budd's Master-at-Arms, John Claggart, is described as "a man about five-and-thirty, somewhat spare and tall" in figure with small, shapely hands and a "notable" face, "the features all except the chin cleanly cut as those of a Greek medallion; yet the chin, beardless as Tecumseh's, had something of strange proturberant broadness in its make. . . . It served Claggart in his office that his eye could cast a tutoring glance."[9] In contrast, Sergeant Huber is "a strongly built, rather heavy man of forty . . . [with] head thrust forward, sunk a little between his powerful shoulders, and the strong jaw . . . pushed out aggressively. But the eyes were smouldering, the face hung slack and sodden with drink" (23). The sergeant's ape-like physiognomy reveals nothing of Claggart's effete cruelty, but the same oral aggression. At the crucial point in the conflict in both stories, both Billy Budd and Bachmann are unable to communicate in speech their anxiety, which derives for Billy from a sense of outraged justice, for Bachmann from a sense of overwhelming shame. Both communicate their feelings with their fists, involuntarily striking their petty officers, thus placing themselves at the mercy of the military justice system, though with direr results in Budd's case than in Bachmann's.

Bachmann, at the beginning of the march, is "bound in a very dark enclosure of anxiety within himself" (23). Experiencing dissociation, he feels his consciousness separated from his body. Later as the soldiers go through the exercises, Bachmann watches, "small and isolated" (24) like a child, as another man, looking insect-like and mechanical, climbs the rampart, and his own bowels turn to water. When his turn comes, Bachmann places the ladder on the rampart and determines to climb. But "at every hitch a great, sick, melting feeling took hold of him. . . . the blind gush of white-hot fear, that came with great force whenever the ladder swerved, and which almost melted his belly and all his joints, and left him powerless" (25). This feeling of powerlessness is manifested in a regressive symptom as Bachmann, unable to maintain urethral control, clings to the ladder with his urine running down his leg and "the echo of the sergeant's voice thundering from below." Lawrence emphasizes Bachmann's overwhelming sense of shame: "He waited, in depths of shame beginning to recover himself. He had been shamed so deeply. Then he could go on, for his fear for himself was conquered. His shame was known and published. He must go on" (25). But even that victory is denied him as the sergeant takes his wrists from above and drags him up over the edge of the earthworks.

"Grovelling in the grass to recover command of himself," Bachmann is overwhelmed by a sense of worthlessness: "Shame, blind, deep shame and ignominy overthrew his spirit and left it writhing. He stood there shrunk over himself, trying to obliterate himself" (25). The voice of the sergeant comes down "on his veins like a fierce whip" (26). The psychological meaning of this image for Lawrence is apparent if one recalls its use in the poem "Discord in Childhood," in which the shrieking, slashing violence of the storm battering the ash-tree outside the house is the metaphor for the family violence within. The first stanza, beginning:

> Outside the house an ash-tree hung its terrible whips,

is paralleled with the second:

> Within the house, two voices rose, a slender lash
> Whistling she-delirious rage, and the dreadful sound
> Of a male thong booming and bruising, until it had drowned
> The other voice in a silence of blood, 'neath the noise of the ash.[10]

In the story, the voice of Sergeant Huber is that of the punitive father threatening violence to the frightened child. The non-commissioned officer appears to Bachmann with the same sense of large animal violence that little Hans had sensed in the falling horse, and the threat of castration at the hands of a primordial father figure that little Hans had feared in the biting horse is implicit to Bachmann in the sergeant's lacerating voice and teeth:

> The brutal, hanging face of the officer violated the youth. He hardened himself with all his might from seeing it. The tearing noise of the sergeant's voice continued to lacerate his body.
> . . . The face had suddenly thrust itself close, all distorted and showing the teeth, the eyes smouldering into him. The breath of the barking words was on his nose and mouth. He stepped aside in revulsion. With a scream the face was upon him again. (26)

Raising his arm defensively, Bachmann involuntarily strikes the sergeant, knocking him backward over the ramparts and into the water of the moat below.

Feeling "deep within him . . . the steady burning of shame in the flesh," Bachmann is unable to "take the responsibility of himself" and decides that "he must give himself up to someone." In this desperate need for mothering, he becomes "obsessed" with the thought of his sweetheart, Emilie: "He would make himself her responsibility" (27). But Emilie "was virgin, and shy, and needed to be in subjection" (32) herself. She acquiesces, somewhat reluctantly, in hiding Bachmann, with the aid of Ida Hesse, the governess, and lies to the soldiers who come looking for him: "she had wanted him as a distant sweetheart, not close, like this, casting her out of her world" (33).

After Bachmann, as a result of severe tension and anxiety, has slept, Emilie comes to his bedside, waiting "as if in a spell." The description, from Bachmann's angle of vision, with her "standing motionless and looming there, [as] he sat rather crouching on the side of the bed," suggests the attitudes of mother and child. As he draws her to him, however, "a second will in him was powerful and dominating" (34). Burying his face in her apron, "he had forgotten. Shame and memory were gone in a whole, furious flame of passion." Afterward, "she lay translated in the peace of satisfaction":

> And he was restored and completed, close to her. That little, twitching, momentary clasp of acknowledgement that she gave him in her satisfaction, roused his pride unconquerable. They loved each other, and all was whole. (34)

Bachmann's successful sexual experience provides him with clear evidence that, despite the castration fears brought to the fore by the imagery of tearing and whipping associated with the sergeant's oral aggression, his genitals, the "widdler" that little Hans feared would be cut off, are still intact and not really threatened.

This does not mean that Bachmann's acrophobia has left him. Earlier, with reference to Bachmann's shame (30), Lawrence wrote in the page proofs, "Yet he dared not touch it, probe it, draw out the thorn, and bear the hurt to its depth."[11] Now, having conquered his shame, he decides that he can live with this phobia as a "thorn in the flesh":

> "If I'm made that way, that heights melt me and make me let go my water"—it was torture for him to pluck at this truth—"if I'm made like that, I shall have to abide by it, that's all. It isn't all of me." He thought of Emilie, and was satisfied. "What I am, I am; and let it be enough." (35–36)

Little Hans, by a combination of analytic understanding and gradual desensitization by repetition of the feared action in company with an admired, powerful other is relieved of his agoraphobia. Bachmann's solution of accepting his acrophobia as a "thorn in the flesh" and getting on with his life is both more ambiguous and more realistic for an adult, whose patterns of response are already well established but who has not necessarily ceased developing. The nodal insight that Bachmann gains through the successful sexual experience is a turning point, a developmental beginning that frees his formerly blocked potential for psychological growth. The allusion to St. Paul's "thorn in the flesh" (2 Corinthians 12:7) suggests obliquely that this solution reflects the compromise with perceived limitations by Lawrence himself, whose autobiographical persona in both *Sons and Lovers* and "The Rocking-Horse Winner" is named Paul.

Filled with plans to escape to France on a bicycle that Ida Hesse will borrow from her lover, Bachmann suddenly remembers the postcard to his mother and gives it to Emilie to post. The sweethearts sleep together again that night. The next day, when the lieutenant and his men arrive, having traced Bachmann to the baron's house by the postcard, the military no longer has the power to violate him. Impassively he joins the mechanical file: "There Emilie stood with her face uplifted, motionless and expressionless. Bachmann did not look at her. They knew each other. They were themselves" (38).

On the evidence of Bachmann's inhibition about writing his weekly postcard to his mother and his wish to have Emilie take maternal responsibility for him, one may infer that his phobia has its pathogenesis in an oedipal conflict. His acrophobia is, I think, more than a simple fear of heights in that it is associated with mounting and with swaying motion, as in sexual intercourse, and with crossing a barrier, as in the stages of psychosexual development. His anger, the concomitant of his fear, is directed toward his sergeant, who stands as a father surrogate who can tell him what to do and punish him for not doing it. Bachmann expresses this hostility first in his failure to control his bladder, a regressive symptom, then in involuntarily striking the officer. If the sergeant, with his bared teeth and tearing voice, threatens castration, like little Hans's biting horse, he falls, like little Hans's falling horse, a symbolically slain father. Bachmann runs to Emilie, like a child to his mother, to be taken care of.

But if Bachmann's phobia is rooted in the oedipal conflict of the phallic stage of psychosexual development, his sense of shame derives from the anal stage, the basic problem of which, according to Erik Erikson, centers on the issue of control. The task one confronts in this stage is a resolution of the conflict between the alternatives of autonomy, on the one hand, and shame and doubt, on the other.[12] Bachmann's difficulties are all in the area of control. He suffers anxiety before the training exercise because he fears the loss of self-control, which he later manifests in his failure to climb the ladder, his inability to maintain urethral control, and his striking the sergeant. His response is a deep sense of shame and humiliation. It is significant that at this point, Bachmann feels shame, not guilt: shame results from a sense that one's perfectionistic self-image has been violated, guilt from a sense that one has violated oedipal prohibitions.

Lawrence's conclusion is a tentatively positive one that does not overstate the hard won development that Bachmann achieves. Psychologically, his transformation is from the anal to the phallic stage. The question to be answered in the anal stage is, "Is my whole being loathsome? Or is it all right for me to *be* a person?" Bachmann has answered that question. The new question of the phallic stage is, "Is it all right for me to *be* as a *sexual* person?" The new polar alternatives to be confronted in answering this question are *initiative* vs. *guilt*.[13] Bachmann has achieved *autonomy*, the task of the anal stage: through ego growth he has, both consciously and emotionally, asserted his own values and separated himself from the outside values of societal expectations. In the context of the story, however, his oedipal guilts remain unresolved, and he has not achieved *initiative*. After his sexual relations with Emilie, Bachmann is reminded—significantly, at the sound of retreat from the nearby army post—to send his postcard to his mother. Whether purposive in intent or not, this action is deterministic in effect, assuring his capture. Moreover, his stoical acceptance of both his phobic affliction and his return to military authority suggests obedient resignation to deserved punishment. Although evidence of oedipal conflict remains, the autonomy that Bachmann has achieved represents a potential for further growth. In a scene paralleling the confrontation between Bachmann and the sergeant, the baron confronts Bachmann in Emilie's room. As master of the house and Emilie's solicitous employer, this aristocrat also stands as a father surrogate to Bachmann, just as the model for the character, Lawrence's father-in-law, Baron Friedrich von Richthofen, stood in relation to Lawrence. Bachmann confronts the fictional baron with autonomy rather than with the castration anxiety he had evinced in response to the sergeant. He feels no shame, for neither the baron nor the military world can have any hold on Bachmann's essential being now.

NOTES

1. D. H. Lawrence, "The Thorn in the Flesh," in *The Prussian Officer and Other Stories*, ed. John Worthen, *The Cambridge Edition of the Letters and Works of D. H. Lawrence* (Cambridge: Cambridge University Press, 1983), p. 38. Citations in the text from "The Thorn in the Flesh" are to the Cambridge Edition, but see also the originally published version of the story, "Vin Ordinaire," in the *English Review* 17 (June 1914): 298–315; and a detailed discussion of Lawrence's revisions by Keith Cushman, "D. H. Lawrence at Work: 'Vin Ordinaire' into 'The Thorn in the Flesh,'" *Journal of Modern Literature* 5 (February 1976): 46–58.

2. Paul Friedman, "The Phobias," in *American Handbook of Psychiatry*, 2 vols. (New York: Basic Books, 1959), 1:293.

3. Ibid., 1:293–94.

4. Sigmund Freud, "Obsessions and Phobias: Their Psychical Mechanism and Their Aetiology," in *The Standard Edition of the Complete Psychological Works of Sigmund Freud*, 24 vols., trans. James Strachey in collaboration with Anna Freud, assisted by Alix Strachey and Alan Tyson (London: Hogarth Press and the Institute for Psycho-Analysis, 1962), 3:80.

5. Ibid., 3:81.

6. Sigmund Freud, "Analysis of a Phobia of a Five-Year-Old Boy," in *The Standard Edition*, 10:24. Subsequent quotations are taken from this edition and volume.

7. See John B. Humma, "Melville's *Billy Budd* and Lawrence's 'The Prussian Officer': Old Adams and New," *Essays in Literature* (Western Illinois University) 1 (1974): 83–88.

8. Herman Melville, *Billy Budd, Sailor* (reading text), ed. Harrison Hayford and Merton M. Sealts, Jr. (Chicago and London: University of Chicago Press, 1962), p. 50.

9. Ibid., p. 64.

10. D. H. Lawrence, "Discord in Childhood," in *The Complete Poems of D. H. Lawrence*, ed. Vivian de Sola Pinto and F. Warren Roberts (New York: Viking, 1971), p. 36.

11. Lawrence, *Prussian Officer*, p. 251n.

12. Erik H. Erikson, *Identity and the Life Cycle: Selected Papers*, published as *Psychological Issues* 1, no. 1 (1959), pp. 65–74. See also Erik H. Erikson, *Childhood and Society*, 2d rev. ed. (New York: W. W. Norton, 1963), pp. 251–54.

13. *Identity and the Life Cycle*, pp. 74–82. See also *Childhood and Society*, pp. 255–58.

12

Odysseus, Ulysses, and Ursula: The Context of Lawrence's *Rainbow*

EVELYN J. HINZ and JOHN J. TEUNISSEN

The eldest boy ran away early to sea, and did not come back.

—The Rainbow

In *The Ulysses Theme: A Study in the Adaptability of a Traditional Hero,* W. B. Stanford concludes his investigation with a discussion of Joyce's famous novel and Kazantzakis's *Odyssey.*[1] In many ways, however, the work that most deserves to climax such a discussion is D. H. Lawrence's *The Rainbow.*[2] For not only does Lawrence's "epic" embrace the major documents of the entire tradition—the redactions of Ovid, Dante, and Tennyson, as well as Homer—*The Rainbow* also provides a striking example of "adaptability," to the point, indeed, of ultimately giving the Ulysses role to a woman—only to have her reject it!

One reason that Stanford overlooked *The Rainbow* might be that Lawrence is simply too subtle, his evocation of Odyssean motifs too organic. And here it is instructive to note Lawrence's own response to the publication of Joyce's novel. "I shall be able to read this famous *Ulysses* when I get to America," he wrote to S. S. Koteliansky, in July 1922; "I doubt he's a trickster."[3] Upon reading the novel, he complained to his agent, Thomas Selzer, that the work "wearied him": "so like a schoolmaster with dirt & stuff in his head: sometimes good, though, but too mental."[4] Nor did his respect for Joyce increase over the years: "My God, what a clumsy *olla putrida* James Joyce is!" he wrote to Aldous Huxley, in August 1928.[5]

If Lawrence is not so "clumsy" as blatantly to call attention to the Odyssean dimension of *The Rainbow,* however, he does include a number of directive allusions—with the first of these appearing in the "retrospective" first part of the first chapter of the novel.

After describing the seemingly timeless old world of the Brangwens,

171

Lawrence focuses upon the factors that occasioned its collapse—and chief among them are the aspirations of the Brangwen women. Identified generally as an orientation toward intellectual and social values, these aspirations are also given a distinctly "Odyssean" coloring:

> The lady of the Hall was the living dream of their lives, her life the epic that inspired their lives. In her they lived imaginatively, and in gossiping of her husband who drank, of her scandalous brother, of Lord William Bentley her friend, member of Parliament for the division, they had their own Odyssey enacting itself, Penelope and Ulysses before them, and Circe and the swine and the endless web.[6]

Purely decorative as the allusion might seem to be, it becomes pointedly instructive when we consider that just as the *Odyssey* is the record of the fortunes of Odysseus after the fall of Troy, so *The Rainbow* is the story of the Brangwen descendants after the world of their paternal ancestors has been overthrown; just as the *Odyssey* reflects a shift from the mythic orientation of the *Iliad* to a more secular and domestic focus,[7] so the point of departure in *The Rainbow* is the transition from the primitivistic Zeitgeist of the Brangwen men to the social values of the Brangwen women.

As these observations—and the eclectic nature of the allusion itself—also suggest, Lawrence is not interested in the *Odyssey* as a structural model for his novel; rather his concern is with the archetypes it contains and the spirit that the figure of Odysseus has come to symbolize. Consequently, in the same way that he goes beyond the *Odyssey,* as it were, to include the context of the *Iliad,* so when he goes on to identify Odysseus's modern counterparts, his emphasis is upon the centrifugal instead of the centripetal features of Homer's hero: "The male part of the poem was filled in by such men as the vicar and Lord William, lean, eager men with strange movements, men who had command of the further fields, whose lives ranged over a great extent" (5).

What the vicar, in particular, also has in common with Odysseus is the nature of his physical stature, and herein again Lawrence seems to be relying as much upon the tradition as upon any specific description in Homer's epic.

In physique, Odysseus deviates from the old heroic norm in that he has unusually short legs, partly compensated for by the development of the upper part of his body and by his being the favorite of Athena. The vicar similarly stands small in contrast to the "full-built" Brangwen man and is preferred by the Brangwen woman because of his "higher" development. He is "dark and dry and small beside her husband," but as

> Brangwen had power over the cattle so the vicar had power over her husband. What was it in the vicar, that raised him above the common men as man is raised above the beast? . . . That which makes a man strong even if he be little and frail beside a bull, and yet stronger than the bull, what was it? It was not money nor power nor position. What power had the vicar

over Tom Brangwen—none. Yet strip them and set them on a desert island, and the vicar was the master. His soul was master of the other man's. (4)

The passage reminds one of the debate between Ajax and Odysseus for the armor of Achilles in Book 13 of Ovid's *Metamorphoses*. To the argument of Ajax (whose name means "of the earth" and has become a synonym for physical strength) that by virtue of his prowess and valor he is the rightful heir of the arms of Achilles, Odysseus answers:

> You are strong, and brainless;
> I think about the future. You can fight,
> We set the time for fighting, Agamemnon
> And I, Ulysses. Only in the body
> Are you worth anything, but I have mind,
> Sense and intelligence. As a ship's captain
> Is better than a rower, as a leader
> Is greater than his soldier, so do I
> Outrank you, Ajax; in my make-up knowledge
> Governs brute force, and therein lies my talent.[8]

The judges of the debate respond to Odysseus's oratorical power and consequently decide in his favor: "what eloquence could do / Was evident; the eloquent man bore off / The brave man's arms." In the Brangwen woman's debate over the respective claims of the vicar and her husband, the decision is similarly in favor of brain over brawn.

In championing the vicar, furthermore, the Brangwen woman also finds her own prototype in the Odyssean tradition, just as a precedent for Lawrence's identification of intellectual forces with the female also comes into focus. For Odysseus too had his female supporter in the form of the goddess Athena, and her qualities are all of a cerebral kind. Born from the forehead of Zeus, she is scornful of the "weaker sex," while her stock epithet is "the bright-eyed." In the same way, the Brangwen woman abhors "blood-intimacy" and her aspirations are repeatedly described in visual terms: "Her house faced out . . . looked out to . . . the world beyond. She stood to see the far-off world. . . . Looking out, as she must . . . she strained her eyes to see what man had done in fighting outwards to knowledge . . ." (3). The militant spirit of the Brangwen woman is also an Athena trait, of course, as is her orientation toward city life; in her cult statues, Athena is pictured as an armed goddess and she is, after all, the patroness of Athens.

As for why she champions Odysseus, Athena's own explanation is to be found in the thirteenth book of the *Odyssey*, when upon his return to Ithaca she approaches him in the disguise of a shepherd. Immediately wary, Odysseus himself adopts a disguise by pretending he is a Cretan refugee. Athena hears his story with amusement, and when he is finished abandons her disguise and applauds his ingenuity; for that, she explains, is the bond between them: " 'We are both adepts in chicane. For in the world of men you have no rival as a statesman and an orator, while I am pre-eminent among the gods for invention and resource.'" She then goes on to notice her continued guardianship of Odysseus, but he is slightly annoyed because he feels Athena deserted him during his sea voyages and also is suspicious that she is mocking him and practicing further deception. To his complaints Athena replies, " 'How like you to be so wary! And that is why I cannot desert you in your misfortunes: you are so civilized, so intelligent, so self-possessed.' "[9] If we return now to the opening of *The Rainbow* we discover that these are similarly the three qualities which the Brangwen woman so greatly covets in the vicar and his circle. It is the "finer bearing" of the vicar, his mental "quickness" and educated sophistication, and the "self-contained manner" of Mrs. Hardy that the Brangwen woman desires in place of the qualities that make the Brangwen man "native to the earth."

Moreover, in the legend of the fall of Troy there is a specific object with which Odysseus and Athena are associated—the wooden horse. Thus in addition to consisting in a triumph of the mind over matter, the defeat of Troy presents an example of the triumph of the mechanical and artificial over the physical and natural, of the machine over the man. Now not only does industrialism find a place in the Odyssean dimension of *The Rainbow,* but also a new frame of reference is given to Lawrence's use of horse imagery. In *The Lost Girl* (which Lawrence was writing concurrently with the first draft of *The Sisters,* though he completed and published it some years later) Cicio, the Italian, observes to Alvina that in England " 'horses live a long time, because they *don't* live—never alive—see? In England, railway-engines are alive, and horses go on wheels.' "[10] To the same effect, whereas the ancestral Brangwen men are characterized by their vital relationship to real horses, after the entrance of the Midland Railway into the Erewash Valley signals that "the invasion was complete," their descendants hear only the "shrill whistle of the trains" (6, 7).

In contrast to their paternal ancestors, the later Brangwen men are sent to school, and it is here that Ursula's grandfather encounters the Victorian version of the Odysseus archetype: "He sat betrayed with emotion when the teacher of literature read, in a moving fashion, Tennyson's 'Ulysses,' or Shelley's 'Ode to the West Wind' " (10). Evocative of the cosmic lifestyle of his ancestors, Shelley's poem especially appeals to Tom, who has been sent "forcibly away" to school (9). But clearly it is Tennyson's poem that would have special attraction for the Brangwen women.

The discontent of Tennyson's Ulysses with his people—"That hoard, and sleep, and feed and know not me"—is in keeping with the prototypic Brangwen woman's discontent with the "blind intercourse of farm-life" and her feeling of superiority to her man (2). The premium placed by Ulysses upon knowledge and experience, action and travel, is similar to the values which the Brangwen woman associates with the "higher" mode of life. "I am become a name," says Ulysses; "For always roaming with a hungry heart / Much have I seen and known; cities of men / And manners, climates, councils, governments." The Brangwen woman yearns for "the far-off world of cities and governments and the active scope of man, the magic land to her, where secrets were made known and desires fulfilled" (3). Most important thematically is the conclusion of "Ulysses": "Made weak by time and fate, but strong in will / To strive, to seek, to find, and not to yield." For if the vicar with his "magic language" symbolizes one of the motivating forces in *The Rainbow*, it is Lord *Will*iam, "member of Parliament for the division," who represents the other. Most important imagistically, and possibly most important of all in view of the title of *The Rainbow*, is Tennyson's image of experience as an arch:

> I am a part of all that I have met;
> Yet all experience is an arch wherethro'
> Gleams that untravell'd world, whose margin fades
> For ever and for ever when I move.

In contrast to the rainbow at the end of the book, whose arch is "the top of heaven" under which life perpetually renews itself and which promises security by reason of cyclicality, here the arch is a perpetually receding doorway *through* which man must journey (in linear fashion) on and on until death.[11]

Appropriately, the first time we meet the Ulyssean arch is in the same context in which we first meet the iron horse, and appropriately, too, the arch is presented in terms of traveling. To connect the newly-opened collieries a canal is constructed across the Marsh meadows: "A high embankment travelled along the fields to carry the canal, which passed close to the homestead, and, reaching the road, went over in a heavy bridge." The Marsh Farm is on the opposite side of the canal from the collieries, "but, looking from the garden gate down the road to the right, there, through the dark archway of the canal's square aqueduct, was a colliery spinning away in the near distance, and further, red, crude houses plastered on the valley in masses, and beyond all, the dim smoking hill of the town" (6).

Not surprisingly, the Ulyssean arch also figures prominently in Lawrence's exploration of Will Brangwen's desire to experience the Absolute, whereby it is also associated with the eschatological orientation of the Judeo-Christian tradition. For Will, the "adventure into unknown realities" begins at the church door, and "eager as a pilgrim" he walks with his wife Anna "up the steep hill" to Lincoln Cathedral: "Here the satisfaction he had yearned after came near, towards this, the porch of the great Unknown, all reality gathered, and there, the altar was the mystic door, through which all and everything must move on to eternity" (203). A generation later the Ulyssean symbol recurs in the more secular form of a school entrance: "She entered the arched doorway of the porch" (369), Lawrence writes, in describing the major event in Ursula's determination "to follow knowledge like a sinking star."

*   *   *

According to one of the few critics who discusses the Homeric reference in *The Rainbow,* the allusion to the *Odyssey* is designed to highlight the inadequacy of the Brangwen men:

> the Brangwen women are not fulfilled; their yearnings for the outside world are only vicariously satisfied. Instead of a living interchange with their husbands, instead of their husbands being the reckless voyagers into the unknown who come back to them and complete them, it is the people of the Hall who provide them with "their own Odyssey," who bring "Penelope and Ulysses before them."[12]

But the thing which one must notice is that the discontent of the Brangwen women and the idea that the life of the Hall constitutes a "higher" mode of being are presented from the women's point of view, and the question one must ask in turn is whether or not Lawrence endorses their perspective. Their aspirations lead to the road taken in *The Rainbow,* but whether Lawrence views that direction as fortunate is a very different matter.

The invocation of an archetypal figure does not by definition constitute a positive context, for every archetypal figure is Janus-faced—Odysseus especially so. Indeed, as Stanford has demonstrated, there are two very different traditions concerning Odysseus: the one focuses upon him as "The Favourite of Athena" and views him as a culture hero; the other emphasizes that he is "The Grandson of Autolycus," the arch-deceiver, and treats him as a trickster and fraudulent counselor. Similarly, there are two opposed ways to interpret Tennyson's poem. One way, Ulysses is an old man who, no longer being needed, masks his impotence by expressing his discontent with the placid life of Ithaca and by announcing his decision to depart. The other way is to view him as a hero in an unheroic world. One way, Ulysses is foolhardy and irresponsible; the other, he is the thirster after knowledge in the best Renaissance tradition. The Brangwen women represent the "positive" interpretation, but as we turn now to another allusion to the Odyssean motif we begin to glimpse the other side of the picture.

As a child, Ursula Brangwen, like her maternal ancestors, attempts to escape from the "heat and swelter of fecundity" (263) by imagining an Odyssean context for herself. But when the time comes for her to go to school in Nottingham, "she must move out of the intricately woven illusion of her life: the illusion of a father whose life was an Odyssey in an outer world . . . then the multitude of illusions concerning herself . . . how in England she was under a spell, she was not really this Ursula Brangwen" (266). What compensates for her loss of this set of illusions is her belief that "she was going to inherit her own estate, when she went to the High School. . . . There she was going to walk among free souls, her co-mates and her equals, and all petty things would be put away." As Lawrence points out, however, what Ursula has done is simply to exchange one set of unrealities for another: "She made a new illusion of school": seated "upon the hill of learning, looking down on the smoke and confusion and the manufacturing, engrossed activity of the town . . . she fancied the air was finer, beyond the factory smoke" (267).

Consequently, it now seems that the intellectual ideals of the ancestral Brangwen women—their Odyssean aspirations—are themselves a kind of Circean snare. In attempting to escape from what they consider to be the drugged existence of their men, they have become victims of a more powerful charm. The "Hall" that fascinates the Brangwen women is the hall of the enchantress; the language of the vicar, the man with "strange movements," is indeed "magic" and it has cast a spell over them. Around Circe's hall are wild animals drugged into mildness; civilization has similarly tamed man's instinctual impulses; Circe turned men into swine; civilization has turned men into mechanical monsters. " 'What are you, you pale citizens?' " asks Ursula after she has become aware that "the civic uniform was a trick played," that civilization is a delusion, an appearance and not a reality, " 'You subdued beast in sheep's clothing, you primeval darkness falsified to a social mechanism' " (448). Behind the "dark and dry and small" vicar who brings "the wonder of the beyond" before the Brangwen women, then, stands the "wily" Odysseus, the craftsman who deceived the Trojans into thinking that the wooden horse was a sacred gift.

To relate industrialism to this aspect of the Odyssean motif Lawrence describes in terms of a spell the reaction of the Brangwens to the building of the canal and colliery:

> At first the Brangwens were astonished by all this commotion around them. The building of a canal across their land made them strangers in their own place, this raw bank of earth shutting them off disconcerted them. As they worked in the fields, from beyond the now familiar embankment came the rhythmic run of the winding engines, startling at first, but afterwards a narcotic to the brain. (7)

Similarly, the machine is presented as a Circean web; from their garden gate the Brangwens see "a colliery spinning away in the near distance" (6). What the machine spins is the illusion of progress, while in actuality all it does is to turn the earthy ancestral Tom Brangwen into the cynical and swinish Uncle Tom, colliery manager:

> His manner was polite, almost foreign, and rather cold. He still laughed in his curious, animal fashion, suddenly wrinkling up his wide nose, and showing his sharp teeth. The fine beauty of his skin and his complexion,

some almost waxen quality, hid the strange, repellent grossness of him, the slight sense of putrescence, the commonness which revealed itself in his rather fat thighs and loins. (346)

It is not only Circe who is associated with the weaving of a web in the *Odyssey*. The endless web was the means whereby Penelope was able to remain faithful to her husband. To defend her husband's interests against the suitors, Penelope told them that she would submit to one of them when she had completed the tapestry upon which she was working, but each evening she undid the weaving. This web is also to be found in *The Rainbow*, and at first it appears to have the same function of symbolizing the woman's role as guardian of the values of the hearth and home. Tom Brangwen and his wife sit together in the evening: "She was sewing. He sat very still, smoking, perturbed. He was aware of his wife's quiet figure, and quiet dark head bent over her needle" (87). What perturbs Brangwen is his intuitive appreciation that her sewing is not in the interests of preserving their relationship but for the purpose of denying and mastering him: "It was too peaceful. . . . His wife was obliterated from him, she was in her own world, quiet, secure, unnoticed, unnoticing. He was shut down by her" (87). It is not an embodiment of faithfulness who sits here sewing, in short, but an embodiment of self-assertion. And what is implicit here becomes explicit in Anna's use of her sewing not as a defense but in defiance of her husband:

> She turned to her sewing. Immediately the tea-things were cleared away, she fetched out the stuff, and his soul rose in rage. He hated beyond measure to hear the shriek of calico as she tore the web sharply, as if with pleasure. And the run of the sewing-machine gathered a frenzy in him at last.
> "Aren't you going to stop that row?" he shouted. "Can't you do it in the daytime?"
> She looked up sharply, hostile from her work.
> "No, I can't do it in the daytime. I have other things to do. Besides, I like sewing, and you're not going to stop me doing it."
> Whereupon she turned back to her arranging, fixing, stitching, his nerves jumped with anger as the sewing-machine started and stuttered and buzzed.

Penelope undid her weaving in anticipation of her husband's homecoming; Anna "tore the web sharply" after her husband comes home.

> But she was enjoying herself, she was triumphant and happy as the darting needle danced ecstatically down a hem, drawing the stuff along under its vivid stabbing, irresistibly. She made the machine hum. She stopped it imperiously, her fingers were deft and swift and mistress.
> If he sat behind her stiff with impotent rage it only made a trembling vividness come into her energy. On she worked. At last he went to bed in a rage, and lay stiff, away from her. And she turned her back on him. And in the morning they did not speak, except in mere cold civilities.

And when he came home at night, his heart relenting and growing hot for love of her, when he was just ready to feel he had been wrong, and when he was expecting her to feel the same, there she sat at the sewing-machine, the whole house was covered with clipped calico, the kettle was not even on the fire. (160)

The sewing-machine, then, like the "colliery spinning away" symbolizes the power of the mechanical over the passional. The "endless web" that Anna sews is not a symbol of the woman's guardianship of the values of the hearth and home but her rejection of those values in the interest of dominance.

That this web of power is also a web of illusion, that the Ulyssean will, like the Ulyssean desire for knowledge, is a destructive rather than a creative principle, Lawrence demonstrates generally through the sexual frustrations and perversions, the suicidal and nihilistic tendencies of those who enjoy it and those who are the product of it. The liberated Winifred Inger, "a fearless-seeming, clean type of modern girl whose very independence betrays her sorrow" is one example; she gives one "altogether the sense of a fine-mettled, scrupulously groomed person, and of an unyielding mind. Yet there was an infinite poignancy about her, a great pathos in her lonely, proudly closed mouth" (335). If she is "proud and free as a man" (336) she also, in her lesbian desires, loves like a man. Initially Ursula admires this modern Greek, this avatar of Diana (she dresses in "a rust-red tunic like a Greek girl's" for her swimming race with Ursula and appears as "firm-bodied as Diana" [336])—but ultimately Ursula begins to recognize the chaos that this mistress, like the other "educated, unsatisfied people" to whom she introduces Ursula, symbolizes (342). For her own part, Winifred senses that Ursula has recognized her destructiveness: "At the bottom of her was a black pit of despair." But she is too proud to admit it and "too hopeless to rage" (343). As such she becomes the perfect mate for the pit-manager, Tom Brangwen:

He too was at the end of his desires. He had done the things he wanted to do. They had all ended in a disintegrated lifelessness of soul, which he hid under an utterly tolerant good-humour. He no longer cared about anything on earth, neither man nor woman, nor God nor humanity. He had come to a stability of nullification. (343)

Literally and figuratively, therefore, the aspirations of the Brangwen women for higher things have led their descendants into the pit. The world that gleams through the arch of the aqueduct is a "dim and smoking" one; the "finer, more vivid *circle* of life" (emphasis added) to which they desire entry is a hellish one. And these observations suggest that Lawrence may be invoking another signature to the Odysseus archetype. At the entrance to Dante's inferno there is also an arch, and in the eighth circle of that hell are to be found the Evil Counselors who are retributively punished for their deceptive words and false counsel by being subsumed in tongues of fire. Because of his agency in the downfall of Troy, Ulysses is the prominent figure among them. The recurrence of circle imagery in *The Rainbow*,[13] coupled with the fact that in "The Widening Circle" chapter Lawrence chronicles Ursula's disillusionment when she discovers that "instead of having arrived at distinction they had come to a new red-brick suburbia in a grimy town" (241), confirm the likelihood that Lawrence has *The Inferno* in mind. Furthermore, in this same chapter, as Ursula wanders in the garden waiting for the rest of the family, she hears the bells of the church ring the *eighth* hour. A closer look at Dante's portrayal of Ulysses is therefore in order.

According to Dante, Ulysses—like the nameless Brangwen son—never returned home. Rather, he left Circe's isle merely to set out in further pursuit of knowledge: " 'not fondness for my son, nor reverence / for my aged father, nor Penelope's claim / to the joys of love, could drive out of my mind / the lust to experience the far-flung world,' " he explains. When on that voyage they come to the Pillars of Hercules, "warning all men back from further voyage," Ulysses exhorts his crew against yielding: " 'You were not born to live like brutes, / but to press on to manhood and recognition.' " As a result he and his crew are drowned, "as it pleased Another to order and command."[14] In Dante's hands, therefore, Ulysses becomes an embodiment of the spirit of the Renaissance and the passion that has come to be considered characteristically Greek—the desire to know. According to Stanford, Dante does not condemn Ulysses for his overweening desire for knowledge, but in making this desire the agent by which he leads his crew into destruction Dante raises the question of whether those who conduct us into new areas of life and thought are culture heroes leading us to higher civilization or fraudulent counselors enticing us to our doom. To a large extent this is the very issue at the heart of *The Rainbow*, but Lawrence unlike Dante is not reluctant to answer: the Brangwen woman's aspiration leads to "Widening" circles, but the wider the circle the greater the sense of frustration and alienation; her desire for the "higher" form of being makes for progress, but the more civilized the character the more materialistic he seems to become.

Tom Brangwen, Ursula's uncle, is the living proof. Like the vicar (and Odysseus), he is "rather short" with "a quick intelligence." He has gone not merely to grammar school but also "High School" and on to further education in London. He is, needless to say, the favorite of his mother, Lydia; like her it is he with "his soft inscrutable nature, his strange repose and his informed air, added to his position in London, who seemed to emphasize the superior foreign element in the Marsh." In her naïveté Ursula thinks him "a romantic, alluring figure"; "He spoke other languages easily and fluently, his nature was curiously gracious and insinuating. With all that, he was undefinably an outsider. He belonged to nowhere, to no society" (237–40). To Ursula's idealistic assertion that the greatest virtue in life is courage, he asks " 'Courage for what?' " Courage for everything, she answers; " 'Everything's nothing,' laughed her uncle" (289).

To this fate, then, has the Odyssean spirit led the modern world, according to Lawrence; in forcing her descendants to become travelers, the Brangwen woman leads them into eternal exile, dooms them to the life of the wanderer. Ulysses' thirst for knowledge leads to the death of his crew; the Brangwen woman's craving for the higher mode of existence leads to death in life.

There is, however, one further probable allusion to the Odyssean complex, and to examine it in context is to discover not merely that the phonetic connection between Ulysses and Ursula is meant to be appreciated but also that Lawrence's heroine is designed as a positive corrective to the tradition.

The allusion appears in the chapter in which Lawrence traces the beginning and forecasts the end of the relationship between Ursula and Anton Skrebensky. Initially she is attracted to Anton because he seems to offer a solution to the impasse she has reached: "Out of the nothingness and the undifferentiated mass, to make something of herself! But what? In the obscurity and pathlessness to take a direction! But whither? How take even one step? And yet, how stand still?" (281). But gradually his emphasis upon the validity that action gives to one's life leads Ursula to suspect that his political involvement and concern with progress are a way of rationalizing his own psychological impotence.

Immediately following a conversation to this effect during one of their walks, the couple come to a wharf just above one of the canal locks, where lying moored is an empty barge. The barge is "the *Annabel,* belonging to J. Ruth of Loughborough," a grimy man with blue eyes and fair hair (i.e., the distinguishing features of the original male Brangwen line). Despite Anton's implicit disapproval, Ursula wants to go inside the barge: "She *did* want to go down" (310). If the name of the place with which Mr. Ruth is associated—Loughborough, i.e., low-district—and that Ursula must go down to enter the place suggest that the episode is designed as a descent into the underworld, the vitality of the bargeman indicates that this underworld is not at all the place of the dead.

Entering the cabin of the barge, Ursula meets the man's wife and an as yet nameless baby, and as Ursula holds the child the couple argue over the issue. Then:

> "What's *your* name?" the man suddenly asked of her.
> "My name is Ursula—Ursula Brangwen," she replied.
> "Ursula!" he exclaimed, dumbfounded.
> "There was a Saint Ursula. It's a very old name," she added hastily, in justification.
> "Hey, mother!" he called.
> There was no answer.
> "Pem!" he called, "can't y'hear?"
> "What?" came the short answer.
> "What about 'Ursula'?" he grinned.
> "What about *what?*" came the answer, and the woman appeared in the doorway, ready for combat.
> "Ursula—it's the lass's name there," he said gently.

. . . .

"It's not a *common* name, is it!" [the mother] exclaimed, excited as by an adventure. (312)

Why the father should be dumbfounded by the name Ursula and the mother should think of it in terms of an "adventure" may require for explanation a knowledge of Lawrence's earlier work. "Pem," the name of the bargeman's wife, was used by Lawrence in his first work, *The White Peacock*, as a variant of Penelope.[15]

*   *   *

Having thus examined the major allusions to the Odyssean tradition in *The Rainbow*—with a view toward demonstrating that their presence is deliberate and for the purpose of showing how the key imagery of the novel derives from this context—we are now in position to appreciate the way in which "the Ulysses theme" is played out in the successive generations of Brangwens, becoming thereby the chief principle of coherence of the work and possibly the secret of its great appeal.

To begin with Ursula's grandfather, then, the event that precipitates his discontent with the life of his fathers is his meeting, in an "upper room" of a hotel in Matlock, with "a small middle-aged man with iron-grey hair and a curious face, like a monkey's but interesting, in its way almost beautiful. Brangwen guessed that he was a foreigner" (18). Warm and instinctive himself,

> Brangwen marvelled over the cold, animal intelligence of the face . . . at the old face turned round on him, looking at him without considering it necessary to know him at all. The eyebrows of the round, perceiving, but unconcerned eyes were rather high up, with slight wrinkles above them, just as a monkey's had. It was an old ageless face. (18–19)

At the same time that he has this inhuman quality, the "man was most amazingly a gentleman all the time, an aristocrat." The foreigner, in short, appears to Brangwen in the same way that the vicar, with his "strange movements" and "magic language" appeared to the Brangwen women, while it is by way of their after-dinner conversation that the prototype for both becomes evident. Their talk is "chiefly of horses," and the words with which the stranger finally takes his leave are " 'Good night, and bon voyage' " (19).

Prior to this meeting, Brangwen resembled his paternal ancestors, but immediately after the contact with the stranger he begins to question and become self-conscious like his maternal ancestors: "What was it all? There was a life so different from what he knew it. What was there outside his knowledge, how much? What was this that he had touched? What was he in this new influence? What did everything mean? Where was life, in that which he knew or all outside him?" (19).

As a result of the Matlock experience, Brangwen dreams of "the meeting with a small, withered foreigner of ancient breeding" (20) and when he meets Lydia Lensky he appropriately announces, " 'That's her' " (24). In her appearance as well as her background, Lydia is equipped to take the place of the nameless foreigner and the vicar (she is also housekeeper at the vicarage): "She was dressed in black, was apparently rather small and slight, beneath her long black cloak, and she wore a black bonnet. She walked hastily, as if unseeing, her head rather forward. It was her curious absorbed, flitting motion, as if she was passing unseen by everybody, that first arrested him" (23). If her bird-like motions also suggest her association with Athena, even more so do her eyes, since in addition to "the bright-eyed," another epithet of the goddess was "the grey-eyed," and it is this feature that Lawrence repeatedly notices in describing Lydia: "the bend of her head was proud, her grey eyes clear and dilated, so that the men could not look at her, and the women were elated by her, they served her" (53); "Then, as he sat there, all mused and wondering, she came near to him, looking at him with wide, grey eyes that almost smiled with a low light" (43; see also 27 and 55).

Though her foreignness initially attracts Tom to Lydia, after their marriage the unknown world from which she comes makes Brangwen both uneasy and frustrated. "She was curiously self-sufficient and did not say much" (55), but occasionally she tells him stories of her past. The one told at some length has to do with a railway-carriage that served as a traveling brothel (56), and the effect of the story is so to disorient Brangwen and to dissolve the reality of the world around him that he begins to wonder whether what he sees is real "or whether it was merely a figment in the atmosphere" (57). Thus just as the horse full of Greeks is the device that throws the Trojans into confusion and ultimately confounds them, so Lydia's story of the railway carriage befuddles and enrages Tom:

> And there she sat, telling tales to the open space, not to him, arrogating a curious superiority to him, a distance between them, something strange and foreign and outside his life, talking, rattling, without rhyme or reason, laughing when he was shocked or astounded, condemning nothing, confounding his mind and making the whole world a chaos, without order or stability of any kind. (56)

Lydia's very mode of speaking, Lawrence seems to suggest, reflects the mechanical motions of the train as well.

As a result of being thus "burned out of cover" by those who had "set fire to the homestead of his nature" (20), Tom is never again able to find perfect contentment; the perennial question always comes to destroy his peace: "But what was at the end of the journey?" (69). On the other hand, he is able to discover a measure of satisfaction through his sexual relationship with his wife, which is presented as a centripetal rather than a centrifugal movement. Whereas the Brangwen women turn their backs on their men and face outward, straining to see the spoken world that gleams through the arch of experience, Lydia and Tom in their passion had "thrown open the doors, each to the other, and had stood in the doorways facing each other" (91). And thus the ideal moment in their relationship and the one that puts at peace the soul of the child Anna is imaged not as an arch through which one must move but as a rainbow under which she no longer need struggle: "She was no longer called upon to uphold with her childish might the broken end of the arch. Her father and her mother now met to the span of the heavens, and she, the child, was free to play in the space beneath" (92).

With the coming of Will Brangwen the invasion of the Marsh is reenacted, as Anna senses in him the way out of the life of the farm: "In him she had escaped. In him the bounds of her experience were transgressed: he was the hole in the wall, beyond which the sunshine blazed" (109). But as we come to know him Will Brangwen is seeking not so much a way out as a way back; Anna is not a native of the Marsh but a transplant there from the world of the beyond. Both of them are second-generation figures, and whereas Tom Brangwen became the restless wanderer, Anna and Will have inherited the discontent and willfulness characteristic of the Odyssean type. With Tom Brangwen we had the setting out on the odyssey; with Will and Anna we are in the middle of the journey. Thus whereas in the Tom section there are only occasional sea images, an extended metaphor of sea voyage and shipwreck provides the background for the Will and Anna sections.

Will Brangwen looks forward to his marriage to Anna as the thing that will satisfy his yearnings, as the end of his voyage: "Like a man who journeys in a ship, he was suspended till the coming to port" (125). For he looks at his relationship to his wife as the means whereby to escape from the social world into the unknown and as the ark in which they will rest secure while the flood engulfs the rest of the world. In marriage he seeks to fulfill his desire for mastery and dominance.

Anna's will to power, however, is as great as his and her yearning is for the type of life enjoyed by Millicent Skrebensky and represented by her husband, the baron, who in form and character is a duplicate of the earlier Brangwen woman's vicar (195–96). As a result she calls her husband a fool for thinking she will submit to him; she thanks the gods for her unconquerable spirit and asserts that she will be the master of her fate and the captain of her soul. "Yet he went on trying to steer the ship of their dual life. He asserted his position as the captain of the ship. And captain and ship bored her." In the face of her ridicule and obstinacy, he feels he has "gone on the wrong tack"; but in view of the spirit of his age, "he felt it hard to give up the expedition" (170).

In consequence, their marriage becomes a battle of wills, an Odyssean struggle for survival in the strait bounded on either side by Scylla and Charybdis with each of them representing these dangers for the other. "She was as the rock on which he stood, with deep, heaving water all round, and he was unable to swim"; but she "beat him off, she beat him off. Where could he turn, like a swimmer in a dark sea, beaten off from his hold, whither could he turn? He wanted to leave her, he wanted to be able to leave her. For his soul's sake, for his manhood's sake, he must be able to leave her" (183). She is "like a fury to him" her eyes bright "with a cold, unmoving hatred," with her hands "breaking his fingers from their hold on her, persistently, ruthlessly" (184). "In his moments of intense suffering, she seemed to him inconceivable, a monster, the principle of cruelty" (185). To Anna, in turn, Will is the dark whirlpool that will suck her down into the subterranean depths; he is the monster with "something dark and beastly" in his will which will destroy her spirit: "Gradually she realized that her life, her freedom, was sinking under the silent grip of his physical will" (182).

With the birth of the child, Ursula, the battle ends, and with "Anna Victrix." But with motherhood Anna also gives up her role as the Odyssean adventurer, and again the surrender of the Ulyssean spirit is imaged in terms of a change from the doorway arch to the rainbow, although the change is not complete and in turn, thematically, the surrender is not a totally satisfactory one. After the birth of Ursula, Anna is less discontented than before:

> Yet still she was not quite fulfilled. She had a slight expectant feeling, as of a door half opened. . . . She was straining her eyes to something beyond. And from her Pisgah mount, which she had attained, what could she see? A faint, gleaming horizon, a long way off, and a rainbow like an archway, a shadow-door with faintly coloured coping above it. Must she be moving thither? (192)

The questioning of questing goes on until Anna becomes pregnant again, "which made her satisfied and took away her discontent. . . . With satisfaction she relinquished the adventure to the unknown." She relinquishes it not because she has found an answer to her question but simply because she has "lapsed into vague content." Nor does she relinquish it entirely, but rather surrenders the burden to the next generation:

> If she were not the wayfarer to the unknown, if she were arrived now, settled in her builded house, a rich woman, still her doors opened under the arch of the rainbow. . . . She was a door and a threshold, she herself. Through her another soul was coming, to stand upon her as upon the threshold, looking out, shading its eyes for the direction to take. (193)

To her daughter Ursula, however, being the mother of future Ulysses figures is not enough; nor is she content to play merely the "supportive" Athena role. Indeed, to this third-generation Brangwen, Anna's "vague content" is the equivalent of the inertia that occasioned Tennyson's hero to set sail, and the inadequacies of the men she encounters make it impossible for her to champion them in any way.

But Ursula's determination "to strive, to seek, to find"—once stated in these Ulyssean terms—is too obvious to require further imagistic or thematic documentation. What do need emphasis are Lawrence's uses of the Ulyssean arch to dramatize her ultimate *disillusion,* and his concurrent use of the "iron horse."

Both figure prominently in Lawrence's description of Ursula's education, with the "tram" being the vehicle in which she is "carried forward, into her new existence" at St. Philip's (Greek, "horse-lover"). "It sidled round the loop at the terminus," Lawrence writes, with the animistic verb keeping the "horse" motif to the fore, as also does the verb he uses to describe her entrance into the vehicle: "She mounted into the wet, comfortless tram, whose floor was dark with wet, whose windows were all steamed, and she sat in suspense." Obvious here too is the evocation of the "wooden horse" motif, especially when Lawrence repeats: "The windows of the tram grew more steamy, opaque. She was shut in with these unliving, spectral people" (368). And when she dismounts, as it were, at the end of her education, it is to wonder at the extent to which she had been taken in by the lure of advancement:

> Always the shining doorway ahead; and then, upon approach, always the shining doorway was a gate into another ugly yard, dirty and active and dead. Always the crest of the hill gleaming ahead under heaven: and then, from the top of the hill only another sordid valley full of amorphous, squalid activity. (436)

Through her relationship with Anton Skrebensky, Ursula similarly begins to question the concept of duty, and in the scene in which she is joined by her Uncle Tom—that other advocate of the utilitarian ethic—to say goodbye to Anton (off to fight the good fight in South Africa), the iron horse again becomes a focusing symbol:

> The three made a noticeable group on the station; the girl . . . pale, tense with youth, isolated, unyielding; the soldierly young man in a crush hat and heavy overcoat . . . his whole figure neutral; then the elder man, a fashionable bowler hat pressed low over his dark brows . . . his whole figure curiously suggestive of full-blooded indifference. (329–30)

As Ursula stands on the platform, she feels "a great emptiness about her," while in his description of the arrival and departure of the train Lawrence makes it a symbol of the Odyssean spirit—with its furious action and determination not to bend: "The train was rushing up"; "The train moved off. . . . The train gathered speed, it grew smaller and smaller. Still it ran in a straight line" (330).

But the key "train" scene is the one which brings the Brangwens' history full circle: it was with Tom Brangwen's meeting of the withered foreigner one Whitsuntide that the odyssey of *The Rainbow* began, and it is also on this day that Ursula has her climactic experience on the downs. "Ursula was always yearning to go to the top of the downs. The white track wound up to the rounded summit. And she must go." She reaches the top and from this perspective experiences a cosmic view of the situation:

Up there, she could see the Channel a few miles away, the sea raised up and faintly glittering in the sky, the Isle of Wight a shadow lifted in the far distance, the river winding bright through the patterned plain to seaward, Arundel Castle a shadowy bulk, and then the rolling of the high, smooth downs, making a high, smooth land under heaven, acknowledging only the heavens in their great, sun-glowing strength, and suffering only a few bushes to trespass on the intercourse between their great, unabateable body and the changeful body of the sky. (463)

From this vision of the majestic and mythological hierogamy, she turns to the historical world of men:

Below she saw the villages and the woods of the weald, and the train running bravely, a gallant little thing, running with all the importance of the world over the water meadows and into the gap of the downs, waving its white steam, yet all the while so little. So little, yet its courage carried it from end to end of the earth, till there was no place where it did not go.

To which mode of life will she pay allegiance is the question with which she is confronted, and her answer consequently determines the meaning of the entire narrative and Lawrence's attitude toward the Odyssean quest. The train looks courageous in its smallness, but "the downs, in magnificent indifference, bearing [sic] limbs and body to the sun, drinking sunshine and sea-wind and sea-wet cloud into its golden skin, with superb stillness and calm of being, was not the downs still more wonderful?"

In describing Ursula's Odyssean aspirations earlier, Lawrence had written: "For there was this world to conquer, this knowledge to acquire, this qualification to attain. And she worked with intensity, because of a want inside her that drove her on. Almost everything was subordinated now to this one desire to take her place in the world. What kind of a place it was to be she did not ask herself" (411). Similarly, though Tom Brangwen had wondered "When did it come to an end? In which direction was it finished?" (131), he too had set out blindly, without knowing where he was going but simply because he had been taught to aspire to the Odyssean life. Now, from the downs and with the fate of herself and her ancestors whereby to judge, Ursula is ready to frame an answer:

The blind, pathetic, energetic courage of the train as it steamed tinily away through the patterned levels to the sea's dimness, so fast and so energetic, made her weep. Where was it going? It was going nowhere, it was just going. So blind, so without goal or aim, yet so hasty! She sat on an old pre-historic earth-work and cried, and the tears ran down her face. The train had tunnelled all the earth, blindly, and uglily. . . . So shortsighted the train seemed, running to the distance, so terrifying in their littleness the villages, with such pettiness in their activity. (463)

In this final image Lawrence makes the train symbolic of the two elements that are basic to the Odyssean archetype—the journey and the fixed will. While in emphasizing the blindness of its goal, the absence of any goal, and the blindness of its progress, he prepares for Ursula's desperate recognition of the nature of the Odyssean life. "'I want to go,'" cries Ursula, at the seaside; "'I want to go,' she cried again, in the high, hard voice, like the scream of gulls." And when Anton asks, "'Where?'" her reply is the pathetic culmination of two thousand years of progress, "'I don't know'" (478).

Where Ursula does discover an answer is in her encounter with "real" horses—an encounter that puts to the test her maternal ancestors' conviction that "any man is little and frail beside a bull, and yet stronger than the bull" because of "knowledge" (4). Upon first sensing the presence of the horses, her first impulse is to ignore them: "She continued her path, inevitably. . . . She pursued her way with bent head [like her grandmother, Lydia]. She did not want to know they were there" (486). But this mind-over-matter strategy fails, and what ultimately enables her to escape is an animal instinct for survival, on the one hand, and a "blood-consciousness" recognition of what she and the horses have in common, on the other.

> She was aware of their breasts gripped, clenched narrow in a hold that never relaxed, she was aware of their red nostrils flaming with long endurance, and of their haunches . . . pressing, pressing to burst the grip upon their breasts, pressing for ever till they went mad, running against the walls of time, and never bursting free. (487)

Similarly, at the outset of her Odyssean career, Ursula "was like a young filly that has been broken in to the shafts, and has lost its freedom. . . . The agony, the galling, the ignominy of her breaking in. This wore into her soul. But she would never submit. To shafts like these she would never submit for long" (407).[16]

Nor does she ever "yield" in the sense of giving up her own quest for self-realization, of course; but after her encounter with the horses, she comes to see that Ulysses is a very unreliable guide to this end. "I cannot rest from travel," vaunted Tennyson's outward-bound protagonist; to Lawrence's homeward-bound protagonist, however, what is "dull" is not "to pause" but continually to be on the move: "She had an idea that she must walk for the rest of her life, wearily, wearily. Step after step, step after step. . . . Step after step, step after step, the monotony produced a deep cold sense of nausea in her" (490). Accordingly, the prelude to her ultimate vision of the rainbow is her "delirious" dream of "taking root" and of developing in accordance with the laws of nature[17] rather than in opposition to them. Or as Paul J. Rosenzweig puts it, she comes to discover that "Only by travelling inward can one paradoxically reach the horizon."[18]

*   *   *

If the "Ulysses theme" is therefore the controlling theme of *The Rainbow*, according to Michael L. Ross it is also the connecting link between that novel and its sequel, *Women in Love*:

The "unknown" toward which [Ursula] ventured with Birkin represents the same goal toward which [her ancestors], with their more trammeled gait, have groped; through all the startling changes of moral climate that mark the two volumes, there still gleams (in the words of a poem that deeply moves the adolescent Tom Brangwen) "that untraveled world, whose margin fades / For ever and for ever" as the protagonists move.

The main difference between the two works, as Ross sees it, is that in *Women in Love* Lawrence's "initial, inspiring confidence in an evolutionary thrust toward ever-expanding possibilities was . . . replaced by a desperate sense of the destructiveness of historical processes"; and reflective of this difference in particular is the way in which the positive arch symbolism of *The Rainbow* is parodied in such scenes as that "in which Gudrun and Gerald kiss under the 'square arch' of the colliery railway overpass." Here, he observes, "the archway leads not toward fulfillment or the 'unknown' but rather toward the threadbare reenactment of sterile patterns of feeling—ultimately, toward the Alpine 'cul de sac' in which Gerald's affair with Gudrun proceeds to its bitter conclusion, the terminal 'unknown' of death."[19] As we have demonstrated, however, the negative arch symbolism is already operative in *The Rainbow* and the optimism of that novel has precisely to do with Ursula's rejection of the Ulysses role—just as the tragedy of Gerald and Gudrun derives from the fact that they are "always roaming with a hungry heart" and obsessed with "piling life on life" in an attempt to fill up the time until "Death closes all."

Of course Lawrence himself was an inveterate traveler, but if we are to trust his explanation in *Fantasia of the Unconscious,* then what he was actually seeking was a place "to be alone with one's own soul. . . . To be at one in my own self. Not to be questing any more. Not to be yearning, seeking, hoping, desiring, aspiring. But to pause, and be alone."[20]

NOTES

1. W. B. Stanford, *The Ulysses Theme: A Study in the Adaptability of a Traditional Hero* (Ann Arbor: University of Michigan Press, 1968), pp. 211–46.

2. Our criticism of Stanford for omitting *The Rainbow* is in no way designed to call the value of his study into question. On the contrary, our reliance upon his research will be obvious throughout our discussion.

3. D. H. Lawrence, *The Collected Letters of D. H. Lawrence,* ed. Harry T. Moore (New York: Viking, 1962), p. 712.

4. John Worthen, *D. H. Lawrence and the Idea of the Novel* (London: Macmillan, 1979), p. 141.

Worthen himself believes that it is *Kangaroo* that has most in common with *Ulysses*—both being experimental novels in which the "apparent digressions are as important as its central narrative." He also argues that Lawrence was consciously competing with Joyce, citing as evidence Lawrence's observation when he finished *Kangaroo:* "such a novel! Even the Ulysseans will spit at it."

Another possibility, however, arises when Worthen observes that upon reading excerpts from *Ulysses* in the *Little Review,* Lawrence complained to Compton Mackenzie that it was "more disgusting than Casanova . . . I *must* show it can be done without muck." The work that immediately comes to mind in this context is *Lady Chatterley's Lover,* an insight which was coincidentally corroborated at the 1981 MLA Seminar on Lawrence when Zack Bowen read a paper on *Ulysses* followed by our paper on *Lady Chatterley's Lover.* Specifically, the similarities between the basic adulterous triangle and the Venus/Mars/Vulcan imagery became everywhere evident. Under the title "War, Love, and Industrialism: The Ares/Aphrodite/Hephaestus Complex in *Lady Chatterley's Lover,*" our revised paper is reproduced in *D. H. Lawrence's "Lady": A New Look at Lady Chatterley's Lover,* ed. Michael Squires and Dennis Jackson (Athens: University of Georgia Press, 1985), pp. 197–221.

5. Lawrence, *Collected Letters,* p. 1075. Henry Miller, who was in effect a contemporary of both, shared Lawrence's opinion of Joyce: "If the *Odyssey* was a remembrance of great deeds, *Ulysses* is a forgetting. That black, endless, never-ending flow of words in which the twin-soul of Joyce is swept along like a clot of waste matter passing through the drains, this stupendous deluge of pus and excrement, which washes through the book languidly seeking an outlet, at last gets choked and, rising like a tidal wave, blots out the whole shadowy world in which this epic was conceived." See *The World of Lawrence: A Passionate Appreciation,* ed. Evelyn J. Hinz and John J. Teunissen (Santa Barbara, Calif.: Capra Press, 1980) p. 110.

6. D. H. Lawrence, *The Rainbow,* introduction by Richard Aldington (New York: Viking, 1961), p. 8. All subsequent quotations are taken from this edition.

7. It is essentially on these grounds that E. V. Rieu, in his introduction to his translation of the *Odyssey,* describes the work as the "true ancestor" of the novel. See Homer, *The Odyssey* (Harmondsworth: Penguin Books, 1946).

8. Ovid, *The Metamorphoses,* trans. Rolfe Humphries (Bloomington: Indiana University Press, 1955), p. 317.

9. *Odyssey,* pp. 210–11.

10. D. H. Lawrence, *The Lost Girl* (New York: Cambridge University Press, 1968), p. 159. And in Book 13 of *The Odyssey,* Athena says to Odysseus that no one would use Ithaca for training horses because the ground is too broken and the meadows are too narrow.

11. In noting the importance of "arch" symbolism in *The Rainbow* but discussing it in terms of the difference between Norman and Gothic architecture, Mark Spilka is representative. See his *The Love Ethic of D. H. Lawrence* (Bloomington: Indiana University Press, 1966).

12. Is Daleski's pun on "vicariously" intended? H. M. Daleski, *The Forked Flame* (Evanston, Ill.: Northwestern University Press, 1965), p. 81.

13. For an extended discussion of this imagery, see Edward Engleberg, "Escape from the Circle of Experience: D. H. Lawrence's *The Rainbow* as a Modern Bildungsroman," *PMLA* 78 (1963): 103–13.

14. Dante, *The Inferno,* trans. John Ciardi (New York: New American Library, 1954), pp. 223–24.

15. This is not to suggest that the parallels with St. Ursula should be ignored but rather that they should be seen in the light of the larger Odyssean context. For discussions along the former lines, see Carol Hasley Kuo, "Lawrence's *The Rainbow,*" *Explicator* 19 (June 1961): item 70; and Ordelle G. Hill and Potter Woodberry, "Ursula Brangwen of *The Rainbow:* Christian Saint or Pagan Goddess?" *D. H. Lawrence Review* 4 (Fall 1971): 274–79.

16. The connection between Ursula's education and the bondaged condition of the horses is noted by Ann L. McLaughlin, who also points out the way in which Lawrence uses horse imagery to characterize the militarist, Anton Skrebensky. She also draws attention to the way in which the horses of *The Rainbow* represent not the vitality which Lawrence associates with this animal in *Apocalypse* but the frustration of that vitality. See "The Clenched and Knotted Horses in *The Rainbow,*" *D. H. Lawrence Review* 13 (Summer 1980): 179–86.

17. Nor is this to speak merely metaphorically or poetically. For as Robert Langbaum points out in *The Mysteries of Identity: A Theme in Modern Literature* (New York: Oxford University Press, 1977), Ursula's concern with being herself is in accordance with the principle of "cellular

identity," and he goes on to quote a specialist in cellular immunology. See pp. 317–18. In passing, one might note that Langbaum associates the grove in which Ursula encounters the horses with Dante's dark wood and sees her encounter with them as the equivalent of his descent into hell.

18. To emphasize this point, Paul J. Rosenzweig ("The Defense of the Second Half of *The Rainbow*," *D. H. Lawrence Review* 13 [Summer 1980]: 150–60) observes the way in which Lawrence counterpoints Ursula's whirlwind travels with Anton across Europe with the real discovery she has when she looks "inward" through a microscope at a speck of life. In commenting on the belief that the more one sees and knows the better, Rosenzweig also seems subconsciously to be registering a critique of the Ulyssean spirit: "Lawrence regarded as anathema this naïve attitude toward 'experience,' as if it were just another case of material accretion building gradually toward a heavenly epiphany" (159).

19. Michael L. Ross, "'More or Less a Sequel': Continuity and Discontinuity in Lawrence's Brangwensaga," *D. H. Lawrence Review* 14 (Fall 1981): 284. Though he does not directly concern himself with Ulysses, Ross does point to similarities between Ursula and Stephen Dedalus in their attempts to escape the "nightmare of history."

20. D. H. Lawrence, *Psychoanalysis and the Unconscious and Fantasia of the Unconscious*, introduction by Philip Rieff (New York: Viking, 1960), p. 168.

13

Purgation by Form in the Poetry of T. S. Eliot

E. L. EPSTEIN

T. S. Eliot wrote many poems in conventional forms, both in traditional meter and rhyme-schemes, and in untraditional but regular forms. In addition, he wrote free-verse poems; however, in these free-verse poems he seems sometimes to be verging toward regularity—sometimes he finally achieves it. This distribution is not arbitrary or capricious. His use of both regularity and freedom is thematic: his free verse and his regular verse express metaphorically two minds—the mind that creates, and the mind that suffers. It is the mind that suffers which creates regular forms; in Eliot's purgatorial world the suffering mind " 'move[s] in measure, like a dancer.' "[1] The more extreme the suffering, the more crystalline the form; the greater the pressure, the brighter the diamond. It is the mind that creates that expresses itself initially as free melismata, free expressions in varying rhythms, binding loosely both dignified and trivial material, creating confused expressions of shifting mood. However, when suffering begins and increases, the free form begins to stiffen in agony. Forcing together its disparate elements by the pressure of the mind that suffers, the complete poem ends up as an ironic jewel.

Some of Eliot's poems in completely traditional form display this process. "Burbank with a Baedeker: Bleistein with a Cigar"; "Sweeney Erect"; "Whispers of Immortality"; "Sweeney Among the Nightingales"—these poems, from *Poems* (1920), exhibit the extremity of hysterical or despairing irony. In these poems the monumental lies next to the comic, in twin meaninglessness. Here pure fear crystallizes into pure form, as fruits crystallize in sugar. These four poems display a Laforguean sorrow, the pain of the clown wounded beyond death, the clown so stricken that his conscious mind cannot begin even to create a song about his sorrow. Like a disturbed pond, the clown's fragmented *sensibilité* can reflect only a comically shattered world, but the clown's suffering mind writes its own independent regular poem.

In some of his poems, therefore, Eliot demonstrates distress hardening into despair; these poems commence with free forms and gradually harden.

However, others begin with the ironic regularity of despair and then fall apart; in these the tone of despair finally finds a small voice for itself to mourn sincerely. In "A Cooking Egg," the quatrain form falls apart into self-mockery. The first seven stanzas are regular in rhyme *(abcb)*, and are generally in iambic tetrameter. However, with line 29 the poem falls apart:

> Where are the eagles and the trumpets?
>
> > Buried beneath some snow-deep Alps.
> > Over buttered scones and crumpets
> > Weeping, weeping multitudes
> > Droop in a hundred A.B.C.'s.

Here the decay of form is a metaphor for the decay of any other kind of form—religious, political, social, psychological. Eliot employs this pattern, *form→decay,* or *confusion→form,* in many of his major poems, and always to signal a purgatorial motion between a deeper level of suffering, of frozen crystalline irony, and another level, the higher level of surface confusion, of meaninglessness, trash, and quotidian complexities.

"Preludes" provides examples of both forms. The first three Preludes begin in loose forms and "harden" into form; the fourth, reversing this pattern, falls apart, reemerging into clowning and confusion.

The meter of the first Prelude is a smooth iambic tetrameter, Eliot's favorite form in metered verse. The second and third Preludes shift to a regular/ irregular syllabic beat. The fourth Prelude begins with iambic tetrameter but falls apart. The rhyme-patterns also proceed from irregular to regular in the first three Preludes and the reverse in the fourth Prelude.

I

Meter		*rhyme*
Iambic tetrameter	The winter evening settles down	a
I.t.	With smell of steaks in passageways.	b
X	Six o'clock.	c
I.t.	The burnt-out ends of smoky days.	b
I.t.	And now a gusty shower wraps	d
X	The grimy scraps	d
I.t.	Of withered leaves about your feet	e
I.t.	And newspapers from vacant lots;	f
X	The showers beat	e
I.t.	On broken blinds and chimney-pots,	f
I.t.	And at the corner of the street	e
I.t.	A lonely cab-horse steams and stamps.	g
I.t.	And then the lighting of the lamps.	g

The rhyme-scheme in Preludes I is irregular at first *(abcbdd)*, but settles down to alternate rhymes *(efefe)* and ends with a couplet *(gg)*. The poem is metrically in a perfect iambic tetrameter broken with an irregular short line (the X-line) in three-line intervals. However, as the *efefegg* rhyme-scheme begins, the poem loses its inserted irregular X-lines, and the last tone of Preludes I deepens from sadness to a deep sorrow; the poem proceeds from preliminary freedom in form to a stiffened despair.

Preludes II also moves from rhyming and rhythmic irregularity to regularity.

II

Syllabic Count		rhyme
8	The morning comes to consciousness	a
6	Of faint stale smells of beer	b
7	From the sawdust-trampled street	c
8	With all its muddy feet that press	a
6	To early coffee-stands.	d
7	With the other masquerades	e
4	That time resumes,	f
6	One thinks of all the hands	d
7	That are raising dingy shades	e
7	In a thousand furnished rooms.	f

	Irregular	*Regular*
Rhyme	*abca'd*	*efdef*
Syllables	8 6 7 8 6	7 4 6 7 7

In the first stanza the *abc* then repeats the *a*, as *a'd*, but the second stanza is more regular than the first in that it echoes the *d*-rhyme from the first stanza. The syllable-count of the poem, chaotic at first (8 6 7 8 6), moves to regularity (7 4 6 7 7). Again the observer, at first observing the garbage of the world with sad irony, then moves to the sorrow of the animate and human, just as in Preludes I.

In Preludes III the same movement toward regularity occurs, the same deepening of the tone. The syllable-count, mixed at first, settles down to regularity (8 9 9 8 9 8 7) (10 10 9 8 8 8 8 7), and so does the rhyme-scheme *(abcdecf) (gghijjhi)*.

III

Syllabic Count		rhyme
8	You tossed a blanket from the bed,	a
9	You lay upon your back, and waited;	b
9	You dozed, and watched the night revealing	c
8	The thousand sordid images	d
9	Of which your soul was constituted;	e[= b'?]
8	They flickered against the ceiling.	c
7	And when all the world came back	f
10	And the light crept up between the shutters	g
10	And you heard the sparrows in the gutters,	g
9	You had such a vision of the street	h
8	As the street hardly understands;	i
8	Sitting along the bed's edge, where	j
8	You curled the papers from your hair,	j
8	Or clasped the yellow soles of feet	h
7	In the palms of both soiled hands.	i

Preludes IV reverses the pattern, and provides a sordid but conclusive exit from the labyrinthine sorrow of the whole "Preludes." The rhythm begins with nine impeccable lines of iambic tetrameter, then falls into syllabics (9 8 11 7/8 9 7/8). The rhyme-scheme attempts to resist the decaying of the form— the first four lines are regular *(abcb);* the second four try to hold themselves together with a half rhyme *(daa'c),* a harking-back to the *a-* and *c*-rhymes. Then the rhymes and rhythms both fall apart in the dusty arena of the trash world *(eefgfhij).*

IV

Meter		rhyme
Iambic tetrameter	His soul stretched tight across the skies	a
I.t.	That fade behind a city block,	b
I.t.	Or trampled by insistent feet	c
I.t.	At four and five and six o'clock;	b
I.t.	And short square fingers stuffing pipes,	d
I.t.	And evening newspapers, and eyes	a
I.t.	Assured of certain certainties,	a'
I.t.	The conscience of a blackened street	c
I.t.	Impatient to assume the world.	e

Syllabic Count		rhyme
9	I am moved by fancies that are curled	e
8	Around these images, and cling:	f
11	The notion of some infinitely gentle	g
7/8	Infinitely suffering thing.	f
9	Wipe your hand across your mouth, and laugh;	h
9	The worlds revolve like ancient women	i
7/8	Gathering fuel in vacant lots.	j

The overall form of the "Preludes" as a whole is *Irregular→Regular; Irregular→Regular; Irregular→Regular;* and *Regular→Irregular.* "Preludes" falls apart at the conclusion, and the trashy confusion of the tone ends the poem. If *Irregularity* equals the sensibility confused and wounded by the modern world, then *Regularity* equals an ultimate point beyond suffering. The *Irregular* is still human in its confusion; the *Regular* moves beyond the commenting mind to the mind that constructs an ironic crystal of pain beyond sighs and rubbish. Then, with Preludes IV the reader exits from the crystal world of suffering into the dirty, sadly-comic world again.

This type of analysis helps to explain the appearance of regularities in long free-verse poems. "The Love Song of J. Alfred Prufrock" drifts in and out of regularity—the Michelangelo jingle, and the blank-verse lines:

> I should have been a pair of ragged claws
> Scuttling across the floors of silent seas.

Then the rest of the poem consists of loose regularities, repetitions, irregularly rhyming verse. However, the end of "Prufrock" becomes ominously regular as Prufrock approaches the center of agony. The epigraph to "Prufrock" suggests that Prufrock, like Dante's Guido da Montefeltro, will never emerge from his lost state. The damned, like the saved, are what they were in life, but concentrated into the essence of themselves, unmixed with any merely human neutral behavior. This state will be theirs forever, and here we find the concentrated essence of Prufrock.

The end of "Prufrock" is regular, in three-line units:

Syllabic Count		rhyme
6	I grow old . . . I grow old . . .	
11	I shall wear the bottoms of my trousers rolled.	
14	Shall I part my hair behind? Do I dare to eat a peach?	a
14	I shall wear white flannel trousers, and walk upon the beach.	a
11	I have heard the mermaids singing, each to each.	a

10	I do not think that they will sing to me.	b
11	I have seen them riding seaward on the waves	c
10	Combing the white hair of the waves blown back	d
10	When the wind blows the water white and black.	d
11	We have lingered in the chambers of the sea	b
10	By sea girls wreathed with seaweed red and brown	e
10	Till human voices wake us, and we drown.	e

Iambic pentameter emerges and sinks, emerges and sinks, and finally, in the last couplet, establishes itself hypnotically. The syllabic-count wavers (6 11 14 14 11), then becomes regular (10 11 10 10 11 10 10). The rhyme-scheme of the last ten lines moves toward complete regularity: *aaa b cdd bee.* It is in these hypnotic crystalline lines that "you and I," the mind that suffers and the mind that creates, becomes "we," and both drown in the depths of their own permanence.

This movement from prosodic irregularity to regularity was not invented by Eliot, though it is employed most effectively by him of all modern poets. In the history of English poetry, the first and, for a long time, the only poet of note to end his irregular "odes" regularly was Dryden. "Ode" designated originally in English any irregular poem. Dryden began to make regular odes, but his example was not followed by any poet of note for a long time. Dryden ends with tercets in his "Ode on St. Cecilia's Day," and "To the Pious Memory of the Accomplished Lady Mrs. Killigrew." Cowley does not follow Dryden's lead, nor does Wordsworth; although there *are* triplets in the "Intimations" ode, there are none at the end. Neither Coleridge nor Keats follows Dryden.

Tennyson, on the other hand, does follow Dryden's example. Three early and irregular poems of Tennyson end regularly, in tercets: "Ode to Memory," "The Sea Fairies," and "The Dying Swan," all written before 1830. After "Lotos-Eaters," published in 1832, there is a long interval. Then Tennyson provides regular, tercet endings to two odes: "Ode Sung at the Opening of the International Exhibition," published in 1862, and "Ode on the Death of the Duke of Wellington," published in 1865. (See also "The Hesperides.") Later, Matthew Arnold follows Tennyson's early practice, with "The Buried Life," published in 1852.

The ending of an irregular poem with regular forms, therefore, seems to be derived from the "ode" tradition established by Dryden and employed by Tennyson. The most sustained example of the ode ending regularly is to be found in the "Choric Song" of the "Lotos-Eaters" by Tennyson, a long, irregular ode, and possibly Eliot's model. In this poem the sufferers of

Odysseus's crew drift from irregular recollections of their hardships and
sorrows into complete hypnotic regularity; at the end of the ode, they sink
into their own depths—the collective "we" is used both by Prufrock and
Tennyson's Greeks—and the lines become regular tercets.

The regularity in "Choric Song" begins with section VII. The rhyme-
scheme of VII is *aabaabcdcd'dd*. The regularities of the first six lines—
aabaab—moves into *cd* and then in the tercet pattern that (except for the
opening couplet of VIII) will persist for the remaining nine tercets of section
VIII. The rhythm of the "Choric Song," generally irregular, settles down in
the last few tercets into regularity; the last sixteen lines have 13, 14, or 15
syllables. The same weariness that had expressed itself in the beginning in
irregular melismata begins to crystallize into hypnosis and chant:

Choric Song.

I.

There is sweet music here that softer falls
Than petals from blown roses on the grass,
Or night-dews on still waters between walls
Of shadowy granite, in a gleaming pass;
Music that gentlier on the spirit lies,
Than tir'd eyelids upon tir'd eyes;
Music that brings sweet sleep down from the blissful skies.
Here are cool mosses deep,
And thro' the moss the ivies creep,
And in the stream the long-leaved flowers weep,
And from the craggy ledge the poppy hangs in sleep.

II.

Why are we weigh'd upon with heaviness,
And utterly consumed with sharp distress,
While all things else have rest from weariness?
All things have rest: why should we toil alone,
We only toil, who are the first of things,
And make perpetual moan,
Still from one sorrow to another thrown:
Nor ever fold our wings,
And cease from wanderings,
Nor steep our brows in slumber's holy balm;
Nor harken what the inner spirit sings,
'There is no joy but calm!'
Why should we only toil, the roof and crown of things?

III.

Lo! in the middle of the wood,
The folded leaf is woo'd from out the bud
With winds upon the branch, and there
Grows green and broad, and takes no care,

Sun-steep'd at noon, and in the moon
Nightly dew-fed; and turning yellow
Falls, and floats adown the air.
Lo! sweeten'd with the summer light,
The full-juiced apple, waxing over-mellow,
Drops in a silent autumn night.
All its allotted length of days,
The flower ripens in its place,
Ripens and fades, and falls, and hath no toil,
Fast-rooted in the fruitful soil.

IV.

Hateful is the dark-blue sky,
Vaulted o'er the dark-blue sea.
Death is the end of life; ah, why
Should life all labour be?
Let us alone. Time driveth onward fast,
And in a little while our lips are dumb.
Let us alone. What is it that will last?
All things are taken from us, and become
Portions and parcels of the dreadful Past.
Let us alone. What pleasure can we have
To war with evil? Is there any peace
In ever climbing up the climbing wave?
All things have rest, and ripen toward the grave
In silence; ripen, fall, and cease:
Give us long rest or death, dark death, or dreamful ease.

V.

How sweet it were, hearing the downward stream,
With half-shut eyes ever to seem
Falling asleep in a half-dream!
To dream and dream, like yonder amber light,
Which will not leave the myrrh-bush on the height;
To hear each other's whisper'd speech;
Eating the Lotos day by day,
To watch the crisping ripples on the beach,
And tender curving lines of creamy spray;
To lend our hearts and spirits wholly
To the influence of mild-minded melancholy;
To muse and brood and live again in memory,
With those old faces of our infancy
Heap'd over with a mound of grass,
Two handfuls of white dust, shut in an urn of brass!

VI.

Dear is the memory of our wedded lives,
And dear the last embraces of our wives
And their warm tears: but all hath suffer'd change:
For surely now our household hearths are cold:
Our sons inherit us: our looks are strange:

And we should come like ghosts to trouble joy.
Or else the island princes over-bold
Have eat our substance, and the minstrel sings
Before them of the ten years' war in Troy,
And our great deeds, as half-forgotten things.
Is there confusion in the little isle?
Let what is broken so remain.
The Gods are hard to reconcile:
'Tis hard to settle order once again.
There *is* confusion worse than death,
Trouble on trouble, pain on pain,
Long labor unto aged breath,
Sore tasks to hearts worn out by many wars
And eyes grown dim with gazing on the pilot-stars.

VII.

But, propt on beds of amaranth and moly,
How sweet (while warm airs lull us, blowing lowly)
With half-dropt eyelid still,
Beneath a heaven dark and holy,
To watch the long bright river drawing slowly
His waters from the purple hill—
To hear the dewy echoes calling
From cave to cave thro' the thick-twined vine—
To watch the emerald-colour'd water falling
Thro' many a wov'n acanthus-wreath divine!
Only to hear and see the far-off sparkling brine,
Only to hear were sweet, stretch'd out beneath the pine.

VIII.

The Lotos blooms below the barren peak:
The Lotos blows by every winding creek:
All day the wind breathes low with mellower tone:
Thro' every hollow cave and alley lone
Round and round the spicy downs the yellow Lotos-dust is blown.
We have had enough of action, and of motion we,
Roll'd to starboard, roll'd to larboard, when the surge was seething free,
Where the wallowing monster spouted his foam-fountains in the sea.
Let us swear an oath, and keep it with an equal mind,
In the hollow Lotos-land to live and lie reclin'd
On the hills like Gods together, careless of mankind.
For they lie beside their nectar, and the bolts are hurl'd
Far below them in the valleys, and the clouds are lightly curl'd
Round their golden houses, girdled with the gleaming world:
Where they smile in secret, looking over wasted lands,
Blight and famine, plague and earthquake, roaring deeps and fiery sands,
Clanging fights, and flaming towns, and sinking ships, and praying hands.
But they smile, they find a music centred in a doleful song
Steaming up, a lamentation and an ancient tale of wrong,
Like a tale of little meaning tho' the words are strong;
Chanted from an ill-used race of men that cleave the soil,

Sow the seed, and reap the harvest with enduring toil,
Storing yearly little dues of wheat, and wine and oil;
Till they perish and they suffer—some, 't is whisper'd—down in hell
Suffer endless anguish, others in Elysian valleys dwell,
Resting weary limbs at last on beds of asphodel.
Surely, surely, slumber is more sweet than toil, the shore
Than labour in the deep mid-ocean, wind and wave and oar;
Oh, rest ye, brother mariners, we will not wander more.[2]

Rhyme Scheme: (1) ababcccdddd
(2) aa′a″bcbbcc′dcdc
(3) aa′bbcdbedeff′gg
(4) ababcdcdcefe′e′ff′
(5) aaabbcdcdee′e″e‴′ff
(6) aabcbdcedefgfghghii′
(7) aabaabcdcd′dd
(8) aabbbcccdddeeefffggghhhiiijjj

Eliot, therefore, had examples in English poetry to draw upon for the appearance of regularity in the middle of irregularity, or at the end of it. In "Prufrock" he gestures to the tradition with the tercet in lines 122–24, rhyming *peach/beach/each*. Then, his debt paid to Dryden, Tennyson, and Arnold, Eliot produces the sad, flat statement, "I do not think that they will sing to me," and ends regularly, with *waves/back/black,* and *sea/brown/drown.*

This sort of analysis can explain the true uses of meter. Any poet who simply uses metered or unmetered verse mechanically, arbitrarily, without thought, is *only* a conventional poet. All major poets see the implications of the forms they use. Eliot found ways to express both the surface of human confusions and the depths of damnation or salvation. Eliot's duple persona—the mind that suffers and the mind that creates—moves in a purgatorial rhythm to and from crystalline forms.

NOTES

1. T. S. Eliot, "Little Gidding," in *The Complete Poems and Plays of T. S. Eliot* (London: Faber and Faber, 1969), 2.93. All subsequent quotations from Eliot's work are taken from this edition.
2. Alfred Lord Tennyson, from "Lotos-Eaters," *Poems,* vol. 1, annotated by Alfred Lord Tennyson, ed. Hallam, Lord Tennyson (London: Macmillan, 1907; reprint, Westport, Conn.: Greenwood Press, 1970).

14

Yoknapatawpha's Indians: A Novel Faulkner Never Wrote

WALTER TAYLOR

Faulkner once called James Joyce "a case of a genius who was electrocuted by the divine fire."[1] He could scarcely have found a happier phrase for the experience he himself underwent during the period when his Yoknapatawpha tales began to materialize in his imagination. Yoknapatawpha, David Minter has asserted, was a "staggering" revelation for Faulkner. "Characters, families, and communities began to proliferate, scenes and actions to multiply with such rapidity that his imagination began leaping from one possibility to the next in frenetic discovery."[2] The language Faulkner used to describe that experience is now familiar. "I discovered that my own little postage stamp of native soil was worth writing about," he said. It had enabled him to create "a cosmos of my own" which was "a kind of keystone in the Universe." There remained only his lifelong struggle to commit his cosmos to paper, for he knew "that I would never live long enough to exhaust it."[3] The experience Faulkner here describes apparently took place during the winter of 1926–27,[4] and is often believed to have focused mainly on his Snopes and Sartoris families. It may well have been merely the most memorable of a series of such experiences, and almost certainly included other characters. "There is startling evidence in Faulkner's early work," Thomas L. McHaney writes, "that most of his characters and thematic preoccupations existed in his mind almost from the beginning of his writing career."[5] At all events, it is clear that by early 1927 a vast but incomplete network of myth about Yoknapatawpha was present in Faulkner's mind, of which the works eventually committed to print represent a relatively small portion.[6]

The existence of this body of private myth controlled Faulkner's methods of composition for the remainder of his career. I do not mean, of course, that Faulkner never conceived the plot of a story or novel at a date later than 1927, that he did not alter this basic structure of myth as he came to understand it better, or that he was never again electrocuted by the divine fire. What I wish to emphasize is the importance of this early experience for Faulkner's later methods of composition. From 1927 on, his most characteristic approach to his work was to be the fleshing out of tales from this body of private myth into individual stories, followed by the gradual reworking of these stories into longer, often episodic, narratives.

Faulkner's career is replete with evidence of this process. An obvious illustration is the history of his Snopes tales. First conceived in 1926, these tales were not brought together as a novel until 1940, with *The Hamlet;* and his Snopes trilogy was not completed until 1959 with *The Mansion*. Few areas of Faulkner's work, however, reflect the process more clearly than his tales of the Yoknapatawpha Indians. There are enough connections between these efforts to suggest that no later than the fall of 1928—the point at which Joseph Blotner places the composition of "A Justice"[7]—Faulkner was drawing on a body of private myth about his Indians, generally complete in his mind, from which a larger work of fiction was taking shape. These tales constitute, in fact, the most closely connected body of Faulkner's work never to have been drawn together into a novel. And because they do, they reveal as do few other areas of his work, the processes by means of which Faulkner moved from his original body of myth toward the creation of individual works about Yoknapatawpha.

Faulkner's Indian tales divide themselves into two segments, roughly according to their distance in date of publication from his original breeding period of Yoknapatawpha myth. The first is a series of five stories that focus on the Indians themselves rather than, as in later stories, on the influence of Indians on white culture: "Red Leaves" (1930), "A Justice" (1931), "Mountain Victory" (1932), "A Courtship" (1948) and "Lo!" (1950). Largely unromanticized (the exception is "A Courtship"), ironic in tone, these stories reveal the Indians' struggle with the impact of European culture up to 1865. The second group reveals a revision of both the original body of myth and its manifestations in the early stories in behalf of Faulkner's developing concern with the significance of Indian culture for whites; it includes material eventually brought together in *Go Down, Moses* (1942), Faulkner's "Appendix: The Compsons" (1946),[8] *Requiem for a Nun* (1951), "Mississippi" (1954), and *The Big Woods* (1955). These later works, often romantic and nostalgic in tone, reveal Faulkner's changing attitudes toward his original body of myth— a point that I shall briefly address later. But it is the earlier group of stories which, because they suggest Faulkner's intention of evolving a novel about his Indians, are most revealing about his methods of composition.

The most obvious problem in approaching these stories is that the time of conception of each of the five is uncertain. Existing manuscripts offer little help, as prior versions probably existed. The first datable record of any of the stories is 24 July 1930 when Faulkner notes having submitted "Red Leaves" to the *Saturday Evening Post*. "Mountain Victory" and "A Justice" may well have been either complete or in advanced stages by that time, as he records having sent the former to the *Post* in September or early October of that year and the latter on 29 November. If "A Justice" was begun, as Blotner argues, in 1927, the other two may have existed in some form for at least as long. Nor is it impossible that the seed ideas for "Lo!" (apparently written during the summer of 1933 and submitted for publication no later than July 1933) or even "A Courtship" (submitted, apparently for the first time, in June 1942) may also date from that period.[9]

The five stories concern two groups of Indians, each sometimes called Chickasaws, sometimes Choctaws. One group, characterized in "A Justice," "Red Leaves," and "A Courtship," is governed by chieftains known as Issetibbeha, Moketubbe, and Ikkemotubbe or "Doom." Another, characterized in "Mountain Victory" and "Lo!," is governed by a family named Weddel. Each is supplied with a rough connection to Mississippi's historical Indians. In "A Courtship" Issetibbeha's tribe contains a woman who is "the second cousin by marriage to the grand-niece of the wife of old David Colbert."[10] A historical Colbert family existed among the Chickasaws.[11] The Weddel family, who claim a French ancestor, recall the historical Greenwood LeFlore and his family; LeFlore, like Faulkner's Francis Weddel, made a trip to Washington to visit the President of the United States.

As is generally the case with myth (and with Faulkner's other Yoknapatawpha tales), disparities exist both between and within the stories. Genealogies, time schemes, even the facts of history, are ignored with cavalier disdain. "I never made a genealogical or chronological chart," Faulkner said of his Yoknapatawpha tales to Malcolm Cowley, suggesting that "perhaps" this was "because I knew I would take liberties with both—which I have."[12] Lewis M. Dabney, in his fine study *The Indians of Yoknapatawpha,* has argued that "there are practical reasons for this." Faulkner's "material comes from the period . . . just before 1800, and the removal of the Indians in the 1830s," he points out, and thus "one generation's experience is expanded into two or three generations, to do justice to its varied possibilities."[13] McHaney is perhaps closer to the mark in defending these inconsistencies on the grounds that Faulkner was merely refusing to allow "his artistry or his imagination" to be "slave to the actual details of any one place." To Faulkner, "discrepancies were not inconsistencies . . . since he was not writing a uniform regional geography or saga. He changed everything—biography, history, geography, his invented characters themselves—to blend into the effects [in a given work] he wanted to create."[14] What is most significant in all this, however, is that while hardly the stuff of fiction, such discrepancies are no more than what is normally expected of raw myth, and suggest the essentially mythical quality of Faulkner's imagination.

More important than Faulkner's discrepancies are the number of points on which he remains consistent from story to story. It is here that the original myth reveals itself most clearly. The most obvious of these are the establishment and history of his two ruling families of Indians. The most complete is the story of Ikkemotubbe's visit to New Orleans, retold in nearly the same form in "A Justice," "Red Leaves," and "A Courtship." All three stories recount how Ikkemotubbe visits New Orleans, acquires the name of Doom, remains seven years, and returns to acquire the title of Man, or chieftain. Probably also part of the original myth are three adjuncts of this tale: the story of his friendship with a Frenchman with the unlikely name of the Chevalier Soeur Blonde de Vitry (recounted in "Red Leaves" and "A Courtship"), the story of the transportation of an abandoned steamboat overland to serve as Doom's house (recounted in "A Justice" and "Red Leaves"), and the story of the slaves brought home by Doom (recounted in "A Justice" and "A Courtship"). It is suggestive that the story of Doom's New Orleans trip and subsequent establishment of himself as "the Man" is not only more complex than any of the plots of the stories in which it appears, it is also more nearly at the heart of the Indians' history; its recurrence in all three stories argues strongly that Faulkner had imagined another, lengthier version.[15]

Each of the stories about the Weddel family also contains fragments of a larger, more complex tale of the founding and history of their family. Its details are only hinted in "Lo!" as the President spots "the face of a Gascon brigand" (389) behind Francis Weddel's Indian features, and as the Secretary tells the President of "that French father of his from New Orleans" who "saw to" the correctness of the Indians' title to their land. But the Weddels' story is revealed in enough detail in "Mountain Victory" to suggest the larger version that existed in Faulkner's mind. Here Saucier Weddel, Francis's son, presents in capsule form the tale that was apparently fleshed out later as "Lo!": "My father drove to Washington once in his carriage to remonstrate with President Jackson about the Government's treatment of his people, sending on ahead a wagon of provender and gifts and also fresh horses for the carriage . . ." (759). Implicit in the fact that Faulkner drew on this material for "Lo!" is the probability that he meant to do a similar thing with the rest of Saucier's tales about his family, which taken together sound remarkably like the plot of a novel. His father "was a Choctaw chief named Francis Weddel," Saucier relates. "He was the son of a Choctaw woman and a French emigré of New Orleans, a general of Napoleon's and a knight of the Legion of Honor. His name was François Vidal" (759). His father met Saucier's mother during the Washington visit. Both are dead, the father serving the United States in the Mexican war, the mother of pneumonia contracted while hiding the family silver from Federal troops. Saucier himself has fought through the war in Virginia. Unmarried, he is the last of the Weddel line. Again, as with the story of Ikkemotubbe, the detail supplied about the Weddels, not wholly necessary for the plot, implies another, more complex story than the one in which it appears.

Fully as suggestive are the ways in which the tales of these two families resemble each other. Each is an account of how the Eden of the Indians is converted to a plantation economy founded on slavery. In each this change is brought about by an ancestor based in New Orleans. And in each the change is paralleled by an influx of alien blood into the veins of the Indians: in the case of Ikkemotubbe and his tribe, the influx of African blood (in "A Justice" and "Red Leaves") and European blood (in "Red Leaves"); in the case of the Weddels, the French blood of Vidal. There are other, more direct connections. In "A Courtship" Faulkner could have been thinking of Greenwood LeFlore's—or Francis Weddel's—trip to Washington as his Indian narrator describes a parley between Issetibbeha and "General Jackson" establishing the boundary of the Indians' territory: "Issetibbeha and General Jackson met and burned sticks and signed a paper, and now a line ran through the woods. . . . It . . . [had] the Plantation on one side of it, where Issetibbeha was the Man, and America on the other side, where General Jackson was the Man" (361). But the most obvious link between the two stories is the similarity of the French emigrés who are instrumental in Europeanizing the two clans of Indians. The names Vitry and Vidal are similar enough to have been connected in Faulkner's mind (one remembers the Suratt of *Sartoris* becoming Ratliff in the Snopes tales). More significantly, the two figures are cut from the same cloth. Saucier Weddel's reminiscences supply a romanticized version of his grandfather,[16] painting Vidal as a man of substance, "a general of Napoleon's and a knight of the Legion of Honor." But the President is closer to the mark in "Lo!" when he spots "the face of a Gascon brigand" behind the Indian features of Saucier's father. The clue needed to form this conclusion is to be found in Faulkner's "Appendix: The Compsons," where he writes that Ikkemotubbe's friend Vitry, "had he not been born too late, could have been among the brightest in that glittering galaxy of blackguards who were Napoleon's marshalls" (704). The statement not only affirms the accuracy of the President's vision of a "Gascon brigand" but also emphasizes the connection of Vitry and Vidal in Faulkner's mind.

The conclusion raises a corollary issue. If the two Indian sequences are in some respects reworkings of the same material, which sequence was imagined first? Dates of submission—the only information available implying dates of conception of the stories—serve more to obscure this issue than to resolve it. Since "Red Leaves," "Mountain Victory," and "A Justice" were submitted for publication within a little over four months of each other—24 July to 29 November 1930—it is possible that all three stories may have existed in manuscript before any of the three was submitted. And since the composition dates of the other two stories are also unknown, it is at least possible that all five may have been begun in 1930 or earlier. A clue, perhaps, may be found in the fact that the Weddels—particularly Saucier Weddel—with their paternalistic sensibility and pride in their ancestors, resemble in many ways the Sartoris family of *Flags in the Dust*, while Ikkemotubbe, with his gross drive toward power and his commitment of his family to intermixture with African blood, resembles such later white patriarchs as Thomas

Sutpen and Carothers McCaslin. Such parallels suggest that Faulkner's original framework of myth may have been structured around the legends of the historical Greenwood LeFlore, a patriotic and responsible paternalist whose image somewhat resembles that of the Sartorises; but that Faulkner's developing interest in the consequences of slavery and racial mixture led him to switch to a figure, Ikkemotubbe, who like Sutpen and McCaslin incurs a curse because of his exploitation of land and people and thus brings about the degeneration of his line. It is equally arguable, however, that whichever of Faulkner's families was conceived first, he was evolving a work with parallel plots, each involving a family of Indians.

What, then, would have been the contours of the novel Faulkner was evolving? Assuming that this work was to feature parallel plots, it is possible to visualize its contours. It was, clearly, a panoramic work whose themes resembled those of *Flags in the Dust* and anticipated those of *The Unvanquished, Absalom, Absalom!* and *Go Down, Moses*. One plot would have traced the rise of the Weddels from their obscure beginnings as the spawn of the "Gascon brigand" Vidal through their acquisition of land and paternalistic sophistication to their eventual destruction in America's wars. It might have fleshed out such tales as Vidal's liaison with the "Choctaw woman"; Francis Weddel's successes in Europeanizing his clan, his trip to Washington, his wooing there of Saucier's mother, his death serving the United States in Mexico; Saucier's French education, his military service for the Confederacy and the loss of his arm in battle, his mother's death from pneumonia, and the death of Saucier on his way home from Virginia while protecting his black groom.

The novel's other plot would have traced the despoiling of the Indians' Eden through the story of Ikkemotubbe's family and a curse they have evoked because of slavery. It might have included the Edenic fellowship between Indian and European described in "A Courtship," Doom's seven-year visit to New Orleans, his encounter with Vitry and notoriety as a gambler, his liaison with the West Indian woman who was to become his wife, his retreat to the Indian settlement to avoid her vengeful brother, his acquisition of the title of Man, the arrival of the pregnant West Indian woman and the birth of their son, Issetibbeha, the transportation of the steamboat overland to serve as Ikkemotubbe's house, the assumption of the role of Man by Issetibbeha upon his father's death, the prosperity of the plantation as a result of Issetibbeha's success at breeding and selling slaves, his trip to Paris, his acquisition of a slave wife, and his murder at the hands of his degenerate son, Moketubbe. This is, of course, a body of material vast enough to be unmanageable even for a Faulkner. Uniting the two plots, however, is the common theme that Europeanization, with its adjunct, the treatment of land and human beings as property, has led both families first to their aggrandizement, then to their downfall.

Why, then, did Faulkner's Indian novel end as another of those pieces stored in what he called his "lumber room," his repository of unused portions of Yoknapatawpha myth, never to be removed and carpentered into a finished product? Writers often become indifferent to unfinished works, but Faulkner's interest in his Indians, as revealed through his incorporation of Ikkemotubbe and others into works like *Go Down, Moses,* remained constant at least until the publication of *The Big Woods* in 1955. One problem may have been financial: Faulkner had little luck marketing his Indian stories. More important, however, would appear to be the fact that Faulkner was struggling in these stories with problems that he had difficulty resolving in other works. There was the obvious problem of which Indian family—the Weddels, with their Sartoris-like image, or Ikkemotubbe's line, with their Sutpen-McCaslin type of image—to focus on. This divided attitude paralleled the divided attitude he brought to his Sartorises, Sutpens, and McCaslins, and centered on the question of racial mixture. The Sartorises of *Flags in the Dust* and *The Unvanquished,* a model paternalistic family, never commit their blood to the blood of slaves;[17] the Sutpens and McCaslins incur a curse by doing so. Four of the five Indian stories deal directly with the consequences of racial mixture, and the fifth, "A Courtship," deals with it by implication in the wooing of an Indian girl by a white steamboat pilot. The Weddels, like the Sartorises, do not mix with their slaves but represent a mix of European and Indian; they have lost the title of Man "to the branch which refused to become polluted" (759). Implicit in the situation is the question as to whether their mixture of European blood has resulted in their rise, and in the sophistication of Saucier Weddel. The Ikkemotubbe tales suggest other issues. Has mixed blood brought about the gentleness and inner strength of the Sam Fathers of "A Justice"? Is it responsible for the degeneracy of Moketubbe in "Red Leaves"?

Although Faulkner never openly endorsed such racist notions, he never fully reconciled his ambivalence toward them,[18] and his inability to commit himself to one or the other of his Indian families foreshadows his struggle with these problems in his later works. To have undertaken a resolution of these in his Indian novel would have elevated it to an important place in his canon. He chose instead to approach them in *Absalom, Absalom!* and *Go Down, Moses,* and in doing so, he preempted the themes that had moved him most deeply in the Indian stories. And by the time the latter novel was published in 1942, Faulkner was entering a different phase of his career. He had defined at length in these works the curse of slavery that ravaged his plantation families; now he was involved in the search for heroes who could transcend it. Which is to say that, in *Absalom, Absalom!* and *Go Down, Moses,* Faulkner had already written the most significant portions of the stories of Ikkemotubbe and the Weddels. To Faulkner in 1942, it must have seemed that there was no longer any point in completing his novel of Indian life.

NOTES

1. William Faulkner, *Faulkner in the University,* ed. Frederick L. Gwynn and Joseph Blotner (Charlottesville: University of Virginia Press, 1959), p. 53.

2. David Minter, *William Faulkner: His Life and Work* (Baltimore: Johns Hopkins University Press, 1980), p. 80.

3. William Faulkner, *Lion in the Garden: Interviews with William Faulkner,* ed. James B. Meriwether and Michael Millgate (New York: Random House, 1968), p. 254.

4. See Joseph Blotner, *Faulkner: A Biography,* 2 vols. (New York: Random House, 1974), 1:527–34.

5. Thomas L. McHaney, "The Elmer Papers: Faulkner's Comic Portrait of the Artist," *Mississippi Quarterly* 26 (Summer 1973): 284 n.8.

6. Minter writes in *William Faulkner* that "since each of its parts implied all the rest . . . [Yoknapatawpha] always included characters and adventures he had not recorded, corners he had not fully explored. If on one side it constituted a world of which he was the only adequate master, on the other it contained multitudes even he could not exhaust" (p. 81).

7. Blotner, *Biography,* Notes 82.

8. William Faulkner, "Appendix: The Compsons" (1946), in *The Portable Faulkner,* rev. ed., ed. Malcolm Cowley (New York: Viking, 1967).

9. See Blotner, 1974, pp. 566, 676, 679, 683, 691, Notes 82 (for "A Justice"); pp. 663–64, 679, Notes 95 (for "Red Leaves"); pp. 669, 679, 688, 808, Notes 98 (for "Mountain Victory"); pp. 808, 854, Notes 115 (for "Lo!"); and pp. 1101, 1253 (for "A Courtship"). See also James B. Meriwether, "The Short Fiction of William Faulkner: A Bibliography," in *PROOF: The Yearbook of American Bibliographical and Textual Studies,* ed. Joseph Kaleg (Columbia: University of South Carolina Press, 1971), 1:293–329; Hans Skei, *William Faulkner: The Short Story Career* (Oslo: Universitetsforlaget, 1981); Skei, *William Faulkner: The Novelist as Short Story Writer* (Oslo: Universitetsforlaget, 1985); James B. Carothers, *William Faulkner's Short Stories* (Ann Arbor: UMI Research Press, 1985).

10. William Faulkner, "A Courtship" (1948), in *Collected Stories* (New York: Random House, 1950), pp. 361–80. All subsequent quotations from "A Courtship," " A Justice" (1931), "Lo!" (1950), "Mountain Victory" (1932), and "Red Leaves" (1930) are taken from this edition, hereafter cited parenthetically in the text.

11. Lewis M. Dabney, *The Indians of Yoknapatawpha* (Baton Rouge: Louisiana State University Press, 1974), p. 37.

12. William Faulkner, *The Faulkner-Cowley File: Letters and Memories, 1944–1962,* ed. Malcolm Cowley (New York: Viking, 1966), p. 55.

13. Dabney, *Indians,* p. 14.

14. Thomas L. McHaney, "The Faulkners and the Origins of Yoknapatawpha County: Some Corrections," *Mississippi Quarterly* 25 (Summer 1972): 264.

15. Faulkner retold the story of Doom's New Orleans trip once more in *Big Woods* (1955), pp. 115–16, altering the material to reconcile it with his later works about Indians.

16. Of the discrepancies between the accounts of the Washington trip in "Lo!" and "Mountain Victory," Blotner writes that they "could . . . be attributed to the differences between the truth and the version of it the son would give years after his famous father's death" (*Biography,* Notes, 115).

17. In "There Was a Queen" Faulkner provides a different version.

18. I have argued this point at length in *Faulkner's Search for a South* (Urbana: University of Illinois Press, 1983).

15

Original Sin in "The Last Good Country": or, The Return of Catherine Barkley

MARK SPILKA

We get to know Nick better here than we have ever done before. And the "Hemingway heroine" is never more real than in her youngest appearance as his kid sister. Right down to the short hair, Littless is the wonderful if slightly unreal child that grew up to be Catherine Barkley and all the others.

—Philip Young

I

On 17 January 1952 Ernest Hemingway roughed out a telegram he meant to send to an editor at Rinehart and Company about Philip Young's critical study of his work. Apologizing for his delay in answering a letter from Young, he said that he had been working hard on his own writing, that he was thinking over Young's letter as Young had taken time to think over his, and added that he would be writing soon. On the same sheet with the telegram, but at the top of the page, there appears the first paragraph of a story he would develop further a few months later:

> I was watching the bottom of the spring where the sand rose in little spurts with the bubbling water. There was a tin cup on a forked stick that was stuck in the gravel by the spring and I looked at it and at the water rising and then flowing clear in the gravel bed beside the road. The road was hot and sandy and from where we sat under the cedars you could watch it both ways. One way went up the hill and the other went down to the dock. Behind us was a cedar swamp.

The story, recast in the third person, would eventually become the long unfinished fragment now entitled "The Last Good Country."[1] Written over a six-year period, from 1952 to 1958, it was the last Nick Adams tale he would try to compose, and seems in many ways the most tender and most person-

210

ally revealing story in that sequence. Its initial placement with the Young telegram may help to explain its genesis.

Hemingway had been disturbed for some time by mysterious reports from Rinehart's first reader, Malcolm Cowley, about the psychoanalytic nature of Young's approach. He had written Cowley that same day complaining about such treatment, imagining the several ills which might be attributed to him— barratry, cowardice, homosexuality, impotence, incest, leprosy, misappropriation of funds, miscegenation, mopery, sedition, untruthfulness—and offering to write a foreword to the book which would make such charges look silly. Later, as he learned more about the manuscript, he would focus his objections on Young's thesis that a traumatic war wound governed his life and work, and upon a notion shared with Cowley and others that his women characters were dream-girls, fantasy creations, without much credibility. But more immediately it was the invasion of his privacy that troubled him.

He had been horrified by the accounts of his life that friendly observers like Cowley and Lillian Ross had recently published; but since he knew and respected these writers, he could indulge their "misunderstandings" with some patience. Academic critics like Young were another matter. They invaded his life without permission, accused him of mental disorders, appropriated and distorted his past, and—most aggravating of all—pretended to know more about it than he did. He was corresponding in a cordial way with one such scholar, Charles Fenton, a fellow war-veteran who wanted to write about Hemingway's apprenticeship in journalism; but when Fenton tried to investigate his years at Oak Park High School, he turned against him and, as with Young, tried to prevent him from publishing his book. Arthur Mizener's life of Scott Fitzgerald seemed to him to epitomize such academic scavenging. When Mizener replied to his letter of protest, "We'll get you in the end," he repeated the statement in letter after letter to his friends. His epithets for such biographical critics—undertakers, bone-pickers, grave-robbers, carrion crow—indicated his justifiable fear of being taken by them as already dead and buried. That morbid fear—and his inability to "think in their heads" as he had thought his way into the heads of the Germans in World War II—made him mean and choleric and inevitably disturbed his writing.

It was the appropriation of his past, however, that finally proved most troubling. If all his fictions were inventions, they were also firmly grounded in past experience. He looked on the past accordingly as stored material for his own imaginative reconstruction. Now that private stockpile was being plundered, and he was unsure how to preserve it for himself. One boyhood incident—the blue heron episode at the tip of Walloon Lake—seemed especially worth salvaging. On 23 September 1951 he had written to the one academic critic he trusted, Carlos Baker, "that two game wardens had once chased him all over Michigan and that he was lucky not to have been sent to reform school."[2] Actually no one had pursued him farther than his doorstep, and reform school was never in question. About a week after his sixteenth birthday (21 July 1915), he had gone boating with his eleven-year-old sister Sunny along the shoreline between Emmett and Charlevoix counties on Walloon Lake, and, in the marshy region at the western tip of the lake, had impulsively shot a blue heron in unwitting violation of the game laws. The son of the game warden from his home county (Emmett) had discovered the bird in their boat when they went ashore to eat a picnic lunch, and had promptly impounded it. When Ernest told him on their return that a man had given it to him, the boy reported the incident to his father; but shortly after, when two game wardens from the relevant counties came looking for Ernest at the Hemingway cottage, Mrs. Hemingway dressed the men down, ordered them off her property at shotgun point, and sent word to Ernest to stay with friends "until further notice." Ernest then fled to the Dilworths' home at Horton Bay, and from there retreated to his Uncle George's summer place at Ironton. A week or so later, acting on his uncle's spoken (and perhaps his father's written) advice, he pleaded guilty before a judge in Boyne City, paid a small fine, and returned home in time for the haying.[3]

As Baker observes, it was a minor scrape that Hemingway "afterwards remembered, and characteristically exaggerated, as the worst of his boyhood. . . . He had tangled with the law. He had been a bad boy. All the rest of his life he regarded game wardens with the utmost suspicion" (B, 31–33). Apparently he looked on academic critics like Young, Fenton, and Mizener with the same suspicion; they were the literary game wardens who threatened to retrace his tracks, impound his illicit trophies, and commit him to that great reform school in the sky. He would tell his own version of the story before they caught him, and tell it well enough—imaginatively but truly—to let posterity judge his boyhood crimes.

Such motives may explain what Baker calls the "puerile" nature of the story. The two game wardens who pursue Nick Adams and encamp in his summer home, hoping to starve him out, are drunken louts who fall asleep while Nick and his sister steal provisions from the cottage pantry and the woodshed outside. Next day the baffled wardens are unable to think out Nick's intentions, and when they question his friends the Packards at their country store, Mr. Packard easily provokes the more dangerous warden from "down state" into a defensive posture, accuses him of a frame-up in a Western town from which they have both long since returned to Michigan, and threatens to expose him if he uses his gun against Nick Adams. Fortunately this Western melodrama ends where it begins. The game wardens are too old and inept to trail the fugitives, and though the local warden's son might do the trailing, that part of the plot never materializes. Hemingway himself must have faltered at the prospect of writing a mere boy's adventure tale; but perhaps he also faltered before the far more difficult task of defining childhood affections.

That spring he had just finished his prize-winning fable, *The Old Man and the Sea,* which he had considered calling *The Dignity of Man.* In its lyric reaches the story had expressed his own tender regard for the sea and its creatures, for the old man who went out too far to bring in his finest catch, and for the young boy on shore who believed in him. His creative mood was by and large beneficent, and his wife Mary had insured its continuity by turning him away from the usual deathly denouement to the old man's final dream of lions.[4] He was on his good behavior that year, trying to avoid rancorous quarrels like those with Young, Fenton, and Mizener, pulling away from them with some success into the creative possibilities of his fiction: and among those possibilities was the secret source of his tender regard for wives like Hadley and Mary, "daughters" like Adriana Ivancich, and fictional heroines like Catherine Barkley, Maria, and Renata, whose credibility is sometimes confused by critics with the dream-like situations which underlie—and in that sense undermine—their realistic portraits.

In "The Last Good Country" the controlling dreamlike fantasy beneath the surface realism is too obvious to undermine the heroine's credibility; but what it expresses—or enables Hemingway to express—is not so obvious. On 24 April 1952 Hemingway had written to Adriana Ivancich, the daughterly model for Renata in *Across the River and Into the Trees,* that he had begun a story "about Michigan long ago" that was inwardly complex but outwardly "very simple" (*B,* 634). Among its inward complexities was a curious notion of original sin. The notion is first broached by Mr. Packard in a flashback conversation with Nick Adams:

> Mr. John liked Nick Adams because he said he had original sin. Nick did not understand this but he was proud.
> "You're going to have things to repent, boy," Mr. John had told Nick. "That's one of the best things there is. You can always decide whether to repent them or not. But the thing is to have them."
> "I don't want to do anything bad," Nick had said.
> "I don't want you to," Mr. John had said. "But you're alive and you're going to do things. Don't you lie and don't you steal. Everybody has to lie. But you pick out somebody you never lie to."
> "I'll pick out you." (*NA,* 84)

Mr. Packard returns the compliment, gives Nick some explicit sexual advice (see Appendix C) which Scribners' fastidious editors have excised from the printed text, but which helps nonetheless to establish Packard as a more useful sexual authority than Nick's father (who in "Fathers and Sons" dismisses all such matters as "heinous crimes" [*NA,* 236–37]), then questions Nick closely about a girlfriend he has lost. Nick says he feels bad about losing her, but proves an apt pupil when he admits that "None of it was her fault. She's just built that way. If I ran into her again I guess I'd get mixed up with her again." Whether the lost girlfriend is Trudy, the Indian girl mentioned earlier in the story, or a girl like Marjorie, with whom Nick hopes to get "mixed up" again in "Three Day Blow" (*NA*, 195–96), is unclear.[5] But the connection between original sin, lost girlfriends, and repentable things worth doing has been firmly made.

On 22 April 1953, about a year after he began to develop "The Last Good Country," Hemingway wrote to Bernard Berenson about his long-dead paternal grandmother, Adelaide Edmonds Hemingway, an Oberlin graduate who sprang from Western pioneer stock and taught botany and astronomy to all her children and grandchildren. In the letter he describes her as a lovely and beautiful woman who wrote excuses for him for school whenever he wanted to box instead, and who told him that the only things she regretted in life were those she had not done. The truthfulness between them, her willingness to cover his truant behavior, and her life-prescription as to doing rather than regretting, are very much the substance of Mr. Packard's relations with and prescriptions for Nick Adams.

Packard's Western experience may also owe something to Hemingway's family heritage. Though his prototype, Jim Dilworth, was a blacksmith, and though the Dilworths were old settlers at Horton Bay, Hemingway's biographers say nothing about their Western background. Hemingway's forebears on both sides had lived in the West, however, as guides and early settlers; and his indulgent paternal grandfather, who gave him his first gun when he was ten, had often told him stories about coming West to Chicago in a covered wagon. Hemingway's special fondness for Anson and Adelaide Hemingway, his implicit preference for them over his own parents, may explain his similar preference for the indulgent Dilworths and their backwoods ethos. Mrs. Dilworth was Aunty Beth to the Hemingway children, as Mrs. Packard in "The Last Good Country" is Aunt Halley. A handsome homespun woman, one who runs a hotel, smells wonderfully of the kitchen on baking day, and still prides herself on being "all the woman" her husband can handle, Mrs. Packard even loves culture in an earthy way, as her husband loves good whiskey; and the cheerful badinage between them must have seemed to Hemingway a happier blend of culture with frontier earthiness than his strict, sober, and essentially suburban parents could offer. Significantly, when Hemingway and his first wife Hadley stayed at a pension in the mountains near Montreux in 1922, the place and the German Swiss family who ran it reminded him of the Dilworths at Horton Bay, and he especially prized the "ideal blend of wilderness and civilization" they afforded; and two years later, while traveling in the Spanish Pyrenees, he liked the Spanish people so much that he called them "good guys" like Jim Dilworth of Horton Bay (*B*, 112, 169). As Mrs. Packard observes while accepting Nick's illegal rainbow trout as dinner fare for her hotel guests, Nick too is "a good boy no matter what anybody says" (*NA*, 62); and Mr. Packard plainly admires and protects his penchant for original sin. "I wish Mrs. Packard was our mother," says Littless in a variant passage in the original manuscript; and as we have seen, Nick has already chosen Mr. Packard as his father-confessor. They are the "good frontier parents," then, who assist Nick and his sister in escaping the game wardens to "the last good country."

If "original sin" means doing things you will regret not having done, and getting into trouble for doing them, then Nick's several violations of the game laws must also come under this heading. As his sister reminds him, he is guilty of at least three such violations: shooting a moose out of season, selling rainbow trout to the Packards, and killing the unmentionable thing the game wardens took from his boat—unmentionable because "that was the [only] proof they had" of his sinful doings (*NA*, 60). Later when the wardens identify their proof as a buck deer shot out of season, the hired girl Suzie tells Mr. Packard that the local warden's boy must have found the meat where Nick "had hung it up in the old springhouse" (*NA*, 89). As that interesting discrepancy suggests, and as the original manuscript confirms, Hemingway had begun with a more likely cargo for Nick's boat—the blue heron from whose slaying this albatross tale derives—and had then changed to the buck deer in the springhouse midway through. Whether for the illegal slaying of bird, beast, or fish, then, found in boat or springhouse, the local warden— who has been after Nick for the last four years because of such misde-meanors—now means to make an example of him by sending him to reform school.

By citing only the proved violation, critics Baker and Young tend to minimize the reasonableness of Nick's and—by the same token—Heming-way's anxieties (*B*, 31–33; *PY*, 10–11). Whatever his capacity for exaggeration, Hemingway's grouping of these offenses must reflect his state of mind at sixteen when charged with killing a protected species. If he was also provid-ing the Dilworths' hotel with trout dinners, as seems likely, if he had violated other game laws, as seems likely, then the prospect of being tried for all such crimes at once must have seemed frighteningly real. He had been raised in a home, moreover, where the list of "punishable offenses," major and minor, was legion; and his exaggerated sense of guilt and punishment may reflect that woodshed outlook. His invention of a Western past for the "down state" pursuer, as for Mr. Packard, was decidedly juvenile; but here again his outlook was familial, albeit in a different and more complicated way. If, as Philip Young argues, the escape to "the last good country" is an American dream, as in Huck Finn's flight to the "territory," it was a dream that all of Hemingway's forebears had realized; and if, as Young also notes, the escape with one's sister is a universal fantasy, as in *Hansel and Gretel* (*PY*, 11–12), it was a fantasy that again linked Hemingway with his forebears, especially as it called for adventurous spirits among his sisters, frontier throwbacks like himself, "original sinners" for whom the suburban family circle had proved unusually confining.

At one point or another each of Hemingway's four sisters seems to have qualified as just such an adventurous spirit; and at one point or another each seems to have qualified also as his favorite sister. Hence each is a likely

candidate for imagined escape from family restrictions. His older sister
Marcelline, for instance, often threatened to run away from home and once
did run off to Chicago by herself. She was closest to Ernest in infancy when,
as we shall see, their mother's twinship experiments established their common hair-length—first long, then short—as a recurring sign for Ernest of male
and female likeness; and she especially prized her companionship with
Ernest during their school days.[6] According to Mary Hemingway, his next
oldest sister, Ursula, about three years younger than Ernest, had become his
favorite by the 1950s when "The Last Good Country" was written. Ernest
then considered her "the nicest and the best" of all his sisters.[7] As Constance
Montgomery points out, Ursula had also run off several times to meet Ernest
in Petoskey, probably when he lived there after World War I.[8] His baby sister
Carol, with whom he shared birthday celebrations at Walloon Lake, was
another favorite, early and late. Ernest considered her the "most beautiful of
the family" and was "absolutely nuts about her," perhaps because "She
looked as a girl exactly as [he] looked as a boy."[9] Hence his consternation
when she ran off to get married in Switzerland in 1933 against his own and his
mother's wishes (*B*, 303, 306). Interestingly, in 1921, in a letter to Carol about
his forthcoming marriage, he called her his very best sister and asked her not
to tell this to anyone because he had always loved her so much better than the
others that it made them jealous! One wonders if he did not say the same
thing, at some point, to all his sisters. Whatever the case, when Ernest was
sixteen—Nick's age in the story—his closest companion was neither Marcelline, Ursula, nor Carol, but his eleven-year-old sister Madelaine "Sunny"
Hemingway, who never ran off with anyone, but who at this time hiked with
him in the woods, fished and boated and picnicked with him, and accompanied him on family errands and odd jobs. It was Sunny, moreover, who was
with him when he shot the blue heron, and whose tomboy adventures and
repentable actions most nearly matched his own. The most athletic and the
least squeamish of all his sisters, and the one who got into trouble most often,
she was also the one whom Ernest most admired and protected during his
adolescent years. As their nicknames for each other—Nunbones and Oin-
bones—indicate, they were also verbally attuned. In childhood they developed a private language that none of the family could penetrate; after
Ernest's return from the war, he taught her "beautiful swear words and
phrases in Italian" and a "really dirty song" that she would sing "on call—
with gusto"; and in adult years Ernest continued to enjoy her sudden ingen-
uous flights into scatological or sexual humor, including sharp digs at his
more chauvinistic assumptions.[10] From Sunny especially, then, but also from
Carol, Ursula, and Marcelline, came adventurous traits and repentable actions that went into his invented portrait of the imagined Littless; and with
Sunny as with the others, there was the imagination of shared difference and
escape.

In a way, all these young Hemingways were their grandparents' rather than their parents' children; all wanted to escape from the family's present circumstances to something like its frontier past. Having been taught to shoot, fish, boat, and swim at Walloon Lake, having been raised on tales of the family's frontier adventures, they felt out of place and ill at ease in the strict environs of Oak Park. They felt different from their neighbors, and, at different stages of conformity or rebellion, they felt different from each other too.

Thus, as "The Last Good Country" begins, Hemingway tells us that Nick and his sister Littless "loved each other and . . . did not love the others. They always thought of everyone else in the family as the others" (*NA*, 57–58); and later, when they reach their forest refuge, Littless tells Nick that "crime comes easy for you and me. . . . We're different from the others" (*NA*, 99). From such imagined difference with each of his four sisters, and from the blue heron episode itself, Hemingway had fashioned Nick's escape with Littless to "the last good country"—a detailed action covering two nights and three days of sibling closeness. More than that he could not imagine without violating the law of failed relations that governs all his fiction: but the wonder is that he could imagine even that much unabashed tenderness. His basic motive for inventing that escape now seems clear: it was something he had always wanted to do in fact and was now able to do in fiction; something he had thought of many times in childhood and regretted never doing; something which, late in life, he wanted to understand better and to affirm, especially as it clarified his lifelong difficulties with affectionate love and challenged his ability to convey such tender feelings. He needed Littless, then, because she gave him access to still another range of "repentable" emotions—one that he had for a long time deliberately underplayed.

II

In revising his original opening paragraph, Hemingway decided accordingly to clarify and expand the scene so as to dramatize Nick's relations with his sister. She is literally given the first word, and her loving concern for her brother's welfare is at once made evident:

> "Nickie," his sister said to him. "Listen to me, Nickie."
> "I don't want to hear it."
> He was watching the bottom of the spring where the sand rose in small spurts with the bubbling water. There was a tin cup on a forked stick that was stuck in the gravel by the spring and Nick Adams looked at it and at the water rising and then flowing clear in its gravel bed beside the road.
> He could see both ways on the road and he looked up the hill and then down to the dock and the lake, the wooded point across the bay and the opening lake beyond where there were white caps running. His back was against a big cedar tree and behind him there was a thick cedar swamp. His sister was sitting on the moss beside him and she had her arm around his shoulders.

"They're waiting for you to come home to supper," his sister said. "There's two of them. They came in a buggy and they asked where you were." (*NA*, 56)

As the expansion makes clear, Nick has positioned himself so as to see both ways down the road on which the game wardens may travel. Though he doesn't want to hear his sister's warning, he has already begun the difficult process of "thinking straight" about his situation (*NA*, 58). Nearby is his illegal catch of twenty-six trout for the Packard hotel dinners. He will have to sell them quickly to get more money for his escape. Leaving his sister will also be difficult: as she forces him to admit, he will be lonely without her. Sliding back out of sight as the game wardens pass by in their buggy, Nick tells his sister that he would like to kill those "sons of bitches." But Littless opposes killing: she will go along to prevent it; she is old enough to go; she has already helped him and will help him more. When he argues that the wardens will look harder for two, that "a boy and a girl will show up more," she tells him that she will cut her hair and "go like a boy," having "always wanted to be [one] anyway" (*NA*, 57). Nick agrees to take her with him, though "only for a couple of days." The clear spring water into which he initially gazes, the cedar swamp behind it, are tangible signs of his dilemma. When he and Littless reach their forest refuge, they will camp beside another clear spring with a cedar swamp behind it. As in his famous early tale, "Big Two-Hearted River," Hemingway again chooses to externalize the simplicities of the "good life" and the complications that threaten it; and as always in his fiction, he tries to make us feel the outward shape and texture of inward complexities. Thus, as the story opens, the wellspring of childhood affection flows fresh and clear. Nick will abide by it as he escapes from threatening complications, if only to stave off loneliness.

On the surface, Nick's decision to bring Littless with him seems like a tactical error. If she will ease loneliness and prevent killings, she will also require considerable care and protection and might well limit the time needed for lying low until the wardens tire of waiting. In a variant version of the opening such considerations weigh so heavily that Littless is forced to trick Nick into taking her against his will. But whether tricked or persuaded, Nick consciously defies still another source of censure: "I shouldn't take you," he says in the published version. "But then I shouldn't have done any of it" (*NA*, 58). The first "shouldn't" refers to family rather than legal restrictions. To flee with Littless is a repentable crime against them, another form of "original sin." Though Littless will leave a note under her mother's door that night, announcing that she has joined Nick to keep him out of trouble (this is her trick on him in the variant version), Nick recognizes his responsibility, as her older brother, for pitting the two of them against his mother's displeasure. If the game wardens overtly threaten his freedom, his mother and the "others" are from the first the essential threat from which, along with Littless, he wishfully flees. Unlike Mrs. Hemingway, who drove the wardens from her property and instructed Ernest to escape to the Dilworths, Mrs. Adams has allowed the fictional wardens to encamp in her cottage, has herself retired with "a sick headache" and left the details of flight and safety to her children (*NA*, 64). As Littless says later, she sees them essentially as "fugitives from justice steeped in sin and iniquity" (*NA*, 105).

That instructive reversal of "how it was" tells us something about Hemingway's prejudicial view of his mother, whose death in 1951 he numbered among his recent emotional burdens but whose funeral he did not attend. But as Littless's frequent references to family fights attest, it was not Mrs. Hemingway's exemplary courage and concern that he wanted to fictionalize, but her supposed inability to face and resolve family difficulties by distinguishing between real and superficial misconduct. The occasion that fits that description is not the blue heron episode but his banishment from the cottage at Windemere shortly after his twenty-first birthday.

On returning from Italy in 1919 Hemingway had gloried for a while in his role as war hero, then floundered aimlessly. Like so many returned veterans, he had trouble in adjusting from wartime tension, excitement, and freedom to the responsibilities and conventions of peacetime society. His leg wounds took a long time to heal. He amused himself meanwhile with boyhood pastimes, mixing adolescent hi-jinks with foreign pleasures, and regressing demonstrably to puerile attitudes. By the summer of 1920 he was performing tasks for his mother at their summer home reluctantly, insulting her openly, taking off on sprees with his wartime friend Ted Brumback, freeloading on his friends and parents. When his sisters Ursula and Sunny invited him and Ted to sneak off on a midnight picnic at Ryan's Point along with four young neighbors, their absence was soon detected and they returned at 4 a.m. to a grim reception. The girls were forbidden late dates for the rest of the summer. Ernest and his friend, judged old enough to know better, were banished to Horton Bay to work for their room and board at the Dilworths. It was at this point that Mrs. Hemingway wrote Ernest her famous letter, likening a mother's love to a bank account full of love and patience on which a child draws for sustenance, but which Ernest had woefully overdrawn. Though critics like Carlos Baker and Scott Donaldson have seized upon the letter's mixture of Christian piety with fiscal ethics, they have chauvinistically neglected its cogent description of the mother's nurturing and supportive role through the several stages of childhood.[11] That description looks better, in these days of raised consciousness, than it did during the previous fifty years of public scorn for maternal bitchery, much of it initially heaped by Hemingway himself. Ironically, he would invoke at least some of his mother's values as his own in "The Last Good Country," where Nick's concern for Littless's health, safety, and feelings is nurturing and supportive.

But in 1920, as in 1952, Hemingway's wounded pride was the major factor. The picnic was an innocent spree; he had been kicked out "over nothing";[12]

in decrying his irresponsibility, his mother was covering her own crime of building a summer music studio for herself with money best used for her children's education (*B*, 98); worst of all, she had shown no faith in his eventual capacity for making good. After a few more months of idleness, her equally righteous son found a job in Chicago and the rift mended. But the memory rankled ever after. The escape to Europe with Hadley in 1921, the African trips with Pauline and Mary, the sporting excursions in Key West, Cuba, Spain, Idaho, were—among other things—flights from the restricting conventions of his mother's world.

"The world's a jail and we're going to break it together," wrote Hadley in an engagement letter in 1921.[13] So Catherine Barkley and Lieutenant Henry attempt to break free of the war's encroachments in *A Farewell to Arms*. So Nick and Littless flee legal and domestic restrictions in "The Last Good Country." For Littless especially the flight is an exuberant liberation: "we may have to be away for years," she argues hopefully at the start (*NA*, 58); "is it always this nice when you run away from home?" she asks along the way (*NA*, 69); and, once they reach their forest camp, she imagines how much fun it would be if they weren't in trouble and wants to stay there always (*NA*, 91, 103).

"Do you think we'll get out west . . . on this trip?" she asks on the second night of their adventure (*NA*, 100). Her Western yearnings have been stirred, apparently, by their passage through a stretch of virgin timber where the trees rise sixty feet before branching and where no sun penetrates their foliage. "This is the way forests were in the olden days," Nick then tells her. "This is about the last good country there is left" (*NA*, 74). "I love the olden days," she responds, and later, as they camp by old Indian firestones, she imagines herself as a whore's assistant in a Sheboygan saloon (*NA*, 96). For like Nick and Ernest Hemingway, Littless lives on an imaginative frontier. Stimulated by books and family legends, her mind reaches back to the Western past or outward to new adventures. In her pack she carries adventure books and romances for campfire reading: *Lorna Doone*, *Kidnapped*, *Wuthering Heights*. In the vaulted forest she wonders if they "can go to Europe some time and see cathedrals" (*NA*, 75). The religious atmosphere of the woods has stimulated this last request. As their discussion now indicates, they are literary and cultural travelers and their forest refuge is that "ideal blend of wilderness and civilization" that Hemingway sought for most of his adult life.

Thus, when Nick tells Littless they will go to Europe once he gets past this trouble and learns to make some money, they begin to talk about his writing. Littless asks if he couldn't make money by writing "cheerfuller things." "That isn't my opinion," she hastens to add. "Our mother said everything you write is morbid" (*NA*, 75). Here Hemingway transposes family objections to his writing from the 1920s back into Nick's adolescent years. In an excised passage, a variant version of the fragment's final page, Nick reminds Littless that Mr. Packard had liked his "story about the whore," which probably refers (anachronistically) to Nick's experience at seventeen in "The Light of the World" (1933). Packard's preference and his earthy tolerance suggest still another story, "Up in Michigan," in which Hemingway had borrowed the first names (but not the age and characters) of Jim and Liz Dilworth for a seduction tale that horrified his parents when it appeared in *Three Stories and Ten Poems* (1923), but that pleased the Dilworths when they read it.[14] Still, as Littless now tells Nick, she and Mr. Packard "are the only ones who like what you write."

Ernest was an established author of such works, including *The Sun Also Rises,* when his sister Sunny wrote early in 1927 to ask if she might visit him and Hadley in Paris. Unknown to her, Ernest had just left Hadley and, surviving the one-hundred-day ordeal she had imposed on him, was about to marry Pauline Pfeiffer. Nevertheless he immediately cabled Sunny to urge her to join him in Paris for a trip to Spain; and when parental disapproval and lack of funds held her back, he was sorely disappointed.[15] As Sunny then informed him, his cable itself had upset their parents:

> Oh, Ernie, if you only had said "Cathedrals" instead of "Fiesta" it might have been better. They have a horror for Fiesta and Spain in general—ever since your book. They can't believe that I would become anything but a prostitute if I even visited such a place. They're afraid of all the drinking etc. Your book was too vivid on the life that is led. They never should have seen the cover even. . . .

As it turned out, Sunny would sail to France with Ernest and Pauline in 1929, a few months after their father's tragic suicide. Having loved his father much, Ernest could forgive him many things. But his bitterness about his mother's original disapproval of Sunny's trip, and its basis in her disapproval of his life and writing, stayed with him. He would draw upon these episodes from the 1920s for the forest conversations between Nick and Littless in 1915.

Still another form of family disapproval emerges on the eleventh of the original thirteen-page start for the tale as Littless asks a pointed question:

> "It isn't dirty for a brother and sister to love each other is it?"
> "Who said it was?"
> "Somebody in the family."
> "I can guess."

"Don't guess," says Littless, and then indicates that it isn't who he thinks it is. Whether the offending member of the family is a jealous sister or some older relative is never shown. But the question of whether a brother and sister can love each other is one that children often ponder; and here, as elsewhere in the tale, Hemingway works to distinguish between the innocence of such affections and the cultural fear of incest which may attend them. When on an early variant page Littless tells Nick "we've done wrong already," and Nick denies it, Littless quickly insists: "I don't mean that kind of wrong like you and Trudy. I mean I've stolen for you and I keep your secrets and now I'm warning you about [the game wardens]." But Nick has taken her cultural point, and when she asks if she can run off with him, he tells her that "People wouldn't understand." In the published text this issue is limited to Nick's musing, in the forest: "He loved his sister very much and she loved him too much. But, he thought, I guess those things straighten out. At least I hope so" (*NA*, 101).

What he means by too-muchness is then illustrated by Littless's innocent prattle about becoming his common-law wife and having children by him while still a minor so that he'll have to marry her under "the Unwritten Law" (*NA*, 104). As the text makes us see, this open testing of half-understood limits is scarcely a neurotic revelation. The issue is easily and playfully aired; the love in question is basic to emotional growth; the affections are, as we say, healthy, and without them we would not be able to love one another tenderly as adults. As in "Soldier's Home," where the returned veteran Harold's "best sister" Helen similarly wants him to be her beau and love her always, the affections are open, uncomplicated, and crucial to any future tenderness Harold may feel for adult women. If he now prefers the easy sexuality he knew with German and French women to the complications of American courtship, he also prefers his sister's easy affection to his mother's demanding and demeaning pieties, even as Nick prefers Littless to the "others."

Reviewers have not been exactly quick to see this affirmation. Their comments on "The Last Good Country"—"barely sublimated incest," "slightly soppy narrative," "a mawkish shard of an abandoned novel," "too much . . . sentimental talk," "the verge of incest," "right out of James Barrie, even to the sexual undercurrents"[16]—suggest how unthinkingly we still operate under the post-Victorian, that is to say Freudian, dispensation. We are so embarrassed, apparently, by any genuine expression of affection that we can only assign it to sentimentality or neurosis. Hemingway himself has contributed to this contemporary attitude, perhaps more than any other modern writer, through the widespread influence of his deadpan style and through popular legends about his stoic toughness; so it is not surprising that reviewers influenced by both have missed the persistent defense of vulnerable feelings in his work, or the constant demand for emotional support in his life, and are now at a loss to account for a direct display of family closeness. It is not the "verge of incest," however, that Hemingway treads in this decidedly revealing story; it is the frontier of childhood affections, rather, which the completely open issue of incest helps to outline. Philip Young almost sees this when he speaks of "hints of physical love" that "highlight the innocence of actual relationships" in such stories, and of "overtones," without which "we would never think to realize how immaculate is the conception" (*PY*, 12). Never, at any rate, in our slightly addled time, when we are unable to distinguish between the sensual closeness of friends and relations and the sexual closeness of lovers.

In "The Last Good Country," however, Hemingway himself seems to understand this distinction. Nick's tender regard for his sister is carefully played off against his sexual connection with the Indian girl Trudy, who though pregnant by him is not even "second best" in his affections. The editors of Scribners have done the fragmented tale a large disservice by cutting out the dialogue pertaining to Trudy; for, surprisingly, the girl who "did first what no one has ever done better" in "Fathers and Sons" (1933; *NA*, 243) is here edged out by Nick's concern for his sister—or not so surprisingly, perhaps, if we recall how Nick is determined to kill the Indian boy Eddie Gilby if he tries to sleep with his sister Dorothy in that earlier tale, though it is all right for Nick to "make plenty baby" with Eddie's half-sister Trudy (*NA*, 239–41). Now, with Trudy literally pregnant and Nick himself an outcast, Nick feels he ought to rejoin her until Littless persuades him to run off with her instead. Though she is plainly jealous of Trudy's sexual hold on Nick, she is willing to help him find her so long as her own innocent hold on his affections is stronger—as it proves to be, once she tricks him into taking her along on his escape. In other words, she saves him from the consequences of his sexual as well as his legal "crimes," and it is this double or—considering his family's disapproval—this triple jeopardy that the editors of Scribners forfeit by their cuts. The whole force and point of the later argument about Trudy, and of Nick's decisive exclamation, "The hell with Trudy," is also lost (*NA*, 70–71); but more to the point, the innocent nature of physical love between brother and sister is needlessly obscured throughout the text.[17]

Thus, early in the tale, when Littless marvels at the idea of knockout drops like those which whores use in rolling lumberjacks, and thinks they "ought to have some for in emergencies," Nick wants to kiss her "just for in emergency" (*NA*, 64); and it is at this point, in the original manuscript, that the missing dialogue about Trudy begins. Among its several lost beauties is Littless's reason for withholding until now her knowledge of Trudy's whereabouts: "I thought we'd go away together and I'd take care of you and you'd take care of me and we'd hunt and fish and eat and read and sleep together and not worry and love each other and be kind and good." The juxtaposition of this innocent option with Nick's baby-making life with Trudy is what the tale is chiefly about; it is an enactment of Littless's dream, which Nick seems to share, or which he at least seems to prefer to life with Trudy, for when he is now reminded of the "sweet-grass" smell he associates with making love to her in "Fathers and Sons" (*NA*, 244), he frankly says: "I'm sorry Littless. . . . I'm not a good brother, and I'm not a good man and I'm not a good friend even," and then acknowledges that he prefers Littless and that finding Trudy is not even his "second best hope."

The discounting here of loveless sex is like the discounting of Lieutenant Frederic Henry's whoring in *A Farewell to Arms*: his love for Catherine Barkley is a different thing entirely. So too is Nick's love for Littless different from his "sweet-grass" love for Trudy, which seems to undergo a radical change with pregnancy at stake. Hemingway is up to something new, apparently, in this story, something he could not altogether work out, but something nonetheless intriguing as far as it goes. Among its more fascinating aspects is the attempt to affirm the innocent closeness between brother and sister as the historic basis for responsible adult love. When Nick and Littless sleep together in the forest and Nick wakes in the cold night to "spread his Mackinaw over his sister," he rolls closer to her for warmth; and feeling "the warmth of his sister's body against his back," he thinks: "I must take good care of her and keep her happy and get her back safely"—and falls asleep again. When he wakes once more in the early light he watches his sister, still asleep, and, admiring her "high cheekbones and brown freckled skin light rose under the brown" and "the beautiful line of her head," he wants to draw her or, at the least, to describe her resemblance to "a small wild animal" and "the carved look" of her sleeping face (*NA*, 101). It seems to me a real failure in moral apprehension to call this "barely sublimated incest" or to speak of sexual undertones or overtones. The too-muchness of his sister's love for him, on which he now remarks, might lead that way if it were intense, obsessive, or cloying; but since it is none of these, it leads instead to Nick's protective and nurturing regard, his parental concern to see her through. For Nick already knows what Lieutenant Henry takes a long time learning: that selfless consideration for another is the crux of love; and like Hemingway himself, he seems to have learned this early from a position of strength, as an only brother surrounded by adoring sisters.

What he did not learn—how many of us do?—was how to love another from a position of equality. Meanwhile his greater strength—his protective and nurturing love—is here appropriate to its subject. He will always have a parental or big brotherly edge on his younger sister, and there is no point in denying its validity as a human bond or doubting its persuasively innocent expression. The real problem that Nick's creator could not solve was how to deal with love between adult men and women of equal strength or status. And here, if anywhere, the question of neurosis and its sentimental expression may be legitimately raised.

In at least three of his major novels, for instance, Hemingway seems unable to connect affection with sexual love without making the Victorian payment for that connection. In Victorian fiction, where incest is often a hidden force, the punishment for sexual love is death. In Hemingway's fiction the same punishment seems to be administered, always by external and physical agencies, to affectionate lovers, as with Catherine's death by childbirth in *A Farewell to Arms*, Robert Jordan's by the approaching enemy in *For Whom the Bell Tolls*, and Colonel Cantwell's by heart failure in *Across the River and Into the Trees*. The selfless heroines of these novels—Catherine, Maria, Renata—are subservient partners like Littless, devoted admirers of their military beaus, willing to do all they can to please them. But they are, alas, unequal admirers; they receive less than they give, and the love they give and receive is in each case overvalued as an adult norm. Its mystification as a mutually selfless exchange—a mixing together of two as one—is accordingly suspect, and we may well want to call it sentimental and, considering its rigged and punitive outcome, neurotic.

"The Last Good Country" provides still other clues to this sentimental overweighting of adult romances. Thus Catherine and Maria share with Littless the wearing or intended wearing of short-cropped hair, a leitmotif used differently in different stories. In "The Last Good Country" Littless crops her hair at the forest camp so she will look like a boy and be less detectable to pursuing game wardens. But the action has other meanings: "I should have asked you," she tells her brother, "but I knew it was something we had to do" (*NA*, 96). Since it is also something she wanted to do anyway, so as to become her brother's companion on a more permanent basis, it may also be something he wanted too. "I like it," he now tells her. "To hell with everything. I like it very much." Huck Finn's break with social expectations is couched in similar terms when he decides to "go to hell" and rescue Nigger Jim. Philip Young cites forbidden but innocent love as the common denominator in these frontier tales (*PY*, 12); but nice as that observation is, it doesn't tell us much about the relevance of hair-length to such love. Perhaps we should turn for a moment to biography for some help.

Everyone knows that Ernest's mother, Grace Hall Hemingway, made Ernest wear Dutch-length hair and dresses like his older "twin" sister Marcelline in infancy. Few realize that she later reversed the experiment and cut Marcelline's hair like a boy's—that is to say, like Ernest's—in the summer of 1906 when Marcelline was eight and Ernest, seven. It was a dreadful experience for Marcelline, who was embarrassed enough when she entered a new school that fall with "partially grown out hair"; but when a new girlfriend decided to "even it out" with even more disastrous results, her now disillusioned mother made her wear one of Sunny's baby bonnets to school to cover her "shameful appearance." A teacher mercifully intervened after two mortifying weeks, and the bonnet was discarded;[18] but the mortification seems to have impressed young Ernest enough to inspire Maria's shameful cropping by Spanish fascists in later years, in *For Whom the Bell Tolls,* and her sponsorship by an older woman, Pilar, as Robert Jordan's ward-like reward. As Hemingway (if not his critics) must have seen, the male twin was favored far more often in his mother's odd experiments than the female twin.

Cropping as unwanted punishment is not the same, of course, as wanted cropping, and none of Hemingway's sisters willingly sheared her locks to please him; but one of them, Sunny, was tomboyish enough to seek his sporting approval, and in 1921, while Ernest was working in Chicago on the *Cooperative Commonwealth,* Sunny led her sisters in defying their father's edict against the Irene Castle bob. "Short hair is unwomanly and I won't have it in my house," her father had told her; but when she pointed out that she had been wearing it short for a week without his noticing it, the edict broke and her sisters followed suit.[19]

Sunny's daring defiance of parental expectations was like her brother's; and like Lady Ashley's defiance a few years later, it reflected the new feminine assertiveness, the new twenties' spirit of comrades-in-arms equality. Ernest seems to have liked it, though, for its implicit tribute to male superiority: the girls were more like men, they were copying male styles, seeking male freedoms for themselves, and that freed him in turn to be more like them, to let his hair grow longer, as Catherine Barkley—who intends to cut hers short to resemble his—asks of Frederic Henry. Ernest could afford to express his tender and affectionate feelings with a woman who wanted to be like him, indeed to *be* him, and to be all mixed up with him, as Catherine and Frederic mix together at night as lovers (*FTA*, 300). Androgyny, then, was for Hemingway a reassurance of manly superiority that allowed him to be womanly. Which is why when Littless says "we" had to do this, Nick likes it, and says "To hell with everything."

Littless is like Catherine in other ways. When she refers to having fun, as she often does, or to having "a lovely time" (*NA*, 71), she even sounds like Catherine. The forest dialogues are especially resonant with such accents. When Littless sits on Nick's lap, rubs her cropped head against his cheek, and amuses him with imagined stories about getting knockout drops for their trip from the Queen of the Whores in Sheboygan, and with her fear of being ruined morally by the taste of stolen liquor, she is Catherine Barkley writ small, the "good girl" we remember from the novel who wants to do "something really sinful" (*FTA*, 152–53), like catching gonorrhea because her lover caught it, or staying with his many bad girls so she can make fun of them to him afterwards (*FTA*, 299). The innocent woman mocking and envying the women her initiated lover has known is common enough in double-standard times; and her dilemma is part of what Hemingway caught in tonal focus in *A Farewell to Arms;* but what he also caught, as "The Last Good Country" reveals, was the appeal for him of uninitiated "good girls" playing with the terms of male privilege—indeed, questioning those dubious freedoms—while at the same time offering redemptive love. As Nick puts it in the excised passage about Trudy, "I'm not a good brother, and I'm not a good man and I'm not a good friend even." But with Littless he becomes all these things, and when Frederic Henry is all these things and more with Catherine Barkley, they have "a lovely time."

As indeed they do. The love and the lovely time may be limited, but they seem to me genuine in all such cases; the women in question—Catherine, Maria, Renata—seem to me credibly portrayed. It is the overweighting and mystification of such romances, the inequality of the exchanges, and the convenient deaths that follow, which seem to me suspect.

III

In "The Last Good Country" Hemingway returns to the place where all such loves began, the Michigan woods he often tramped in boyhood with some currently favored sister. When Nick worries about whether Littless is eating or sleeping well, or performing her daily ablutions, or when he performs his own carefully detailed outdoor tasks—fishing, hunting, cooking—the author's pride in the survival skills of his frontier children informs his loving prose. Their pastoral home away from home is a testament to the idyllic summers Hemingway spent in Michigan; and their imagined escape from wardens, family restrictions, and sexual consequences is a revealing instance of the author's many imagined escapes to lost frontiers. The many parallels with *A Farewell to Arms* are accordingly instructive: two loving fugitives who have committed "crimes" feel different from the "others"; their several "crimes" and their escape to "the last good country" are sanctioned by redeeming love; their repentable action may have serious consequences but is better done than left undone and regretted; once beyond the social pale they talk of common-law marriage; they care for each other selflessly and bravely; the "good girl" amuses her protector with imagined tales of being bad; she crops her hair to be more like him; and their pastoral retreat, where they will read romantic books and talk often about writing, is an "ideal blend of wilderness and civilization" like the Swiss chalet in the mountains near Montreux where Ernest stayed with Hadley in 1922 and where Frederic stays with Catherine in 1918. Indeed, as the long fragment ends, Nick is about to read aloud to Littless from *Wuthering Heights,* a romantic novel about another British heroine named Catherine who enjoys both moor and mansion but dies in childbirth, and who so identifies with the boy with whom she was raised ("I *am* Heathcliff") as to remind us of Catherine Barkley's selfless love for Frederic Henry—who (like Heathcliff) mourns her loss long after she is dead!

There is of course no death in childbirth in "The Last Good Country"; but Prudence Boulton, the model for pregnant Trudy, was said by some Petoskey natives to have died in childbirth, and Ernest was rumored to be the father of her child. Though the rumor has since been proven false,[20] Hemingway does imagine Nick as Trudy's lover and impregnator; and if we imagine for him her death in childbirth, one "criminal" consequence is conveniently resolved. That hypothetical resolution helps also to dramatize the separation Hemingway now makes between sex and affection. What he had joined together so tragically in *A Farewell to Arms* he now deliberately sunders. It seems almost as if he returns to the childhood source of his adult affections for selfless and adoring women so as to affirm his own investment in redeeming love. Or perhaps, by again separating such love from loveless sex, he hopes to clarify its puzzling dissolution in adulthood. But as we have seen, he cannot face his even greater stake in inequality. He can only create a legitimately disequal love; and there the affection plot breaks off.

What he did create, in opposition to redeeming childhood love, was an almost unredeemable form of childhood anger. If Mr. Packard has for the time being taken care of the game wardens, Nick still must deal with the relentless tracking of the local warden's son; and in the fragment's final pages his forest idyll is disturbed by reminders of that approaching nemesis. Nick feels sick and uncertain as he tries to think out what might happen if the boy should find them, a predicament that moves him to the curious pronouncement: "I have to think about things now for the rest of my life" (NA, 110). That seems to be the price for original sin, or for doing repentable things worth doing, and though Nick seems ready to pay it, he is almost overwhelmed by the desire to kill the boy who forces that moral fate upon him. He knows that Littless can feel that desire "because she is your sister and you love each other" (NA, 113); but he tries nonetheless to enlist her in the fiction that nobody ever talked or thought about killing. He knows that he "can't do it while she's along" (NA, 111); but that only means that, without her restraining presence, he is helpless before his own murderous impulses. It seems evident at this point that the game warden's boy, like those academic biographers whom Hemingway detested, is a symptom of deep-seated hostility against punitive pursuers, censor-figures, shamers, blamers, disapprovers: a symptom then of paranoia. Against it we may range such gentling images as Nick's stroking of his sister's head when she crawls through a fence on their journey and he asks if she is tired; his fondness for her in the morning light; and the coldness and freshness of the water they now drink from the forest spring. But the force of Nick's anger, and its origins in family strictness and disapproval, are left unexplored. All we have—in considerable strength—is the countervailing force of family affection, the wellspring of childhood love.

A few more biographical clues will help to underscore the importance of that force in Hemingway's romantic fiction. When Ernest took his sister Sunny along with him to Florida in 1928 to help with the typing of A Farewell to Arms, he asked her to tell him stories about her nursing experiences in Chicago. Two or three years earlier she had written him about one experience that may have reminded him of his wartime romance with the American nurse, Agnes von Kurowsky, from which the novel largely sprang.[21] After graduating from high school in 1924, Sunny had gone into nurse's training at West Suburban Hospital in Oak Park, had fallen in love with one of her patients—a newspaperman like her brother—and had written Ernest for advice. As she tells it in her memoir, the story takes on unintended resonance:

> After two years' training, I thought I was in love with a patient named Robert St. John. I enjoyed our secret meetings and note-passing when I was off duty. Bob influenced me to stop nurse's training and try college.
> I remember writing Ernie at the time for his opinion of this man. He answered promptly, honored that I had consulted him, and allowed as how any guy who could work as a rewrite man on that particular Chicago newspaper must be a good guy and just might be worthy of his kid sister.
> But Bob and I fell out of love as easily as we had fallen in.[22]

This story about secret meetings and note-passing between an off-duty nurse and a patient who must measure up to her may have been the catalyst for Hemingway's famous novel about wartime love. Though Hemingway drew on his romance with Agnes von Kurowsky for the central situation in that novel, Agnes seems to have been a much more confident and flirtatious woman than Catherine Barkley. She was also older and more experienced than Ernest, his superior in age and wisdom, and her nature and her eventual rejection of him seem to have been reworked in the novel into a type and situation closer to the heart's desire. As we have seen, Catherine's admiration for Lieutenant Henry, her desire to please him and be like him, are like the admiration and fondness that Sunny and her sisters had for brother Ernie; and it seems to me something like a tribute to them all that he created such qualities in adult heroines like Catherine—whose social defiance and whose bravery in the face of death may owe something also to their post-pioneer courage. Of course, Hemingway's adoring first and second wives, Hadley and Pauline, are the conscious models for Catherine Barkley; but by the 1950s he was drawing consciously on their forerunners, Sunny and her sisters, for those healthy family affections that he had often betrayed or discounted or suppressed, but that had nonetheless sustained him as that good androgynous man—friend, brother, husband, son, lover—he was always capable of being. Interestingly, the last date on his unfinished manuscript is 20 July 1958, which means that it was broken off so he could complete his long unpublished novel about androgynous couples, *The Garden of Eden* (*B*, 684). Meanwhile he had effectively created their original childhood types, a tomboyish sister who may be little-or-less than Catherine Barkley but who seems far more likely to survive, and her nurturing and protective brother, who already knows what Frederic Henry took a long time learning, and then "was always able to forget" (*FTA*, 14).

APPENDIX A

Grace's Banking Analogy, 24 July 1920:

A Mother's love seems to me like a Bank. Each child that is born to her enters the world with a large and prosperous Bank Account, seemingly inexhaustible.

For the first five years, he draws, and draws—physical labor and pain, loss of sleep, watching and soothing, waiting upon, bathing, dressing, feeding, amusing: the Mother is practically a body slave to his every whim. There are no deposits in the Bank Account during all the early years. "Cheery—" thinks the mother, some day he will be a comfort to me, and return all I'm doing for him. Then for the next ten years or so, up to adolescence, while the Bank is heavily drawn upon for love and sympathy, championship in time of trouble or injustice, nursing through illness, teaching and guiding, developing the young body and mind and soul at all and any expense to the often exhausted parents:—during this time, there are a few deposits of pennies, in the way of little services willingly done, some thoughtfulness and thank yous.

Now comes the trying time of adolescence, when the mother must make constant excuses for overwrought nerves, when the child she has so lovingly borne and reared, turns and tongue-thrashes her, sneers at her advice and precautions, considers her quite out of date. She hears it all, hopes for the best, and makes allowances.

Truly the Bank Account is perilously low, and there is nothing coming in, no deposits unless occasional spells of regret for past conduct make him come to her with an "I'm sorry and will truly try to do better."

But now, adolescence is past, full manhood is here. The Bank is still paying out love, sympathy with wrongs, and enthusiasm for all ventures; courtesies and entertainments of friends, who have nothing in common with Mother, who unless they are very well bred, scarcely notice her existence. But, the Bank goes on handing out understanding and interest in budding love affairs, joy in plans of every kind.

The account needs some deposits, by this time, some good sized ones in the way of gratitude and appreciation. Interest in Mother's ideas and affairs. Little comforts provided for the home—a desire to favor any of Mother's peculiar prejudices, on no account to outrage her ideals. Flowers, fruit, candy, or something pretty to wear, brought home to Mother with a kiss and a squeeze. The unfailing desire to make much of her feeble efforts, to praise her cooking, back up her little schemes. A real interest in hearing her sing, or play the piano, or tell the stories that she loves to tell—a surreptitious paying of bills, just to get them off Mother's mind.

A thoughtful remembrance and celebration of her birthday and Mother's Day. The sweet letter, accompanying the gift of flowers, she treasures it, most of all. These are merely a few of the deposits which keep the Account in good standing.

Many mothers, I know, are receiving these and much more substantial gifts and returns from sons of less abilities, than my son.

(The "dressing down" cited by Baker and Donaldson, in which she tells Ernest *"You have overdrawn,"* follows at this point.)

APPENDIX B

The Trudy Excision, ms. pp. 11–13, second opening, *NA,* 64:

"Let me kiss you," her brother said. "Just for in emergency."

"Who will you kiss when you go away?"

"Nobody," he said. "Trudy maybe if I can find her."

"I thought you were through with her."

"I was. But I'm not sure now."

"You wouldn't go and make her another baby, would you?"

"I don't know."

"They'll put you in the reform school for that if you keep on doing it."

"I heard that."

"Well let's not talk about it," his sister said. "I promised myself I'd never even think about it. I don't want to think about that while you're gone and have the family talk about it and we know it's true. Where's she now?"

"I'm going to find her."

"Really? Nicky you shouldn't. Please don't."

"I think I have to, Littless."

"I know where she is if you have to find her."

"Where is she?"

"At the Indian Play."

"Really?"

"Why would I tell except to keep us from having trouble finding her? Why wouldn't I tell you the truth when I love you?"

"Why didn't you tell me before?"

"Nicky you ought to learn not to ask too much. I thought we'd go away together and I'd take care of you and you'd take care of me and we'd hunt and fish and eat and read and sleep together and not worry and love each other and be kind and good."

"When did you find out?"

"This afternoon. I saw Joubert on the bridge fishing when I went home. He asked about you and said Trudy was at the play and Billy had a job there too. He tried to get a job but they wouldn't take him. He can't swim well enough to play water baseball."

"Was that all he said?"

"He said for me to ask you if you had forgotten what sweet grass smells like."

"I'm sorry Littless," Nick said. "I'm not a good brother, and I'm not a good man and I'm not a good friend even."

"But you would have taken me truly if you thought I wouldn't make trouble, wouldn't you?"

"Of course."

"And this is your second best hope, isn't it?"

"It isn't even that."

"I don't mind as long as it's second best."

"Let's go down and watch them drinking," Nick said. "I'd like to hear them talk sitting in our house."

APPENDIX C

The Packard-Nick Excision, ms. p. 84, *NA,* 49:

"All right," Nick said. "I'll never lie to you."

"I don't mean I want you telling me everything," Mr. John said. "Like if you jerk off."

"I don't jerk off," Nick told him. "I fuck."

"I guess that's as simple a word for it as any," Mr. John said. "But don't you do it any more than you have to."

"I know. I started it too early I guess."

"So did I," Mr. John said. "But don't do it when you're drunk and always make water afterwards and wash yourself good with soap and water."

"Yes Sir," Nick had said. "I don't have much trouble with it lately."

"What became of your girl?"

NOTES

1. The fragment appears in *The Nick Adams Stories,* ed. Philip Young (New York: Bantam Books, 1973), pp. 56–114; hereafter *NA* in the text. The original opening epigraph and the Young telegram are from the Hemingway Collection at the Kennedy Library in Boston. Unless otherwise indicated, other references to Hemingway's letters and manuscripts, and to his mother's and his sister Sunny's letters, are drawn from this source and are used here with the permission of Mary Welsh Hemingway and—for Sunny's letters—Madelaine Hemingway Miller. Later references to the Scribner paperback edition (New York, 1969) of *A Farewell to Arms* will appear in the text after the initials *FTA.* See Young's foreword to the revised edition of his book, *Ernest Hemingway: A Reconsideration* (University Park: Pennsylvania State University Press, 1966), pp. 1–28, for a full account of his difficulties with Hemingway in getting the original edition published.

2. See Carlos Baker, *Ernest Hemingway: A Life Story* (New York: Bantam Books, 1970), pp. 33, 720; hereafter *B* in the text.

3. This version of the blue heron episode is pieced together from five discrepant accounts by Carlos Baker, Leicester Hemingway, Marcelline Hemingway Sanford, Madelaine "Sunny" Hemingway Miller, and Mary Welsh Hemingway. I have relied chiefly on Grace Hemingway's extensive report on the incident in a letter to her husband in the summer of 1915, cited in Leicester's *My Brother, Ernest Hemingway* (Cleveland and New York: World, 1962), pp. 35–37, and on regional maps that explain its reference to "Game and Fish Wardens for both counties, Emmett and Charlevoix." Since both counties are northern, the "down state" origin of the "dangerous warden" in the story, as cited in the text, was pure invention. Presumably "down state" was for Hemingway a more legally ominous region than the familiar northern counties. It was from an MLA meeting in "down state" Detroit, Michigan, incidentally, that Philip Young had sent Hemingway his disturbing summary of psychoanalytic approaches to the author's life and work.

4. See Mary Welsh Hemingway, *How It Was* (New York: Ballantine Books, 1977), pp. 361–62.

5. As Constance Montgomery observes in *Hemingway in Michigan* (New York: Fleet, 1966), p. 133, Hemingway's girlfriend, Marjorie Bump, the model for Marjorie in "The Three Day Blow," had waited on tables at the Dilworths' hotel when Hemingway stayed there in 1919–20. This might explain Mr. Packard's awareness of Nick's lost girlfriend. But Nick is only sixteen in "The Last Good Country," and if his life follows Hemingway's, as Philip Young believes, he would not meet Marjorie until after the war (see Young's case for the dating of the Marjorie stories in "Big World Out There: *The Nick Adams Stories,*" *Novel: A Forum on Fiction* 6 (Fall 1971): 14; hereafter *PY* in the text). Trudy therefore seems the likelier girlfriend. As Nick tells Mr. Packard in the flashback, "Somebody said she was working up at the Soo" (*NA,* 84). But as he learns in an earlier excised passage, Trudy is actually working at the "Indian Play" in Petoskey, where the wardens think—with some justice—that Nick may flee.

6. See Marcelline Hemingway Sanford, *At the Hemingways: A Family Portrait* (Boston and Toronto: Little, Brown, 1962), pp. 178, 184.

7. Mary Welsh Hemingway, *How It Was,* pp. 360, 286.

8. Montgomery, *Hemingway in Michigan,* p. 90.

9. Mary Welsh Hemingway, p. 286.

10. See Madelaine Hemingway Miller, *Ernie: Hemingway's Sister "Sunny" Remembers* (New York: Crown, 1975), pp. 36–37, 71, 90, 120–21.

11. See Baker, p. 97, and Scott Donaldson, *By Force of Will: The Life and Art of Ernest Hemingway* (Harmondsworth: Penguin Books, 1978), pp. 14–15, 293. Both critics skip the actual banking analogy and quote only the letter's punitive conclusion. For the heart of Grace's argument, see Appendix A.

12. Miller, *Ernie,* p. 68.

13. See Alice Hunt Sokoloff, *Hadley: The First Mrs. Hemingway* (New York: Dodd, Mead, 1973), pp. 1, 68.

14. Montgomery, p. 123.

15. Miller, pp. 106–8.

16. *Ernest Hemingway: The Critical Reception,* ed. Robert O. Stephens (New York: Burt Franklin, 1977), pp. 483, 485, 488, 493.

17. Philip Young says that such cuts and changes "were either necessary, to piece together two long and different openings present in the manuscript, or desirable, where the text was wordy, or the pace slow, or the taste dubious. The job has been skillfully done by Scribner's" (*PY,* 6). As my complaints indicate, I believe they botched the job in several major and minor respects. Hemingway had begun the tale, for instance, with a thirteen-page account of Nick's departure with Littless that does not develop their return to the summer cottage for supplies or their trip to the Packards' store to sell the trout. He decided to include these episodes, along with other changes, and began writing a new version of the opening events which comprises the bulk of the 102-page manuscript. The new version begins on a page numbered 3, which plainly indicates his intention to cut back into the original opening on that page. But Scribner editors decided to include six of the original thirteen pages as the opening, thereby creating the discrepancy (which Hemingway would have avoided) of illegal game found in both boat and springhouse. Hemingway's decision to have Littless trick Nick into taking her rather than persuade him is also violated, with some damage to sense when Nick is upset by the letter Littless leaves for her mother (*NA,* 66), although she has already told him she would leave it (*NA,* 59). Littless's resourcefulness and astuteness, and her stake in the escape, are also diminished by these changes, as by the Trudy cuts in the second opening cited in the text. For the Trudy excisions, see Appendix B.

18. Sanford, *At the Hemingways,* pp. 109–11.

19. Ibid., pp. 206–7.

20. For the rumor, see Montgomery, p. 28; for its disproof, see Paul Smith, "The Tenth Indian," in *Ernest Hemingway: The Writer in Context,* ed. James Nagel (Madison: University of Wisconsin Press, 1984), pp. 67–68, 73–74. Smith reveals here that Prudence Boulton died at sixteen in February 1918 in a suicide pact with her young white lover, whose child she was then carrying. Hemingway may have learned this when he returned to Michigan in April 1918 for a last fishing trip before going off to war.

21. The date of this letter is uncertain. Though Sunny speaks in her memoirs of meeting Robert St. John after two years of nurse's training, which would be in 1926, she mentions "Bob" in a letter to her brother in December 1925 as being jealous of another man (Frank Hines) with whom she had taken a recent trip. She passes off his jealousy lightly ("I'm not a sort to worry. I have others—tra! la!"), which would seem to indicate that their romance was dissolving and that her letter asking Ernest for advice about him had been sent earlier in 1925. Its reception came, in any case, when Ernest was either in the midst of writing *The Sun Also Rises* or finished with it, and ripe for the seeds of a new novel.

22. Miller, p. 105.

16

The Quincunx Quiddified: Structure in Lawrence Durrell

IAN S. MacNIVEN

"Yet obstinately I dream of such a book, full of not completely discrete characters, of ancestors and descendants all mixed up—could such people walk in and out of each other's lives without damaging the quiddity of each other?"

—Durrell, *Constance*

Lawrence Durrell's "Quincunx," now commonly referred to as *The Avignon Quintet,* has been called a *roman fleuve,* and as such it could be considered a revival of modernism in the manner of Ford Madox Ford's *Parade's End;* Durrell himself has suggested the nested boxes of the *gigogne* as a pattern;[1] and in the third novel of the *Quintet, Constance: or, Solitary Practices* (1982), one of the characters, Sutcliffe, the fictive novelist and putative creator of parts of the Quincunx, proposes writing

> that ideal book—the titanic do-it-yourself kit, *le roman appareil.* After all, why not a book full of spare parts of other books, of characters left over from other lives, all circulating in each other's bloodstreams—yet all fresh, nothing second-hand, twice chewed, twice breathed. Such a book might ask you if life is worth breathing, if death is worth looming.[2]

These possible labels are contradictory in a way: the *roman fleuve* and the *roman appareil* both imply the disorderly flow of associational discourse,while the *gigogne* is based upon careful craftsmanship where structure, if not an end in itself, is at least an integral part of meaning. Durrell himself has disclaimed the first of these methods, claiming that his *Quintet* "ne deviendra jamais un roman fleuve."[3]

Those familiar with the somewhat ostentatiously proclaimed "relativity" scheme of *The Alexandria Quartet* expect elaborate structure from Durrell, and need no reminders of his relationship to the great early modernists. Thus we find in the "soup-mix" of the *Quartet* "three sides of space and one of time,"[4] a conscious departure from the Proustian-Bergsonian sense of duration; there is also a Joycean awareness of the importance of structure, shifting styles, and esoteric language; a Conradian gift for the exotic and suggestively sinister foreign setting; a Lawrencean skill in evoking place and an even more unembarrassed treatment of sex. Durrell also shares with many important authors writing in English the fact that he is not in the mainstream of English literature. Lawrence to be sure *is,* but Conrad, Ford, Joyce, T. S. Eliot (Durrell's editor at Faber and Faber and for years his mentor in poetry), and Woolf clearly are not of the line of Jane Austen, Dickens, George Eliot, Hardy, Huxley, C. P. Snow, and Graham Greene. The fact that Durrell belongs with the modernists and not in the direct current may help explain his often harsh handling by English critics who would prefer to write off modernism after 1930, by which time Lawrence was safely dead and Joyce had moved into the obscurities of *Finnegans Wake.* The more significant question to consider is whether Durrell, modernist or not, has succeeded in moving his *Quintet* into the new territory he claims for it.

"Five colours mixed make people blind," goes the Chinese proverb Durrell quotes as one of the epigraphs to *Livia: or, Buried Alive* (1978), the second novel of *The Avignon Quintet.* But there is no reason why the five books of the *Quintet* should produce the effect the Chinese sage warns us against, arranged as they are in a quincuncial pattern with finely tuned structural and symbolic underpinnings. To begin with the obvious: the quincunx mentioned in the first novel, *Monsieur: or, The Prince of Darkness* (1974), describes a planting pattern not uncommon in medieval and Renaissance arboretums: five trees arranged like the dots on the five in dominoes. This quincunx of trees is said to be the key to the lost Templar treasure, for which various characters search throughout Durrell's series. Is the Templar hoard a tangible treasure of gold and precious stones, as Lord Galen the banker believes, or is it a gem of spiritual knowledge, a gnosis, such as the mystic Akkad expounds in *Monsieur?* Wisely, I think, Durrell never resolves the question: no treasure, once found, can match the allure of the still-elusive trove. Durrell's treasures match the preoccupations of his characters, appropriate in a work in which "fiction" creates "reality."

There is a second medieval referent to Durrell's five-part structure: "quincunx" also describes ancient reliquaries formed of four equal squares hinged to the sides of a fifth square to make an equal-armed cross when open, a cube when closed. The central square held the key religious relic, while the four outer squares carried complementary decorations. The reliquary imitated in miniature the cathedral, and in the final volume, *Quinx: or, The Ripper's Tale* (1985), Durrell wrote, "In architecture the quincunxial shape was considered a sort of housing for the divine power—a battery, if you like," and added that the Templar treasure was to be found in a "quincunx of little cells."[5] The centerpiece of the reliquary contained the object of real value for the faithful. Inverting the usual storyteller's practice of presenting a "real" framework to enclose a narrative at a further remove from reality, in *The Avignon Quintet* Durrell has made his centerpiece, and by placement his treasure, "fictional" according to the narrative frame of the sequence, and the outer parts, the outer four books, "real." He has also narrated the "fiction," *Monsieur,* first, the "real" framework second. These reversals of expectation set the precedent, as we will see, for a whole series of structural and thematic inversions.

An examination of the *Quintet* from the perspective of structure must consider the degree of immanence of the author's proclaimed quincuncial pattern, along with certain emphasized integers, specifically one, two, and three, found respectivly in monotheism and the other mono-prefixed subjects, in a dualistic philosophy centered around gnosticism, and in various triads of lovers illustrating pluralistic relationships. Twining about the various number patterns, especially the pastoral quincunx suggestive of Eden, is the *S*-curve of the serpent, from the literal cobra-worshipers of Macabru in *Monsieur* to the sinuous tracks of the various train, road, and river journeys the characters make in search of the wisdom of the serpent, of enlightenment. Inseparable from both the quincunx pattern and its link to the supposed Templar treasure and heresies and to the beliefs of the desert gnostics, followers of the serpent Ophis, is the pattern of inversions beginning, theologically, with the usurpation of the throne of Christ by the Prince of Darkness, and finding expression in the novels in the various sexual inversions and poly-partnered matings. Monotheism and monogamy—indeed all simple, single answers—are suspect in Durrell's world.

While Durrell can be as jokey as Joyce, we cannot afford to ignore his pronouncements on his art. In a recent interview in *Egoïste,* Durrell pinned his justification of the five-pattern of his then work-in-progress to the earlier *Quartet,* and made it clear that the *Quintet* was intended to explore a new structural device:

> "J'ai voulu faire un roman pour célébrer Einstein, et ses quatre dimensions; et un autre pour les tibétains et le nombre cinq, puisque chez eux il n'y a pas le conscient et l'inconscient, mais cinq paniers avec des éléments, des attributs. Ce qui est très près Einstein, aussi. Je n'ai jamais cherché à être original, mais contemporain."[6]

Many critics have been lured by the preface to *Balthazar* in which Durrell proclaimed his structural plans for the *Quartet:* a play on relativity in which the "truth" of events depends upon the position of the observer, and in which time is relative or is even allowed to break the forward progression of the novels by repeating itself. Although there have been both supporting arguments and reservations voiced as to the applicability of Einsteinian relativity to Durrell's "word continuum," I think it is safe to say that the viability of his basic structure has been established. The *Quintet* also is close to Einstein, as Durrell claims in the *Egoïste* interview, with the important difference that elements of the story are not only retold by different observers-participants, but they are retold as a fiction written by one of the characters.

Durrell has also taken pains to tie his multi-novel structures to nature, human sexuality in the case of the love-oriented *Quartet,* which he introduced with an epigraph from Freud ("I am accustoming myself to the idea of regarding every sexual act as a process in which four persons are involved"), and to the pattern of fives—five fingers, five senses, five dimensions—for *The Avignon Quintet.* In a letter written shortly after he completed the *Quintet,* Durrell states that he had switched from the four-part structure of the *Quartet* to the five-part *Quintet* because of his perception of the Eastern view of humanity:

> [Man] fitted into our behavioristic notion of individual psychology as consisting of two parts, conscious and unconscious, male and female—materially making up a cube anatomically; a four-power animal with the possible existence of a fourth dimension! This was our religion. But in oriental terms this isn't true for the human personality is far from discrete, it is five-powered and five-sided. It ain't stable but a "congeries" of elements. Seen in this way my five-power novel should give a much more "flou" effect for its personas are not wholes but collections of spare parts. They *could* be each other by a simple slip of contingency. As for death which, like matter, rules the western novel, that doesn't exist either. Oriental thinking regards it as simply changing your violin case for another! Nor does reality itself have outlines, borders, because it is provisional and not fixed and demarcated. The multiplicity of possible lives in each of us is quite overwhelming—how to reduce it to an artistic formula is the problem? I have tried to do so while still remaining a European.[7]

Thus, Durrell set out to show in the *Quintet* this interchangeability of personalities, events, and even such states as life and death.

The "reality" presented in the volumes *Livia, Constance, Sebastian: or, Ruling Passions* (1983), and *Quinx* records the incestuous, conjugal, and deviate loves of the siblings Livia, Constance, and Hilary. The novelist Blanford is married, for a time, to the "formidable quaire" Livia, and he turns out to be the "author" of *Monsieur.* Blanford has created an "alter ego," the novelist Robin Sutcliffe, who is credited with having written the "Venetian Notebooks" section of *Monsieur.* Much later in *Sebastian* (but earlier in "real" chronology), Sutcliffe and Blanford discuss the "double concerto" of a novel, apparently *Monsieur,* which they are writing together. Says Sutcliffe, "You could sign yourself OREPSORP and I could sign myself NABILAC. It's the other side of the moon for Prospero and Caliban. . . . In other words *enanteiodromion,* everything would be turning into its opposite."[8] Later Blanford tells his double, "Your version of our book gives the presence of events, mine the absence" (143). The reader is invited to play the game of deriving the characters and actions, in retrospect, of *Monsieur* from the other books, in a parody of the way critics search for sources in an author's life. In a quasi-comic subplot, the Templar treasure mentioned rather fleetingly in *Monsieur* becomes in the subsequent volumes the object of an intensive search by Lord Galen, Prince Hassad, Quatrefages, and the German double agent, Smirgel.

As the reader progresses through the five novels, he realizes that *Monsieur* is the hub about which the others rotate like stepchildren, both in themes and in structural devices. Said Durrell of *Monsieur*, "It's a groundplan."[9] Some have seen instead the hub in *Constance,* the longest and perhaps the most clearly narrated of the novels, and it does stand in somewhat the same relationship to the *Quintet* as *Mountolive,* in Durrell's words a "straight naturalistic novel,"[10] does to the *Quartet.* But of the Quincunx novels, *Monsieur* alone spans everything, from the suppression of the Templars by Philippe le Bel to the torture of Quatrefages and others by the Nazis and their surrogates; from Durrell's condemnation of "the four Ms—which characterise our age with such depth of focus. . . . Monotheism, Messianism, Monogamy, and Materialism,"[11] to his views of pluralistic social relationships as truer to man's nature; from his belief in the breakdown of the discrete ego to his Eastern-leaning view of the multiplicity of personalities inherent in the individual; from the gnostic theory that evil has supplanted good as the controlling supernatural impulse, a religious inversion, to the sexual inversions of many of the characters; and so on. The characters succeed or fail depending on how well they can cope with these issues—especially the four *M*s—relevant to each; and the various groupings of individuals invite consideration as microcosms of society. In keeping with his five-part structure, Durrell adds another *M* to his four-*M* list: "The Freudian analysis of absolute value [is] based upon infantile attitudes towards excrement. Gold and excrement, that is poetic indeed! The cornerstone of culture then is another M—*merde*. The gold bar is the apotheosis of the human turd" (*Monsieur,* 142). Wealth is shown up for what, in Durrell's eyes, it essentially is: "the smoked dung of merchant enterprise" (*Monsieur,* 278).

Before we examine Durrell's *M*s more closely, a word about possible sources. Durrell has practiced yoga and studied oriental religions for many years, and his readings in Tao and the *I Ching,* Tantrism, and Milarepa are well documented, both in his correspondence with Henry Miller and in his book on his meetings with Jolan Chang, *A Smile in the Mind's Eye* (1980). Durrell's discussions with Chang, author of *The Tao of Love and Sex,* have included consideration of the psychic and physical benefits of the withheld orgasm, a Tantric method held to lead to the cessation of mental processes and to the ultimate achievement of oneness with the reality of the universe. An important element of Tantrism is the *pancamakaras,* a grouping of five symbol-rich elements whose names begin with *M: madya* (wine), *mamsa* (meat), *matsya* (fish), *mudra* (female partner), *maithuna* (sexual union). These have been interpreted both literally and as representing aspects of the psycho-physiological Hatha Yoga. I am not suggesting a direct correspondence between Durrell's five *M*s and those of Tantrism, but the very concept of employing five *M*s—monotheism, messianism, monogamy, materialism, and *merde*—as a *truc* on which to hang the thematic structure of the *Quintet,* is a coincidence too seductive to be ignored.

Beyond this is the vital significance of the meanings expressed or implied by the Tantric *pancamakaras* in Durrell's contexts. Wine: both as pledge of friendship and as mystic communion, the vintages flow at almost every meeting, and console the solitaries. A drugged wine appears at the Ophitic communion at Macabru in *Monsieur,* and in the next novel Livia and an unnamed lover pledge their carnality in blood drained from the neck of a living cow, a parody of the Christian blood-into-wine and a commentary on monotheism and blood-soaked Christianity. Meat: meals are very important in the *Quintet,* including a banquet redolent of Trimalchio's feast, an orgy of material delights, at the end of *Livia.* In *Monsieur* one of the feasts is a communion at which real *mummia*—mummy flesh—is consumed by the initiates. Meat in the most carnal sense appears as Trash and Pia make love to blood-stained butchers, and hug one another in a lesbian embrace inside the half-carcass of a slaughtered cow. Fish: Durrell is a fine swimmer and a Piscean with a casual interest in astrology who floats naturally into an aquatic lotus position in Peter Adam's BBC-TV documentary, *Spirit of Place: Lawrence Durrell's Greece* (1975), and most of his characters take to the water, often in a baptismal sense. They swim in the river near Verfeuille in *Monsieur* and in the lily pond at Tu Duc in the other novels; they swim at Macabru, the desert oasis, after the Ophitic initiation; they swim in the Mediterranean before Akkad's spiritual teachings; Blanford and Hilary swim in the rock pools above the Pont du Gard, which is finally identified in *Quinx* as the fortuitous monument over the supposed Templar treasure. Blanford's rehabilitation from his war wound is aided by a dip in the lily pond. Female partner: both men and women tend to have female partners in the *Quintet,* and it is the female who seems most often to bring fulfillment, self-knowledge, and wisdom: the sisters Livia and Constance shock and educate Blanford; Constance learns that she is a "man's woman" through Silvie. Attempts at monogamous marriages are destroyed by the agency of a succession of seducing lesbians: Trash, Thrush, Livia herself, Silvie. Sexual union: this is the nexus—sometimes inverted, hence *merde,* sometimes normal— joining many of the characters in the *Quintet.* "Sperm against specie," as Durrell writes in *Monsieur* (223). Constance, as befits her name, is at the pivotal center of several relationships: she marries Sam in what is largely a physical attraction, a betrayal of her inner nature, and, significantly, their child is aborted just before Sam is killed in a wartime accident. A more balanced relationship with Sebastian, described in the novel of that name, is marred by the conflict awakened in him between his love and his driving religious thrust—messianism, in other words—and he is destroyed, murdered by the madman Mnemidis while he, Sebastian, is in an abject state that precludes any resistance. Finally, Constance's reciprocated love for Blanford helps rehabilitate him from his spinal wound (an injury, be it noted, to the site of the five higher Tantric *chakras* or psychic centers) and leads to his emergence as a writer. The implication here is that the highest progeny that can be born of a human relationship is a work of art. All these points suggest, at least, that the Tantric *pancamakaras,* as psycho-physiological keys, have a more than casual applicability to the themes of the *Quintet.* In *Quinx* Durrell links his pattern of fives to Eastern mysteries: "All nature consents to the code of five. (Five wives of Gampopa, five ascetics in the Deer Park, five skandas)" (134).

To return to the five *M*s Durrell evokes specifically. I have already stated that anything single is suspect in the cosmos of the *Quintet.* Durrell plays with the inversion of each of his *M*-terms in order to analyze them. Christian monotheism is seen from the inverted gnostic viewpoint: some diabolical force has taken the place of Christ, and the eye of the godhead now in control is the glittering eye of the serpent, Ophis. Western man's blind acceptance of monotheism has prevented him from realizing this and therefore from coping with evil, just as the "good" people in *Sebastian,* Constance, Schwartz, and Sebastian Affad, are unable to understand, control, or regenerate Mnemidis, whose morality is inverted, for whom "all love was the genius of misgiving, which rules the human heart" (22). Mnemidis thus becomes symbolic of modern man, locked in the worship of a monotheism whose basic morality has become inverted, ignorant of his plight and unable to see the peace possible through the comfortable passivity of Tibetan Buddhism, or through some other pluralistic religion or philosophy. Messianism, which Durrell's Akkad defines as a "foolish personal fate" (*Monsieur,* 142), can be inverted to produce the self-effacing teaching of the Tibetan lamas who sought personal extinction but not the glories of martyrdom, or the example of the gnostics who defied Monsieur by arranging one another's deaths. Possessive monogamy is discarded in favor of multi-leveled, multi-personed companionship. The large number of inverts of both sexes—some of them fixed in monogamous, unisexual relationships of deadly intensity—and the three-sided loves suggest that monogamy is unrealistic, given the complexities of human nature. Exclusive claims lead to the destruction of the relationship, and often of one or both of the partners; but Blanford, having let Constance go her own way at the end of *Quinx,* retains her affection and friendship even beyond her death, as his evenings spent in communion with her attest, although to observers he is "talking in whispers to an empty alcove" (*Monsieur,* 305). Materialism, based on "infantile attitudes toward excrement," is practiced mainly by Durrell's wealthiest and at once most childlike people, the bankers Lord Banquo, Lord Galen, and the Egyptian Prince Hassad. This road leads to Monsieur-le-Prince, corruption, and torture—of the Templars in the fourteenth century, of Quatrefages in the twentieth. From materialism we have only to nudge a symbol to arrive at the fifth *M, merde*. But *merde* is not a true equivalent for materialism, despite the "apotheosis of the human turd." Apostrophizing on Marius, the *"pompe à merde"* he has seen evacuating the cesspools of Avignon, Blanford quotes, *"Inter faesces et urinam nascimur."*[12] The places of excrement and of generation exist side by side. Constance, of Durrell's characters the one most to be heeded, defines Marius as the "anal-oral machine most appropriate to our time" (*Livia,* 262). Re-invert mankind's focus from the *merde*-fixation and we can produce the glory and center of creative life: "We can make amends by loving correctly" (*Monsieur,* 144). It is the fifth *M* that must be at the center of Durrell's Quincunx, signaled by inversions of values: from Eastern polytheistic toler-ance to Western monotheism, from self-effacing passivity to individualistic messianism, from non-possession to materialism, from sperm to feces. And it is *merde* that is the fitting emblem for Monsieur, the Prince of Darkness, to invoke the full title in the English edition of the novel at the structural center of the Quincunx. Re-invert, says Durrell, re-invert. Thus the five-part thematic structure, both in the implied Tantric philosophy and in the declared five *M*s, coincides with the outer form of the *Quintet.*

The Alexandria Quartet provides an important clue to the structure and symbolism of the *Quintet.* In one of the most useful studies to date of the *Quartet,* Carol Peirce has identified over a score of characters and situations that correspond to the major and minor arcana of the Rider Tarot deck.[13] Since the Tarot is mentioned in the *Quintet* as the fortune-telling medium employed by Sabine, it seems not unlikely that a similar study of the later novels would be rewarding. For our present purposes, however, it should be sufficient to follow through on the pattern of fives. In the Tarot the most obvious five-pattern occurs in the minor arcana suit of Pentacles, identified by the pentagram and associated in mantic contexts with money and interest. The suit of Pentacles points toward the superstitious treasure-seekers Lord Galen and Prince Hassad, both of whom have their fortunes told by the Gypsies in *Quinx.* If the love of wealth is indeed tied to infantile attitudes, then we should not be surprised to find these gentlemen among the most childish in their affective natures: Lord Galen naïvely trusts Hitler, and the Prince sports in half-naked innocence with young children.

The pentagram, *inverted,* also appears on one of the cards of the major arcana, Key 15 or The Devil:

A horned devil with wings like those of a bat sits on a half-cube which signifies the half-knowledge of only the visible, sensory side of existence. His right hand is upraised; an inverted flaming torch, symbolic of black magic and destruction, is in his left. On his forehead, the inverted pen-tagram between his horns shows that man's place in the universe is here reversed. From a ring in the half-cube, chains are carried to the necks of a man and a woman. The chains are loose enough to be slipped off, suggest-ing that much of bondage is imaginary.[14]

This description fits almost exactly the main themes and action of the *Quintet:* the protagonists operate on half-knowledge, especially in their often futile application of that incomplete science, psychoanalysis; black magic is suggested as a means of combatting Hitler; the destruction of the Jews, Gypsies, and French Maquisards during the Second World War complements the ancient violence done the Templars, so central to *Monsieur;* the pattern of inversion covers not only man's loss of his natural place as lord of terrestrial creation, guaranteed in Genesis, but the many sexual inversions that poison at least three of the marriages; finally, the bondage theme is everywhere: from Sutcliffe as "bondsman" to his creator, Blanford, to the bondage of Lord Galen to the Templar treasure, to the bondage of various lovers to one another. Some of these bondages in the *Quintet* are, as they are described, imaginary albeit binding, in parallel with the symbolism of the Key 15 Tarot card. Cards reveal the future in *Quinx,* and the power of the storyteller works a similar magic in the *Quintet* as a whole to turn fiction into future reality.

Another vital structural motif, beside the quincunx and the pentagram, is the serpent, Ophis, literally worshiped at Macabru in *Monsieur.* The arboreal quincunx is a tamed pastoral, a man-made Eden, and into this Eden must come, of course, the Serpent: temptation, wisdom, gnosis, evil (or *evol,* love spelled backward or inverted, already coined in the mirror-world of *Justine* [1957], the first volume of *The Alexandria Quartet*). But Durrell's Ophitic serpent, "a symbol of the caduceus of Aesculapius, of the spinal column, of the kundalini-serpent of the Indians" (*Monsieur,* 134), also represents good, the knowledge that prevents man, ancient gnostic or modern mystic, from living a lie. All these motifs present no contradiction in Durrell's dualistic, often triune world. Just as he exploits the patterns of fives, so the *S*-pattern twines itself around the elements of Durrell's various Edens in the *Quintet.* *Monsieur* opens with a train journey down the *S*-curves of the rail line that skirts the Rhone on its way south to Avignon; this is succeeded by the winding procession of Piers's funeral, "a long glowworm of light" (69). In *Livia* there is another *S*-journey down the Rhone, this time by steam barge, and in *Quinx* the rail route to Avignon is covered again; and there are many other examples. Durrell specifically ties the *S*-structure to his narrative method in his description of the reminiscences and musings of Blanford, which take up most of the first 166 pages of *Livia:* "The long serpentine thought, after so many parentheses, came at last to rest in his silent mind" (167).

Some of the literal journeys are as meandering as the one the reader takes through Blanford's mind: Felix Chatto's insomniac rambles about Avignon; Blanford's nocturnal wanderings about the same city in search of Livia; Sabine's travels with the Gypsies. These less directed movements suggest the paths of persons lost in labyrinths, and the labyrinth is another recurring structural device in the *Quintet.* Piers originally wanted to study archaeology and explore the labyrinth at Gortymna, but ends up investigating the gnostic mysteries and his own mind; and the putative Templar treasure is said to be hidden in a labyrinth under the Pont du Gard, a labyrinth protected, as are all truly mythological labyrinths, by a dangerous monster, in this case by the system of explosive mines planted by Austrian sappers. Constance and Blanford stay away from this labyrinth until just before the tunnels are to be breached at the end of *Quinx,* perhaps symbolically indicating at once their rejection of merely material treasure and their solution of their personal labyrinths of the emotions. Other labyrinths are more purely intellectual—for instance, Toby's exploration of the blind passages and false leads to the mystery of the destruction of the Knights Templars. Another puzzle, both labyrinthine and serpent-shaped, is the "death-map" on which Piers records the deaths of his friends, and through which he tries to predict his own ritual murder. "The snake symbolises process, even time itself" (*Monsieur,* 35), says Bruce Drexel, explaining the shape of his friend's death chart. Durrell in his early novel *The Dark Labyrinth* (1947) had already used the maze as a laboratory for psychological enquiry; *The Avignon Quintet* too is the portrait of a labyrinth, physical as well as mental. However, unlike the earlier novel, the *Quintet* investigates the pattern of fiction-into-reality and its inverse, reality-into-fiction, in an attempt to redefine the process of creation, the relationship of the author to his fictions.

"We are treading a very narrow path between reality and illusion," Durrell has Akkad say in *Monsieur* (167), and to demonstrate this thesis Akkad plants a fake article "exposing" as hoaxes his mystic séances at Macabru. That Piers continues to believe the truth of the gnostic initiation despite the evidence of the fake publication proves, claims Akkad, the "truth" of the religious experience. Along the scheme of the *gigogne,* Durrell explores the frame-within-frame patterns, implying that the series could continue indefinitely. In the "Envoi" to *Monsieur* he writes:

> So D.
>> begat
>>> Blanford (who begat Tu and Sam and Livia)
>>>> who begat
>>>> Sutcliffe
>>>> who begat
>>>> Bloshford.

Then Durrell suggests inverting the pattern, when Sutcliffe claims that Blanford could turn out to be "the fiction of one of his fictions" (*Livia,* 53). On the scale of reality, the outermost "box" of the *gigogne* is the existence of a shadowy "begetter" named D.; which encloses a box containing *Livia, Constance, Sebastian,* and *Quinx;* which in turn contain *Monsieur;* which holds several boxes, including "The Venetian Documents," a medley of

Sutcliffe's novel fragments and of his daily life as well, and a "Life with Toby" box holding Toby's historical study of the Templars. Sutcliffe's "Documents" section also contains what could be considered separate interior boxes, among them Piers's diary and the exploits of Bloshford and Oakshot, characters invented by Sutcliffe and therefore at a still further remove from reality. But Sutcliffe is not fixed on the reality scale, and it is instructive to consider the progressive levels of his emergence as "real." At the end of *Monsieur* he is clearly identified as a character invented by Blanford; in *Livia* he talks back to Blanford on the telephone, but Blanford keeps reminding him he is a fiction; in *Constance* Sutcliffe "materialises" beside Blanford and plays billiards with the "real" Constance; in *Quinx* he appears as Blanford's "alter ego," conversing normally with him on ways to "heighten the colour" of Sutcliffe's marriage "in the interests of my [Blanford's] fiction" (30). Finally Sutcliffe has to remind Blanford, "But you are talking as if I am real" (37). We come to doubt the fictional nature of fiction, which is exactly what Durrell wants. Freud's old leather couch, rescued in the "fictive" *Monsieur,* shows up as part of Blanford's dream in "real" *Livia,* and as a tangible object in *Constance.* Invented Sutcliffe refuses to remain dead, although according to Blanford he had cooperated in his suicide. Durrell implies that since we routinely question the reality of reported events, why not, conversely (or inversely), question the fictional nature of fiction, even fiction which the author assures us is invented? Once again, the inversion is a useful signpost to meaning. Reality is what we take to be real, so that fictions can and do become real.

In addition to its intricate and obviously purposeful structure, the *Quintet* is a modernist work in another sense: society and manners are curiously absent. Yes, there are many characters, but there is little sense of a shared community, of shared values. As Marie-Anne Pini has noted, Avignon is seen, for the most part, at night and deserted.[15] When the citizens do appear in force, at the end of *Constance,* it is simply as part of the hysterical mob that cheers on the murderer of Nancy Quiminal. Nor are the main characters united by any sense of community or even, necessarily, by common interests, but often only by chance geography. Durrell's people in large groups can be narrowly defined: a frenzied mob, Prince Hassad's criminal associates, Quatrefages's lunatics. In no meaningful sense are they a community, a society. As part of his definition of modernism as it operated in the 1920s, Malcolm Bradbury wrote: "Secular, mobile, heterodox . . . society seems less like a community than an impersonal crowd, men are constantly compelled to create their identities, their aspirations, their values."[16] This is precisely what Durrell's characters are forced to do: redefine themselves, over and over. In this process of redefinition they lose any claim to the traditional stable ego, which once established the parameters for decorum in the author's delineation of character.

Durrell has often proclaimed his impatience with the discrete ego, just as

one of his acknowledged masters, D. H. Lawrence, did on 5 June 1914, in a
letter to Edward Garnett:

> You mustn't look in my novel [*The Rainbow*] for the old stable *ego*—of the
> character. There is another *ego,* according to whose action the individual is
> unrecognisable, and passes through, as it were, allotropic states which it
> needs a deeper sense than any we've been used to exercise, to discover are
> states of the same single radically unchanged element.[17]

Lawrence explains his concept of the ego by reference to the various states of
the element carbon: coal, soot, diamond. Similarly, Durrell has Blanford say,
"What always bothered me was the question of a stable ego—did such a thing
exist? . . . Myself, I could hardly write down the name of a character without
suddenly being swamped by an ocean of possible attributes, each as valid
and as truthful as the other" (*Livia,* 37).

Durrell deliberately ties this instability of the ego to the Tibet he claimed as
an inspiration for the *Quintet.* He has Blanford discuss a letter from his
estranged wife, Livia:

> "But the letter . . . was written from Gantok [*sic*] and she had headed it,
> 'On the road to Tibet.' It was long, rambling and inconsequential, and . . . I
> destroyed it. But I remember one part in which she wrote: 'You cannot
> imagine what it is like to find myself in a land where beautiful six-armed
> Tsungtorma raises her lotus-soft palms.' It was a fair enough criticism of
> my literary method—why not six-armed psyches? Would it be possible, I
> wondered, to deal fairly with a multiplicity of attributes and still preserve a
> semblance of figurative unity in the personage described? I was dreaming
> of a book which, though multiple, embodied an organic unity." (*Livia,* 38)

Note that Durrell, if Blanford can be taken as his spokesman in this discussion of literary method, is aware of the need to maintain the *semblance* of
unity, even while disbelieving in it. Alexandra David-Neel in *Magic and
Mystery in Tibet,* a book to which Durrell has referred elsewhere, quotes one
of her mentors, Daling lama, as saying, "A living being is an assemblage, not
a unity."[18] "On the road to Tibet" echoes David-Neel's book, a large part of
which describes her difficulties on the way to her goal, but even more
pertinent to the *Quintet* is her statement that "Plurality of personalities in the
apparently single individual is, of course, not peculiar to Tibetan lamas, but it
exists in them in a remarkably high degree."[19] An important part of the
Tibetan understanding of the plurality of personalities was reincarnation,
which Durrell in *Livia* ties to multiple-volume works: Blanford envisages "a
series of books through which the same characters move for all the world as
if to illustrate the notion of reincarnation. After all, men and women are
polyphonic beings. . . . Pia into Livia, Livia into Pia, what does it matter?—
somewhere in that recess of time they are conscious of each other, of their
origins" (41–42).

Durrell's fascination with Tibet goes back at least to *The Black Book* (1938), which is introduced by an epigraph in Tibetan, and there are many illustrations of the "multiplicity of attributes" and the "plurality of personalities" in the *Quintet*. Livia herself is protean, as Blanford realizes:

> "The Livia of that epoch was dark and on the thin side. . . .her black soft hair seemed to fly out of the crown of her head and flow down the sides in ringlets reminiscent of Medusa—the snake is quite an appropriate metaphor. . . . and from time to time an expression came into her eyes, a tense fierce expression, and one suddenly saw a man-at-arms peering at one out of a helm." (*Livia*, 38–39)

Preoccupied by memories of sexual conquests, Livia could take on yet another attribute: "I saw her face suddenly go dead and transform itself into the resolute face of a tough little sailor" (*Livia*, 36). The mystic Akkad in *Monsieur* goes through astonishing physical changes, reflecting his inner states: "He sometimes looked heavy and fat, sometimes thin and ascetic" (105). Some characters change states even more dramatically: as we have seen, Blanford "invents" Sutcliffe, causes him to commit suicide, and then discusses his resurrection with him. Other characters are cross-pollinated through several books: the sage Akkad in *Monsieur* appears to have gotten his name from a "criminal type" mentioned fleetingly in the "real" *Livia*, and his personality and interests from Sebastian Affad—surely Durrell's illustration of the evil-good duality of man.

If the discreteness of the ego is for Durrell an unsound assumption, everything mono- is also suspect, as we have seen. If we accept the gnostic premise of the usurpation of Christ's cradle and throne by the Prince of Darkness, we live under a dualistic reign, evil in opposition to good, but with the former in the ascendant, an inversion of orthodox Christianity. Monogamy is doomed to failure because it runs counter to mankind's nature. Analyzing the situation of Piers, Bruce, and Silvie in *Monsieur*, Sutcliffe says, "I suddenly saw the underlying unity of the three children as a total *self*, or the symbol of such an abstraction. Against the traditional duality-figure of our cosmology I placed a triune self, composed of two male and one female partner—a gnostic notion, if I remembered correctly" (220). Here is another parallel to D. H. Lawrence: the Gerald Crich, Birkin, and Ursula friendship in *Women in Love*. That both these triune relationships fail does not mean that either writer repudiated them *in theory*. In the *Quintet* there is a second triune love-grouping that also stands distinct from the traditional love-triangles of conflicting, competing individuals: Hilary, Livia, and Blanford. In the first triad of lovers in the *Quintet*, Bruce is attracted homosexually to Piers and heterosexually to Silvie; Silvie loves her brother incestuously and Bruce within the bonds of legitimate marriage. Durrell seems to be implying that such relationships cannot prosper in our society:

Silvie drifts in and out of insanity, deeply burdened by guilt. In the other triad, Livia becomes destructive and finally commits suicide, and Hilary behaves jealously toward his brother-in-law Blanford. The monogamy taboos of Western society operate too strongly via the superego for such tripartite relationships to work; but in the Tibet that Durrell claims as inspiration for both *Quartet* and *Quintet*, polygamy and polyandry operate within families—sisters sharing a husband, brothers sharing a wife.

Clearly, Durrell has planned far more carefully than the often rambling narrative and involuted fiction-reality switches might suggest. The quincunx pattern mandates a focus on the central novel, *Monsieur*. The five-part structure, true to nature, counterpoints the overriding theme of the books: that the five *M*s run *contrary* to the inherent patterns of nature which must be followed if the human organism is to be healthy. Misused, monotheism, messianism, monogamy, and materialism lead to destruction, and *merde* represents a symbolic inversion of all values. Duality is truer to reality as Durrell sees it than simple, single states, and the triune relationships, even though perhaps doomed to failure, hold out a tantalizing promise. The *S*-pattern of the serpent stands as a map to the treasure of knowledge, a path that can lead us out of, as well as into, the labyrinths of ignorance. Even the Tarot may be a guide to knowledge for those who believe in the power of the cards. As Durrell wrote in "Cities, Plains and People":

> All rules obtain upon the pilot's chart
> If governed by the scripture of the heart.[20]

The treasure—Templar, physical, psychological, spiritual, intellectual—is there for us to find, if we seek it in the proper frame of mind.

NOTES

1. James P. Carley, "An Interview with Lawrence Durrell on the Background to *Monsieur* and Its Sequels," *Malahat Review* 51 (1979): 46.

2. Lawrence Durrell, *Constance: or, Solitary Practices* (New York: Viking, 1982), pp. 122–23.

3. Jean-Maurice de Montremy, "Lawrence Durrell et Variations: Avignon, troisième mouvement," *La Croix* (Paris), 1 December 1984, 24.

4. Lawrence Durrell, Author's "Note" in *Balthazar* (New York: E. P. Dutton, 1958).

5. Lawrence Durrell, *Quinx: or, The Ripper's Tale* (New York: Viking, 1985), pp. 131–32. Subsequent quotations are taken from this edition.

6. Michel Braudeau, "Lawrence Durell [*sic*]—Michel Braudeau: 'Après ça, J'aurai Tout Dit,'" *Egoïste* (Paris), no. 8 (June 1984): 52.

7. Lawrence Durrell, letter to Ian S. MacNiven, 15 December 1984 (unpublished).

8. Lawrence Durrell, *Sebastian: or, Ruling Passions* (New York: Viking, 1984), p. 123. Subsequent quotations are taken from this edition.

9. Carley, "Interview," 46.

10. George Wickes, ed., *Lawrence Durrell–Henry Miller: A Private Correspondence* (New York: E. P. Dutton, 1963), p. 320.

11. Lawrence Durrell, *Monsieur: or, The Prince of Darkness* (London: Faber and Faber, 1974), p. 142. Subsequent quotations are taken from this edition.

12. Lawrence Durrell, *Livia: or, Buried Alive* (New York: Viking, 1978), p. 263. Subsequent quotations are taken from this edition.

13. Carol Peirce, " 'He so bewitched the cards': Lawrence Durrell's Magical Tarot Deck," "Proceedings of the Third International Lawrence Durrell Conference," 13–14 April 1984 (publication forthcoming).

14. Eden Gray, *The Tarot Revealed* (New York: Bell Publishing, 1960), p. 92.

15. Marie-Anne Pini, "Is Durrell's Avignon in France?," "Proceedings of the Third International Lawrence Durrell Conference," 13–14 April 1984 (publication forthcoming).

16. Malcolm Bradbury, "The Novel in the 1920's," in *The Twentieth Century*, ed. Bernard Bergonzi, *History of Literature in the English Language*, vol. 7 (London: Sphere Books, 1970), p. 184.

17. Harry T. Moore, ed., *The Collected Letters of D. H. Lawrence* (New York: Viking, 1962), p. 282.

18. Alexandra David-Neel, *Magic and Mystery in Tibet* (New York: Dover, 1971), p. 59. First English edition published by Claude Kendall (New York, 1932).

19. Ibid., p. 99.

20. Lawrence Durrell, *Collected Poems*, ed. James A. Brigham (New York: Viking, 1980), p. 163.

17

The Other Doris Lessing: Poet

PAUL SCHLUETER

Most notable writers are distinguished by their mastery of one, possibly two genres; those rare authors such as Robert Penn Warren who move dexterously across generic lines seem to be the exception. Many writers, however, have produced memorable work in genres other than those for which their chief acclaim has resulted; one thinks, for example, of Donald J. Greiner's excellent *The Other John Updike* (1981) as one especially astute examination of these secondary genres. Yet the fact remains that such fugitive or ephemeral works are usually self-evidently inferior when compared to their authors' best work or to comparable writing by others. As fascinating as, say, the poetry of a Faulkner or a Hemingway may be for the dissertation-topic seeker, ultimately these authors' reputations will be based on more enduring work in other genres. Doris Lessing is a similar case in point: internationally known for her novels and her short stories, she is also a frequent essayist.[1] She has written a dozen or so plays,[2] and she has occasionally turned her hand to writing poetry—she even produced a small collection of verse relatively early in her career.[3] While her essays and plays have much to offer the careful researcher and have received some attention, her poetry has scarcely been acknowledged.[4] On the one hand, a reader can see why this is, since the verse is mostly pedestrian or topical; on the other, her poetry does suggest a good deal about the beginnings of her career and about a few of her persistent themes and concerns.

The fact that twenty of the forty-odd poems that Lessing has published appeared in various Rhodesian journals during the 1940s is a clear indication of the increasingly minor position genres other than the novel have occupied in Lessing's career, for all of these twenty appeared before she emigrated to London in 1949 and published her first novel, *The Grass Is Singing* (1950). Her occasional appearance in print as a poet since then has included minor snippets of verse in her disowned novel, *Retreat to Innocence* (1956), and in *Briefing for a Descent into Hell* (1971), and poetry and song are both used repeatedly in *The Marriages Between Zones Three, Four and Five* (1980), the second in her *Canopus In Argos: Archives* series of "space fiction" novels. In these cases, however, the verse is either ostensibly written by one of her characters (thus not really permitting criticism of Lessing as poet), or it simply serves as a kind of counterpoint to plot or character (thus taking it from the category of poetry per se and permitting it to serve merely as a more lyrical rendition of what would otherwise normally be prose). It is more useful, I believe, to consider Lessing's more recent effusions in verse in such journals as the *New Statesman* and the *Listener,* in the autobiographical *Going Home* (1957), and in *Fourteen Poems* (1959), some of the contents of which clearly hearken back to her days in Rhodesia, where two poems in the collection were originally published. Her last published poem to date, "Dear Jack," appeared in a collection of tributes to poet-translator Jack Lindsay in 1980[5] and suggests that even if poetry had been a genre in which Lessing had originally decided to take an interest, her development in technique and awareness of the nuances of language not only never matured but actually regressed.

Lessing's earliest published poem, aside from whatever might have appeared during her schooldays, appeared in July 1943, when she was twenty-three; all of her early work appeared under the byline Doris M. (or D. M.) Wisdom, for at the time she was married to Frank Charles Wisdom; the marriage ended the same year, though the Wisdom name, given magazine publishing schedules, continued to appear till the following spring. This first poem, "The Envious," is a conventional, mostly rhymed elegy for those who had died in war; the "white boys" are "undefeated" and yet "cheated" because they were not aware of how hopes turn to lies because of "rusting systems" strangling their "thrusting lives" and thus promising ever more wars. She concludes by stating that the survivors, not the dead, are the envious ones. As a wartime expression of patriotic sympathy, tinged with the kind of sardonic, muted outrage one might find in Thomas Hardy, the poem, though well-meaning, takes a safe stance, even during wartime, in denouncing the "systems" that create the wars.

Contrasting with such a conventional piece is "Fable," also published in 1943. Discarding rhyme and regular stanzas in this poem, Lessing utilizes an impressionistic approach in which her free verse effectively recreates the moment of transition for a young girl from childish carelessness and dream-like escapism to a more mature awareness of the destruction wrought by the passing of time and changed relationships. Some especially effective images are used: "threaded rain" blowing, shadows "crouching on the walls," a scene as "quiet and warm as a hand." Such a romantic vision of course contrasts sharply with the topical horrors of war; but a similar contrast between youthful innocence and exaltation in simply being alive, on the one hand, and in sensing walls rotting, on the other, reminds the reader of the sudden transformation of youthful innocence and joy into chilly awareness of death and chaos. The "new wind" that blows between the two years described in the poem not only "rotted the walls" but also enabled the "hud-dled band" (presumably those attempting to escape the predations of war) to see "wolves' muzzles thrust aside the fallen beams" and only longingly remember the "far-off, youthful voices singing." The poem is moderately effective, with the sharpness of contrast particularly well done. Of greatest interest to Lessing readers, however, is the fact that the poem contains the plot of *Memoirs of a Survivor* (1974) in miniature, especially with the same longing for lost youth that enables the unnamed protagonist of that novel to envision, even to recreate, a simpler childhood in a similar "long, warm room" before the cataclysm of war. Significantly, "Fable" is one of only two poems that Lessing reprinted in *Fourteen Poems,* a clear suggestion that she wished to preserve not only the poem itself but the concept as well.

These first two poems appeared in *The New Rhodesia,* where a dozen more of Lessing's poems were published until she emigrated; *The New Rhodesia* claimed to have "no connection with any political party, being entirely independent, and therefore able to speak freely on every matter of interest to the public."[6] Her other Rhodesian work appeared in *The Labour Front;* in *N.B.,* successor to *The Labour Front;* and in *Rafters: An Air Force Magazine;* some of her early, disowned stories also appeared in these maga-zines. Even when these journals claimed political impartiality, however, they seemed especially open to political statements in literary guise, and some of Lessing's early poetry is considerably more political in tone and subject than the first two published poems. Indeed, the categories for these early poems given by Robin Graham, who had the advantage of residing and teaching in Rhodesia, where copies of the most elusive of the early poems were avail-able, cited the political as one of Lessing's major emphases in these works, with nature, "the fabulous," and satire being the others.[7] While it would be hard to provide other groupings for such a small sampling of poems—again, she only published forty or so poems altogether, with no more than twenty of these from her Rhodesian days—it should be noted that those that could be categorized as concerned with "nature" seem fully as concerned with im-plicit intrusion by the violence of war and impending social change as they are with the natural world. For one theme is overriding in Lessing's verse, aside from a few almost purely lyrical pieces, and that is the clash between the world of man and the world of nature. The recent observation that Lessing "uses imagery in contrasting pairs (sea/land, darkness/light, silence/sound),"[8] while undeniably true, is also so familiar a dichotomy that one could say that virtually all poets, and most particularly lesser ones, lean on this juxtaposition for some of their ideas.

"Wet Day," for example, seems almost imagistic in its delicate recreation of trees "shrieking in pain" because of wind and rain; but Lessing, in the poem's second stanza in which an artificial world of blue sapphires and jade is posited against the Rhodesian setting, creates a sharp contrast between the natural and the man-made as being parallel to the real and the fictive; one immediately thinks of such parallels as Wallace Stevens's "Anecdote of the Jar," but with Lessing having little of Stevens's verbal and symbolic density. A companion poem, "Wet Night," also describes storminess, but with flooding and the sense of the extremes to which Rhodesian weather could go—from drought to floods—leading her to invoke the rain as a sentient, volitional force, almost animistic in nature. A similar romantic quality, especially one with a Shelleyan sense of nameless, undefinable loss, can be found in others of these early poems. "Conversation," for example, takes the form of what appears to be a dialogue while the speaker is walking down a road, or so it seems until we realize that the speaker is alone, that the one with whom she was speaking was an alter ego of a kind, a speaker or force that would enable the speaker to face the future without fear of annihilation; she strains to hear the "murmur" in the "ever-moving seas / Mourning for me and the nameless wounds that bleed."

A similar vision in which primeval innocence is contrasted sharply with ultimate chaos can be found in "On the Beach," in which the speaker, standing on the shore, watches the "wave rear that hides America from view"; that is, she looks beyond the limits of her known world to the promise of the ever-diminishing world before her. Even here, though, she assumes an apocalyptic stance:

> Knowing that dare I clear my eyes I'd see the earth
> Smoulder as it spins, so close its final end
> When it bursts into flame to light the voids beyond.

Lessing, of course, has increasingly given an apocalyptic emphasis to her fiction, not only including her most vivid account of Armageddon, *The Four-Gated City* (1969), but also by implication several of her recent "space-fiction" works in the *Canopus in Argos: Archives* series. Such an early poem as "On the Beach," predating as it does Nevil Shute's novel of the same title and theme by some eleven years, is particularly vivid in its suggestion that fear has been driven from "small familiar things" but, presumably, that dramatic, world-shaking forms of fear have increasingly dominated the speaker's imagination. Lessing would, she says in "Poem," prefer to "live by an older lore, like swallows," as one means of reconciling death with life. Similarly, in "Landlocked," a title she later gave to part four of the *Children of Violence* series, Lessing decries the "treacherous unease" that makes an exile of her and that forces her to choose the "thin lights" of the town over the voice of nature as heard in the sounds of the sea.

Recurring again and again in Lessing's poems touching on the natural order are the opposing images of drought and water, especially the sea. Not only in the poems just mentioned but also in several others as well, she pictures the dryness of southern Africa as an all-controlling force, a force that both controls and diminishes human activity (as it does in *The Grass Is Singing,* the title of which is from Eliot's *The Waste Land*). On the other hand, her use of water as a motif sometimes suggests the coming of life and even an earthly salvation. "In Time of Dryness," for example, a poem that first appeared in *Going Home* (1957) and was reprinted in *Fourteen Poems,* offers a particularly effective handling of the theme, with images of flesh burning, skulls bleaching in the dust, and the dust itself clinging to "everything that lived and grew." The drought described in the poem is both searing and unrelenting; ironically, the earlier version of the poem (in *Going Home*) offers a final stanza about relying on "memories of waterfalls" and "bright drops squeezed from leaves," a stanza dropped from the later publication. Whether or not the poem is "more cohesive and ultimately more forceful" without that stanza, as has been claimed,[9] is open to question, though it is undeniable that the poem is more unified and foreboding without the glimmer of a promise of relief, even if this occurs only in memory.

Others of Lessing's early poems deal similarly with the contrasting worlds of man and nature, but with little thematic or emotional variation from these. "The House at Night," for example, presents a suburban town house, one of a "herd" of such houses, seen in perspective from a distance and appearing to be on a level with "circling mountains, on a level with the hawks that wheeled over the fields."[10] Other poems, such as "Dark Girl's Song" and "Night-Talk," remind one of the work of nineteenth-century Romantic poets, while still others call to mind earlier twentieth-century poets, such as Lawrence or Hardy, Eliot or Joyce, not poets of Lessing's own generation. "New Man" has been called imitative of "literary expressionism,"[11] but it seems to be more a failed effort at a messianic prophecy taking the form of repetition of key words and some slight degree of stanzaic variation:

> This new man comes.
> He comes
> He comes
>
> From the great salt sea
> From the great salt land.

This "new man" from elsewhere seems to be the focus of "Song" as well, a poem telling of such a man who moves from disdain for familiar locales to a return to "the small unchanging valley" and to his learning "to talk to children, after all." A similar sentimental *Weltschmerz* over lost childhood, over "The innocent, from five uneasy continents, / Wandering homeless," appears in "Exiled," a poem celebrating the speaker's dreaming of returning home vicariously and "like invalids / Of pale contaminated shores and unreal ghosts / With hands as soft as clouds." (One has to recall that by the time *Fourteen Poems* was published in 1959, Lessing was not only an emigrant from Rhodesia but also a "prohibited alien" because of her writings about Africa and—a particularly grotesque bit of bureaucratic sophistry—because of her status as an "Asian" by virtue of having been born in Persia. *Going Home* is her account of her one prolonged return visit to Rhodesia.)

While most of the poems in *Fourteen Poems* derive from Lessing's earlier life, a few seem clearly based on her new life in England. The two poems titled "Older Woman to Younger Man" deal with a familiar motif in Lessing's fiction (as, for example, with similar pairings in such novels as *The Summer Before the Dark* [1973] and *The Four-Gated City,* among others). The first poem contrasts the woman's current lover with all her former lovers; after she swears "to love [him] for love's sake," the younger man will conclude not "She bound me" but "She set me free." The second poem, reflecting a greater awareness of the decline of life, presents the woman, "sunk in sap," hearing in her lover's voice "the small / Murmur of moving leaves and men." In both cases the mood is sad but resigned, tender but aware of perpetual change.

Some seven years separate *Fourteen Poems* from Lessing's first appearance as a poet in British journals, however, and the half-dozen poems she published in the *New Statesman* and the *Listener* during the mid-1960s, when her creative productivity in other genres was especially great, all appeared within a space of a year and a half. In a period of only seven years, from 1962 to 1969, she published *The Golden Notebook, Play with a Tiger* (a play), *A Man and Two Women* (stories), *African Stories, Landlocked* (part four of *Children of Violence*), *Particularly Cats* (a memoir), and *The Four-Gated City* (part five of *Children of Violence*). It is not surprising, therefore, that there was little time for or interest in verse during these years, and that she published only six poems.

The first of these poems, "Here," is a slight sixteen-line piece in which the narrator compares himself/herself with others who have stood in the same place, "All with our flowering branches." But if one begins the poem by believing it to be a conventional comparison of man with a natural object, this conclusion is quickly dispelled by references to mysterious and unexplained things, such as the five locked doors behind the speaker and the others, and the beasts snarling behind the doors, beasts that "licked our hands before." The repeated reference to the darkness suggests that this may be death, especially with the series of rhetorical questions that are offered:

> Who shut the doors?
> Who taught our beasts to snarl?
> Who, what brought me here?

The poem ends with a kind of redundant doubletalk: if the narrator is standing "where the dark came close," then, we are told twice in slightly varying form, the dark itself must close. Whether the subject be death or something more eschatological in nature, the poem does not say. Nor does it offer any clue; the poem merely suggests some sort of symbolic stance of the individual against the darkness.

The second of these poems, "A Visit," is a short free-verse fable about the surprise visit of a young blond king to the place called Alturnun, a visit that stirs the narrator's memory to desire Alturnun long after the event, despite the king's reputation of "laugh[ing] as the blood runs" and of "kiss[ing] and kill[ing] in a hard thriving time." The narrator yearns for the natural and human distinctives of Alturnun; but since it is "Hard to get there," he or she says it has been done through "tricking [his or her] way between dead thoughts." To some extent the vision of a visit by a dashing, vigorous king reminds a reader of Lessing's later *The Marriages Between Zones Three, Four and Five,* but the comparison cannot be extended because a twenty-line poem describing such a visit in the guise of a dream cannot be very precise. The poem also reminds one of escapist Romantic verse treating mythical visions.

"For the Doomed Children," by contrast, is both specific and moving in its occasionally sharp, vivid imagery. The poem, running some twenty-seven lines, cryptically relates an exodus of children; whether set in the historical past (as in the Children's Crusade) or present (as in mass evacuation from a war-zone) is never specified. The picture of chaos and desolation normal in a writing about war is intensified in this poem by Lessing's crisply-realized figures of speech (the opening "thin arms of smoke" wind their way through the narrator's sleep and "loop in death the centuries' trees," the ending with a river "crammed with sprouting limbs and plants" as the result of panicked crowding in trying to cross "cruel rivers"). The water motif is repeated with several variations: the scene is presented "as if viewed through water," an image of feeding in "green depths" is employed, and storms are imminent over the plains. The soldiers, masked against infection and hesitant even to touch each other's hands, find the young corpses in the river, here serving more as a watery grave than anything resembling the source of life and fertility; despite the poem's emphasis on language evocative of such fertil-ity—green, for example, is mentioned five times—the overall vision is one of meaningless destruction and waste of a generation. As a whole the poem is particularly effective in its balance between the horrors of war, destroying as it does even the young and innocent, and the thwarted, twisted hopelessness even in the restoration to life implied by the natural order.

"Hunger the King" and "A Small Girl Throws Stones at a Swan in Regents Park" were published simultaneously in 1967. "Small Girl" is the lesser of the two; the Regents Park setting is not mentioned in the poem but instead serves merely as the presumed scene that prompted the poem, for the small girl ostensibly envisions herself as a prince's daughter waiting for the enchanted swan to carry her to an idyllic island retreat. The mere rumor of such enchanted swans, we are told, "caused even the marketplace to shut its noise in wonder," thus suggesting not only a "Prince Charming" quality but an even more supernatural overtone with echoes of the Leda myth. In the poem's last lines, however, mundane reality intrudes—first with the mirror image of the swan reflected in the pond and then with the girl's presumed realization that the "too perfect swan" is deceiving her with her own voice, not with its sound. In other words, her projection through fantasy has come full circle to the point where she realizes that her wishful thinking is all she hears, not the escapist promise of living happily ever after, hence the stone-throwing as retribution for promises unfulfilled.

"Hunger the King" is more abstract in its approach to language, though redeemed somewhat by the image of disparity between word and reality. Of a dozen words a man is given to say, "Hunger first, with cold its brother" are most profoundly those that endure through a person's life. "Give me" is the refrain of youth, but "hunger" and "cold" serve "that great table spread for middle life," long after childish impatience and eagerness are gone from one's life, from one's "table." After "all the guests have gone" (i.e., when one is alone in middle age) and all the countless words have been uttered, "hunger" and "cold" still remain. The poem is certainly not a profound exploration of the demarcation between carefree youth and somber middle age, but it does set up a vivid dichotomy between the demands of youth and the needs of age, for "hunger" and "cold" have an infinite array of implications beyond those that would occur to youth.

Lessing's last poem from the 1960s, "The Islands," suggests at first a return to a fabulistic setting and theme—especially in her "wondering / If it's angels or devils that hold them [the islands]." But she quickly shifts to an emphasis on subtle, small, loving gestures such as tutoring a child or putting out plants to grow, thus leading the reader to conclude that the "islands" are those within the individual's consciousness identified with loneliness and isolation. Those who have been especially vigorous in life (those for whom "life beats too strong") are those most affected by the "underdrag of lethargy" when vigor and vitality are diminished and therefore are all the more in need of someone to "smooth white sheets or draw a cover up." For this "daily adding of small act to act," which once was "food for the dulling of the heart," is in reality the necessary activity of the present just as "frontiers are held by patience after war." The one who does what must be done, in short, restores order and calm to a "damaged house" through such small gestures as a way to connect the islands. One immediately thinks of Donne's "No man is an island," of course, but since Lessing does not develop the metaphor but merely uses it to introduce her theme, there is little clear-cut connection. The poem is well-meaning and expresses a truism moderately effectively, though without exploring many of the implications of either the symbol or of the theme.

Thirteen years after these last poems appeared, in 1980 Lessing again turned to verse, this time as the initial offering in a collection of tributes to Jack Lindsay, Australian-born Marxist poet, novelist, and translator who was especially popular in England during the 1930s, on the occasion of Lindsay's eightieth birthday. Such gatherings of encomia are no doubt harmless and well-meaning enough; yet Lessing's poetic tribute seems particularly effusive, maudlin, and unconvincing. After each of three unrhymed stanzas, Lessing inserts roughly phonetic renderings of a cat's meowing as a way of extending an image of a cat's sounds and movements, especially of two "cats" in a symbiotic scratching of each other's back. Lessing's wish for Lindsay, twenty years her senior, is that in an additional twenty years he can still "rub [her] ears" and "smooth [her] fur." Indeed, she reiterates exaggeratedly, her wish is that in forty years they can still "rub each other's ears and purr." No doubt Lessing had known both Lindsay and his work for many years by this time; the only possible connection that comes immediately to mind is the same surname used for an old revolutionary of heroic proportions in the *Children of Violence* novels. Nonetheless, this piece of verse is not at all effective, especially as the opening entry in a volume containing tributes by such others as Alan Sillitoe, Roy Fuller, David Holbrook, and Edgell Rickword.

Lessing cannot be considered a significant poet, nor does she consider herself one any more than she considers herself a dramatist; she has disowned most of these earlier phases of her life, just as she has one novel *(Retreat to Innocence),* yet by no means should all of this earlier material be relegated to critical and publishing oblivion. For aside from whatever thematic relevance such earlier writing might have in relation to her career as a writer of fiction, and aside too from any autobiographical parallels that might shed light on her formative experiences, the fact remains that there are occasionally small gems among the masses of dross, gems that deserve more than to be buried forever in obscure Rhodesian journals from the Second World War era. After several early poems, Lessing wisely dropped attempts at rhyming and conventional meter in favor of free verse. Her handling of free verse is sometimes effective, sometimes mere unparagraphed prose. Her sharply realized images are as vivid in her verse as in some of her more nonrealistic novels, but rarely are they developed at sufficient length to enable the reader to play with the logical extensions of the images as they affect both poem and reader. The poems, in short, are sometimes too pedestrian in language and theme to deserve reprinting, beyond whatever light they may shed on her subsequent career and concerns. As a whole, her poetry is less impressive than her still-unexplored plays, much less vigorous in language and impact than her essays, and far less enduring than her novels which, despite their shortcomings, constitute a major creative accomplishment of the twentieth century. Except for an essay such as this, however, the interested reader has no way of judging for himself, simply because of the unavailability of many of the poems themselves and the lack of accurate, readily available bibliographic references to the poems. The fact that she published some forty poems in a period of almost the same number of years, though, and that they vary as greatly as they do, fully warrants the interest of scholars who remain fascinated by "the other Doris Lessing."

APPENDIX: POEMS BY DORIS LESSING

The chronological list below is based in part on Jennie Pichanick et al., comp., *Rhodesian Literature in English: A Bibliography [1890–1974/5]* (Gwelo, Zimbabwe: Mambo Press, 1977).

"The Envious" (as by Doris M. Wisdom). *New Rhodesia,* 30 July 1943, p. 8.

"Fable" (as by D. M. Wisdom). *New Rhodesia,* 3 September 1943, p. 22; reprint, *Fourteen Poems* (Northwood, Middlesex; Scorpion Books, 1959), p. 21; reprint, *Zambesia: Journal of the University of Rhodesia* 6 (1978): 211.

"To a Middle-Aged Lady" (as by D. W.). *Rafters,* December 1943, p. 19. Journal also called *Rafters on Safari* or *Safari.*

"The Song of a Bourgeois" (as by D. M. Wisdom). *New Rhodesia,* 3 March 1944, p. 17; reprint, *Zambesia: Journal of the University of Rhodesia* 6 (1978): 211.

"Conversation." *New Rhodesia,* 28 July 1944, p. 22.

"South Africa." *Labour Front,* January 1945, p. 26.

"Politics." *New Rhodesia,* 7 September 1945, p. 21.

"Aeroplane." *New Rhodesia,* 16 November 1945, p. 20.

"Poem." *New Rhodesia,* 21 December 1945, p. 21.

"Wet Night." *New Rhodesia,* 4 January 1946, p. 17.

"On the Beach." *New Rhodesia,* 12 July 1946, p. 18.

"Landlocked." *New Rhodesia,* 20 December 1946, p. 5.

"Lobengula: Swing Song." *New Rhodesia,* 31 January 1947, p. 19.

"After." *New Rhodesia,* 13 June 1947, p. 22.

"Cleopatra." *New Rhodesia,* 14 November 1947, p. 23.

"Wet Day." *New Rhodesia,* 2 July 1948, p. 21.

"Plea for the Hated Dead Woman." *N. B.,* February 1949, p. 19; reprint, *New Statesman and Nation* 51 (30 June 1956), 768; reprint, *Fourteen Poems,* pp. 12–13.

"Under My Hand." *Trek* 13 (February 1949), 25.

"After a War." *N. B.,* April/May 1949, p. 15.

"The Two Cities." *N. B.,* August 1949, p. 16.

"The Revolutionary." *N. B.,* December 1949, p. 16.

"The House at Night." *Going Home* (London: Michael Joseph, 1957; rev. ed., New York: Ballantine Books, 1968), pp. 42–43.

"In Time of Dryness." *Going Home,* p. 234; *Fourteen Poems,* p. 22 (with final four-line stanza omitted).
"The Lilies." *Going Home,* pp. 186–87.
"Bars." *Fourteen Poems,* p. 14.
"Dark Girl's Song." *Fourteen Poems,* p. 15.
"Exiled." *Fourteen Poems,* pp. 19–20.
"Jealousy." *Fourteen Poems,* p. 23.
"New Man." *Fourteen Poems,* p. 16.
"Night-Talk." *Fourteen Poems,* p. 17.
" 'Oh Cherry Trees You Are Too White for My Heart.' " *Fourteen Poems,* p. 20.
"Older Woman to Younger Man (1)." *Fourteen Poems,* p. 10.
"Older Woman to Younger Man (2)." *Fourteen Poems,* p. 11.
"Song." *Fourteen Poems,* p. 18.
" 'Under a Low Cold Sky.' " *Fourteen Poems,* p. 9.
"Here." *New Statesman* 71 (17 June 1966), 900.
"A Visit." *New Statesman* 72 (4 November 1966), 666.
"For the Doomed Children." *Listener* 74 (10 August 1967), 164.
"Hunger the King." *New Statesman* 74 (24 November 1967), 731.
"A Small Girl Throws Stones at a Swan in Regents Park." *New Statesman* 74 (24 November 1967), 731.
"The Islands." *Listener* 78 (30 November 1967), 689.
"Dear Jack." *A Garland for Jack Lindsay* (St. Alban's, Herts.: Piccolo Press, 1980), p. 6.

NOTES

1. The only published collection of essays by Lessing thus far is *A Small Personal Voice: Essays, Reviews, and Interviews,* ed. Paul Schlueter (New York: Alfred A. Knopf, 1974).

2. Most of Lessing's plays were written for British television, though several were staged as well. Most of the dozen or so have never been published and these—as well as her poems—are unlikely to be published during her lifetime, since she has repeatedly stated that these early efforts were ill-advised, unsuccessful, and worthy of being forgotten. A proposal that the University of Rhodesia publish Lessing's early poems and stories (see Robin Graham, "Twenty 'New' Poems by Doris Lessing," *World Literature Written in English* 18 [1979]: 90–98, especially p. 98 n.5) was vetoed by Lessing (G. R. Brown, head of the English department at the University of Rhodesia, in a letter to Paul Schlueter, dated 26 April 1982). References are hereafter cited as *WLWE.*

See also Paul Schlueter, "Lessing's Unpublished Rhodesian Materials," *Doris Lessing Newsletter* 9, 1 (Spring 1985): 13.

3. *Fourteen Poems* (Northwood, Middlesex: Scorpion Press, 1959); this book was published in a limited edition of five hundred copies, of which the first fifty were signed by Lessing; it has never been reprinted.

4. On the plays, see Agate Nesaule Krouse, "Doris Lessing's Feminist Plays," *WLWE* 15 (1976): 305–22; Malcolm Page, "Lessing's Unpublished Plays: A Note," *Doris Lessing Newsletter* 1, 2 (Fall 1977): 6, 3; entries in various encyclopedias of modern drama; and brief

discussions in most book-length studies of Lessing. On the poems, see Graham (cited above, n.2); and Mona Knapp, *Doris Lessing* (New York: Frederick Ungar, 1984), pp. 68–71.

5. A chronological listing of Lessing's poems and sources appears in the Appendix above.

6. Quoted in Graham, "Twenty 'New' Poems," p. 91.

7. Ibid., p. 92.

8. Knapp, *Lessing,* p. 68.

9. Ibid., p. 69.

10. Doris Lessing, *Going Home* (London: Michael Joseph, 1957; rev. ed., New York: Ballantine Books, 1968), p. 43.

11. Knapp, p. 69.

18

Mario Vargas Llosa's *The Green House*: Modernist Novel from Peru

CHARLES ROSSMAN

Mario Vargas Llosa spent the first nine years of his life outside his native Peru, in Cochabamba, Bolivia. Then, in 1945, he moved with his family to Piura, a provincial town in the coastal desert some five hundred miles north of Lima and nearly a thousand miles from his birthplace far to the south, Arequipa. The family spent only a year in Piura before moving on to Lima. Nevertheless, Vargas Llosa remembers that year as the most formative period of his life.[1]

In Piura, a startling new world engraved itself on the nine-year-old's imagination. There he had his first glimpse of the ocean and of the dunes of blowing, desert sands. There he was intrigued by the sights and sounds of the Mangachería, a tough neighborhood where many of the people lived in mud huts but where, nevertheless, a vivid nightlife of bars and musicians flourished. Above all, the young Vargas Llosa's imagination was piqued by a mysterious, green house on the sandy outskirts of town, a building that lay strangely silent by day but exploded with music and laughter after dark, when it attracted numerous male visitors.

Seven years later, in 1952, Vargas Llosa returned with his family to Piura for a second year of residence. The Mangachería was still there, of course, as was the mysterious green house. But whereas the house had fascinated the nine-year-old, necessarily a distant observer, with a kind of mythical aura, the same green building revealed itself to the sixteen-year-old, who visited it as a patron, as merely a tawdry brothel. As Vargas Llosa has put it, the "green palace of the dunes" now appeared as "primitive and very poor, the dream-mansion was merely a cheap whorehouse."[2]

A decade later, Vargas Llosa derived the title of his second novel, *The Green House,* from that Piuran brothel. In addition, both the "green house" and the Mangachería appear as major settings of the novel. The other major locales of *The Green House*—the jungles and rivers of the Peruvian Amazon region—similarly reflect Vargas Llosa's own experiences.

261

Vargas Llosa first visited the Peruvian jungle in 1958. He had finished his studies at the University of San Marcos in Lima and was looking forward to graduate work at the University of Madrid when Juan Comas, a Mexican anthropologist, arrived in Lima. Comas had come to organize a four-week expedition to study the Indians living along the Amazon headwaters of Peru. Vargas Llosa became intrigued by the project and joined Comas's small group. Traveling by hydroplane and canoe, the adventurers made their way to the region of the Aguaruna and Huambisa tribes by the Upper Marañon river, and to Santa María de Nieva, a small outpost of civilization amidst the jungle. Both the Upper Marañon and Santa María de Nieva later became settings of *The Green House,* as did Iquitos, the largest settlement in the Peruvian jungle.

It was unusual, in 1958, for a youth from coastal Lima, with Vargas Llosa's background, to want to visit the jungle. Not surprisingly, the excursion jolted him. "There I discovered a face of my country completely unknown to me. . . . There I discovered that Peru was not only a country of the twentieth century . . . but that Peru was also part of the Middle Ages and the Stone Age."[3] As with his visit to Piura at the age of nine, Vargas Llosa's experiences in the jungle abruptly and permanently transformed his consciousness.

According to Vargas Llosa's own account, after completing his first novel, *The City and the Dogs* (1962), he thought that it might be less exhausting to write two novels simultaneously, rather than undertake another single work. He reasoned that he could avoid the fatiguing concentration required for a single book by alternating between two different projects. The two narratives that he undertook dealt with, respectively, his memories of Piura—the "green house" and the Mangachería—and of the Amazon jungle.

After a time, Vargas Llosa reports, the characters from one narrative began to intrude into the other. The two novels sought to invade one another, with characters, situations, and settings overlapping and intertwining. Eventually, he conceded to the mandates of the two fictional worlds that refused to be kept separate. He decided to blend them, to write a single novel that would draw on both strands of his experience, the desert coast and the jungle.

While forging his newly unified novel, Vargas Llosa read everything in the libraries of Paris, where he was then living, that dealt with the Peruvian jungles. He absorbed everything in print about the Indians, rivers, trees, birds, and animals of the Amazon. He haunted museums and zoological gardens. Nevertheless, when he finished a draft of the novel in 1964, he felt compelled to return to Peru for a second trip to the jungle to verify his impressions. In the tradition of Balzac, Zola, Flaubert, and the Joyce of *Ulysses,* Vargas Llosa took great pains to render the realistic surface of *The Green House* with factual accuracy.

Within a year of his return to the jungle, Vargas Llosa finished the fourth and last version of *The Green House.* The book was published in Barcelona in March 1966 and met with stunning success. *The Green House* captured three important literary prizes: the Spanish Critics' Award for 1967 (which *The City and the Dogs* had also won in 1963), Peru's own National Award for the Novel, and grandest of all, the Rómulo Gallegos Award. The Rómulo Gallegos Award was a special prize given by the National Institute of Culture and Fine Arts in Venezuela to "the best novel written in the Spanish language during a five-year period," and it carried with it a cash stipend of twenty-two thousand dollars. When Vargas Llosa accepted the prize in Caracas on the night of 4 August 1967, the thirty-one-year-old author became an instant celebrity.

As his acceptance speech, Vargas Llosa delivered an impassioned manifesto concerning the writer's relationship to society. The speech, published as "Literature is Fire," begins with a moving evocation of an almost forgotten Peruvian poet, Oquendo de Amat, who had died in Spain some thirty years before. What interests Vargas Llosa, in particular, is Oquendo de Amat's neglect by his own countrymen. He regards Oquendo de Amat's fate—the hostility and indifference that he suffered—as typical of the relationship between the Latin-American writer and his culture.

"Literature is Fire" carries the argument a bold step further. Regardless of the responses an artist provokes, says Vargas Llosa, even in an ideal society that has rid itself of injustice and that nourishes the artists in its midst, the writer's necessary task is to be perpetually unsatisfied with reality. By his very nature, the writer is a rebel, a professional malcontent. "The writer's very reason for being is protest, contradiction and criticism."[4]

"Literature is Fire," then, expounds a theory of the social value of literature. As Vargas Llosa sees it, literature exposes human and social imperfections to enable their improvement. By depicting unpleasant realities, literature compels readers to acknowledge what they prefer to ignore, thereby activating their ethical wills. Such was Vargas Llosa's goal with *The City and the Dogs*, in fact, although that book neither conveys a simple, didactic message nor recommends an explicit course of action. *The Green House* similarly depicts a corruption that afflicts individuals and institutions alike, and that leads to acute human suffering. The reader not only perceives these events, but necessarily *evaluates* them: we are forced, owing to the book's disjunctions of time, place, and even character, to discover the causes of actions and to assess their consequences.

Whereas *The City and the Dogs* involves three narrative strands, a basic time-span of only a few months, and two principal settings, *The Green House* recounts five separate histories embracing some forty years and set in three far-flung locations: Piura, Santa María de Nieva, and the jungle rivers. The separate histories do not unfold one at a time in chronological sequence. Rather, each is divided into numerous fragments that recur throughout the book in a consistent pattern, first a fragment of story number one, then a fragment of story number two, and so forth, rather like a narrative braid.

Ultimately, the exclusivity of each strand in the braid, of each narrative history, collapses. Characters from one sequence become intertwined in the other personal histories, and characters from one setting also appear in other often remote settings, sometimes with different names. Some narrative sequences are approximately simultaneous, while others reveal widely separated phases of the same lives. Altogether, the five narratives of *The Green House* are dispersed among seventy-two distinct episodes, many of which are further fragmented by flashbacks, sometimes occurring in mid-sentence.

One of the reader's main tasks in *The Green House,* then, is merely to discern the five distinct narratives as continuous and unified, a task considerably complicated by the fact that the individual narratives gradually blend and intertwine. Moreover, Vargas Llosa has set perceptual traps, has posed barricades to understanding, such as pairs of characters with the same name, or the same character appearing with different names, or two different bordellos both called the "Green House." The reader must reorder and unify the various events and settings, the different times, the diverse characters from disparate social classes, and the odd, frequently misleading bits of information, in order to discover, ultimately, the complex whole that the five interwoven strands create.

Following are brief summaries, rearranged in chronological sequence, of the five separate histories in the order that they recur throughout the novel:

1. *Bonifacia and the Sergeant in Santa María de Nieva:* Bonifacia, an Indian girl, is one of the oldest pupils at a small missionary school in Santa María de Nieva. Bonifacia takes pity on two Aguaruna Indian girls who have been forcibly brought to the mission to receive a "Christian education." She helps all the girls escape. The nuns, shocked by Bonifacia's ungrateful behavior, expel her. Adrift in the village without family or means, Bonifacia is taken in by Nieves the river pilot, his woman, Lalita, and their children. A Sergeant of the civil guard proposes that Bonifacia and he marry upon his return from a jungle trip in search of rubber bandits. Because Nieves has once worked for the bandits, the Sergeant finds it his painful duty to arrest his friend. Nieves goes to prison, and the Sergeant and Bonifacia, newlyweds, leave the jungle to begin married life in his distant hometown, Piura.

2. *Fushía, in the Santiago-Marañon river area:* Fushía escapes from jail in Brazil and flees to Iquitos in Peru's Amazon basin. There he gains the confidence of Don Fabio and his boss, Julio Reátegui, local governor and wealthy rubber trader. Fushía runs off with some of Reátegui's money and goods, and with Lalita, a fifteen-year-old girl. Fushía and Lalita hide out on an isolated island, which Fushía uses as a base to steal rubber from the Indians who normally sell to Reátegui. Eventually, Lalita runs away with Nieves, a river pilot who works for Fushía, and they establish a home in Santa María de Nieva (which Bonifacia and the Sergeant visit years later, in another narrative strand). Fushía, who has contracted leprosy, is taken to a leper colony by his friend, Aquilino, who continues to visit Fushía until he is too old to make the difficult river journey.

3. *Anselmo and the original Green House in Piura:* The first scene depicts Piura in the early 1920s as a sandy and quiet place that visitors find too isolated and sleepy. One day, Anselmo rides into town on muleback. At first, Anselmo does little more than drink, eye the women boldly, and gossip about the townspeople. Then Anselmo suddenly builds a brothel called the Green House, on the sand dunes outside of town. Customers flock to it, but Father García excoriates it as the work of the devil. Anselmo cannot contain his passion for Antonia, a sixteen-year-old blind waif, and he carries her off to become his lover and the mother of his child. Antonia dies in childbirth, provoking the wrath of Father García and a group of citizens who burn the Green House. After a long decline and a terrible drunkenness, Anselmo ends up as a peaceful harp player in the chica bars of Mangachería. Years pass, and Anselmo, nearly blind, becomes a beloved member of a popular musical group that performs in the Green House, a brothel owned by Anselmo's daughter, Chunguita. Over the years, the reality of the original Green House becomes shrouded in legend. People wonder if it really existed.

4. *Jum, in numerous jungle settings:* Corporal Delgado goes on a furlough, taking the new recruit, Nieves, as his river pilot. They plunder an Indian village, Urakusa, and when the Indians attack in defense, Nieves escapes (he shows up as a refugee on Fushía's island, in another narrative strand). Delgado, his captain, and Reátegui set out to punish the Indians, both for the attack and for attempting to form a rubber cooperative, rather than sell to Reátegui at exploitative prices. They whip the men, rape the women, beat the Indian's leader, Jum, and steal Jum's young daughter. The daughter is left at the nuns' school in Santa María de Nieva—it is Bonifacia. Jum is left hanging by his wrists—alive, but whipped and with his head shaved—near the dock in Santa María de Nieva to serve as a warning to other Indians who might get ideas about cooperatives.

5. *The Unconquerables and the second Green House:* Lituma returns to Piura after ten years in the civil guard, bringing with him the woman, Bonifacia, whom he married in Santa María de Nieva. He falls in with his old gang of toughs, called the Unconquerables, and lands a job as a sergeant in the Piuran police force. One of the Unconquerables, Josefino, vows to seduce Lituma's wife. One night while drinking at the Green House, Lituma challenges a braggart to Russian roulette. The braggart kills himself, Lituma goes to prison in Lima, and Bonifacia is left behind, pregnant. Josefino succeeds with her. They live together a while, and Bonifacia has an abortion. Josefino eventually abandons her, and she becomes a prostitute in the Green House, where she is called "Wildflower" because of her jungle origin, and where she is working when Lituma returns from prison. Lituma gets his revenge by beating up Josefino and scorning Bonifacia.

Each of these five narratives has its unique perspective, tone, and style. The most conventional sequence is the first, that of Bonifacia and the

Sergeant in Santa María de Nieva, which is told from an orthodox, third-person perspective. The narrator clearly identifies setting and speakers, uses quotation marks to indicate speech, describes a speaker's manner and appearance, but rigorously confines himself to objective presentation of what can be observed and heard. Here are the opening words of the first sequence:

> A door slammed, the Mother Superior raised her face from her desk, Sister Angélica burst into the office like a meteor, her livid hands fell onto the back of a chair.
> "What's wrong, Sister Angélica? Why do you look that way?"
> "They've run away, Mother!" Sister Angélica stammered. "There isn't a single one of them left, God save us."[5]

This is the stuff of the traditional novel, and the reader, on familiar ground, quickly becomes oriented. Even in this sequence, however, the mode soon becomes more elaborate. In the first fragment of the sequence, a paragraph of commentary, inserted without warning or transition into an intensely dramatic moment, calmly describes the geographical setting of Santa María de Nieva in a style reminiscent of a travel guide, after which the dramatic scene, taking no notice of the intrusion, continues. In successive fragments of this sequence, more and more of these descriptions intrude, until they develop into a contrapuntal narrative. While Bonifacia is being questioned by the nuns about the escape of the pupils in the main narrative, the contrapuntal insertions dramatize that very escape.

The fifth sequence treats the Unconquerables and the second Green House in a variation of this technique. We again have an objective, third-person narrator who presents the scene in a traditional fashion, again limiting his own knowledge to what any observer might note. The variation consists of frequent cutaways, in cinematic style, to simultaneous events relevant to the main scene, or to past events that respond to allusions in the main scene. For example, when Chunguita and the band describe the fatal game of Russian roulette to Wildflower, the narrative rapidly shuttles from the present in the Green House, to the night of the killing, and back. All scenes from any time or setting are narrated in the present, as though they are occurring for the first time. The effect of simultaneity is something like the literary equivalent of a musical chord.

The second sequence, recounting the history of Fushía, elaborates the techniques of cutaway and flashback. As before, a typical fragment will begin in the conventional third person. But two specific variations intrude. First, a narrator speaks in summary fashion, blending commentary, narrative, and quotation, without bothering to identify speakers or use quotation marks. For example:

> He had gone to school and that was why the Turk had given him a job in his warehouse. He kept accounts, Aquilino, in some big books called

debits and credits. And even though he was honest in those days, he was already dreaming about getting rich. How he used to save, old man, he ate only one meal a day, no cigarettes, no drinking. He wanted a little capital to set up a business. (23)

The voice here is nearly that of Fushía himself, except that Fushía is referred to in the third person: "How he used to save, old man." A conventional narrative would recast these words as: " 'How I used to save, old man,' said Fushía," using quotation marks to indicate a specific speaker. Vargas Llosa has blended narrator and character, using the voice of the character but the perspective of a third-person narrator.[6]

The second narrative variation in Fushía's otherwise orthodox third-person sequence is the abrupt flashback in mid-conversation. For example:

"But you already told me about that when we left the island, Fushía," Aquilino said. "I want to hear how you escaped."
"With this picklock," Chango said. "Iricuo made it from the wire on his cot. We tried it out and it can open the door without any noise. . . ." (23)

Here Aquilino is quizzing Fushía about his past as the two navigate the Marañon en route to the leper's island. The first paragraph poses Aquilino's question about how Fushía escaped the Brazilian jail. The second paragraph replies by taking us directly back to the jail and to the words of one of Fushía's cellmates, Chango. Chango is presumably answering a similar question posed years before by Fushía himself.

The most innovative sequence, and the most demanding of the reader, is the fourth, the history of Jum and the soldiers in the jungle. This sequence employs an elaborate version of the blended narrator-character that often appears in the Fushía narrative. Here is a typical instance: "Julio Reátegui wipes his forehead, looks at his interpreter; he had gone against the authorities, that was not right and he would pay for it: translate it for him. The clearing at Urakusa is small and triangular . . ." (140). Description, commentary, and dialogue are here blended, undistinguished by quotation marks or discriminating pronouns. "He had gone against the authorities," one finally understands, is Reátegui's remark to an interpreter, but directed to an Indian being whipped.

Speeches by individual characters are even more difficult to distinguish in passages like this: "The officer turns to the Sergeant, was that business about the girl true? and Jum, girl!, very violently, shit! and Fats sh-h-h, the Lieutenant was speaking, and the Sergeant shush, who could tell, they stole girls every day here, it could be true" (173). Here the Lieutenant asks the Sergeant whether Jum's complaint that the soldiers have stolen his daughter is true. Jum angrily butts in to reiterate the word "girl" and utter the epithet "shit." Fats and the Sergeant both attempt to calm Jum (read, for example: "And the Sergeant also urged Jum, 'Shush' "). The sergeant then replies to the Lieutenant's question: "who could tell, they stole girls every day." At their most elusive, the voices in such passages mingle nearly indistinguishably, a chorus of human voices seemingly detached from explicit human sources.

The question naturally arises: Why has Vargas Llosa fragmented his narrative sequences, violated chronological order, exploded personalities and events throughout dozens of brief episodes, and narrated the whole in a variety of difficult styles? That is, why has he made it difficult for the reader to apprehend even the surface facts of his novel, and what relationship does that difficulty have to the meaning of those facts?

One explanation for the intricacies of form and technique in *The Green House* is historical. The 1960s were a time in Latin-American fiction when writers consciously sought to forge a new novel. Writers in the movement known as the "boom" in Latin-American fiction—such men as Gabriel García Márquez, Julio Cortázar, Carlos Fuentes, José Lezama Lima, and Vargas Llosa himself—were impressed by the technical innovations that had transformed European and North-American fiction into a high art form. The "boom" novelists repudiated the naïve realism, pious moralizing, and flowery style that characterized many of their Latin-American predecessors. They turned instead toward such models as Gustave Flaubert, Marcel Proust, André Gide, Franz Kafka, James Joyce, and William Faulkner. Hence, the major "boom" novels of the 1960s are all consciously experimental: Cortázar's *Hopscotch,* Fuentes's *The Death of Artemio Cruz,* Vargas Llosa's *The Green House,* García Márquez's *One Hundred Years of Solitude,* and Lezama Lima's *Paradise,* to cite only the most obvious examples.

But aside from whatever literary movements and historical precedents nourished the technical innovations of *The Green House,* the reader must evaluate the effectiveness of the novel's particular and unique formal qualities. At times, a reader may in fact experience the elaboration of technique in *The Green House* as an exuberant self-indulgence on the author's part, as verbal pyrotechnics for their own sake. But on closer examination, *The Green House* proves vastly more successful than most experimental fiction. Vargas Llosa possesses the necessary combination of skills—his compelling vision and his power with language—that enables technical virtuosity to achieve thematic significance.

For example, Vargas Llosa's techniques both express and evoke a particular attitude toward his characters. The five sequences, seventy-two episodes, transmuting styles, and elusive voices do not recount the histories of discrete "personalities," in the tradition of the nineteenth-century novel. Unlike the classical *Bildungsroman,* for instance, which traces the evolution of a unique self responding to its environment, *The Green House* deals with *clusters* of people who simultaneously shape one another while forming a transcendent, supra-personal whole. Vargas Llosa has explained: "What I've done is almost totally suppress individual personalities, and tried to present collective personalities, that is to say, groups of people who belong to, and embody, various different realities."[7] By dividing his story into dozens of achronological and nonsequential episodes set in scattered locales, Vargas Llosa has rendered human beings as less a matter of "selves," of unique psychological entities, than of aspects and functions of a social milieu. His characters are living intersections in a complex network of the intersecting paths of human beings and cultural forces. The effect of impersonality is heightened by Vargas Llosa's presentation of character from the outside. He rarely registers the thoughts or feelings of a character. Rather, he confines the reader to external appearances, to what a character says and does. As Vargas Llosa himself has put it, his novel is "basically a description of acts."[8]

As a corollary to his conception of character as more impersonal function than subjective self, another effect of Vargas Llosa's disjointed chronologies is their exposure of the ironies of the will and its fate. For example, Fushía recites the story of his youthful escape from prison and his subsequent schemes to become rich and powerful as, ironically, he floats downstream under cover of darkness, a crippled fugitive who will spend the rest of his days in dependence and poverty in a leper colony. As another example, we see Bonifacia as a prostitute in the Green House before we experience either the Sergeant's love for her, their joyous wedding, or their hopes for the future as they leave for Piura from the jungle. Similarly, we learn that Antonia has died even before we discover that Anselmo has captured her out of irresistible love.

Such inversions of chronology poignantly underscore the gulf between human designs and ultimate consequences. Because we know the end of a process before learning of its antecedents, we rarely build up expectations about the future of a character or the repercussions of an action. Instead, we ponder the reversals of fortune that plague all but the powerful and the lucky. In particular, the poor, the powerless, and the primitive—that is, half-breeds, children, women, and Indians—can rarely implement their desires. Indeed, their hopes and expectations often seem pathetically irrelevant both to the causal forces at work and to the final results. A reader observes the unfolding destinies of these submerged people as arbitrary conclusions to incidental desires.

Perhaps the chief effect of the technical variety of *The Green House* is the reader's detachment from the characters. To be sure, Vargas Llosa's narrative methods compel the reader's energetic and alert participation in the novel. Yet the fractured narratives and shifting perspectives prevent deep emotional involvement with the characters. The point becomes clearer if we compare *The Green House*, once more, to the classical novel of the nineteenth century.

The nineteenth-century novel typically immersed the reader in the evolving subjective life of the hero or heroine. One result was that the distance between character and reader often became very slight. One thinks, above all, of how Charles Dickens's characters routinely provoked sympathetic laughter and tears. *The Green House* extends a counter tradition that also springs from the nineteenth century, chiefly in the work of Gustave Flaubert, in which characters are treated more objectively, increasing the distance between a character and reader. Vargas Llosa severely limits the reader's emotional involvement with the characters. We are curious, sometimes shocked and touched, occasionally outraged at cruelty and injustice. But our reactions are to circumstances, events, and forces rather than to individuals with whom we have learned to empathize. Vargas Llosa's techniques make reading *The Green House* more an intellectual than an emotional experience. We watch, experience a surge of feeling, then interpret and judge.

Among those things that we perceive and judge is the impact of the unequal distribution of power. Individuals and groups exploit one another in ascending order of power, from children, women, and Indians on up through the military and the Church to the civil government and the wealthy (often, of course, the same people). One sustained illustration is the Catholic Church, as exemplified by the nuns at the mission school in Santa María de Nieva. The mission school also vividly demonstrates the distinction between human intentions and eventual consequences. From the nuns' point of view, the school is an outpost of civilization and Christian virtues amidst heathen savages. They bring religion and education to a lucky group of Indian girls. From the reader's perspective, the nuns form an unconscious alliance with the military and the governing class to eradicate Indian culture and provide Peruvian society with sufficient washerwomen, household servants, and prostitutes.

As the novel opens, a river launch with five civil guards and two nuns arrives at the Indian village of Chicais. They find the village deserted, but they wait. A group of Aguarunas soon arrives: two men, an old woman with sagging breasts, two little girls and a small boy, all three naked. Although the nuns fastidiously insist that the soldiers should not steal a loose chicken, it becomes clear that they plan to take the girls, even if they must steal them with armed force. A violent scene develops. The Indian men are held at gun point while the nuns recite the rosary and the soldiers kidnap the kicking, clawing girls. The old woman goes into a frenzy, twisting and moaning. The last we see of her, she is prostrate in the sand, her head slumped forward in defeat, weeping with shock and grief.

Later, two of the guards, Shorty and the Sergeant, disapprove of their own actions. But the rest of the soldiers are offended by their companions' doubts. They justify the nuns' behavior with a variety of prejudices about the Indians, ranging from their diets to their religious beliefs. When that doesn't convince Shorty, the soldiers threaten him with physical violence. The nuns, of course, believe that they are improving the Indians, helping to "incorporate those girls into the civilized world," while they also "gain a few souls for God" (101).

The reader sees more than do the soldiers or the nuns. We are struck by the moral blindness of invoking God's commandment against stealing a chicken, in the very act of stealing a mother's two daughters. And we soon learn what it really means to "incorporate those girls into the civilized world." This is made quite clear in the opening section of book two, when Julio Reátegui visits the school in search of servants for his wife and a friend. The nuns momentarily balk, but eventually they concede to power and patronage. After all, Reátegui is the governor and his wife is a strong financial supporter of the school. Therefore, Reátegui leaves with one servant girl and has the nuns' permission to take Bonifacia, as well. He leaves her behind out of mercy for her fearful reluctance.

The opening scene incorporates many themes developed throughout the book: the violation of motherhood and family, often in the name of Christian principles; the smug ethnocentricism that enables such violations simply by regarding Indians as subhumans with no familial bonds; the use of "legitimate" force (the government, the Church) to coerce people without recourse; the overt abduction of humans to fulfill purposes not their own. Abduction, in particular, is a commonplace in *The Green House*. Nieves is abducted to serve in the army. Jum is abducted to teach all Indians a lesson. Bonifacia and the other girls are brought to the school for a Christian education. Indian women by the score are stolen to serve the sexual pleasures of Fushía and his band. Antonia is carried off by Anselmo. Repeatedly, people with power simply capture those without who might be of use to them.

The fate of lower-class women aptly symbolizes much of the social order in *The Green House*. Fushía comments early in the book that a poor woman will usually end up "a washerwoman, a whore, or a servant" (63). But we discover as the book proceeds that Fushía has been too generous in describing a woman's options. Even if she escapes whoredom and becomes a washerwoman or a servant, she is unlikely to escape sexual exploitation. To illustrate:

> There . . . drunken soldiers station themselves at dawn and dusk. Washerwomen coming back from the river, servant girls from the Buenos Aires district on their way to market are caught by groups of soldiers and thrown down on the sand, their skirts are lifted over their heads, their legs are opened, and one after another the soldiers have them and run away. (121)

Although women suffer special abuse, their abstract circumstances are similar to those of all people at the bottom of the social pyramid. All are exploited by someone with greater power, all are treated unfeelingly like utilitarian objects. Even the soldier-rapists described above may have been forcibly "recruited" into the army to serve the interests of the rich and powerful.

Reátegui, at the top of the pyramid, is vastly different from the soldier-rapists. Except where Indians are concerned, his methods of exploitation have been refined well beyond the crudity of overt rape. With a smile, smooth talk, and assurances of respect and future favors, Reátegui can extract a servant from the nuns, obedience from the military officers, and loyalty from Don Fabio, his hand-picked successor as governor. His victims often conspire in their own exploitation, in hopes of some profit of their own. If rape is a fundamental metaphor for social relationships in *The Green House,* so is prostitution. The selling of self and the accommodation of principles to power are endemic. It is entirely appropriate that a pair of brothels should give the novel its name, and that a prostitute should be its heroine.

The most pathetic victims of institutionalized exploitation in *The Green House* are those who, like the Poet and Lieutenant Gamboa in *The City and the Dogs,* expect social justice. They must painfully learn that power over others is the reality, that suffering and brutality are the price of power, and that injustice is the rule.

For example, Jum continues to demand justice, even though he hardly understands the white man's system of government. He knows, spontaneously, that he has been wronged by the soldiers who laid waste his village, raped the Indian wives before the eyes of their anguished husbands, themselves beaten into submission, stole his daughter, and left him, whipped and tortured, hanging above a river dock. Time after time, Jum lodges complaints with the officials. But government officials regard him as a mere nuisance. One even cynically suggests that he file a written protest with the Bureau of Indian Affairs in Lima. Finally, Jum simply disappears, without authorial explanation.

Nieves the pilot believes most innocently in the justice of the "system" and is the one most injured by his faith. He is abducted into the army, escapes, and joins Fushía as his pilot. Later, Nieves abandons Fushía, taking Lalita and her child with him. They make their way to Santa María de Nieva, where they establish a home. That home is disrupted when the soldiers go into the jungle after Fushía and discover that Nieves has worked with the rubber bandits. Nieves refuses to escape arrest, even though the Sergeant and Lalita beg him to flee.

Nieves has twice fled previous situations that threatened him—the army and Fushía. But he loves his family too much to spend the rest of his life running. Instead, he decides to rely on the justice, honesty, and good will of the authorities, of "the sisters, the Lieutenant, the governor, too" (299), as he puts it. He reasons that he has been a mere pilot, rather than a major member of the outlaw group. He will serve his time—which he expects to be only a few months—and return to his family. As it happens, the authorities throw the book at him (just as the nuns showed Bonifacia no mercy), seizing on him as scapegoat. He spends years in prison, and he never sees Lalita or his children again. After his release from prison, which the reader learns about casually through a conversation, Nieves quietly disappears from the novel, like Jum, without explanatory comment.

These examples reveal that justice in *The Green House* is a sentimental trick of consciousness, an idea incidental to events. Individual acts of kind-ness offer the only hint of redemption in a world given over, for the most part, to rapacity. Bonifacia, for instance, is spared from rape in the jungle and, later, from life as an unwilling servant by the sympathy of Reátegui. When she is expelled from the mission school for helping the pupils escape, Lalita and Nieves take her into their home. Bonifacia's own effort to free the pupils, however inept or misguided, is itself an act of kindness. So is Aquilino's gift of yellow cloth to Bonifacia, from which she makes her wedding dress, as is the month that he devotes to transporting Fushía down-river to the leper colony. Most charitable of all is Juana Baura, the sick and impoverished washer-woman who first provides a home for the orphan, Antonia, then for Antonia's own daughter, Chunguita. Such acts of kindness, spontaneous and unre-warded, underscore the pervasive heartlessness of the social world of *The Green House.* Yet they also demonstrate that individual human beings can be more than predators.

   The Green House, like *The City and the Dogs,* portrays a bleak vision of social reality. Also like *The City and the Dogs,* that vision is morally com-plex. We see the rife corruption, the abuse of powerless individuals, and the needlessness of much human suffering. But we cannot easily point fingers of blame at specific individuals. Guilt seems oddly impersonal and collective, something that transcends individuals and accrues to the whole network of human activities. Caught up in the quest for money and power, like Fushía, or in the urge to impose a deeply inconsistent morality, like the nuns, or in the throes of uncontainable passion, like Anselmo or even the soldier-rapists, most of the people in *The Green House* are so elemental and unreflective that *all* moral considerations, not just the idea of justice, strike us as largely incidental to human activity that is essentially amoral. Individuals do not entirely escape responsibility, of course, especially Julio Reátegui, who is at the pinnacle of wealth and power and therefore is subject to the least social coercion. Still, *The Green House* indicts the entire social and economic system, rather than individuals. That system, *The Green House* makes clear, offers little more than the law of the jungle or the ethics of the brothel as standards of behavior.

NOTES

   1. Mario Vargas Llosa, *Historia secreta de una novela, Cuadernos Marginales 21* (Barcelona: Tusquets Editor, 1971), p. 9.
   2. Ibid., p. 20; my translation.
   3. Ibid., p. 25; my translation.
   4. Mario Vargas Llosa, "Literature is Fire," in *Doors and Mirrors,* trans. Maureen Ahern, ed. H. Carpentier and J. Borf (New York: Viking, 1973), p. 434.
   5. Mario Vargas Llosa, *The Green House,* trans. Gregory Rabassa (New York: Avon Books, 1965), p. 18. All subsequent quotations are taken from this edition.
   6. In the original Spanish, the blend of third-person narrator and first-person character is

more pronounced than in English translation, owing to the fact that the first- and third-person forms of the imperfect tense are identical in Spanish. In many of the Spanish passages, then, Fushía simultaneously uses the "I" and the "he" form of the verb. Thus, "cómo ahorraba, viejo," means both "how he saved, old man" and "how I saved, old man," depending on the context. Vargas Llosa exploits this ambiguity.

7. Quoted in Luis Harss and Barbara Dohmann, *Into the Mainstream* (New York: Harper & Row, 1967), p. 361.

8. Ibid., p. 360.

19

Drabbling in the Tradition: *The Waterfall* and *The Mill on the Floss*

KEITH CUSHMAN

Margaret Drabble is the most literary of contemporary English novelists. While publishing nine novels in thirteen years and raising a family, she has managed something like an academic career in literature on the side. Drabble, who took a double first in English at Cambridge, has edited Jane Austen and written a critical study of Wordsworth and an important biography of Arnold Bennett. She teaches at the University of London and has recently edited *The Oxford Companion to English Literature*. But literature for Drabble goes more deeply than these trappings of the academic life might suggest. Margaret Drabble writes fiction that is firmly rooted in the masterpieces of the English literary tradition.

Literary allusion comes as naturally to Drabble as it did to the great Victorian novelists with whom she feels such a kinship; like them, she has read everything and takes literature very seriously. Intertextuality is a significant aspect of her narrative method. It is not a question of "decorating one's books with literature"; rather "literature is a part of life."[1] Drabble, in the words of Nancy Hardin, transforms "a variety of literary references into something very much [her] own."[2]

Drabble's novels "echo with the literary heritage of England,"[3] but in this essay I am interested in something more substantial than echoes. Drabble works naturally and habitually within the formal tradition of allusion. Behind the surfaces of many of her novels one senses the presence of an earlier work of literature. Such allusion "differs from mere source-borrowing, because it requires the reader's familiarity with the original for full understanding and appreciation; and from mere reference, because it is tacit and fused with the context in which it appears." The sort of allusion I am referring to is structural in nature: Drabble gives form to her novel "by suggesting the structure of an older work."[4] Her own novel is given shape and meaning by the way it plays off the work she alludes to.

In *The Millstone* (1965) Rosamund Stacey is a graduate student doing research on Samuel Daniel, author of "The Complaint of Rosamund," and the novel seems a contemporary version of complaint literature.[5] As Drabble wrote *The Needle's Eye* (1972) she was "very conscious of" James's *The Wings of the Dove,*[6] and she has also spoken of her use of *The Prelude* in *The Needle's Eye.*[7] Her most recent novel, *The Middle Ground* (1980), is a contemporary rewriting of *Mrs. Dalloway*. Drabble interrupts her Arnold Bennett biography to identify a striking example of her habit of allusion:

> I should acknowledge at this point my own debt to Bennett, in my novel *Jerusalem the Golden*. . . . The girl . . . like Bennett's first hero, is obsessed with escape, and she too is enraptured by trains and hotels and travelling: she feels she has "a rightful place upon the departure platform" of her home town. There is a good deal of Hilda Lessways in her too. . . . Perhaps it is irrelevant to mention these matters, but to me they are so much bound up together that my novel is almost as much an appreciation of Bennett as this book is meant to be.[8]

In this essay I will be exploring the uses Drabble makes of *The Mill on the Floss* in her fifth novel, *The Waterfall* (1969). I hope not only to illuminate Drabble's novel but also to provide a representative example of her use of structural allusion. My contention is that the meaning of Drabble's novel emerges in part from the interplay between Jane Gray's story in *The Waterfall* and Maggie Tulliver's. At the same time that Drabble borrows from literary tradition, she also updates and revises it.

Drabble's interest in George Eliot is well documented in various interviews. In 1974 she described Eliot as "my ideal novelist in a sense."[9] In 1975 Nancy Poland reported that Drabble was pleased to be "called the George Eliot of her generation,"[10] and more recently Drabble has said that she admired "George Eliot so much because she's so inclusive. She does tackle a very large range of subject matter."[11] It is also common enough for critics to compare Drabble to Eliot.[12]

Nor does the presence of *The Mill on the Floss* go unspoken in *The Waterfall*, ostensibly the book Jane Gray, an Oxford graduate in English, writes in her effort to make sense of her affair with her brother-in-law James Otford. Jane in telling her story, both in the first- and third-person, makes constant reference to a wide range of writers and literary works. In the midst of an introspective outburst in which she expresses her guilt and her sense that her relationship with James is doomed, she compares herself with Maggie Tulliver several times. Perhaps she will drown herself "in an effort to reclaim lost renunciations, like Maggie Tulliver,"[13] she muses. She is haunted by Maggie, by the parallels between their lives, and also by the radical differences between the faraway world of the Tullivers and Dodsons and the world she inhabits:

Maggie Tulliver had a cousin called Lucy, as I have, and like me she fell in love with her cousin's man. She drifted off down the river with him, abandoning herself to the water, but in the end she lost him. She let him go. Nobly she regained her ruined honor, and ah, we admire her for it: all that superego gathered together in a last effort to prove that she loved the brother more than the man. She should have, ah well, what should she not have done? Since Freud, we guess dimly at our own passions, stripped of hope, abandoned forever to that relentless current. It gets us in the end: sticks, twigs, dry leaves, paper cartons, cigarette ends, orange peel, flower petals, silver fishes. Maggie Tulliver never slept with her man: she did all the damage there was to be done, to Lucy, to herself, to the two men who loved her, and then, like a woman of another age, she refrained. In this age, what is to be done? We drown in the first chapter. (*W*, 161–62)

Jane recognizes that there is more than a little "Maggie Tulliver in me," especially in her capacity for "infinite self-sacrifice" (163).

These direct references to *The Mill on the Floss* alert the reader to be on the lookout for Eliot's novel. But for the most part Drabble's allusions function tacitly. First, there are basic parallels of character, situation, and plot. Second, these parallels are reinforced by an imagistic motif taken from *The Mill*. Third, *The Mill* helps Drabble explore a larger philosophical concern, the question of fate and accident. None of the allusions I will be pointing out is perfectly parallel nor is it meant to be. Drabble is writing her own novel, not somehow reproducing Eliot's. But the structural presence of *The Mill* behind *The Waterfall* is unmistakable, whether Drabble is closely following Eliot's novel or playing off it by way of contrast.

Drabble's heroine is a Jane rather than a Maggie, but the two women have more in common than Jane acknowledges in the novel. The other characters in Eliot's love-quartet also have opposite numbers in *The Waterfall*. Lucy Otford is drawn from Lucy Deane, and Lucy Deane's suitor Stephen Guest can be found in James Otford. There are also two rejected males: Philip Wakem in *The Mill* and Jane's husband Malcolm in *The Waterfall*. Of course, there is no Tom Tulliver in *The Waterfall*, nor is there a Mr. Tulliver. *The Mill* is a broader and more ambitious novel, for example, in its treatment of English social history. Nevertheless, Drabble's four central characters are all related to characters in Eliot's novel.

Barbara Hardy has commented that "the heroines of George Eliot's novels . . . all suffer the *ex officio* disability of being women."[14] As Tom Tulliver tells his sister, she is "only a girl."[15] Jane Gray is acutely aware of the problems of being a woman, which is one of the reasons she feels haunted by Maggie.

Maggie is a warm-spirited, generous person who is much given to resignation, though she has interludes of impetuosity. Maggie is insecure and unassertive, depending all her life on her brother's opinion of her. She has a streak of self-renunciation, which is to some extent endorsed by Eliot. In her unhappiness Maggie becomes a passionate devotee of Thomas à Kempis's

Imitation of Christ, a book that reinforces her own inclination to resign herself to her situation. "Everywhere of necessity thou must have patience, if thou wilt have inward peace" (253). This sacred validation of her own nature is so appealing to her that she overdoes it, throwing "some exaggeration and wilfulness, some pride and impetuosity, even into her self-renunciation" (256). Philip Wakem has to warn Maggie that "stupefaction is not resignation" (286).

Maggie seems like a sleepwalker in the episode that leads to her downfall: as she lets Stephen Guest row her down the river, she feels that she is in the hands of some "stronger presence that seemed to bear her along without any act of her own will" (407). Maggie finds "an unspeakable charm in being told what to do" (409).

Though Jane Gray lacks Maggie Tulliver's impetuousness, she suffers from an extreme form of Maggie's passivity. She has escaped the problem of what to do with her life by locking herself away in her stagnant marriage with Malcolm. James makes his advances when she is at her most passive, helpless, and traditionally female, just after she has given birth to her second child. In bed she is James's "prisoner," and, like a damsel in distress, she asks him to "rescue" (38) her. She is so unable to act that a trip to the zoo with her two children becomes a major undertaking, and she is bewildered about the organized play-group she puts her pre-school son in. She is articulating a serious problem when she says that "sometimes . . . I think that . . . any human effort is pointless in the extreme" (53). There is something rather disturbed about Jane's passivity, and indeed Drabble has called her the "dottiest, the nearest to madness" of all her characters.[16]

Jane speaks of herself as being "split" (*W,* 120), just as Maggie Tulliver is made up of "opposing elements" (*M,* 261). Like Maggie, Jane is a "creature full of eager, passionate longings" (*M,* 208). Her good fortune is that James materializes to answer these longings. Jane is confused about her identity, feeling herself "to be nothing, nebulous, shadowy, unidentifiable" (*W,* 148). Maggie, divided between dutiful daughter and passionate young woman, also struggles to establish her identity.

Lucy Deane and Lucy Otford stand out as embodiments of desirable female beauty in their respective ages—and how times have changed. Lucy Deane, altogether "pretty and neat" (*M,* 77) with her blonde "ringlets," "soft hazel eyes," "little shell-pink palm" (316), and her conformity to the wishes of her elders, is not far removed from the stereotypical mid-Victorian heroine. Several generations later the "beautiful" Lucy Otford, liberated in the England of the 1960s, is a casual femme fatale, spending her Oxford years sleeping around and making men (and herself) miserable, settling on James when she becomes pregnant. The Victorian Lucy of unquestioning virtue has modulated into the contemporary Lucy of unthinking promiscuity. Neither Lucy Deane's enslavement to social convention nor Lucy Otford's freedom from it has much to recommend it.

But as different as the two young women are, Drabble clearly wants the reader of *The Waterfall* to think of them together. She makes that evident by means of a parallel motif: both Maggie Tulliver and Jane Gray are powerfully jealous of their cousins. This jealousy helps to explain the behavior of the two heroines. The rivalries in the two novels are more reminiscent of the relationship between sisters than between cousins. In *The Waterfall* there are several situations in which Jane, the surrogate wife, is taken for Lucy, and she also reports that Lucy was "more nearly my sister than my own sister was" (120). (The two sisters motif is almost obsessive in Drabble's fiction.)

Some of the most familiar episodes in the childhood portion of *The Mill* involve Maggie's jealousy of her cousin. The young Maggie is "fond of fancying a world where the people never got any larger than children of their own age, and she made the queen of it just like Lucy, with a little crown on her head, and a little sceptre in her hand. . . . only the queen was Maggie herself in Lucy's form" (55). When Tom favors Lucy and rejects his sister, Maggie's response is "to push poor little pink-and-white Lucy into the cow-trodden mud" (91). Maggie is the ugly duckling who grows up to be the beautiful princess. But the princess is always in exile until Stephen Guest, tacitly engaged to Lucy, shows interest. Maggie's love for Stephen and her trip down the river with him complete the psychological pattern established in the childhood scenes. At last she is triumphing over Lucy.

In a flashback to the childhood of Jane and Lucy in *The Waterfall*, Jane's cousin momentarily seems the reincarnation of Lucy Deane: "She was wearing an embroidered white shirt under a red pleated pinafore dress, and she looked (as my mother said, in a vain search for idiom) cute" (122). As in *The Mill*, it is the rival who garners the parental favor and the male attention. But unlike Maggie, Jane is consciously aware of her rivalry with her cousin: "Sometimes I think that I married because Lucy married. I got a house because Lucy had a house. I had a baby because Lucy had a baby" (136). One of the reasons for loving James is because Lucy had him. "One could diagnose jealousy, no doubt" (129). Jane loves him "because he belonged to my cousin" (70).

After the death of Maggie and Tom we see Stephen, deepened by his sorrow, visiting Maggie's grave, and of course there is "a sweet face beside him" (457), for Lucy has become the helpmate she was always destined to be. In the contemporary world, the affair between Jane and James simply continues, with Lucy and Jane "locked in passionate exclusive discretion" (249). Presumably Lucy Otford loathes herself as much as ever. At least Lucy Deane must have enjoyed the illusion of happiness.

Stephen, the handsome scion of the wealthiest and most socially prominent family in St. Ogg's, has his counterpart in James. The rather dandified Stephen, with his "diamond ring, attar of roses, and air of nonchalant leisure" (316), has always taken his lumps from modern critics. F. R. Leavis called him a "mere hairdresser's block,"[17] and many have commented on his insubstantiality. It is also something of a commonplace to observe that Drabble's females are more convincing than her males, and the case of James Otford offers no exception. Like Stephen, he is an elusive figure, almost a creature of fantasy. Jane seems to *want* him to be something of a fantasy figure, someone to play the strong male and with whom to dwell in "that isolated world of pure corrupted love" (*W*, 137).

Stephen and James are both handsome male specimens, and their good looks are an eminent part of their appeal to the sexually deprived heroines. Stephen is a "striking young man of five-and-twenty, with a square forehead, short dark-brown hair standing erect, with a slight wave at the end, like a thick crop of corn" (317). James has "a hard face, curiously softened by the soft color of his hair: his hair was blond" (28). In contrast to their male rivals, Philip Wakem and Malcolm, Stephen and James are forceful and traditionally masculine. In fact James actually seems "a dangerous man" (29) at first. Passive Maggie and passive Jane are keen to meet their masters. Both men are also rather idle and consequently ready and able to fill their days with love, Stephen because of his wealth and social position, James because his income is derived from the garage and automobile shop he is rather mysteriously a part owner of.

Stephen longs for Maggie to acknowledge his love; James wants to break out with Jane from their enclosed existence. Consequently, each man takes his woman on a journey, and each journey becomes the ill-fated, climactic event of the novel. The automobile trip toward the Norway ferry is reminiscent of the rowboat ride on the Floss. This episode is one of Drabble's most direct allusions to Eliot.

The trip with Stephen brings "the sudden exalting influence of a strong tonic" (407) to Maggie's mind. With Jane's children in the back seat, the lovers in *The Waterfall* attempt to leave behind the "solipsist universe" (190) of their love, traveling toward the coast in a new Aston Martin. Both journeys are highly sexualized. Maggie observes "the breath of the young unwearied day" and "the delicious rhythmic dip of the oars," and "some low, subdued, languid exclamation of love came from time to time, as he went on rowing idly" (407). What better way to update this erotic journey than to place it in a sleek, fast, dangerous sports car. Indeed Jane and racing are the two loves of James's life.

Both journeys seem unreal to the heroines. Maggie feels that "thought did not belong to that enchanted haze in which they were enveloped" (407), and before their trip, Jane considers discussion of it to be "a theme for fantasy" (177). In fact, there is a fantasy quality about each journey. Stephen is making a desperate attempt to put Maggie into a position where she must marry him; he insists that "the tide is carrying us out" and that "everything has come without our seeking" (408). James's fantasy is more domestic: he is play-acting that Jane is his wife and the children are theirs. He even plans to pass Jane off as his wife to his old Norwegian grandfather. Both plans are exceedingly fragile, and both come badly a-cropper. There is almost a sense that fate will not let them get away with such plans.

The final set of analogous characters consists of Philip Wakem and Jane's husband Malcolm. Again it seems appropriate to the times that Philip is the rejected suitor while Malcolm is the rejected husband. In the structure of *The Mill*, Philip plays the weak, almost feminine male, a foil to Tom and Stephen. Malcolm serves the same function, counterpointed against James in *The Waterfall*.

Philip is a sensitive, perceptive, nervous young man and a talented artist as well. He is hunchbacked and, as a result, shy, introspective, and self-pitying. There is something less than male about Philip: Maggie stoops "to kiss the pale face that was full of pleading, timid love—like a woman's" (295). He appeals only to "her pity and womanly devotedness" (359), and when Stephen enters the scene, Philip can only stand helplessly aside.

Like Philip, Malcolm is an artist: a successful classical guitarist and singer who specializes in the music of the English Renaissance. The cultivated, elitist nature of Malcolm's artistry marks his isolation from the mainstream of contemporary life, just as Philip is a skilled draftsman in a society whose values are commercial. Like Philip, Malcolm is both feminine and vulnerable: "He had a thin, sensitive girl's face; fair, rather wavy hair, with a parting and a forelock; he was small and slight and had a kind of pleasing intensity about him, a nervous energy." He has a "vulnerable boyish air" (91), and his failed sexual relationship with Jane makes her suspect that he is latently homosexual. As with Philip, the dynamics of the interlocking relationships dictate that he will lose, and, as with Philip, there is nothing he can do about it. When he learns of his wife's affair, Malcolm comes round in the night seeking his revenge, but he is capable of only an impotent gesture: he breaks a downstairs window and departs.

Jane and Maggie, Lucy Otford and Lucy Deane, James and Stephen, Malcolm and Philip: each of Drabble's main characters is shadowed by a character from *The Mill on the Floss*. We have two passive heroines, two attractive rivals named Lucy, two strong males, and two weak males. Drabble seized upon the Maggie-Lucy-Stephen-Philip quartet in *The Mill* as a starting-point for her own imagination. Eliot's characters exist as ghostly presences in *The Waterfall* and they provide an interpretive counterpoint that enriches and adds dimension to Drabble's novel. This element of "doubling" also has the effect of giving Drabble's characters more weight and making them more archetypal.

One other important plot element of *The Waterfall* is reminiscent of *The Mill on the Floss*, and that is Jane's upbringing. Her parents are consumed by their need to be respectable and keep up appearances. When Jane's mother comes to see the baby, all she can really see is "the thick dust, the round stains, the dirty stove, the tarnished spoons" (41). Her hypocritical parents are "obsessed by the notion of class and rank" (61). Jane recognizes that her love for James is in part an attempt to break out of the sham of her upbringing: he is the destroyer of "decades of careful pretense" (63). The love affair is "irresponsibility glorified, a meaningless, involuntary, undirected swipe at the years of her silent girlhood" (214).

Jane has the same difficulty with her parents that Maggie Tulliver has with her mother and her Dodson aunts. The Dodsons are masterful embodiments of the Protestant ethic in action, their values all centered upon respectabiity and materialism. Family should be the basic center of love and community, but the Dodson family, "respectable for many generations" (107), has only material values to sustain it in time of crisis. When Mr. Tulliver, who has lost the mill through his rash lawsuit, is close to death after falling off his horse, Mrs. Tulliver can only worry about her china, tablecloths, and imminent drop in status. Maggie watches "with gathering anger" (181) before sharply rebuking her mother. Like Jane, Maggie must try to escape the false values of her family.

Drabble also borrows a crucial image from George Eliot. "If I were drowning I couldn't reach out a hand to save myself" (7), Jane Gray says in the first sentence of the book, making us aware from the first of her passivity—and also alerting us to the presence of *The Mill on the Floss.*[18] Few novels can compete with *The Waterfall* when it comes to moisture. "So liquid we are, inside our stiff bodies" (201), Jane comments, and the novel is awash with blood and milk and with tears and sweat as well (not to mention a waterfall). But most interesting for my purposes are the repeated allusions to drowning. Early in the novel when James declares his love, he is making "a willing blind suicidal dive into such deep waters" (37). After their first lovemaking "they fell asleep, damp, soaked in a flood of emotion." Though Jane has always feared the "wetness" of love, now she lies with James, happily "drowned in a willing sea" (46). Always she "lay there, drowned was it, drowned or stranded, waiting for him, waiting to die and drown there" (70). Marriage to Malcolm had seemed no more fatal than "ether or deep water" (104); as she reaches climax with James she is "half dead but not dead, crying out to him, trembling, shuddering, quaking, drenched and drowned, down there at last in the water" (159). These passages are but a small sampling of the allusions to drowning and deep water in *The Waterfall*. The motif is most important as it reflects Jane's rebirth through her sexual relationship with James. Jane is like the "leafless withered unwatered" (42) plant in her house; through James she is brought back to life. The rebirth is registered primarily through the pattern of death—and regeneration—by water.[19]

This motif is obviously drawn from *The Mill on the Floss,* which is also replete with water imagery. The drowning at the end of Eliot's novel attempts the tragic. In their final moment, brother and sister embrace and are reconciled, "living through again in one supreme moment the days when they had clasped their little hands in love" (456). This final scene of suffering offers meaning and even revelation. In sharp and specific contrast, when Jane is certain that James will die after the crash, death "denied me the final vision, the final revelation" (197). Even as he slowly returns to life, "there would be no amount of revelation, no sudden light" (233). *The Waterfall* is Drabble's most romantic novel, though its affirmation of romantic love is ambiguous and laced through with strongly anti-romantic elements. The drowning motif seems to suggest that we come closest to revelation—if but briefly, if indeed only illusorily—through our sexuality. At the same time *The Waterfall* seems to criticize Eliot's attempt to overlay life's ordinariness with tragic meaning. Here Drabble's use of *The Mill on the Floss* involves the juxtaposition of two different conceptions of human experience, the Victorian and the contemporary.

The odd one-paragraph "postscript" at the end of *The Waterfall* alludes further to the tragic denouement of *The Mill*. Though James doesn't die, there is a death after all: "the little, twentieth-century death" (256), his impotence. "All true fictional lovers die" (207). But in real life there is no tragic grandeur; in fact "there isn't any conclusion" (248). Drabble ends her novel with all too literal an anticlimax.

In her interview with Nancy Hardin, Drabble speaks at length about fate and accident, which she believes "fit frightfully well together. . . . You're just completely at the mercy of fate. It's planned but accidental in some peculiar way."[20] Drabble discusses *The Waterfall* to illustrate her ideas about this large question. Once again *The Mill on the Floss* is an important presence behind Drabble's novel.

Eliot is the mid-Victorian novelist most closely associated with deterministic theory. She voiced her belief in this theory when she wrote John Chapman "that the thought which is to mould the Future has for its root a belief in necessity."[21] Eliot "saw a deterministic universe as a marvelously complex unit in which all parts are intricately related to each other, where nothing is really isolable, and where past and future are both implicit in the present."[22] At the same time, she leaves room in her theory for free will. Few actions are so narrowly determined that no effort to change them can succeed, for cause is not the same as compulsion. Furthermore, in her opinion each person's character is one of the causes of what he becomes. Thus, we can help shape our own destiny.

Determinism is a structural idea in *The Mill on the Floss*, most notably in Eliot's treatment of Tom and Maggie, of Dodsons and Tullivers. Biology is fate, for the destinies of Tom and Maggie are significantly shaped by the traits they inherited from their parents. Many critics have provided detailed catalogues of the Dodson and Tulliver characteristics as they determine the choices of Tom and Maggie.[23]

The narrator also points to Maggie's ignorance of "the irreversible laws within and without her" (252), laws that cannot be escaped. The love between Maggie and Stephen is understandable as an illustration of "the laws of attraction" (349). Maggie resists her feeling for Stephen, but he makes her feel as if she is "borne along by a wave too strong for her" (366), just as subsequently in the rowboat she and Stephen will be "borne along by the tide" (401).

But it must not be forgotten that Eliot's idea of determinism includes the belief that the individual is not entirely helpless before his fate. In *The Mill on the Floss* Maggie Tulliver falls back on a sense of absolute determinism in which the will has no freedom—what Eliot would have called necessitarianism—as a rationalization for her own passivity. "Our life is determined for us," she declares to Philip, "and it makes the mind very free when we give up wishing, and only think of bearing what is laid upon us" (264). Her behavior with Stephen is a disastrous case in point. Maggie dazedly lets the experience happen to her, and Eliot finds her culpable for doing so. She can justify her participation in the elopement only by pretending to herself that she is being carried off by Stephen Guest and by fate.

At the outset of *The Waterfall* Jane declares that she is "unwilling . . . to set myself up against my fate" (7). Fate, as word and concept, resonates throughout the novel. When Jane recounts the story of a family Christmas before the beginning of the affair, she says that it was "all foreordained" (64). She loves James "inevitably, of necessity" (50). "It was all predestined: a fate handed down by necessity through generations" (83). Not long before the automobile trip she asserts that "one is not released from the fated pattern, one must walk it till death" (169). The automobile crash seems to demonstrate that "fate and accident fit frightfully well together": the brick in the road that James runs over when, for once, he is not speeding, the instantaneous death of the driver of the other car while Jane and the children are barely scratched, the miraculous survival of James. The sense of the "fated pattern" in this episode is strong.

The love affair itself seems fated, for "people could not change . . . they were predetermined, unalterable, helpless in the hands of destiny" (243). James had been hurt by the ongoing promiscuity of his wife and needed to reassert his maleness. "The baby thing attracted him as much as it repels most men" (220), and the affair began with Jane in bed with a newborn, at her most purely and helplessly maternal. For her part, passive Jane needed someone to come play a forceful male role, and she was ready for sexual awakening after years of bitter frustration with Malcolm. Furthermore, Jane and James as in-laws had been secretly attracted to each other for some time. And then there are the almost irresistibly overripe circumstances of their coming together: in the overheated room, cut off from the rest of the world, the milk and the blood and the sweat all flowing.

Drabble's thinking about determinism is much less systematic, much less formed than Eliot's. At the same time she seems to believe, like Eliot, that fate does not eliminate free will. "There had never been a question of choice" (160), Jane says. And then she adds, "A fine evasion" (161). Like Maggie

Tulliver, only more so, Jane Gray sees life in terms of fate partly to rationalize her difficulty in making choices. "It is our duty to endeavor in the face of the impossible,"[24] but Jane finds such endeavor difficult.

There is something curiously old-fashioned, even Victorian, about Drabble's fascination with fate. Fate is an issue important English novelists have not been concerned with since the days of Hardy. The example of *The Mill on the Floss* helps her explore this grand but rather unfashionable interest. It is as if Drabble invokes the sanction of literary tradition in order to be comfortable about injecting such concerns into a contemporary novel. Each novel presents a deterministic universe, but each also seems to offer the individual the possibility of choice. In each instance the novelist attempts to believe at once in fate and responsibility.

In character and situation, in motif and image, in quasi-philosophical concern, *The Waterfall* alludes extensively to *The Mill on the Floss*. Eliot's novel functions almost as a paradigm for Drabble. One important question remains: why does Drabble make such large-scale use of *The Mill?*

In the first place, it seems simply to be a creative habit for her to make use of masterworks from the past in this way. Filled with literature, she draws quite naturally on literary tradition, and, in doing so, reaps important aesthetic benefits. The task of invention is minimized: she was able to begin *The Waterfall* with an imaginative structure, drawn from a classic novel and so well known to her as to be internalized, firmly in place. *The Mill on the Floss* allows Drabble a potential solution to artistic problems of shape and structure. George Eliot's strategies come ready-made for her to work with in whatever way she chooses.

It is also significant that the mid-Victorian *Mill on the Floss* possesses a moral clarity that is unavailable to our own age. Eliot's certitude is attractive to a novelist who must write without such certitude. Eliot is Drabble's "ideal novelist" partly because of Eliot's strong, unquestioning sense of moral and intellectual conviction. *The Mill on the Floss* functions in this regard as something like a "control" for Drabble as she tells her own more problematic, ambiguous story. Maggie and Tom's epitaph declares resoundingly that "in their death they were not divided" (457). In more troubled and confused times Jane can only hazard that "we would, in death, have been forgiven" (208). The moral security of the traditional novel puts into greater perspective the moral openness of the contemporary work.

Moreover, the relationship between the two novels is reciprocal. If Drabble's open-endedness calls into question Eliot's tragic form and moral conviction, just as surely for readers in the late twentieth century does *The Mill on the Floss* comment on the appropriately modern ambiguities of *The Waterfall*. As Borges has shown, the art of allusion can involve an act of reinterpretation of works from the past.[25] But the past also helps us understand the present.

In *The Waterfall* Drabble draws on literary tradition extensively and complexly. The countless resonances and points of contact between the two novels allow the reader to experience both continuity and counterpoint, to appreciate how our culture has remained rooted in our shared past while at the same time has broken with that past. In creating a novel that plays off a nineteenth-century work so insistently, Drabble is making an intricate commentary on two cultures, one traditional and one modern. *The Waterfall* demonstrates that the lessons of T. S. Eliot's "Tradition and the Individual Talent" are second nature to Margaret Drabble.

NOTES

1. Diana Cooper-Clark, "Margaret Drabble: Cautious Feminist," *The Atlantic Monthly* (November 1980), p. 71.

2. Nancy S. Hardin, "An Interview with Margaret Drabble," *Contemporary Literature* 14 (Summer 1973): 279.

3. Cooper-Clark, "Margaret Drabble," p. 71.

4. Earl Miner, "Allusion," in *The Princeton Encyclopedia of Poetry and Poetics*, ed. Alex Preminger (Princeton: Princeton University Press, 1974), p. 18.

5. Hardin, "Interview," p. 280.

6. Iris Rozencwajg, "Interview with Margaret Drabble," *Women's Studies* 6 (1979): 337.

7. Cooper-Clark, p. 72.

8. Margaret Drabble, *Arnold Bennett: A Biography* (New York: Knopf, 1974), pp. 47–48.

9. Rozencwajg, "Interview," p. 336.

10. Nancy Poland, "Margaret Drabble: 'There Must Be a Lot of People Like Me,'" *Midwest Quarterly* 16 (April 1975): 255. This essay is primarily an account of a question-and-answer session with Drabble.

11. Cooper-Clark, p. 71.

12. Elaine Showalter, *A Literature of Their Own: British Women Novelists from Brontë to Lessing* (Princeton: Princeton University Press, 1977), p. 302.

13. Margaret Drabble, *The Waterfall* (New York: Popular Library, 1977), p. 161. All subsequent quotations are taken from this edition (cited as *W* when reference is ambiguous).

14. Barbara Hardy, *The Novels of George Eliot* (London: Oxford University Press, 1959), p. 47.

15. George Eliot, *The Mill on the Floss,* ed. Gordon S. Haight (Boston: Houghton Mifflin Riverside Edition, 1961), p. 32. All subsequent quotations are taken from this edition (cited as *M* when reference is ambiguous).

16. Hardin, p. 290.

17. F. R. Leavis, *The Great Tradition: George Eliot, Henry James, Joseph Conrad* (London: Penguin Books, 1962), p. 53.

18. In fact, drowning is introduced even before the first page, in the Dickinson poem that serves as the novel's epigraph: "Drowning is not so pitiful / As the attempt to rise."

19. There are also numerous allusions to being borne along by the current. For example, as Jane begins to live for James's visits, she is "submitting herself helplessly to the current" (*W*, 39).

20. Hardin, p. 283.

21. George Eliot to John Chapman, 24–25 July 1852, *The George Eliot Letters*, 7 vols., ed. Gordon S. Haight (New Haven: Yale University Press, 1954–55) 2:49.

22. George Levine, "Determinism and Responsibility in the Works of George Eliot," *PMLA*

76 (June 1962): 270. Levine's impressive essay is the standard treatment of determinism in George Eliot.

23. See, for example, Felicia Bonaparte, *Will and Destiny: Morality and Tragedy in George Eliot's Novels* (New York: New York University Press, 1975), pp. 63–70.

24. Cooper-Clark, p. 73.

25. Borges's essay, "Kafka and His Precursors," is particularly interesting in this context. Borges argues for the impact of Kafka on our reading of a poem by Browning.

Selective Annotated Bibliography

This bibliography was selected to present a variety of texts that discuss modern British and American literature from different, sometimes conflicting, points of view. It is intended to serve only as a guide to the study of conceptions of modernism that have gained currency over the past twenty-five years. We have excluded texts written before 1960 for the sake of economy, given necessary spatial limitations. There are also some works written in the last few years which, again because of limited space, have not been included but which should, perhaps, be noted; for example, Carlos Baker's *The Echoing Green* (Princeton, 1984), Cathy Jrade's *Rubén Darío and the Romantic Search for Unity* (Austin, Tex., 1983), Michael Levenson's *A Genealogy of Modernism* (London, 1984), Donald Stanford's *Revolution and Convention in Modern Poetry* (Newark, Del., 1983), and Alan Young's *Dada and After: Extremist Modernism and English Literature* (Manchester, 1981). Many of the books listed provide bibliographies that extend what we have included, in particular Bradbury and McFarlane's collection, *Modernism: 1890–1930,* and Faulkner's *Modernism.*

Allen, Walter. *Tradition and Dream: The English and American Novel From the Twenties.* London: Phoenix House, 1964. This book completes Allen's comprehensive study of the history of the novel. It covers the principal works of the major modernist novelists in England and America.

Bergonzi, Bernard. *Innovations: Essays on Art and Ideas.* London, Melbourne, and Toronto: Macmillan, 1968. This collection of essays by major commentators on the modernist tradition such as Leslie Fiedler, Frank Kermode, Ihab Hassan, Martin Green, David Lodge, and Bernard Bergonzi is an indispensable source for anyone interested in the subject.

Bradbury, Malcolm, and James McFarlane, eds. *Modernism: 1890–1930.* Harmondsworth, Middlesex: Penguin Books, 1976. This wide-ranging collection of essays discusses the writers, works, ideas, social tensions, and cultural backgrounds that form the defining context for modernism in Europe and North America between 1890 and 1930.

Brun, Gerald L. *Modern Poetry and the Idea of Language: A Critical and Historical Study.* New Haven: Yale University Press, 1974. Brun develops a dialectic between literary language conceived of as the making of hermetic structure on the one hand, and the text "in relation to its situation, that is, in terms of its historical existence" (262) on the other. He illustrates his analysis with texts and authors chosen from late nineteenth- and early twentieth-century contexts.

Chiari, Joseph. *The Aesthetics of Modernism*. London: Vision Press Ltd., 1970. Chiari's work offers a sensitive study of the modernist sensibility from a so- ciological point of view, considering artistic, philosophical, and religious attitudes and their bases in the complex stresses of modern culture.

Chipp, Herschel B., ed. *Theories of Modern Art: A Source Book of Artists and Critics*. Berkeley and Los Angeles: University of California Press, 1968. This volume collects a representative sample of fundamental theoretical documents of twentieth-century art that explain the basic concepts of modern art, many of which have profoundly influenced modernist literature.

Cronin, Anthony. *A Question of Modernity*. London: Secker & Warburg, 1966. Cronin considers a "characteristic 'modernity' " shared by such different writers as Joyce, Eliot, Pound, and Samuel Beckett. His method is to present a series of essays that discuss individual writers and, in the later essays, critics, as soundings of that "modernity" he recognizes is difficult to define.

Davie, Donald, ed. *Russian Literature and Modern English Fiction*. Chicago: Univer- sity of Chicago Press, 1965. Major writers and critics of modernist literature discuss either themselves or other major figures of the modernist tradition as they have been influenced by or reacted to Turgenev, Dostoevski, Tolstoy, Chekhov, and Gogol. A brief discussion of "The Contrary Traffic" is included, i.e., a discussion of Dickens's influence on Russian writers.

Dembo, L. S. *Conceptions of Reality in Modern American Poetry*. Berkeley and Los Angeles: University of California Press, 1966. Dembo focuses on literary and philosophical issues in twentieth-century American poetry. He examines "con- ceptions of reality in this poetry" which involves "an inquiry into the relations between subject and object, between the poetic sensibility and the world that is to be revealed" (vii).

Donoghue, Denis. *The Ordinary Universe: Soundings in Modern Literature*. New York: Macmillan, 1968. In an engagingly written and provocative study of modern- ist writers and their private worlds, which are often at variance with the public world, Donoghue considers primarily poets, some novelists and dramatists.

Ellmann, Richard. *Yeats Among Wilde, Joyce, Pound, Eliot and Auden*. New York: Oxford University Press, 1967. The mutual acquisition of each others' themes, vocabularies, material, effects, and other devices of their craft by such writers as Yeats, Wilde, Joyce, Pound, Eliot, and Auden is studied by Ellmann with Yeats occupying the focal position.

Ellmann, Richard, and Charles Feidelson, Jr., eds. *The Modern Tradition: Back- grounds of Modern Literature*. New York: Oxford University Press, 1965. This collection of primary materials is an invaluable tool for students of the modernist tradition. It includes significant statements of key ideas, attitudes, and interpreta- tions of man, nature, mind, art, etc., representative of the development of the "modern tradition" from the eighteenth to the twentieth centuries.

Engelberg, Edward. *The Unknown Distance: From Consciousness to Conscience, Goethe to Camus*. Cambridge: Harvard University Press, 1972. Engelberg consid- ers the growth of a "Conscience and Consciousness" duality from the eighteenth to the twentieth centuries. He traces the divorcing of consciousness (awareness and knowledge) from conscience (a sense of value and judgment), and argues that "conscience and consciousness [must be restored] to their original unity" (250). His illustrations derive mainly from English and German literatures.

Faulkner, Peter. *Modernism*. London: Methuen, 1977. This book is one of *The Critical Idiom* series edited by John W. Jump. It attempts to define the term, trace the development of the period, and exemplify its characteristics by discussing a series of representative writers.

Feder, Lillian. *Ancient Myth in Modern Poetry*. Princeton: Princeton University Press, 1971. Feder's book discusses the uses of ancient Greek and Roman myths in twentieth-century poetry. She considers a number of poets, in particular Yeats, Pound, Eliot, and Auden.

Foster, John Burt, Jr. *Heirs to Dionysus: A Nietzschean Current in Literary Modernism*. Princeton: Princeton University Press, 1981. This book focuses particularly on Gide, Lawrence, Malraux, and Mann in studying the influence of Nietzsche on the modernists.

Friedman, Alan. *The Turn of the Novel*. New York: Oxford University Press, 1967. Friedman studies the changes in the novel during the first part of the twentieth century. He shows a gradual but clear movement from a closed to an open-ended form of the novel.

Glicksberg, Charles I. *The Tragic Vision in Twentieth-Century Literature*. With a preface by Harry T. Moore. Carbondale: Southern Illinois University Press, 1963. In his preface Harry T. Moore suggests that, despite some areas of disagreement, Glicksberg's study complements George Steiner's *The Death of Tragedy* in that Glicksberg considers in the modernist period what Steiner dealt with in the eighteenth and nineteenth centuries: the difficulty of developing a tragic vision in the modern era.

Gould, Eric. *Mythical Intentions in Modern Literature*. Princeton: Princeton University Press, 1981. Gould reexamines myth criticism, especially that based on Jungian archetypes, using structuralist theories of myth, psyche, and language. He considers the gap between event and meaning in the sign and the development of fiction responding to that gap. His main focus is on writers such as Joyce, Lawrence, and Eliot.

Gross, Harvey. *Sound and Form in Modern Poetry: A Study of Prosody from Thomas Hardy to Robert Lowell*. Ann Arbor: University of Michigan Press, 1964. Gross has developed a refreshingly clear, intelligent, and de-mystifying explanation of modern experiment with prosodic structures. He identifies the poetry "which survives the wreckage of experiment" and the "qualities of all great poetry" (315) that persist in the best of the modernists.

————. *The Contrived Corridor: History and Fatality in Modern Literature*. Ann Arbor: University of Michigan Press, 1971. Gross studies a limited selection of modern writers, i.e., Henry Adams, T. S. Eliot, W. B. Yeats, André Malraux, and Thomas Mann, in order to reveal the "heightened consciousness of history" in modern literature and the modern writers with historical knowledge in a period filled with a sense of crisis.

Hamburger, Michael. *The Truth of Poetry: Tensions in Modern Poetry from Baudelaire to the 1960s*. London: Weidenfeld & Nicholson, 1969. Hamburger attempts to identify "the tensions and conflicts apparent in the work—or behind the work—" (viii) of every major modern poet beginning with Baudelaire. He examines specific poems, poets' remarks on their own works, and poetry in general. He discusses poets' uncertainty about identity, the function of the poet's self, the creation of personas, and poets' reactions to war, technology, and the city.

Heller, Erich. *The Disinherited Mind: Essays in Modern Literature and Thought*. New York, London: Harcourt Brace Jovanovich, 1975. Primarily a study of German literature and thought from Goethe to Kafka, this work ranges widely and says much about the growth of the modernist sensibility. Of particular interest are the chapters "The Hazard of Modern Poetry" and "Yeats and Nietzsche: Reflections on a Poet's Marginal Notes."

Hermans, Theo. *The Structure of Modernist Poetry*. London: Groom Helm, 1982. The purpose of Hermans's study is "to offer a descriptive and comparative study of some fundamental structural aspects of the Modernist mode of poetic writing" (9). He considers, in particular, poets associated with cubism, expressionism, and imagism and vorticism, in the French, German, and English languages, around the time of World War I.

Hoffman, Frederick J. *Death and the Modern Imagination*. Princeton: Princeton University Press, 1964. Hoffman examines twentieth-century literature using death as a central concern, i.e., attitudes toward death organized around three terms—grace, violence, and self. The dying of belief in immortality—one's personal persistence beyond death—has meant a sharp change in attitudes toward death in modern literature.

Howe, Irving, ed. *Literary Modernism*. New York: Fawcett, 1967. This collection of influential statements by major contributors to criticism of the modernist tradition was compiled by one of the most important commentators of the period—Irving Howe. He includes comments by Spender, Ortega y Gasset, Jarrell, Camus, Burke, Harold Rosenberg, Joseph Chiari, Adorno, and Delmore Schwartz, among others.

Kahler, Erich. *The Inward Turn of Narrative*. Translated by Richard and Clara Winston. Princeton: Princeton University Press, 1973. Kahler was a major figure in twentieth-century German intellectual history, and this volume includes a sampling of his insights into the growth of the modernist sensibility. He studies "the internalization of narrative—the movement from external action and epic adventure to the ever-deeper and more intense exploration of character and personality" (viii).

Kampf, Louis. *On Modernism: The Prospects for Literature and Freedom*. Cambridge, Mass., and London: The MIT Press, 1967. Through a study of the sources—in the past and in the twentieth century—of the difficulties that gave rise to styles and roles assumed by modernist artists and intellectuals, Kampf attempts to confront "the discouraging confusions of our times," without attempting to eradicate the confusions at the cost of positive values.

Kenner, Hugh. *A Homemade World: The American Modernist Writers*. New York: Alfred A. Knopf, 1975. Kenner discusses a number of American poets and novelists, e.g., Williams, Stevens, and Moore, Fitzgerald, Hemingway, and Faulkner, in order to trace a "fifty-year reshaping of the American language." Kenner argues that these poets and novelists "rethought and altered, perhaps permanently, the novel and especially the poem" (xviii).

Kermode, Frank. *The Sense of an Ending: Studies in the Theory of Fiction*. London: Oxford University Press, 1966. This book is an important study by one of the more prolific and influential critics of modernist literature. Kermode explores the "apocalyptic spirit" in literature from Plato and St. Augustine to the modernists. He discusses, in particular, Yeats, Eliot, and Joyce, as well as Sartre and Beckett.

Kiely, Robert, ed. *Modernism Reconsidered*. Cambridge: Harvard University Press, 1983. The editor of this collection states his purpose as "to reconsider authors who, for one reason or another, have been excluded by critics from the great modern constellation" and "to examine works by major writers that are not usually regarded as among their most typical or greatest achievements." The collection also explores "received opinion about modernist theories and the assumptions that inform the literature of the period" (vi).

Korg, Jacob. *Language in Modern Literature: Innovations and Experiment*. New York: Barnes and Noble, 1979. Korg discusses linguistic experimentation as an essential component of literary modernism. This verbal revolution was "a search for new expressive resources and new ways of understanding the world" (3). He considers the major poets and novelists and the major movements of the period.

Levin, Harry. *Memories of the Moderns.* New York: New Directions, 1980. Author of a seminal study of James Joyce and a number of other basic studies of modernists, Levin here includes a series of prose pieces that combine criticism and personal recollections of his contact with a number of major modernist writers, such as Eliot, Pound, Joyce, Mann, Hesse, Hemingway, and Sartre.

Paterson, John. *The Novel as Faith: The Gospel According to James, Hardy, Conrad, Joyce, Lawrence and Virginia Woolf.* Boston: Gambit, 1973. Paterson endeavors to describe the essence of the novel as a form by discussing six major novelists from the period between 1870 and 1940. He attempts to define the aesthetic of each writer considered and concludes with an attempt to synthesize his findings to determine something about the essential nature of the novel.

Perkins, David. *A History of Modern Poetry from the 1890s to the High Modernist Mode.* Cambridge: Harvard University Press, 1976. This is the first of two volumes presenting the history of English and American poetry in the twentieth century. The second volume covers "From the 1920's to the Present." This is one of the most comprehensive attempts to deal with the poetry of the modernist era.

Pratt, William. *The Imagist Poem.* New York: E. P. Dutton, 1963. A companion volume to Edward Engelberg's *The Symbolic Poem,* this book provides a brief but very helpful introduction to imagism and the imagist poem by providing key statements of the important contributors to the movement and examples of the poetry.

Scott, Nathan, Jr. *Negative Capability: Studies in the New Literature and the Religious Situation.* New Haven: Yale University Press, 1967. This optimistic study argues a rapprochement between literary and theological concerns resulting from a kind of Keatsian "negative capability" that has displaced the "great 'rage for Order'" (xiv) of the "classic canon" (xiii) of modernist literature. It identifies aspects of modernism by their contrast with contemporary sensibilities.

Shapiro, Karl. *Prose Keys to Modern Poetry.* New York: Harper & Row, 1962. Shapiro has attempted to bring together "the chief prose documents upon which modern poetry is based" (vii). The ordering of the selections is based on "tendency" (viii), e.g., "the symbolist tendency" from Poe to Mallarmé, the "metaphysical tendency," and theories of myth and mythmaking.

Shorer, Mark, ed. *Modern British Fiction.* New York: Oxford University Press, 1961. This collection of essays by such critics as F. R. Karl, Dorothy Van Ghent, F. R. Leavis, R. P. Blackmur, Frederick Crews, David Daiches, and Erich Auerbach, and essays also by Virginia Woolf, E. M. Forster, and D. H. Lawrence, attempts "to define twentieth-century British fiction . . . to show how it is different from fiction that came earlier" (vii).

Spears, Monroe K. *Dionysus and the City: Modernism in Twentieth-Century Poetry.* New York: Oxford University Press, 1970. Spears proposes an inclusive definition of modernism by considering the word, the complex of ideas it relates to, and the literary movement it is used to identify in twentieth-century British and American poetry.

Spender, Stephen. *The Struggle of the Modern.* London: Hamish Hamilton, 1963. In this collection of essays by an important participant in the later development of the modernist tradition, Spender discusses such matters as the modern imagination, the situation of the modernist writers, and the passing of the modernist tradition.

Starkie, Enid. *From Gautier to Eliot: The Influence of France on English Literature*. London: Hutchinson University Library, 1960. Starkie's purpose is to deal with the English writers "who indubitably gained something from their connection and sympathy with France and her literature . . . who definitely experienced her seminal influence . . . solely from the point of view of the impact France made upon them" (ii). She begins, briefly, with Arnold, considers Swinburne and Pater in poetry, and then discusses Moore and James in the novel, as a prelude to her discussion of the modernists.

Stead, C. K. *The New Poetic*. New York: Harper & Row, 1964. This book offers a judicious study of the rise of the modernist poetry from the early shift in Yeats from his nineties to his modernist manner. Stead considers in some detail Eliot's development and conception of poetry.

Stromberg, Roland N., ed. *Realism, Naturalism, and Symbolism: Modes of Thought and Expression in Europe, 1848–1914*. New York: Harper & Row, 1968. This series of primary readings was chosen to illustrate the development of European literary and, to some extent, artistic philosophic thought after the revolutions of 1848 in France, Germany, Austria, and Italy, up to the publication of the first novels of Proust, Lawrence, and Joyce, and the development of imagism.

West, Paul. *The Modern Novel*. Vols. 1 and 2. London: Hutchinson University Library, 1963. West offers a wide-ranging study of the development of the modern novel, seen against the background of modern society's evolution toward an increasingly indifferent and alien cultural milieu.

White, Allon. *The Uses of Obscurity: The Fiction of Early Modernism*. London, Boston and Henley: Routledge and Kegan Paul, 1981. White's book examines the appearance of obscurity "as an important, positive aspect of nineteenth-century English fiction." He attempts to analyze the fiction of the last decades of the nineteenth century "as part of a deep cultural transformation and as individual literary projects carried through in equivocal relation to this transformation" (1).

Wilde, Alan. *Horizons of Assent: Modernism, Postmodernism, and the Ironic Imagination*. Baltimore and London: Johns Hopkins University Press, 1981. By examining the different kinds of irony used by the writers of this century and by examining "the movements that both generate and are generated by these various ironies [as] one of 'mutual implication,' " Wilde traces the development of modernism through the century in a "roughly . . . phenomenological" manner. Irony is treated as a way of imagining the world and not simply as a device.

Williams, Raymond. *Modern Tragedy*. Stanford: Stanford University Press, 1966. Williams studies selected dramatists and novelists and their contribution to modern tragedy. He considers the ideas of tragedy in human experience, in tradition and in a contemporary context, and in modern drama and, briefly, in the novel.

———. *The English Novel: From Dickens to Lawrence*. New York: Oxford University Press, 1970. Williams studies the novelist's "exploration of community: the substance and meaning of community" (ii). He traces these explorations from Dickens, in particular in *Dombey and Sons,* to Lawrence, with particular stress on *The Rainbow, Women in Love,* and *Lady Chatterley's Lover*. He also considers Hardy, Wells, James, Conrad, and Joyce.

Ziolkowski, Theodore. *Disenchanted Images: A Literary Iconology*. Princeton: Princeton University Press, 1977. Ziolkowski traces the "disenchantment" of the image from the Enlightenment to the modernist period as reflective of "changes in the general cultural consciousness" (viii). This study provides a new and interesting approach to the study of the background and development of modernism.

Notes on Contributors

ARMIN ARNOLD has taught at the University of Alberta, Edmonton (1959–61), at McGill University in Montreal (1961–82), and at the Höhere Wirtschafts- und Verwaltungsschule Olten (Switzerland) since 1982. In 1978 he was elected Fellow of the Royal Society of Canada. He has edited *D. H. Lawrence: The Symbolic Meaning* (1962), and written *D. H. Lawrence and German Literature* (1965) and a German biography of Lawrence: *D. H. Lawrence* (1972). He is the author of several books on Joyce, Shaw, Heine, Dürrenmatt, expressionism, paraliterature.

CARL BODE is Professor Emeritus of English and American Studies at the University of Maryland. Much of his more recent creative writing can be found in *Practical Magic,* a book of his poems, which was published in 1981. In the same year he edited a new Emerson anthology in collaboration with Malcolm Cowley. Interested in a variety of literary rebels, he has published a good deal about the life and writings of Thoreau and Mencken. Currently he is engaged in applying reader-response criticism to the principal works of Emerson's prime.

TED BOYLE is Professor of English at Southern Illinois University, author of *Symbol and Meaning in the Fiction of Joseph Conrad* and *Brendan Behan.* He has also written several articles on modern authors including Amis, Golding, Fowles, and Mansfield.

JAMES C. COWAN is the founder and former editor (1968–83) of *The D. H. Lawrence Review.* He is the author of *D. H. Lawrence's American Journey: A Study in Literature and Myth* (1970) and the compiler and editor of two volumes of bibliographical abstracts, *D. H. Lawrence: An Annotated Bibliography of Writings about Him,* vol. 1 (1982) and vol. 2 (1985). He is the first recipient of the Harry T. Moore Award presented by the D. H. Lawrence Society of North America "for distinguished scholarship . . . in the development of Lawrence studies."

KEITH CUSHMAN, Professor of English at the University of North Carolina at Greensboro, is the author of *D. H. Lawrence at Work* (1978) and the co-editor of *The D. H. Lawrence—Amy Lowell Letters* (1985). His many essays include studies of such moderns as Lawrence, Joyce, Kafka, Beckett, Anaïs Nin, Bellow, Philip Roth, Joyce Carol Oates, Ted Hughes, and Philip Larkin. He is the President-Elect of the D. H. Lawrence Society of North America.

EMILE DELAVENAY began research work on D. H. Lawrence when teaching in London in 1931. After a career in London journalism, the BBC in war time, then the United Nations and UNESCO, from which he retired as Chief Editor, he completed *D. H. Lawrence, l'Homme et la Genèse de son Oeuvre, les Années de Formation, 1885–1919,* (1969), translated by Katharine M. Delavenay as *D. H. Lawrence, the Man and his Work* (1972). He also published *D. H. Lawrence and Edward Carpenter, A Study in Edwardian Transition* (1971), and many articles and book reviews on Lawrence and twentieth-century literature. He was Professor of Contemporary English Literature at the University of Nice from 1967 until his retirement in 1974.

EDMUND L. EPSTEIN is Professor of English at Queens College, City University of New York and at the Graduate Center, CUNY. He is editor of *Language and Style: An International Journal,* and has written or edited five books on modern literature and linguistics and many articles. He is at present at work on a book about the use of language by Yeats, specifically on Yeats's use of time.

JAMES FLANNERY is currently Chairman of the Department of Theater Studies at Emory University, Atlanta. He is the author of *W. B. Yeats and the Idea of a Theatre: The Early Abbey Theatre in Theory and Practice* and has staged professional productions of Yeats's plays in Dublin, Belfast, Montreal, Ottawa, Toronto, New York, and Atlanta.

ALAN WARREN FRIEDMAN, Professor of English at the University of Texas at Austin, is the author of *Lawrence Durrell and "The Alexandria Quartet": Art for Love's Sake* (1970), *Multivalence: The Moral Quality of Form in the Modern Novel* (1978), and *William Faulkner* (1985). He is the editor of *Forms in Modern British Fiction, Mario Vargas Llosa, Critical Essays on Lawrence Durrell,* and *Beckett Translating/Translating Beckett.* Friedman is currently completing *Fictional Death,* a study of mortality in the twentieth-century novel.

LAWRENCE B. GAMACHE, Associate Professor of English at the University of Ottawa, has written on Lawrence, Eliot, and modernism, and has edited textbooks on writing skills for Canadian use. He was Secretary-Treasurer of the D. H. Lawrence Society of North America (1983–84) and is currently its Program Chairman.

SUZANNE HENIG is Professor of English at San Diego State University. Her books include *Ululations* (poetry, 1972), *The Age of the Assassin* (poetry, 1976), and *The Literary Criticism of Virginia Woolf* (1968), and she has edited and introduced Woolf's previously unpublished first novel, *A Cockney's Farming Experiences* (1972). She has written widely on twentieth-century British literature, non-Western literature, and modern art, and is founding editor of the *Virginia Woolf Quarterly.* She is currently collecting the scientific work of Dr. Virginia Livingston-Wheeler for the National Cancer Institute, and is working on a volume of poetry.

EVELYN J. HINZ is Professor of English at the University of Manitoba. Her publications include criticism *(The Mirror and the Garden),* an edition of scholarly essays *(The World of Anaïs Nin),* and an edition of Nin interviews and lectures *(A Woman Speaks).* She has edited *Mosaic* since 1979. Among her scholarly articles is a discussion of marriage as an index of genre, which was awarded the William Riley Parker Prize for an outstanding essay published in *PMLA* for 1976. She is the authorized biographer of Anaïs Nin.

RICHARD D. LEHAN, Professor of English at UCLA, is the author of *F. Scott Fitzgerald and the Craft of Fiction, Theodore Dreiser: His World and His Novels,* and *A Dangerous Crossing: French Literary Existentialism and the Modern American Novel.* He was a Fulbright scholar in 1974–75 and a Guggenheim Fellow in 1978–79. He is presently completing a book on the city in history and literature.

IAN S. MACNIVEN is Associate Professor of English at the State University of New York Maritime College. In collaboration with the late Harry T. Moore, he co-edited *Literary Lifelines: The Richard Aldington—Lawrence Durrell Correspondence* (1981). He has also written articles on various modern authors and is currently completing an authorized biography of Lawrence Durrell.

PAUL J. MARCOTTE, Professor of English at the University of Ottawa, is the author of *The God Within: Essays in Speculative Literary Criticism* (1964); *Priapus Unbound: The Concept of Love in Six Early Works of Shakespeare* (1971); and *Quebec Revisited and Other Poems* (1973). His three-volume work, *Priapus Undone: Shakespeare's Concept of Love Inferred from the Problem Works,* is forthcoming.

CHARLES ROSSMAN, Associate Professor of English at the University of Texas at Austin, has published numerous essays and reviews on modern writers—chiefly D. H. Lawrence and James Joyce—in a wide variety of journals and books. He has also edited or co-edited four volumes of essays: one each on Mario Vargas Llosa, Carlos Fuentes, Gabriel García Márquez, and Samuel Beckett (forthcoming). He is on the editorial boards of the *D. H. Lawrence Review, The James Joyce Quarterly, Studies in the Novel,* and *Texas Studies in Literature and Language.*

KEITH SAGAR is Reader in English Literature in the Extra-Mural Department at the University of Manchester. He has written and edited several books on Lawrence, including *The Art of D. H. Lawrence* (Cambridge, 1966), *The Life of D. H. Lawrence* (Pantheon, 1980), and *D. H. Lawrence: Life into Art* (Penguin/Viking and Georgia University Press, 1985). He has also published three books on Ted Hughes.

PAUL SCHLUETER was Harry T. Moore's first doctoral student at Southern Illinois University. He lives in Easton, Pennsylvania, where he writes, edits, arranges conferences, occasionally teaches, and lectures. Among his books are *The Novels of Doris Lessing* (1973), *A Small Personal Voice: Essays, Reviews, and Interviews by Doris Lessing* (1974), *Shirley Ann Grau* (1981), *The English Novel: Twentieth Century Criticism, Vol. II* (1982), *Modern American Literature: Supplement Two* (1985), and *British Women Writers* (1986), the last three with his wife, June Schlueter.

MARK SPILKA teaches English and Comparative Literature at Brown University, where he also helps to edit the journal *Novel: A Forum on Fiction.* He is the author of *The Love Ethic of D. H. Lawrence* (1955), *Dickens and Kafka: A Mutual Interpretation* (1963), and *Virginia Woolf's Quarrel with Grieving* (1980), and the editor of *D. H. Lawrence: A Collection of Critical Essays* (1963) and *Towards a Poetics of Fiction* (1977). He recalls with gratitude that Harry Moore was the outside reader for his first book on Lawrence and a genial academic friend thereafter. He is presently at work on a book-length study of Hemingway's androgynous propensities and their Victorian sources.

WALTER TAYLOR has taught at Georgia Tech, Louisiana State University, and the University of Southwestern Louisiana, and is presently Professor of English at the University of Texas at El Paso. He has published articles in *American Literature, Southern Review, South Atlantic Quarterly,* and other periodicals; his book *Faulkner's Search for a South* was published by University of Illinois Press in 1983.

JOHN J. TEUNISSEN is Professor of English at the University of Manitoba. He has co-edited Roger Williams's *A Key into the Language of America* and Henry Miller's *The World of Lawrence;* in addition, he has edited *Other World: Fantasy and Science Fiction Since 1939.* Author or co-author of numerous essays on American, British, and Canadian literature, he edits the *Canadian Review of American Studies.*

Index

Page numbers in bold type refer to entire chapters.